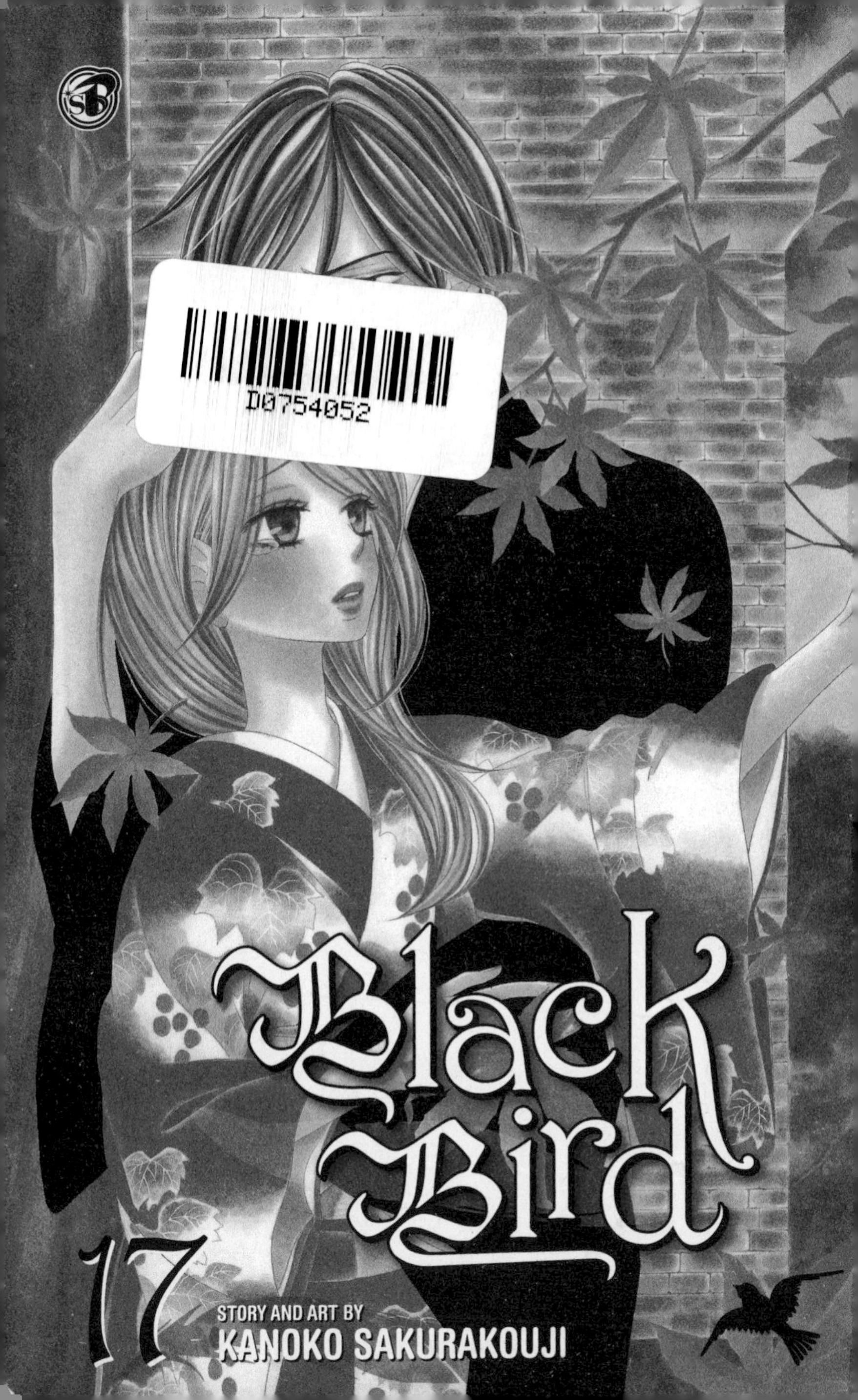
Black Bird
17
STORY AND ART BY
KANOKO SAKURAKOUJI

# Black Bird

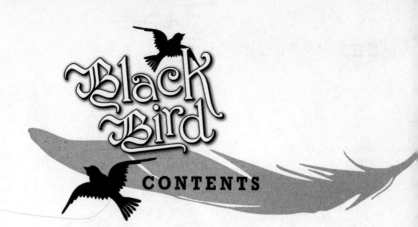

# CONTENTS

# CHARACTERS

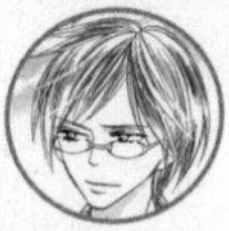

**TADANOBU KUZUNOHA**
Close childhood friend of Kyo's. Current leader of Kitsune clan.

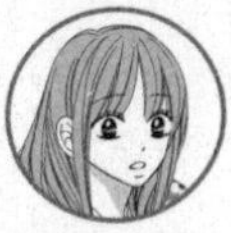

**AYAME**
Wife of Sagami, who is a member of the Eight Daitengu.

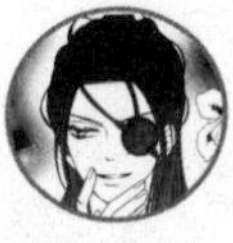

**SHO USUI**
Kyo's older brother an ex-member of the Eig Daitengu. He is also kn as Sojo. His attempted failed and he later die a duel against Kyo.

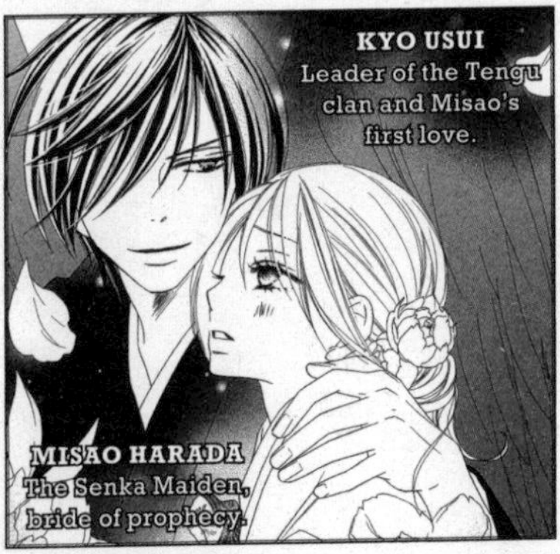
KYO USUI
Leader of the Tengu clan and Misao's first love.
MISAO HARADA
The Senka Maiden, bride of prophecy.

**THE EIGHT DAITENGU**
Kyo's bodyguards. Their names designate their official posts.

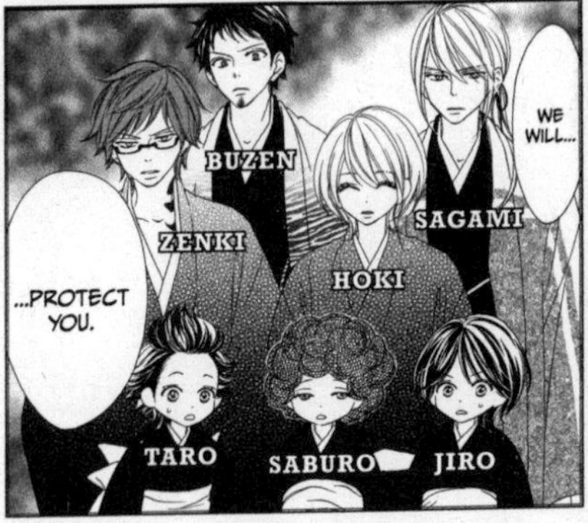
WE WILL...
...PROTECT YOU.
BUZEN
ZENKI
SAGAMI
HOKI
TARO
SABURO
JIRO

**STORY THUS FAR**
Misao can see spirits and demons, and her childhood sweetheart Kyo has been protecting her since she was little.

*"Someday, I'll come for you, I promise."*
Kyo reappears the day before Misao's 16th birthday to tell her, "Your 16th birthday marks 'open season' on you." She is the Senka Maiden, and if a demon drinks her blood, he is granted a long life. If he eats her flesh, he gains eternal youth. And if he makes her his bride, his clan will prosper...And Kyo is a *tengu*, a crow demon, with his sights firmly set on her.

Kyo avoided sleeping with Misao because he knew that sex with a demon is somehow dangerous for the Senka Maiden, but when poison nearly killed him, he finally gave in and took Misao.

Now that Kyo's powers have no equal, his older brother Sho, presumed dead, reappears. After a brutal battle, Kyo finally defeats Sho. With his last breath, Sho ominously predicts that Kyo will end up killing Misao.

Not long after, Misao's pregnancy comes to light. The Senka Roku, record of the fate of the previous Senka Maiden, is still missing. But a surviving Nue clan member tells them that "...the Senka Maiden will die the instant her baby is born"!

Despite Kyo's arguments, Misao is determined to continue with her pregnancy, and now Kyo is desperately seeking some way to save her. But time is quickly slipping by...!

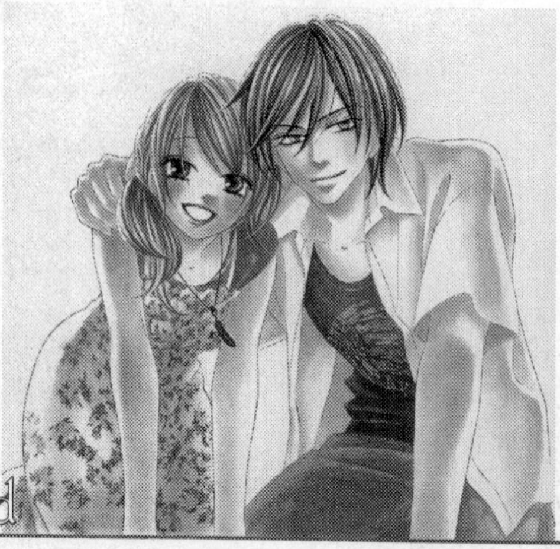

Black Bird

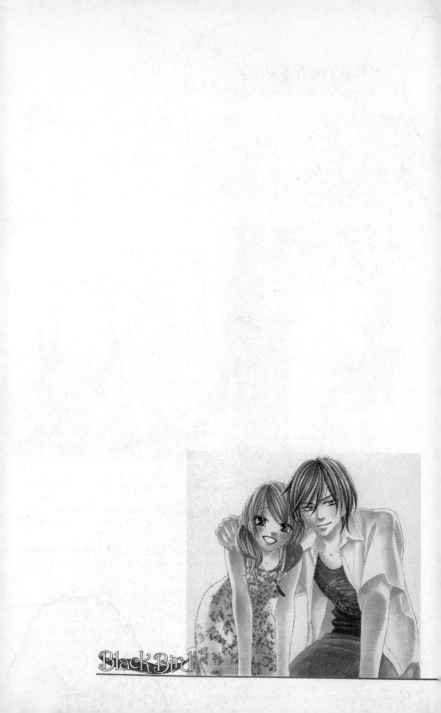

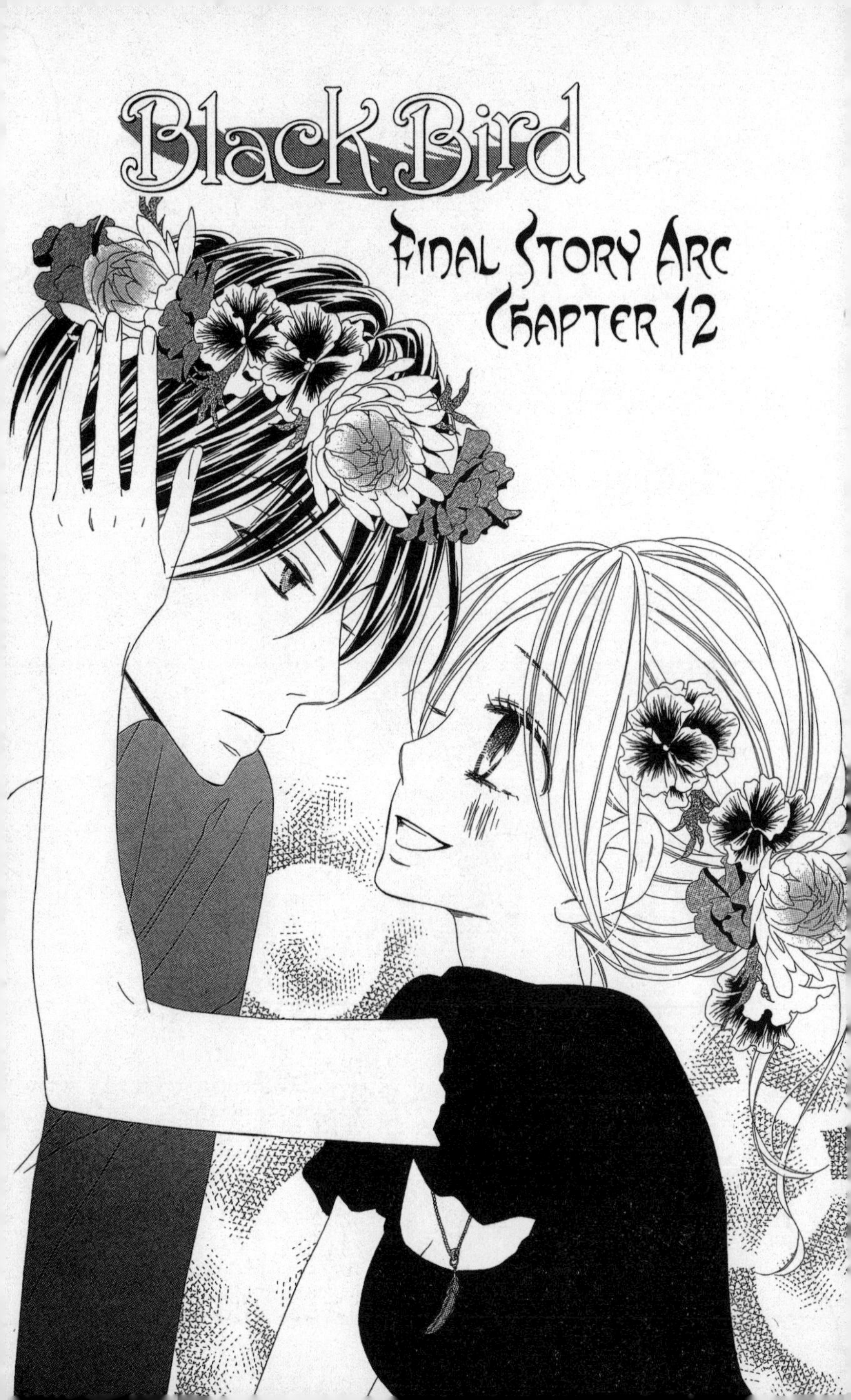
Black Bird
Final Story Arc
Chapter 12

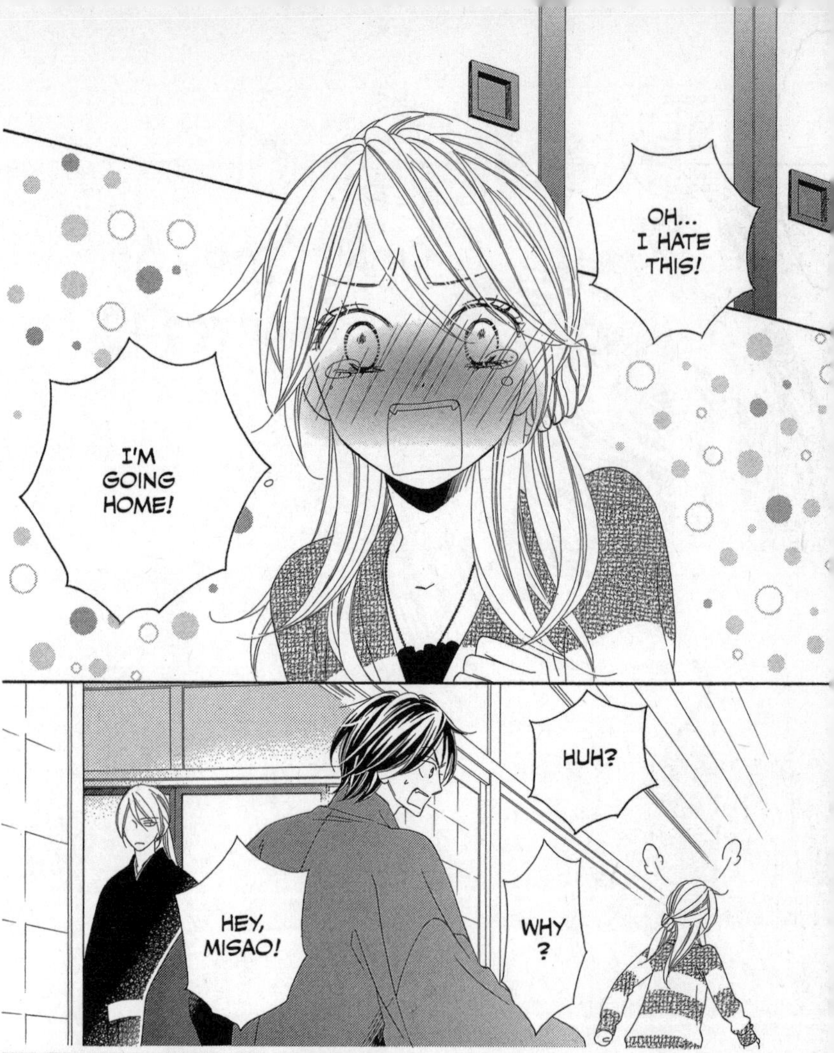
OH... I HATE THIS!
I'M GOING HOME!
HUH?
WHY?
HEY, MISAO!

Hello. Sakurakouji here. I hope you enjoy *Black Bird* Volume 17.

← In this volume I will show you each character's cooking skills. Of course, Taro is as good as a pro...

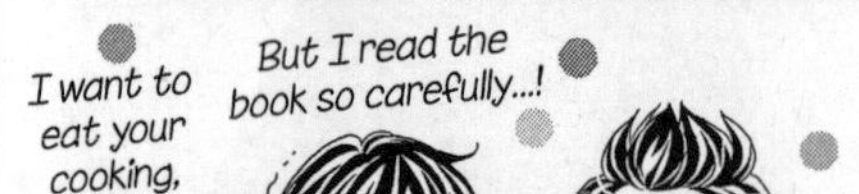
But I read the book so carefully...!
I want to eat your cooking, Taro...
JAPANESE COOKING LIKE THE PROS

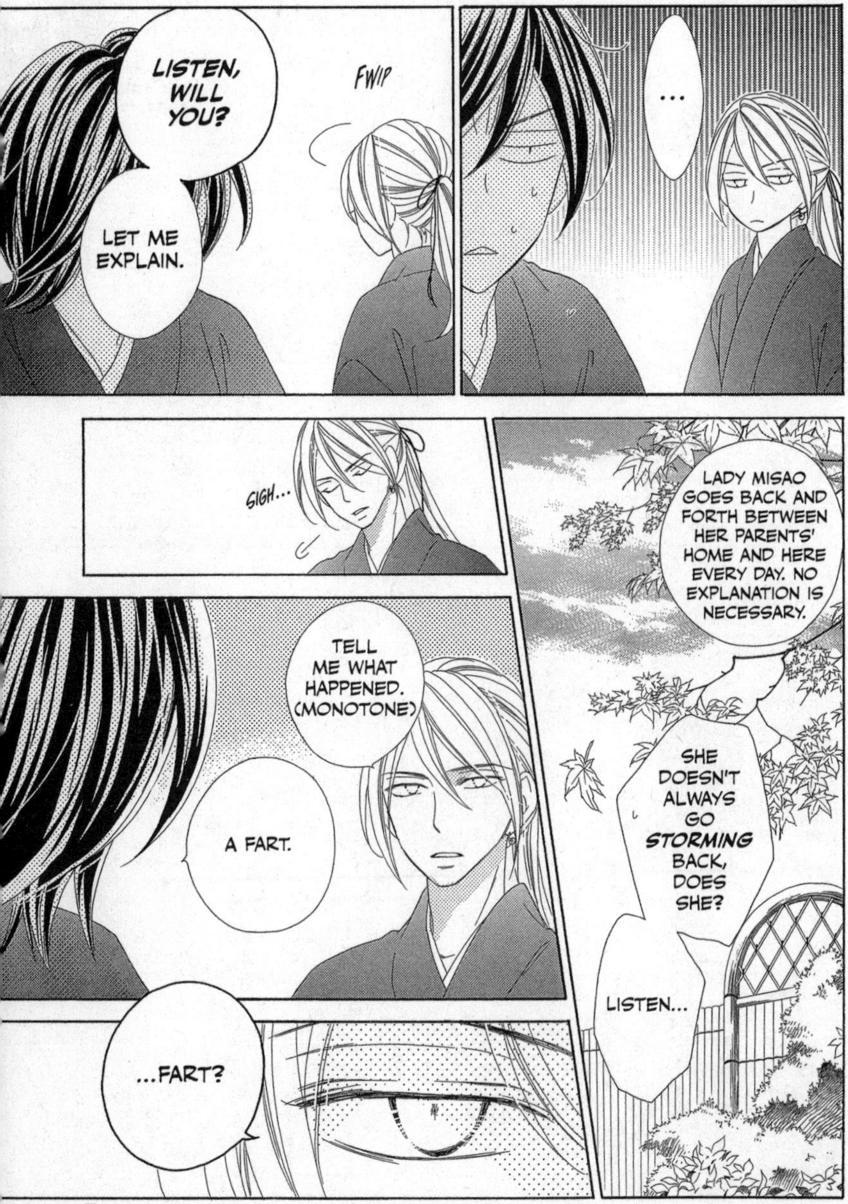
...
LISTEN, WILL YOU?
LET ME EXPLAIN.
FWIP
LADY MISAO GOES BACK AND FORTH BETWEEN HER PARENTS' HOME AND HERE EVERY DAY. NO EXPLANATION IS NECESSARY.
SHE DOESN'T ALWAYS GO *STORMING* BACK, DOES SHE?
LISTEN...
SIGH...
TELL ME WHAT HAPPENED. (MONOTONE)
A FART.
...FART?

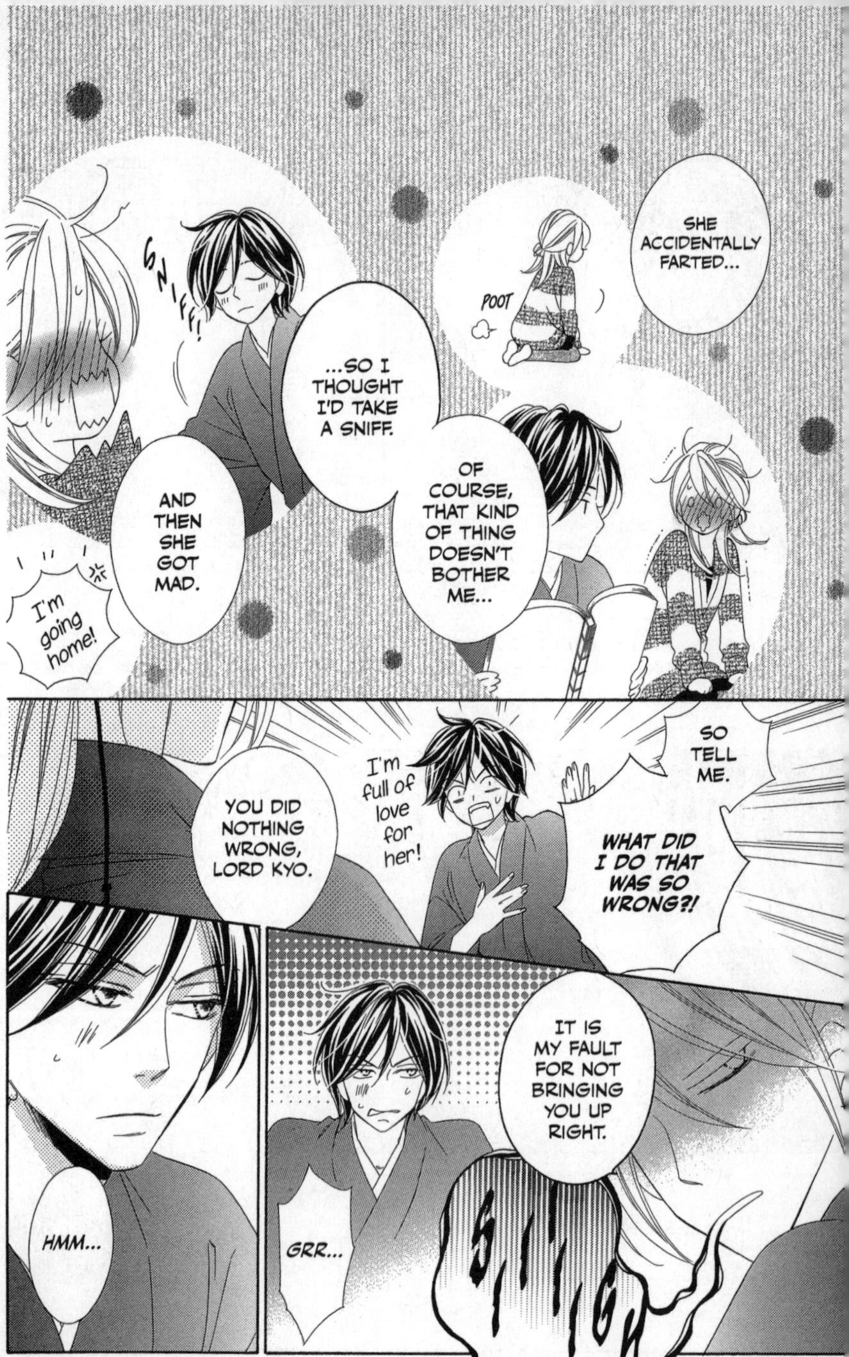
SHE ACCIDENTALLY FARTED...
POOT
OF COURSE, THAT KIND OF THING DOESN'T BOTHER ME...
...SO I THOUGHT I'D TAKE A SNIFF.
SNIFF!
AND THEN SHE GOT MAD.
I'm going home!
SO TELL ME.
WHAT DID I DO THAT WAS SO WRONG?!
I'm full of love for her!
YOU DID NOTHING WRONG, LORD KYO.
IT IS MY FAULT FOR NOT BRINGING YOU UP RIGHT.
SIIIGH
GRR...
HMM...

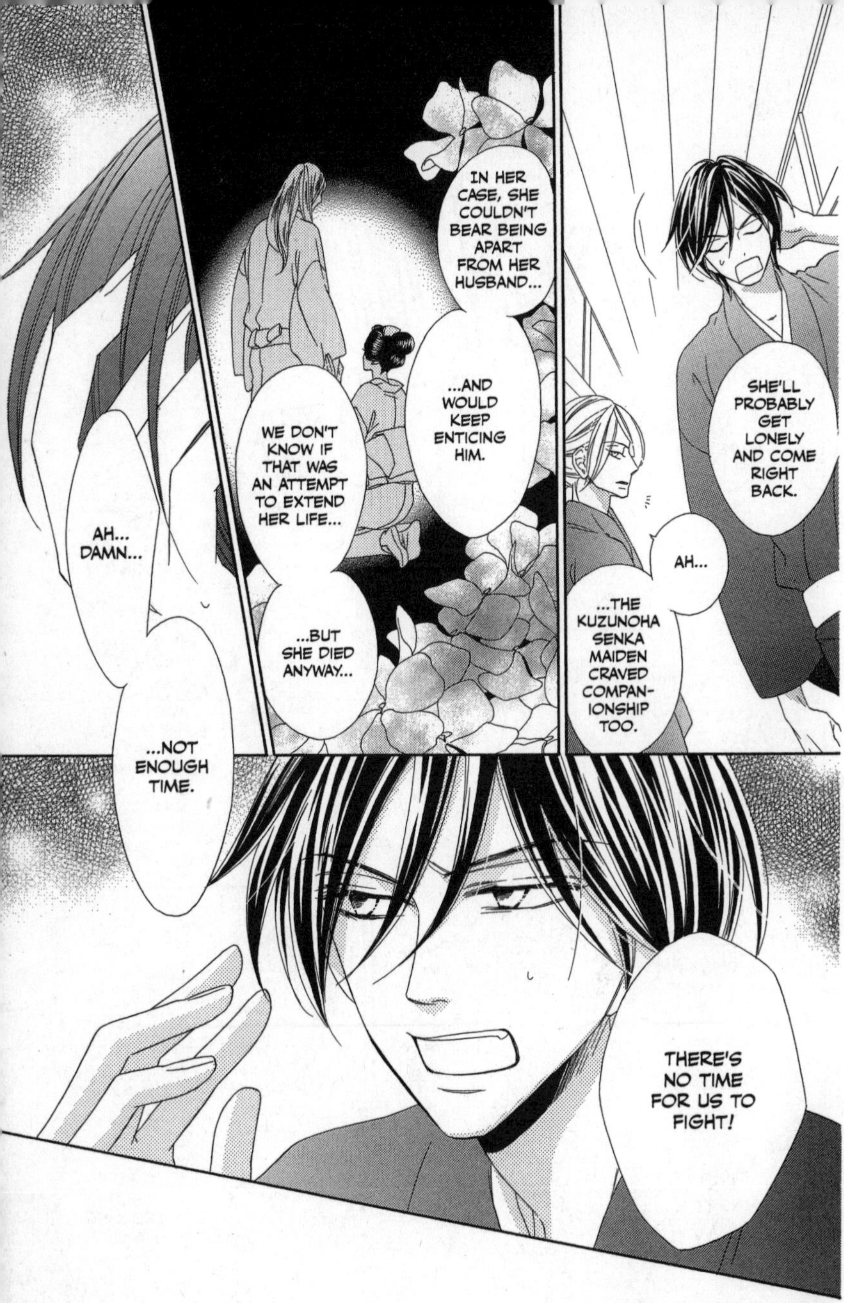
SHE'LL PROBABLY GET LONELY AND COME RIGHT BACK.
AH...
...THE KUZUNOHA SENKA MAIDEN CRAVED COMPANIONSHIP TOO.
IN HER CASE, SHE COULDN'T BEAR BEING APART FROM HER HUSBAND...
...AND WOULD KEEP ENTICING HIM.
WE DON'T KNOW IF THAT WAS AN ATTEMPT TO EXTEND HER LIFE...
...BUT SHE DIED ANYWAY...
AH... DAMN...
...NOT ENOUGH TIME.
THERE'S NO TIME FOR US TO FIGHT!

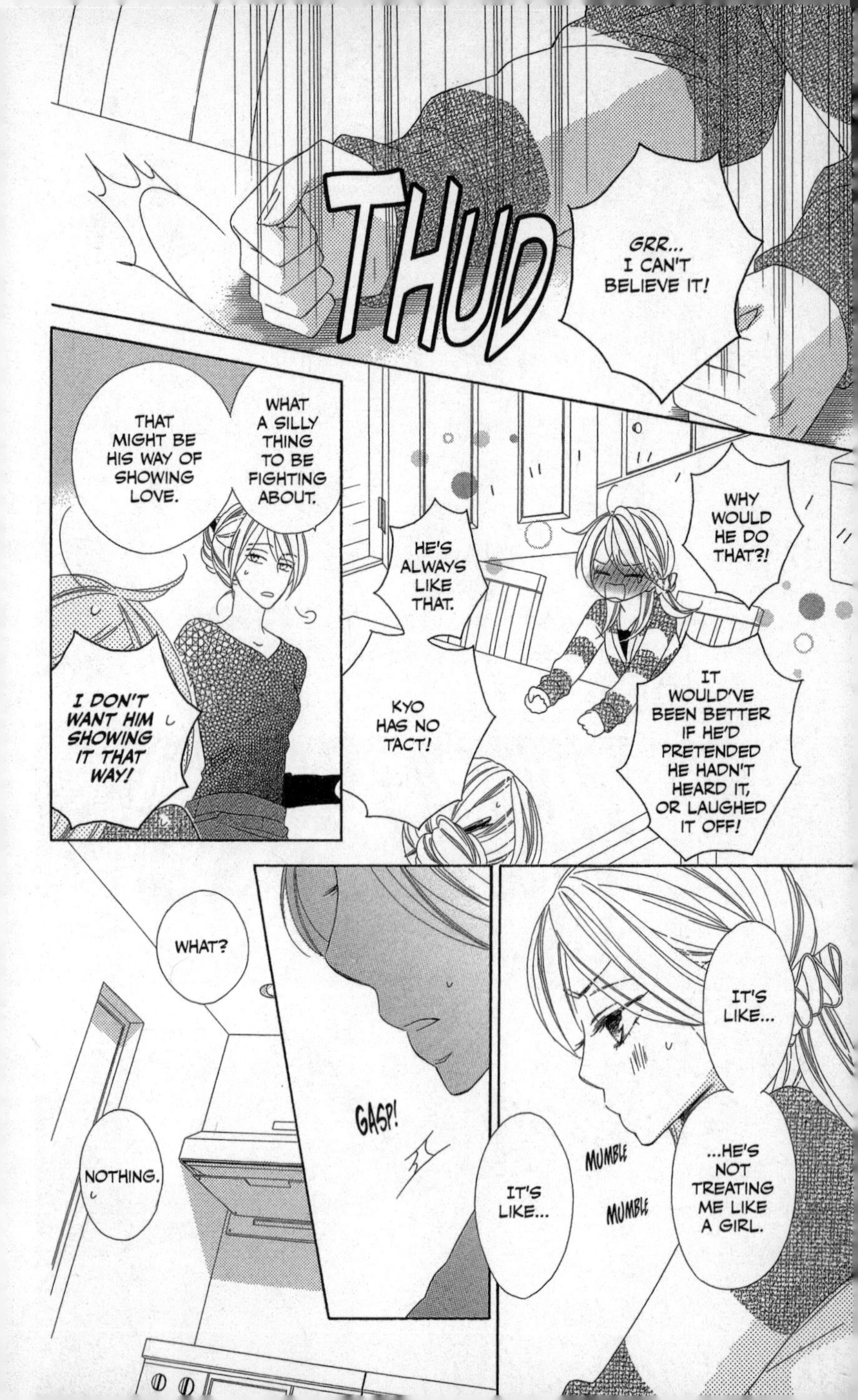
THUD
GRR... I CAN'T BELIEVE IT!
WHY WOULD HE DO THAT?!
IT WOULD'VE BEEN BETTER IF HE'D PRETENDED HE HADN'T HEARD IT, OR LAUGHED IT OFF!
HE'S ALWAYS LIKE THAT.
KYO HAS NO TACT!
WHAT A SILLY THING TO BE FIGHTING ABOUT.
THAT MIGHT BE HIS WAY OF SHOWING LOVE.
I DON'T WANT HIM SHOWING IT THAT WAY!
IT'S LIKE...
...HE'S NOT TREATING ME LIKE A GIRL.
MUMBLE
MUMBLE
IT'S LIKE...
GASP!
WHAT?
NOTHING.

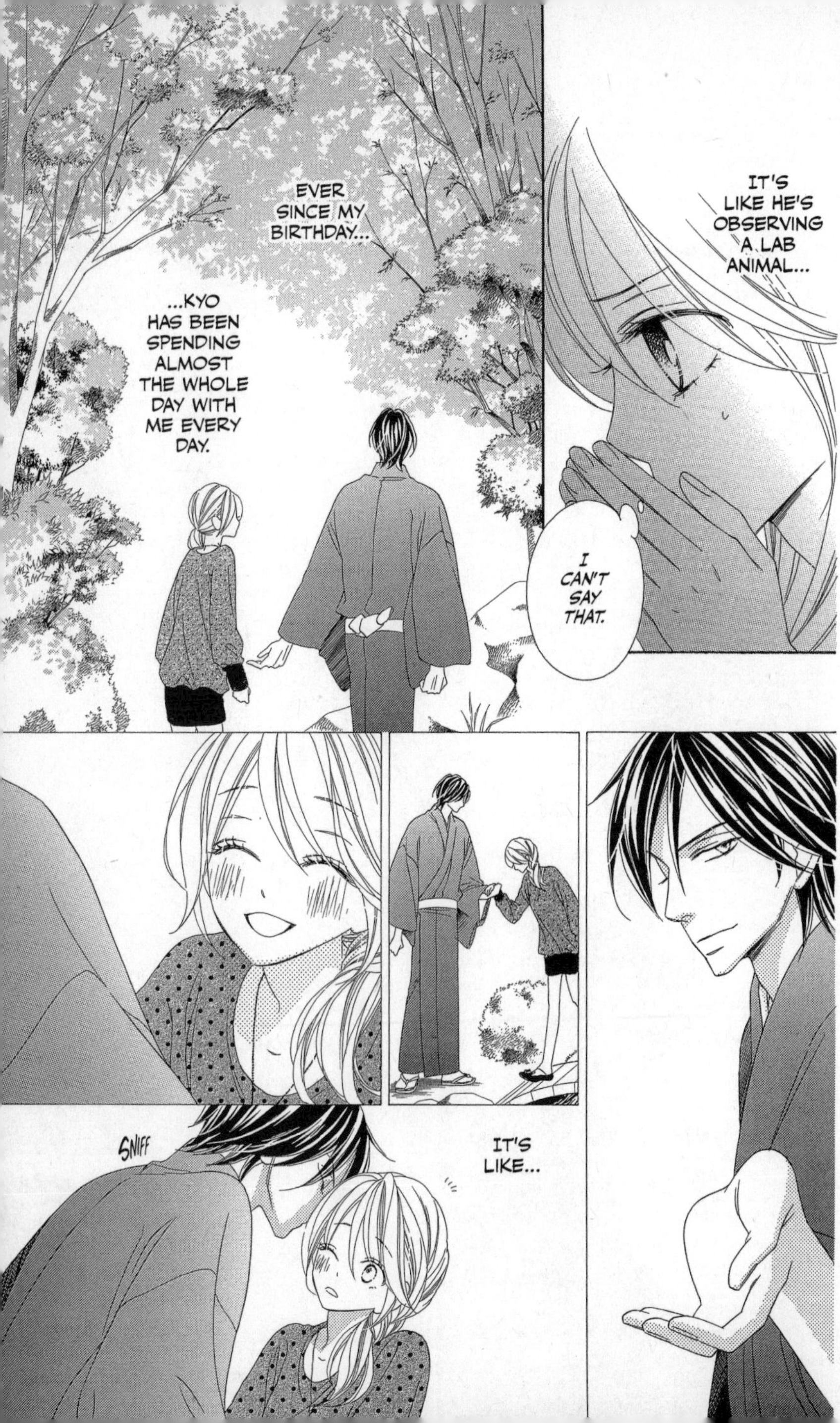
IT'S LIKE HE'S OBSERVING A LAB ANIMAL...
I CAN'T SAY THAT.
EVER SINCE MY BIRTHDAY...
...KYO HAS BEEN SPENDING ALMOST THE WHOLE DAY WITH ME EVERY DAY.
IT'S LIKE...
SNIFF

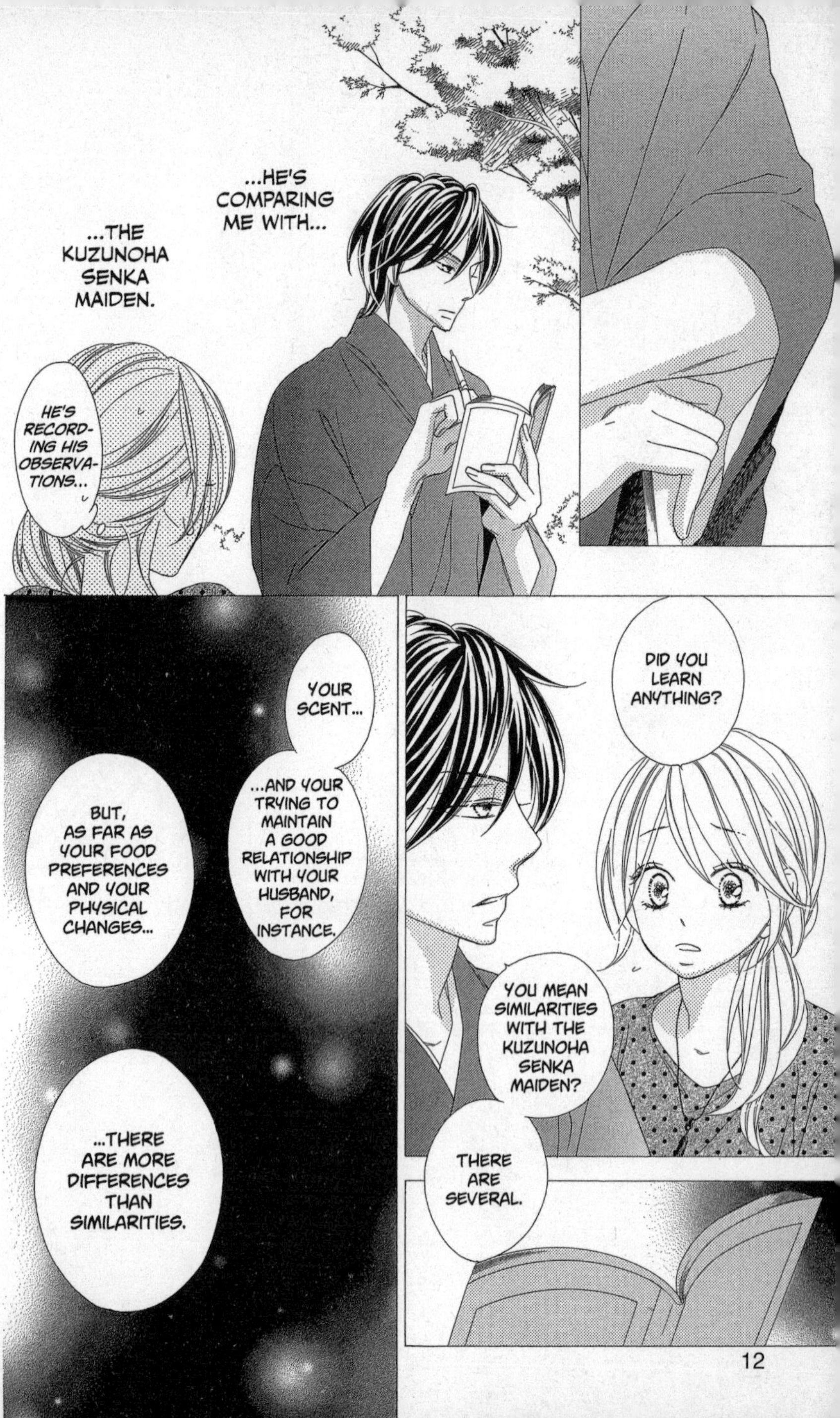
...HE'S COMPARING ME WITH...
...THE KUZUNOHA SENKA MAIDEN.
HE'S RECORDING HIS OBSERVATIONS...
DID YOU LEARN ANYTHING?
YOU MEAN SIMILARITIES WITH THE KUZUNOHA SENKA MAIDEN?
THERE ARE SEVERAL.
YOUR SCENT...
...AND YOUR TRYING TO MAINTAIN A GOOD RELATIONSHIP WITH YOUR HUSBAND, FOR INSTANCE.
BUT, AS FAR AS YOUR FOOD PREFERENCES AND YOUR PHYSICAL CHANGES...
...THERE ARE MORE DIFFERENCES THAN SIMILARITIES.

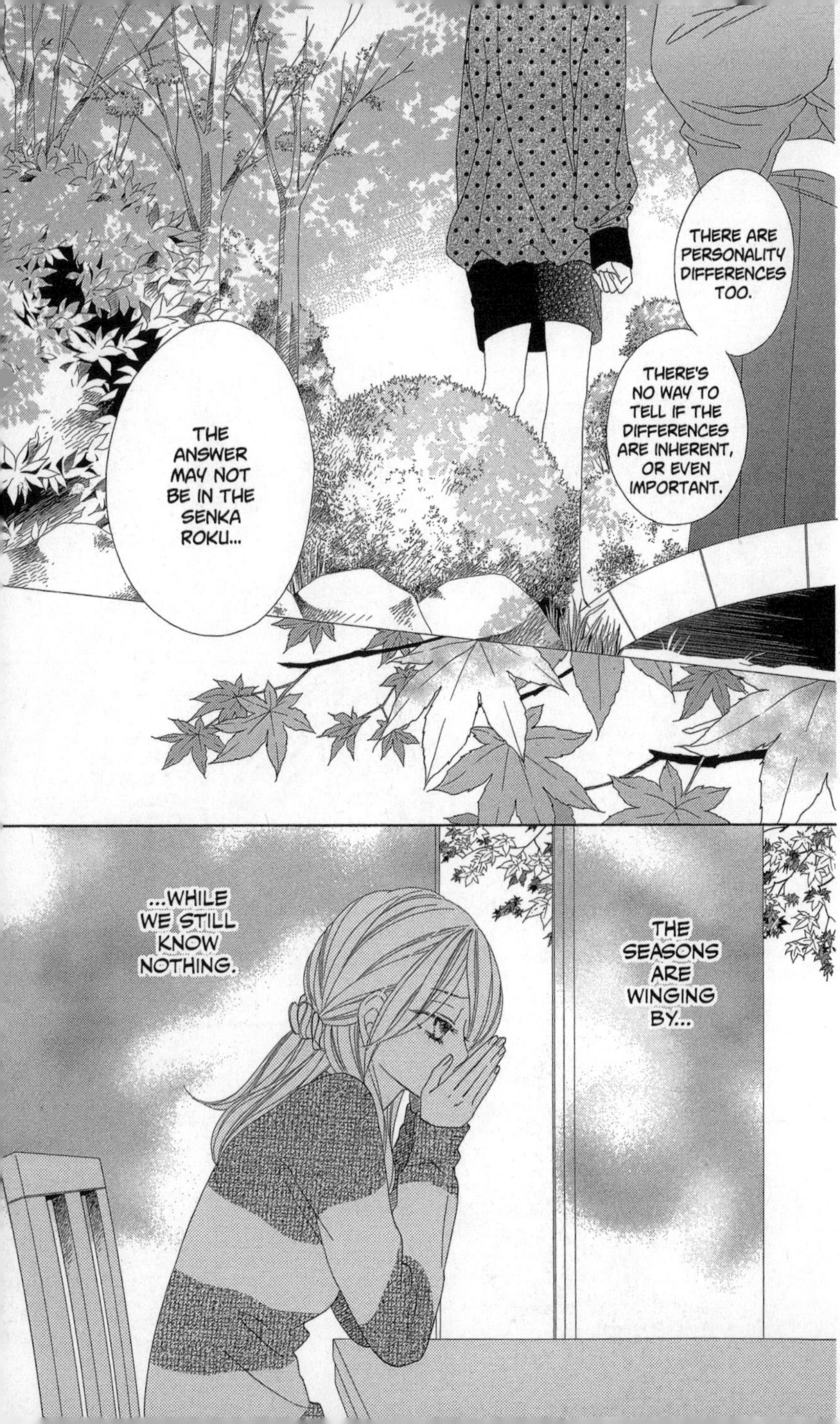
THERE ARE PERSONALITY DIFFERENCES TOO.
THERE'S NO WAY TO TELL IF THE DIFFERENCES ARE INHERENT, OR EVEN IMPORTANT.
THE ANSWER MAY NOT BE IN THE SENKA ROKU...
THE SEASONS ARE WINGING BY...
...WHILE WE STILL KNOW NOTHING.

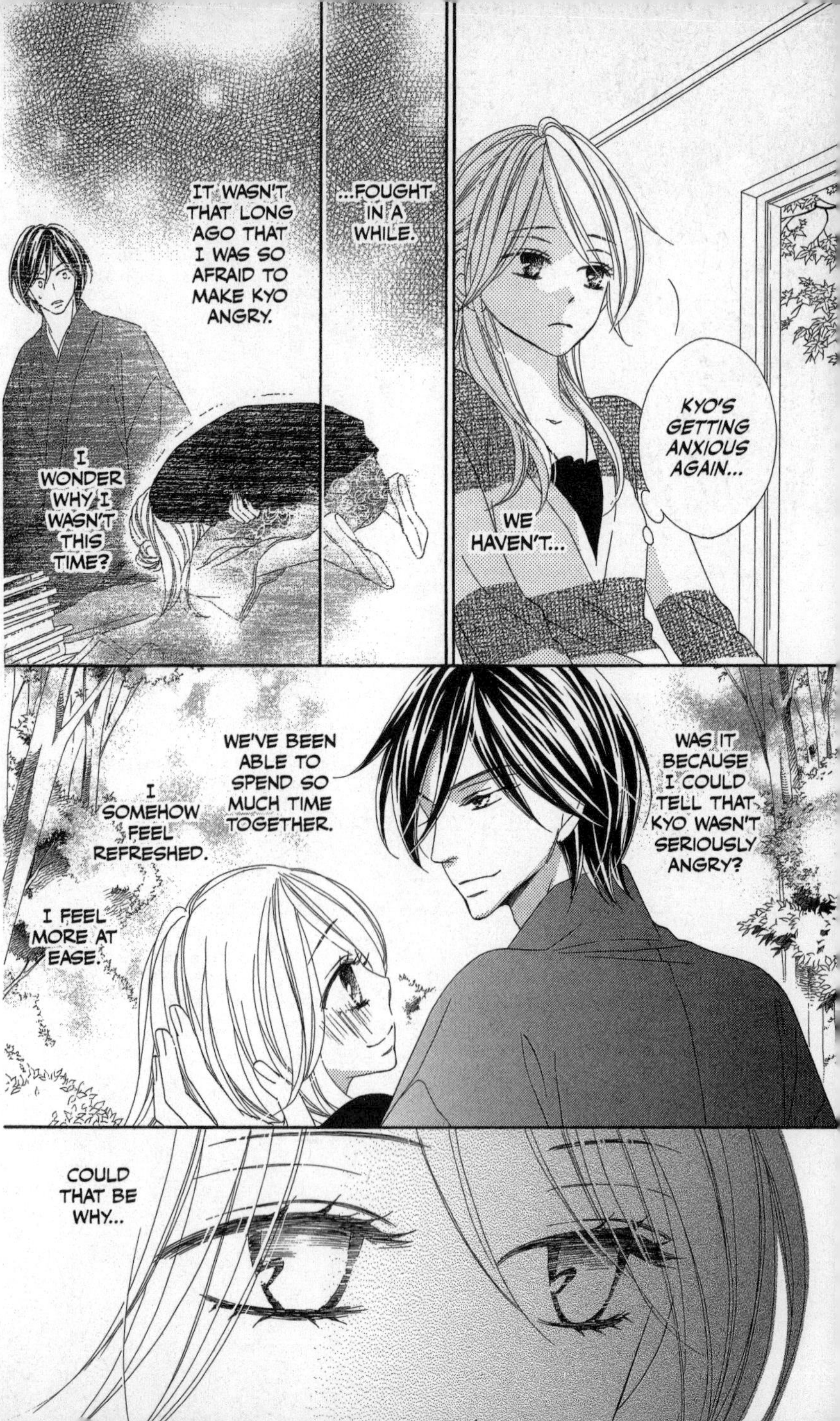
KYO'S GETTING ANXIOUS AGAIN...
WE HAVEN'T...
...FOUGHT IN A WHILE.
IT WASN'T THAT LONG AGO THAT I WAS SO AFRAID TO MAKE KYO ANGRY.
I WONDER WHY I WASN'T THIS TIME?
WAS IT BECAUSE I COULD TELL THAT KYO WASN'T SERIOUSLY ANGRY?
WE'VE BEEN ABLE TO SPEND SO MUCH TIME TOGETHER.
I SOMEHOW FEEL REFRESHED.
I FEEL MORE AT EASE.
COULD THAT BE WHY...

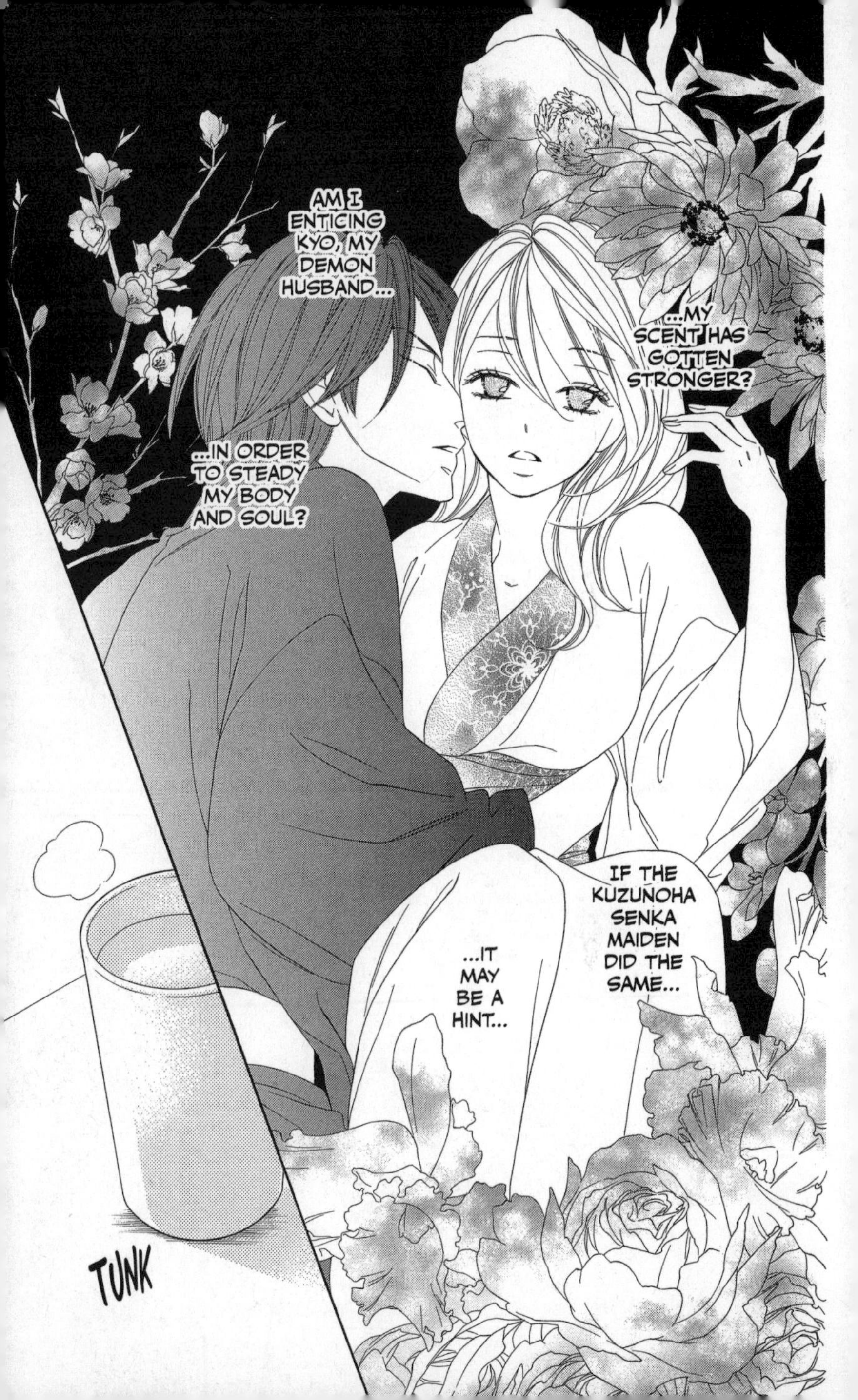
...MY SCENT HAS GOTTEN STRONGER?
AM I ENTICING KYO, MY DEMON HUSBAND...
...IN ORDER TO STEADY MY BODY AND SOUL?
IF THE KUZUNOHA SENKA MAIDEN DID THE SAME...
...IT MAY BE A HINT...
TUNK

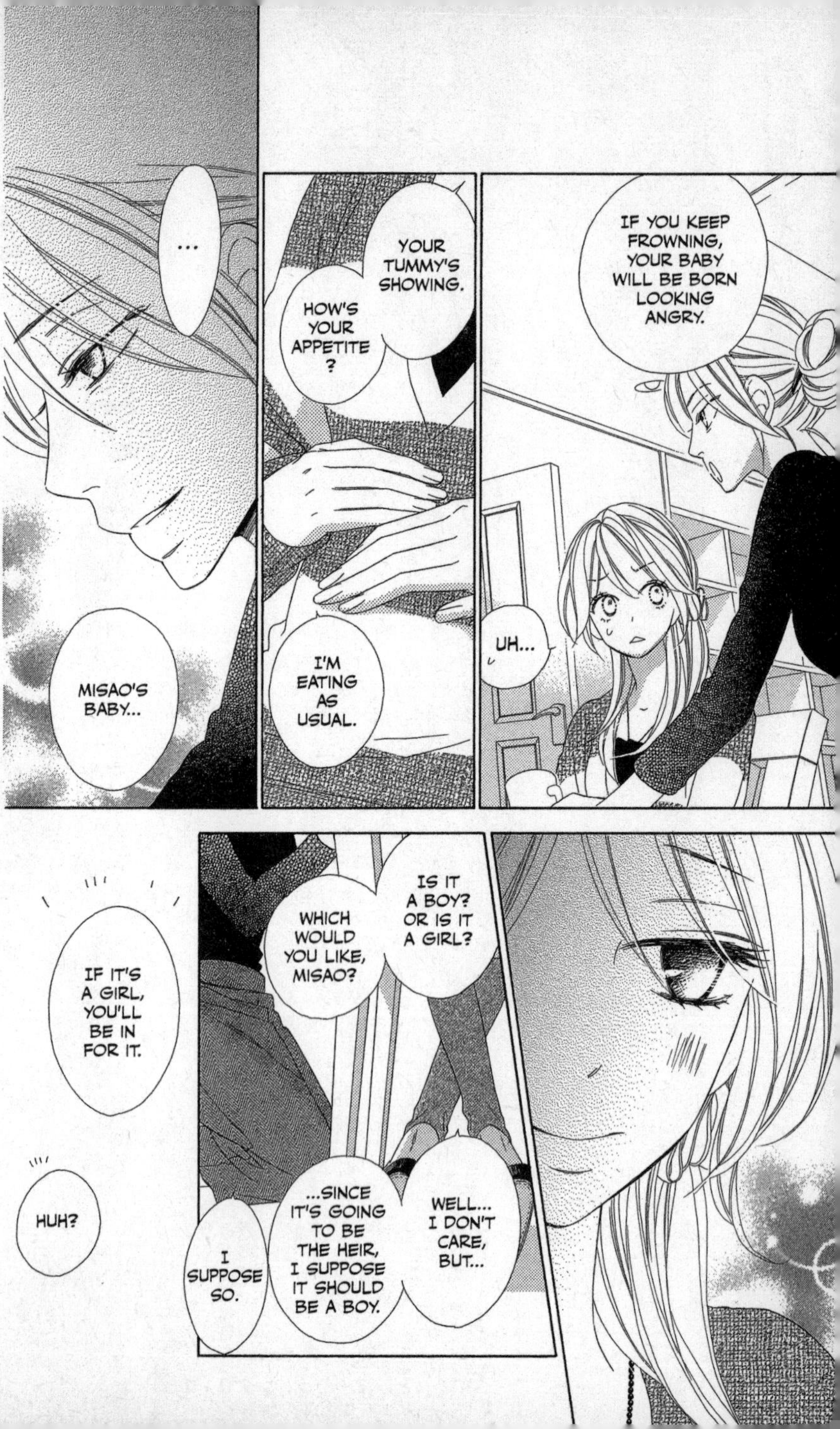
IF YOU KEEP FROWNING, YOUR BABY WILL BE BORN LOOKING ANGRY.
UH...
YOUR TUMMY'S SHOWING.
HOW'S YOUR APPETITE?
I'M EATING AS USUAL.
...
MISAO'S BABY...
IS IT A BOY? OR IS IT A GIRL?
WHICH WOULD YOU LIKE, MISAO?
WELL... I DON'T CARE, BUT...
...SINCE IT'S GOING TO BE THE HEIR, I SUPPOSE IT SHOULD BE A BOY.
I SUPPOSE SO.
IF IT'S A GIRL, YOU'LL BE IN FOR IT.
HUH?

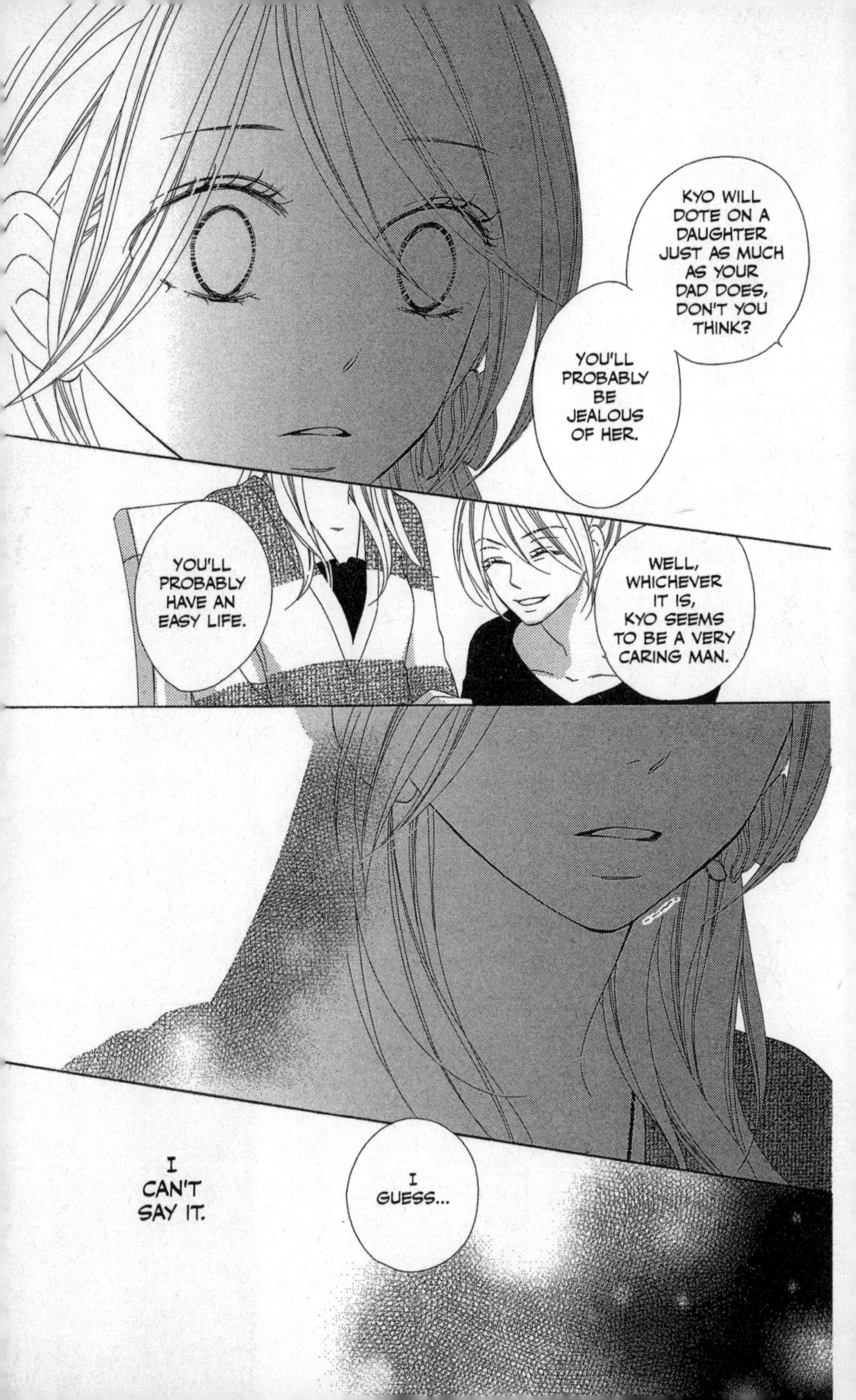
KYO WILL DOTE ON A DAUGHTER JUST AS MUCH AS YOUR DAD DOES, DON'T YOU THINK?
YOU'LL PROBABLY BE JEALOUS OF HER.
WELL, WHICHEVER IT IS, KYO SEEMS TO BE A VERY CARING MAN.
YOU'LL PROBABLY HAVE AN EASY LIFE.
I GUESS...
I CAN'T SAY IT.

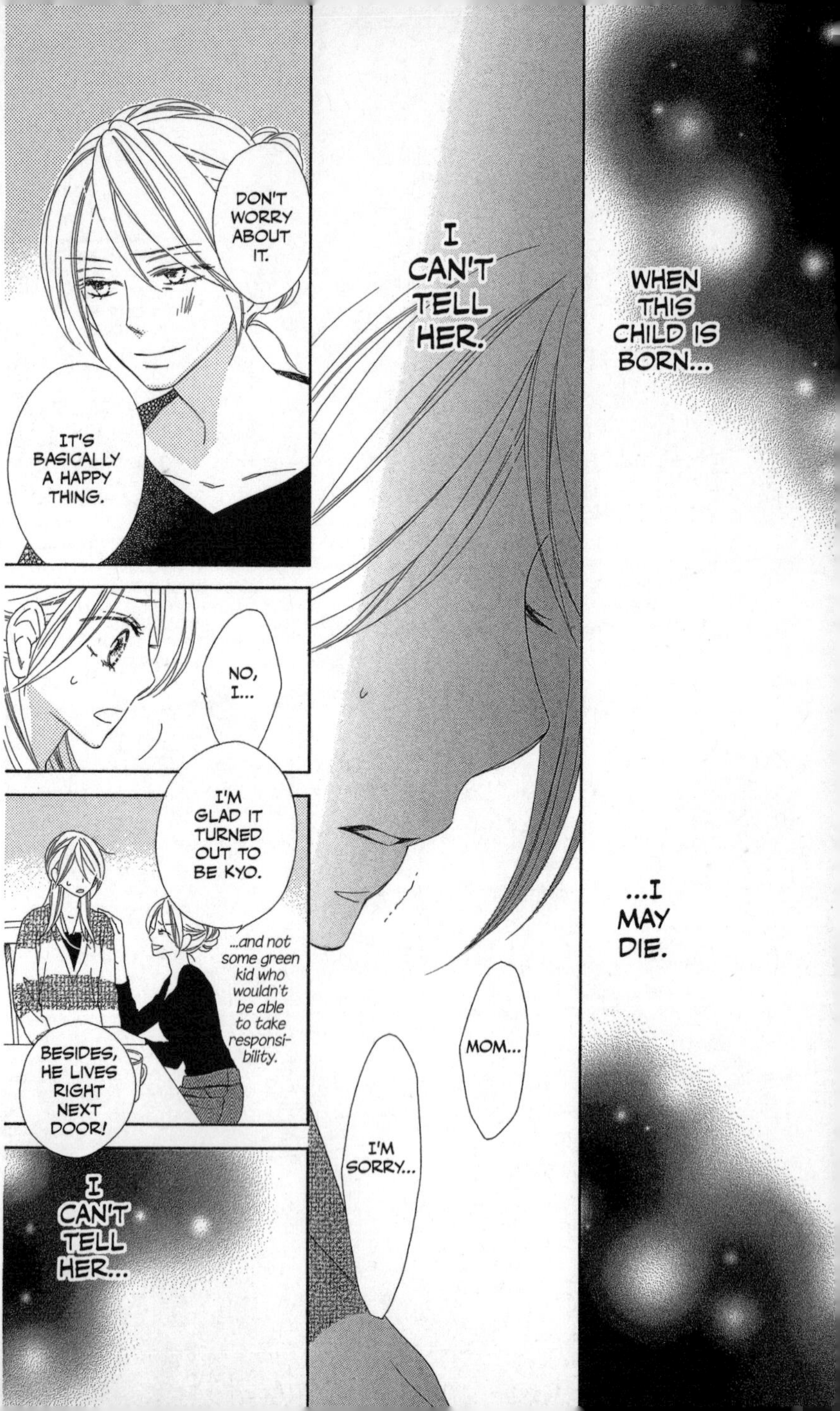
WHEN THIS CHILD IS BORN...
...I MAY DIE.
I CAN'T TELL HER.
MOM...
I'M SORRY...
DON'T WORRY ABOUT IT.
IT'S BASICALLY A HAPPY THING.
NO, I...
I'M GLAD IT TURNED OUT TO BE KYO.
...and not some green kid who wouldn't be able to take responsi-bility.
BESIDES, HE LIVES RIGHT NEXT DOOR!
I CAN'T TELL HER...

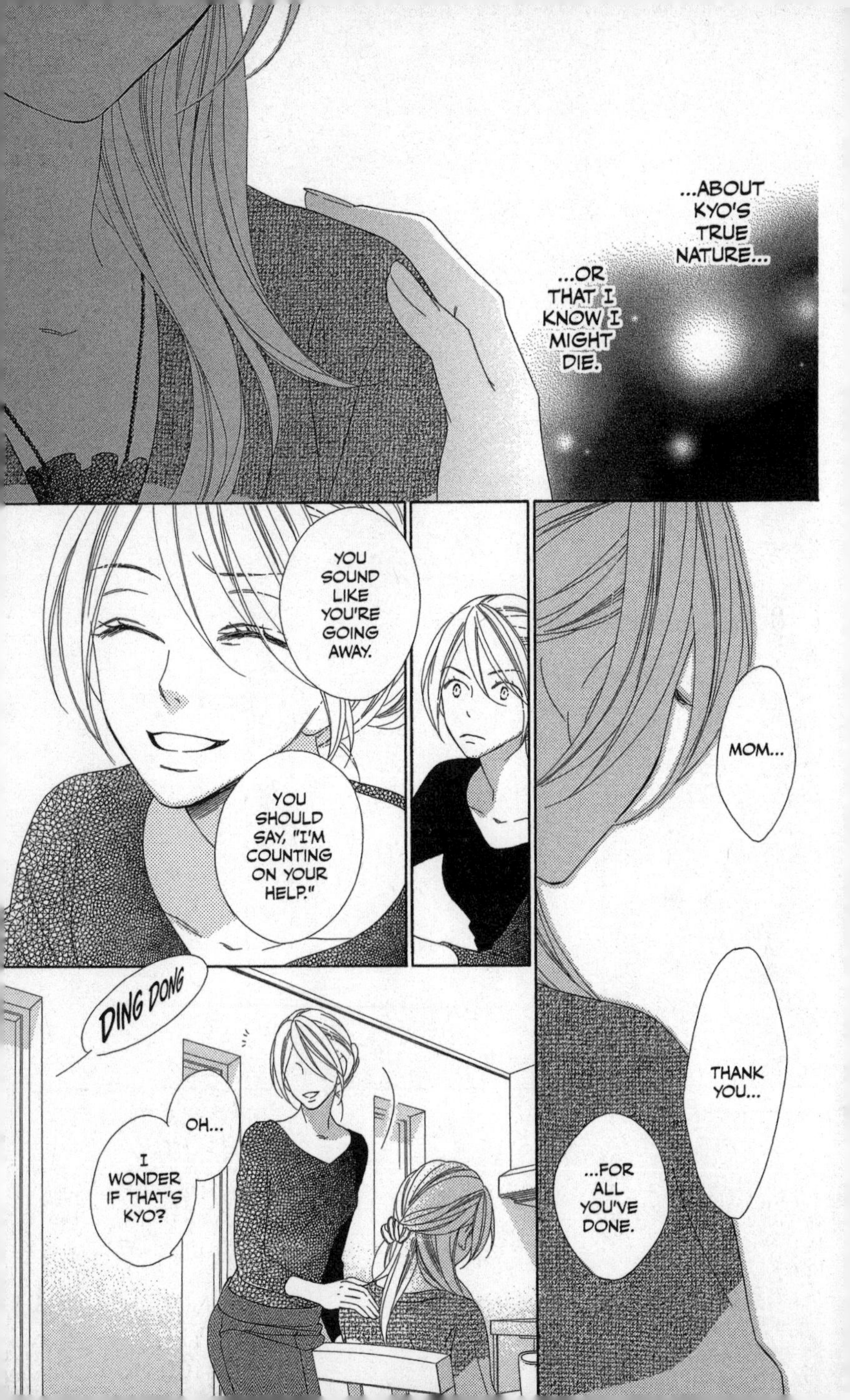
...ABOUT KYO'S TRUE NATURE...
...OR THAT I KNOW I MIGHT DIE.
MOM...
THANK YOU...
...FOR ALL YOU'VE DONE.
YOU SOUND LIKE YOU'RE GOING AWAY.
YOU SHOULD SAY, "I'M COUNTING ON YOUR HELP."
DING DONG
OH...
I WONDER IF THAT'S KYO?

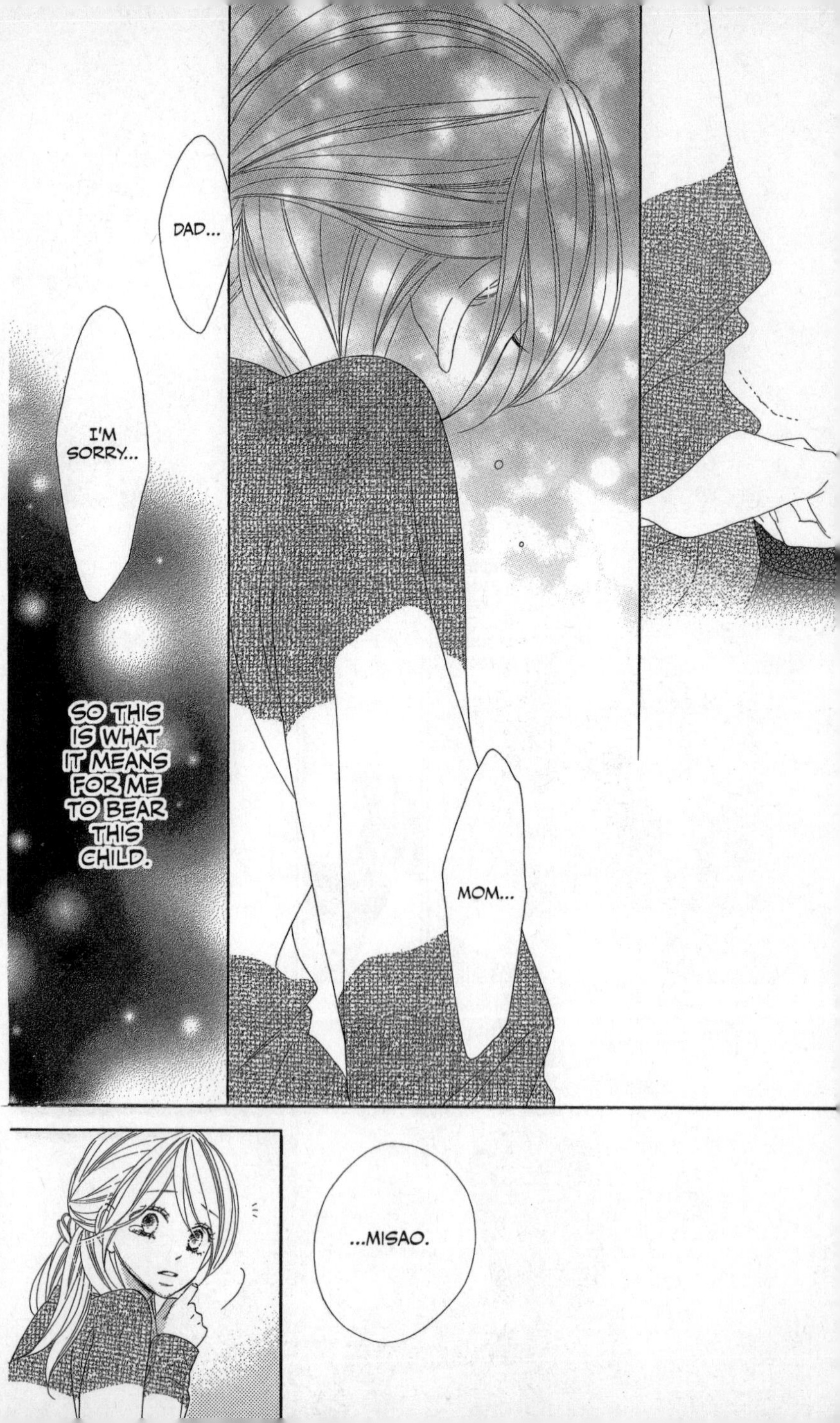
MOM...
DAD...
I'M SORRY...
SO THIS IS WHAT IT MEANS FOR ME TO BEAR THIS CHILD.
...MISAO.

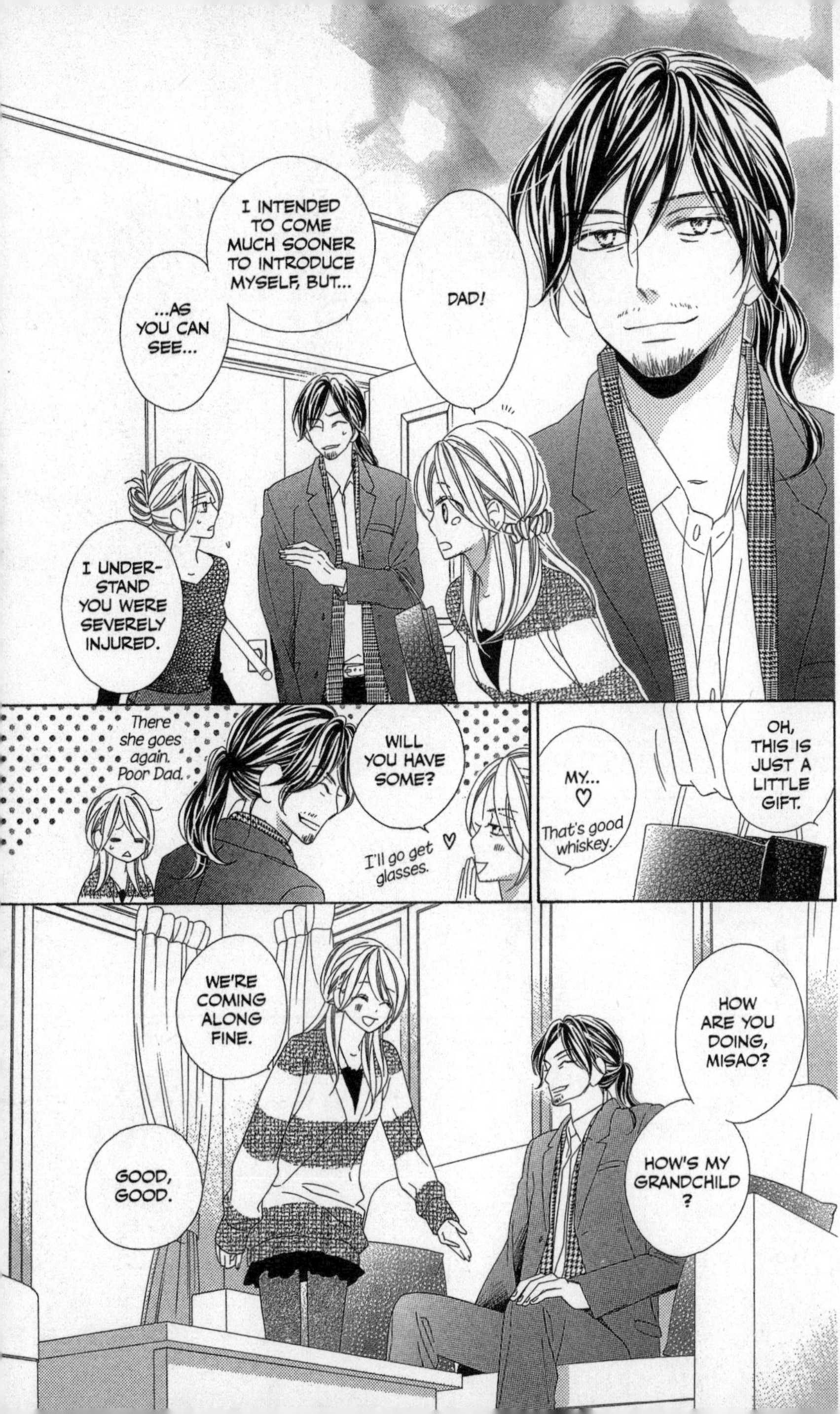
DAD!
I INTENDED TO COME MUCH SOONER TO INTRODUCE MYSELF, BUT...
...AS YOU CAN SEE...
I UNDERSTAND YOU WERE SEVERELY INJURED.
OH, THIS IS JUST A LITTLE GIFT.
MY... ♡
That's good whiskey.
I'll go get glasses. ♡
WILL YOU HAVE SOME?
There she goes again. Poor Dad.
HOW ARE YOU DOING, MISAO?
HOW'S MY GRANDCHILD?
WE'RE COMING ALONG FINE.
GOOD, GOOD.

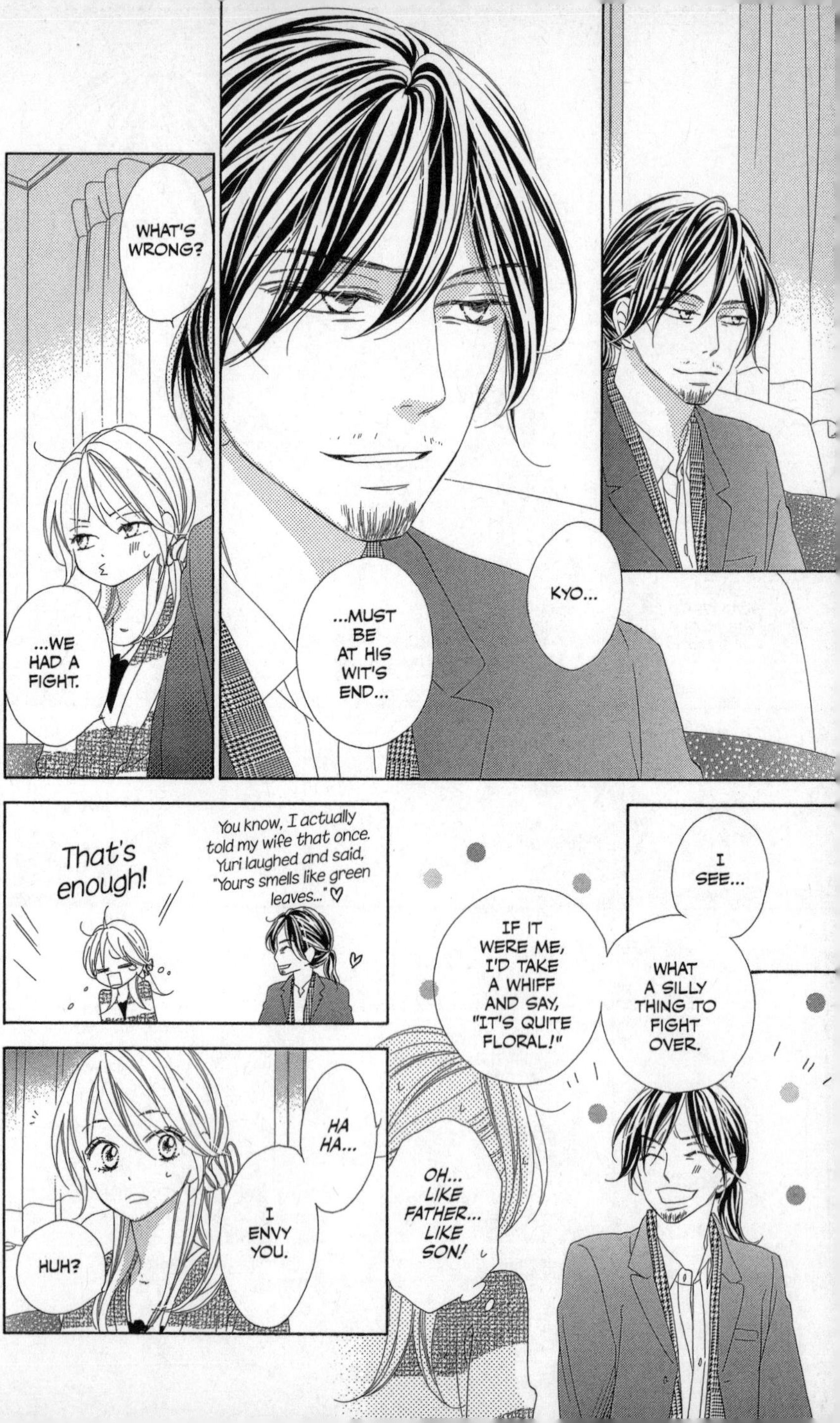
KYO...
...MUST BE AT HIS WIT'S END...
WHAT'S WRONG?
...WE HAD A FIGHT.
I SEE...
WHAT A SILLY THING TO FIGHT OVER.
IF IT WERE ME, I'D TAKE A WHIFF AND SAY, "IT'S QUITE FLORAL!"
OH... LIKE FATHER... LIKE SON!
You know, I actually told my wife that once. Yuri laughed and said, "Yours smells like green leaves..."♡
That's enough!
HA HA...
I ENVY YOU.
HUH?

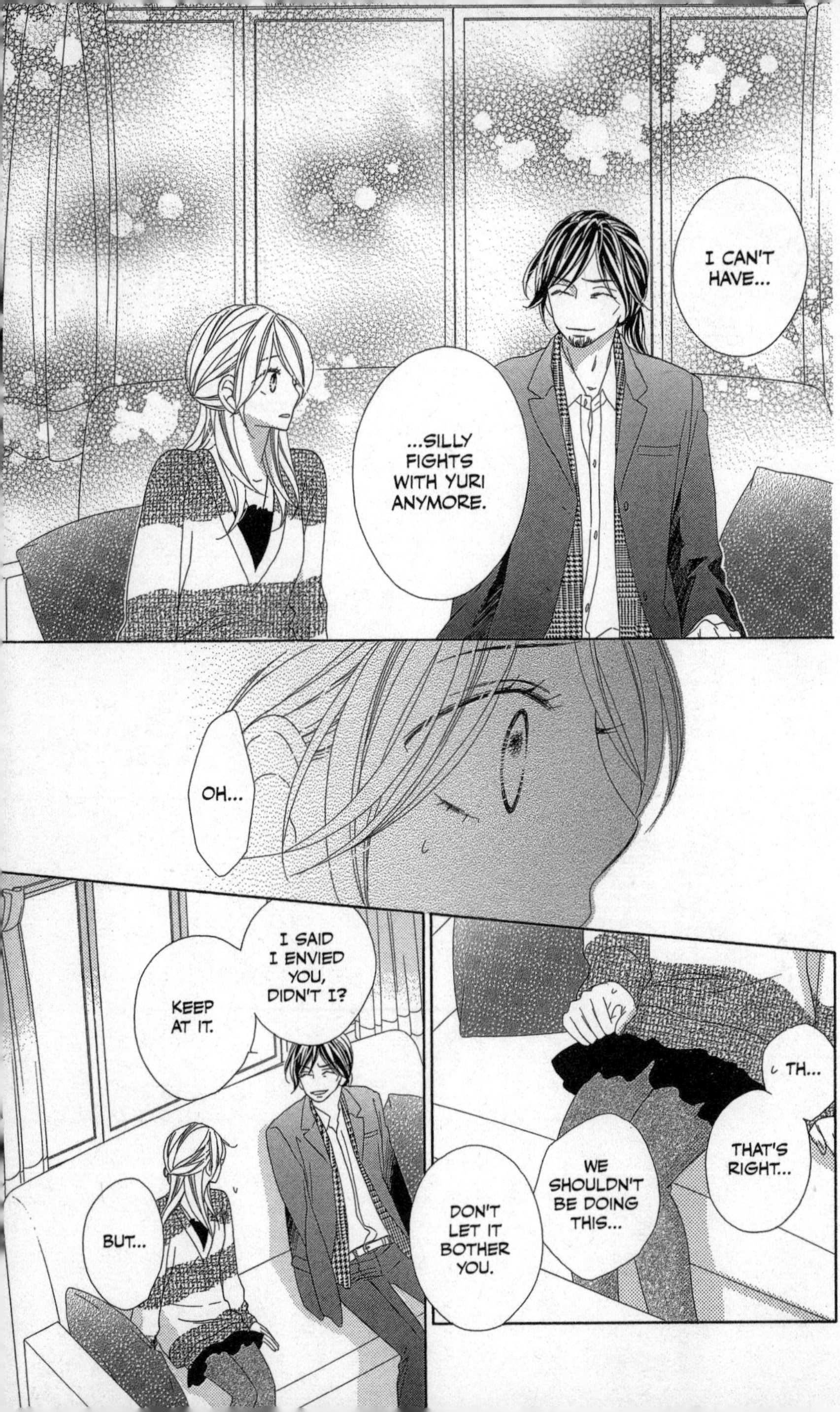
I CAN'T HAVE...
...SILLY FIGHTS WITH YURI ANYMORE.
OH...
TH...
THAT'S RIGHT...
WE SHOULDN'T BE DOING THIS...
DON'T LET IT BOTHER YOU.
I SAID I ENVIED YOU, DIDN'T I?
KEEP AT IT.
BUT...

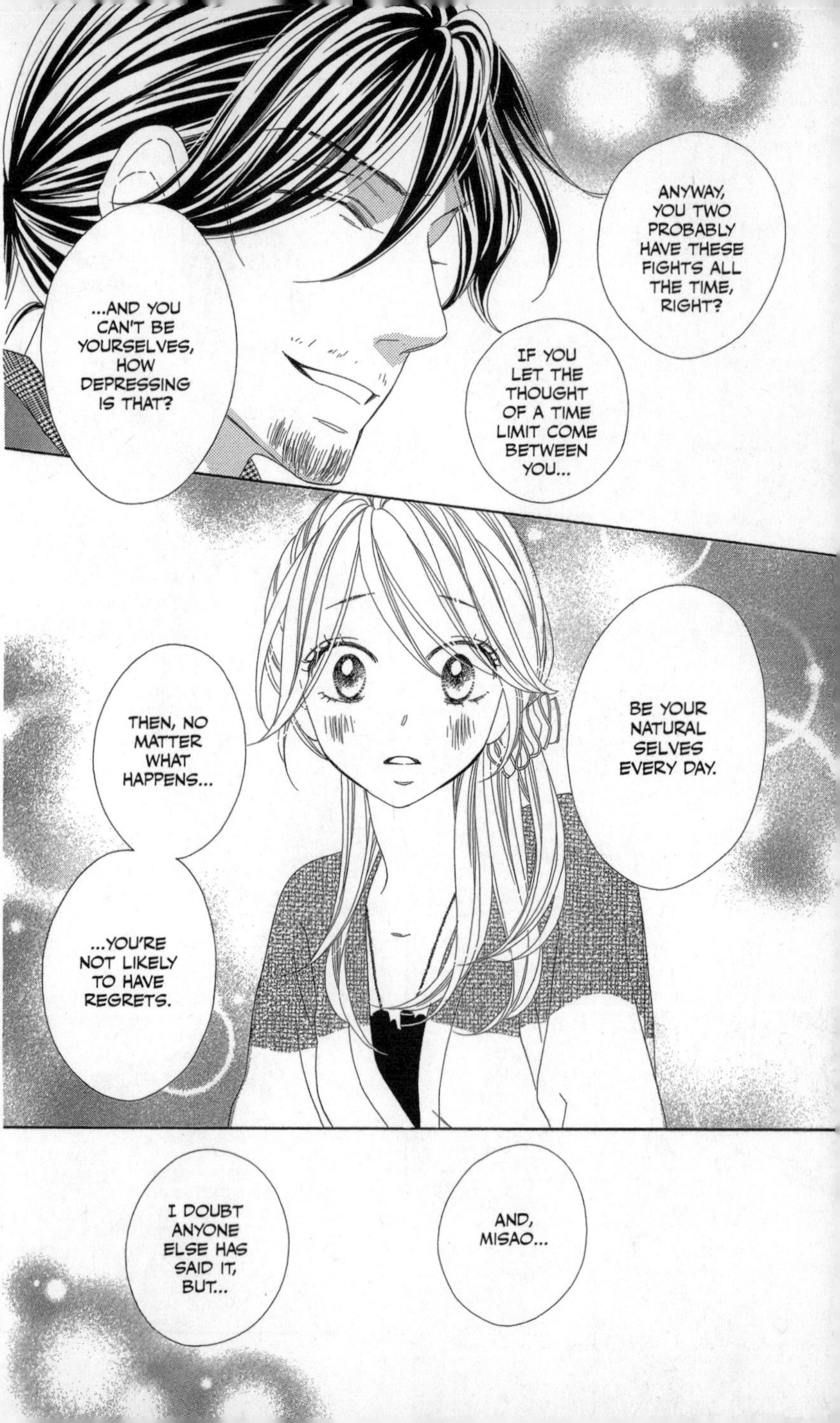
ANYWAY, YOU TWO PROBABLY HAVE THESE FIGHTS ALL THE TIME, RIGHT?
IF YOU LET THE THOUGHT OF A TIME LIMIT COME BETWEEN YOU...
...AND YOU CAN'T BE YOURSELVES, HOW DEPRESSING IS THAT?
BE YOUR NATURAL SELVES EVERY DAY.
THEN, NO MATTER WHAT HAPPENS...
...YOU'RE NOT LIKELY TO HAVE REGRETS.
AND, MISAO...
I DOUBT ANYONE ELSE HAS SAID IT, BUT...

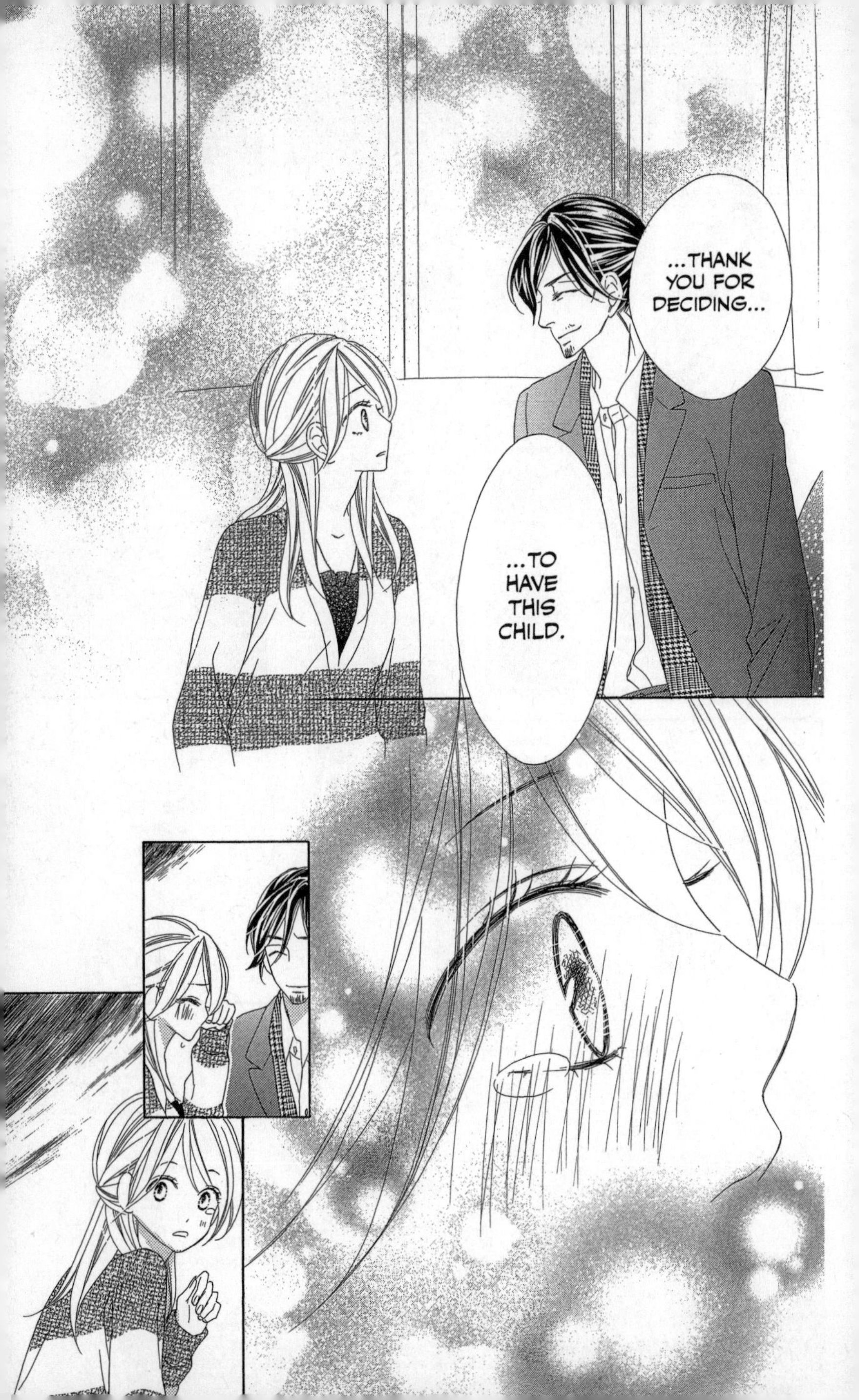
...THANK YOU FOR DECIDING...
...TO HAVE THIS CHILD.

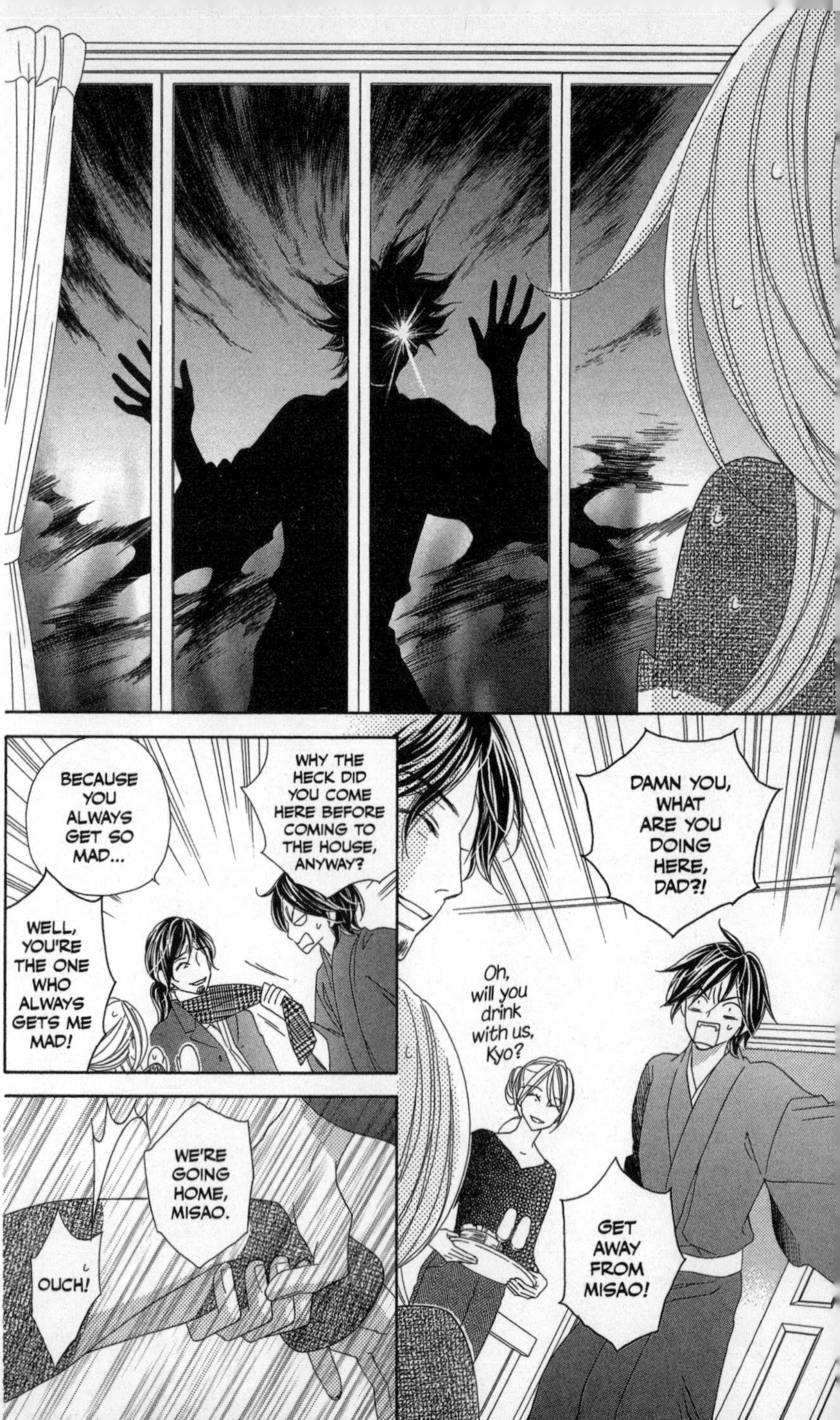
DAMN YOU, WHAT ARE YOU DOING HERE, DAD?!
Oh, will you drink with us, Kyo?
GET AWAY FROM MISAO!
WHY THE HECK DID YOU COME HERE BEFORE COMING TO THE HOUSE, ANYWAY?
BECAUSE YOU ALWAYS GET SO MAD...
WELL, YOU'RE THE ONE WHO ALWAYS GETS ME MAD!
WE'RE GOING HOME, MISAO.
OUCH!

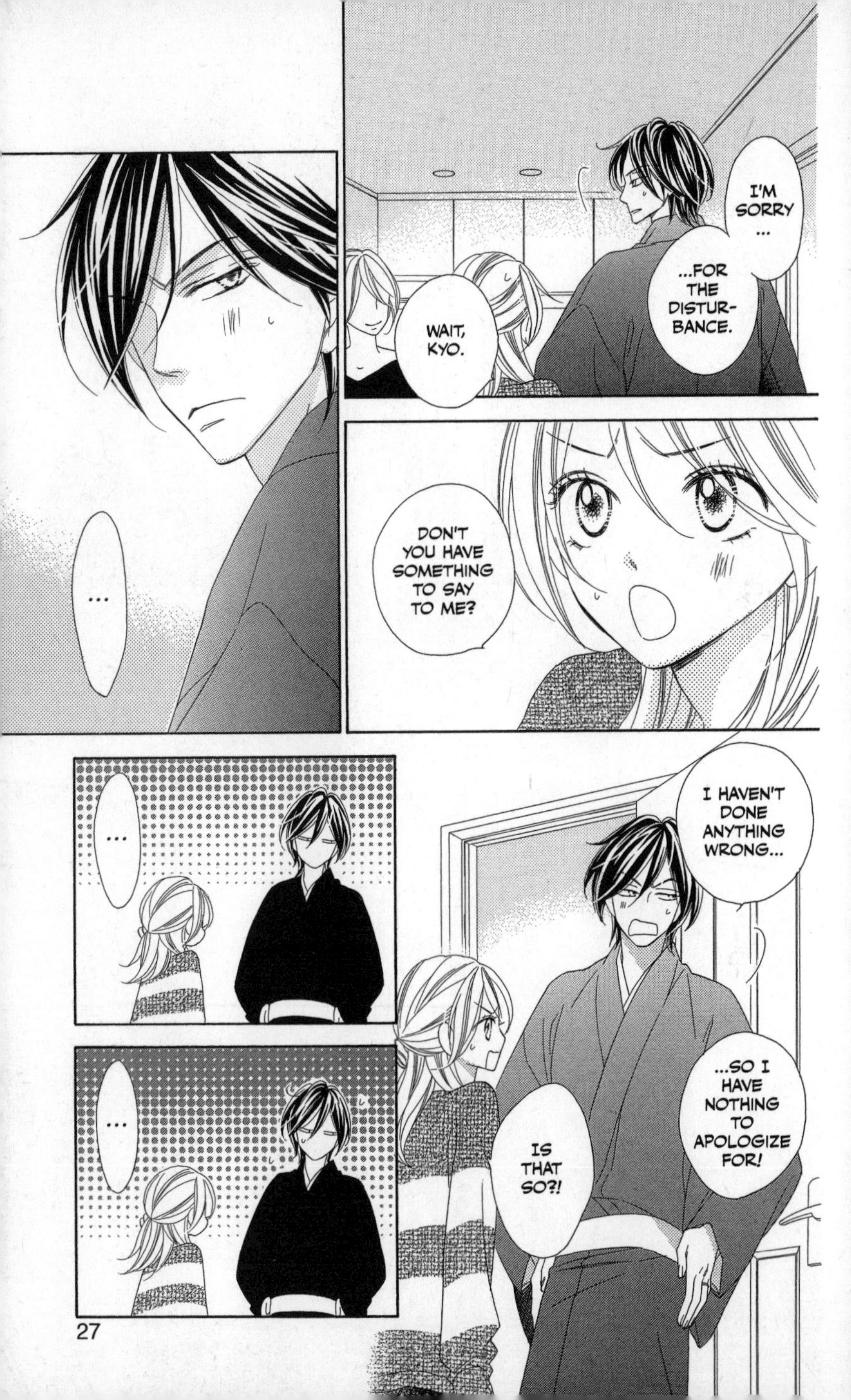
I'M SORRY...
...FOR THE DISTURBANCE.
WAIT, KYO.
DON'T YOU HAVE SOMETHING TO SAY TO ME?
...
I HAVEN'T DONE ANYTHING WRONG...
...SO I HAVE NOTHING TO APOLOGIZE FOR!
IS THAT SO?!
...
...

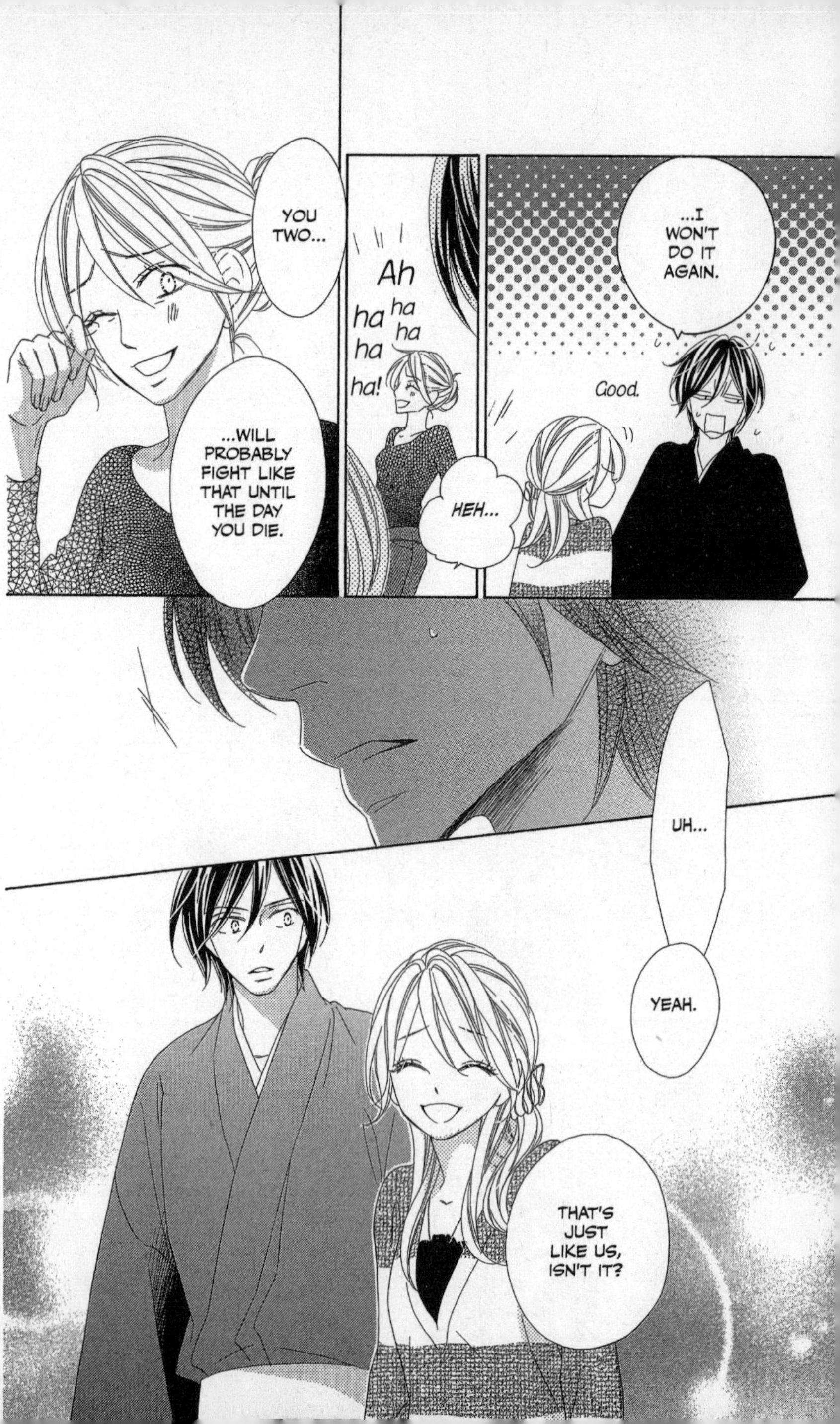

...I WON'T DO IT AGAIN.
Good.
HEH...
Ah ha ha ha ha ha!
YOU TWO...
...WILL PROBABLY FIGHT LIKE THAT UNTIL THE DAY YOU DIE.
UH...
YEAH.
THAT'S JUST LIKE US, ISN'T IT?

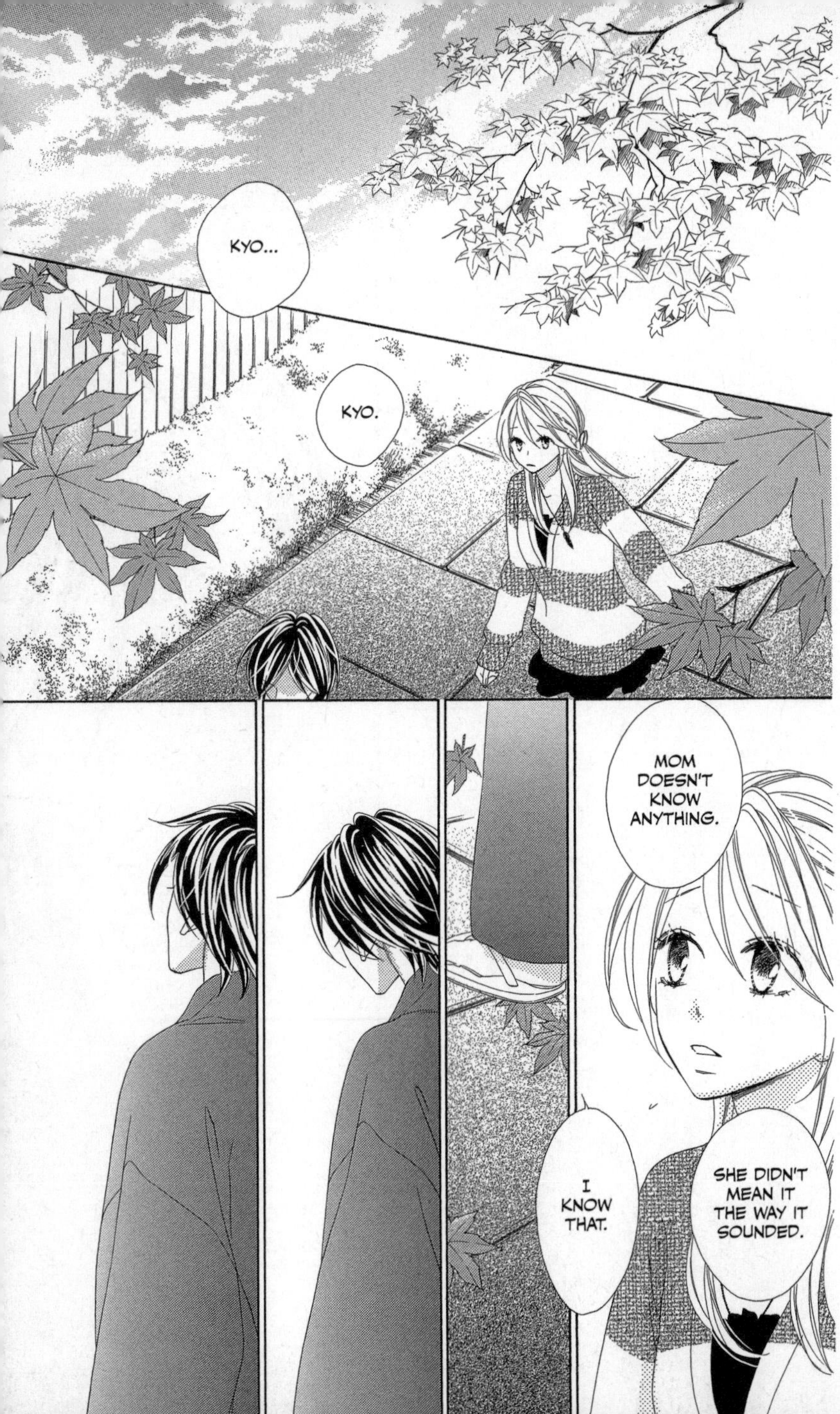
KYO...
KYO.
MOM DOESN'T KNOW ANYTHING.
SHE DIDN'T MEAN IT THE WAY IT SOUNDED.
I KNOW THAT.

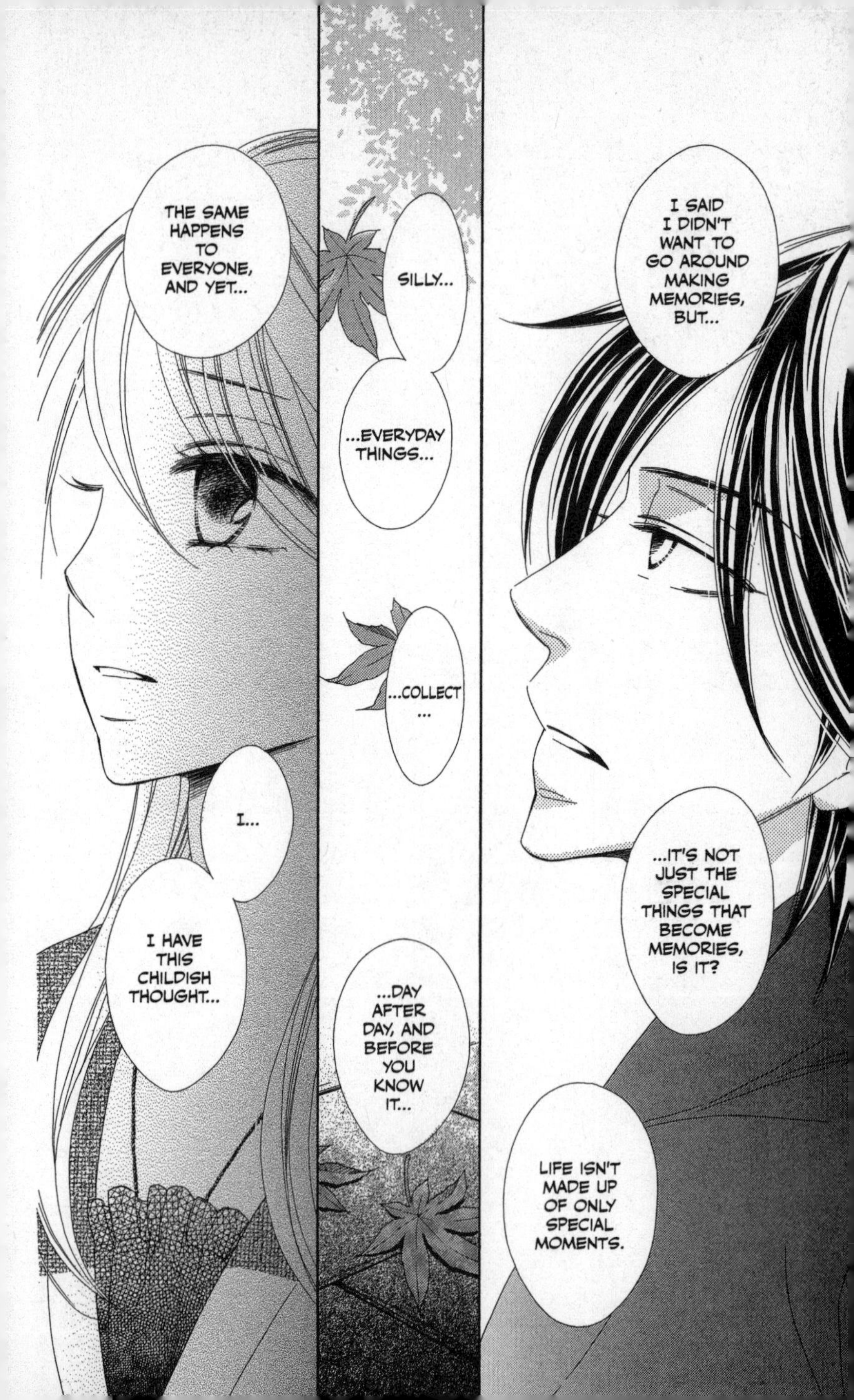
I SAID I DIDN'T WANT TO GO AROUND MAKING MEMORIES, BUT...
...IT'S NOT JUST THE SPECIAL THINGS THAT BECOME MEMORIES, IS IT?
LIFE ISN'T MADE UP OF ONLY SPECIAL MOMENTS.
SILLY...
...EVERYDAY THINGS...
...COLLECT ...
...DAY AFTER DAY, AND BEFORE YOU KNOW IT...
THE SAME HAPPENS TO EVERYONE, AND YET...
I...
I HAVE THIS CHILDISH THOUGHT...

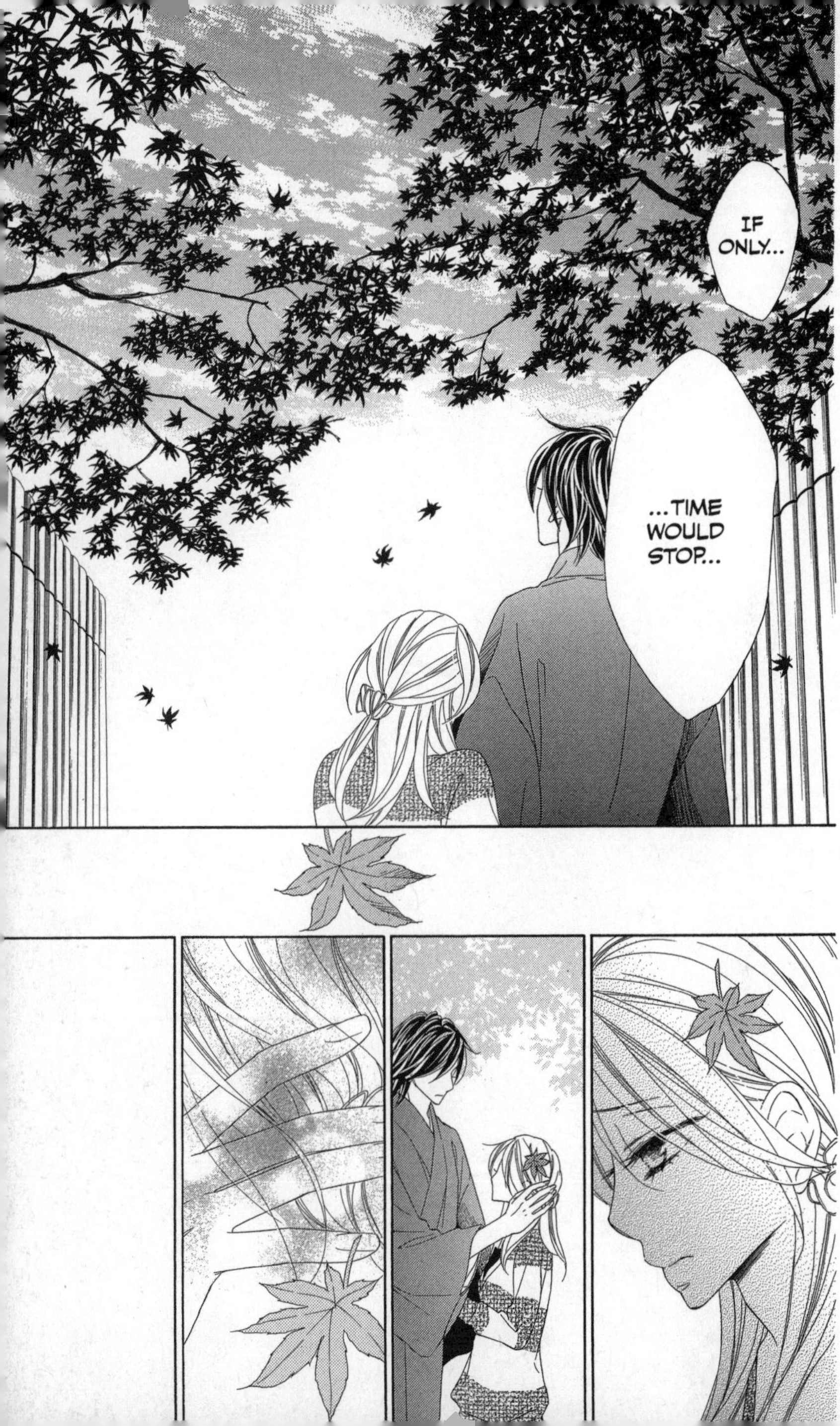
IF ONLY...
...TIME WOULD STOP...

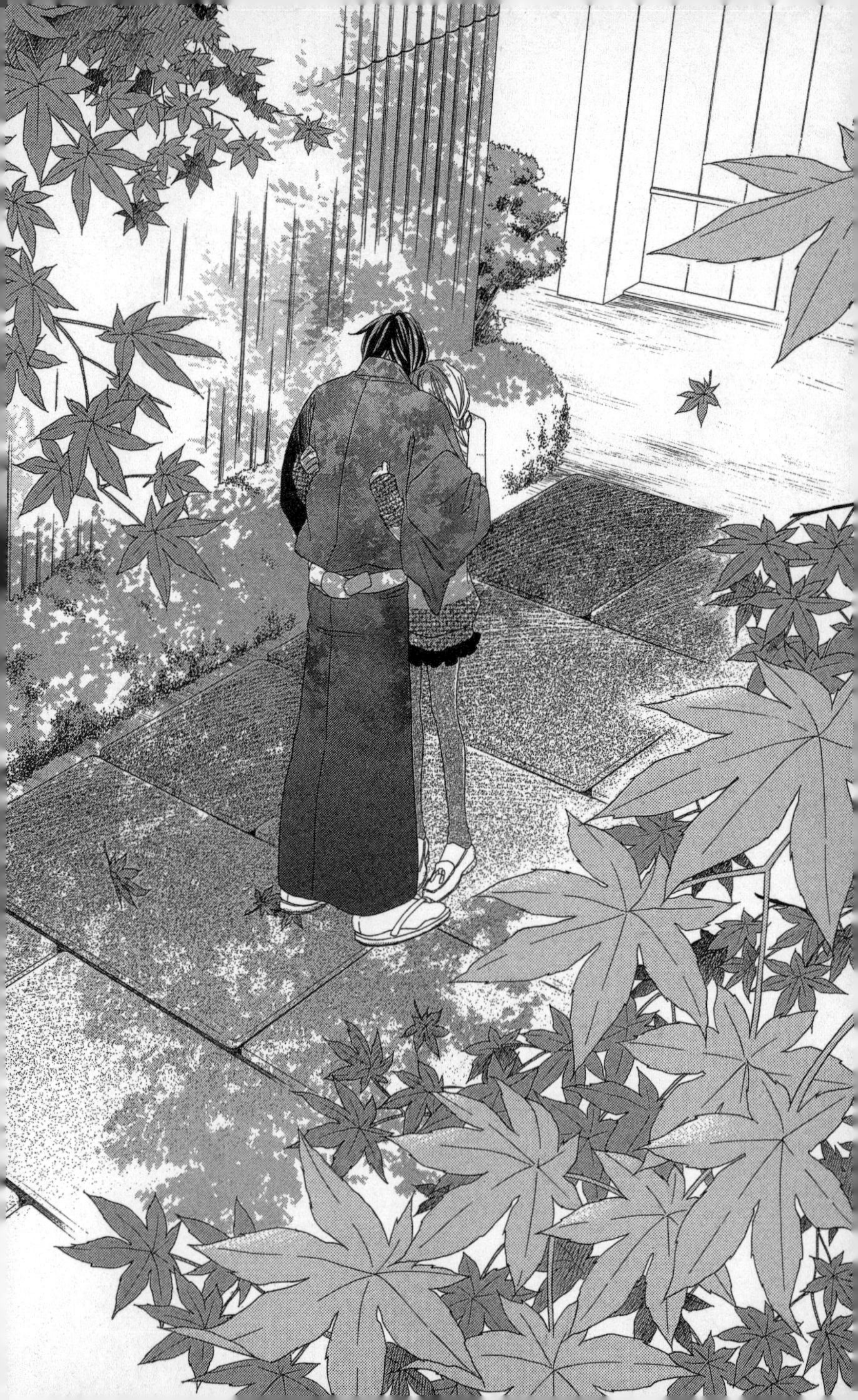

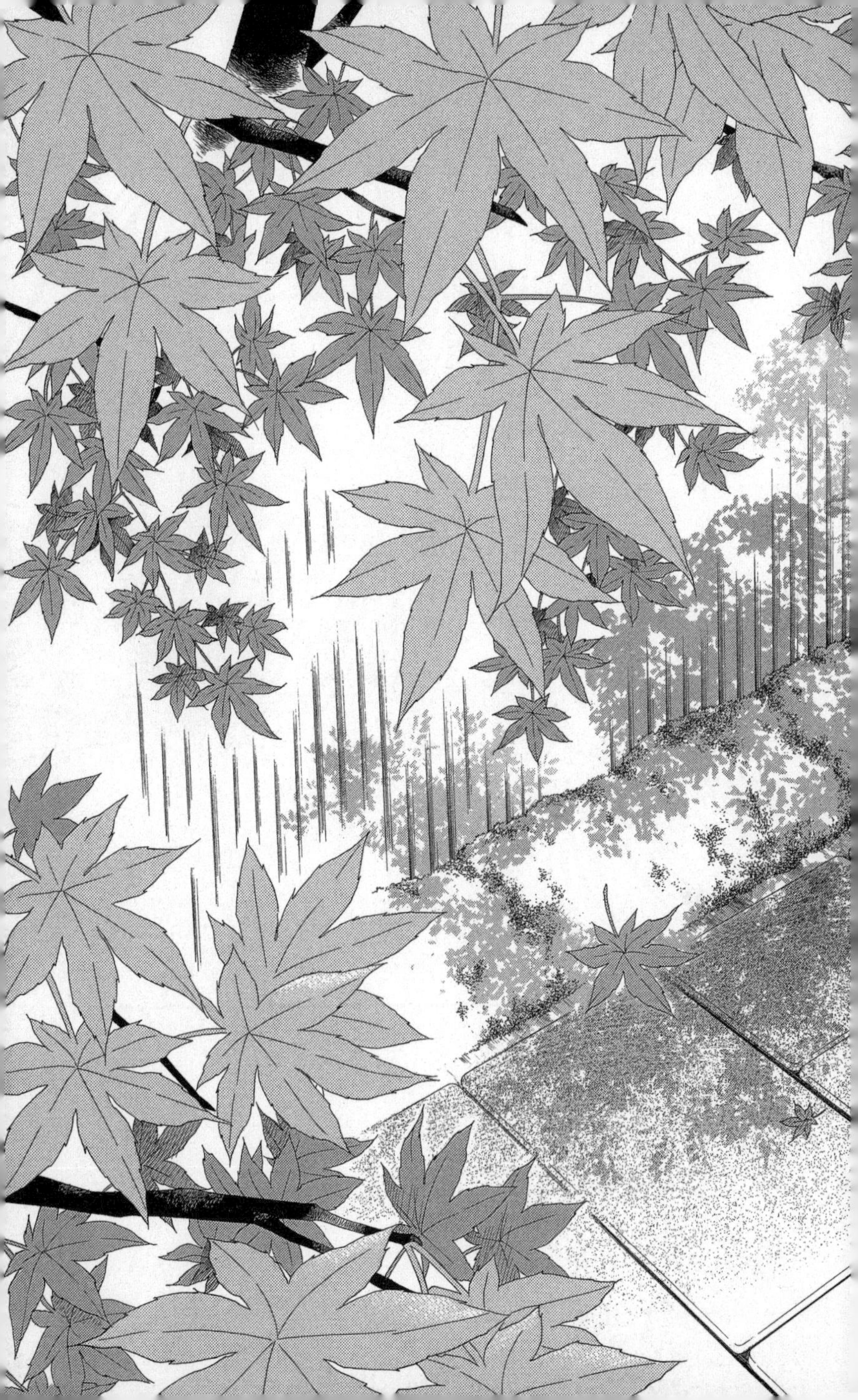

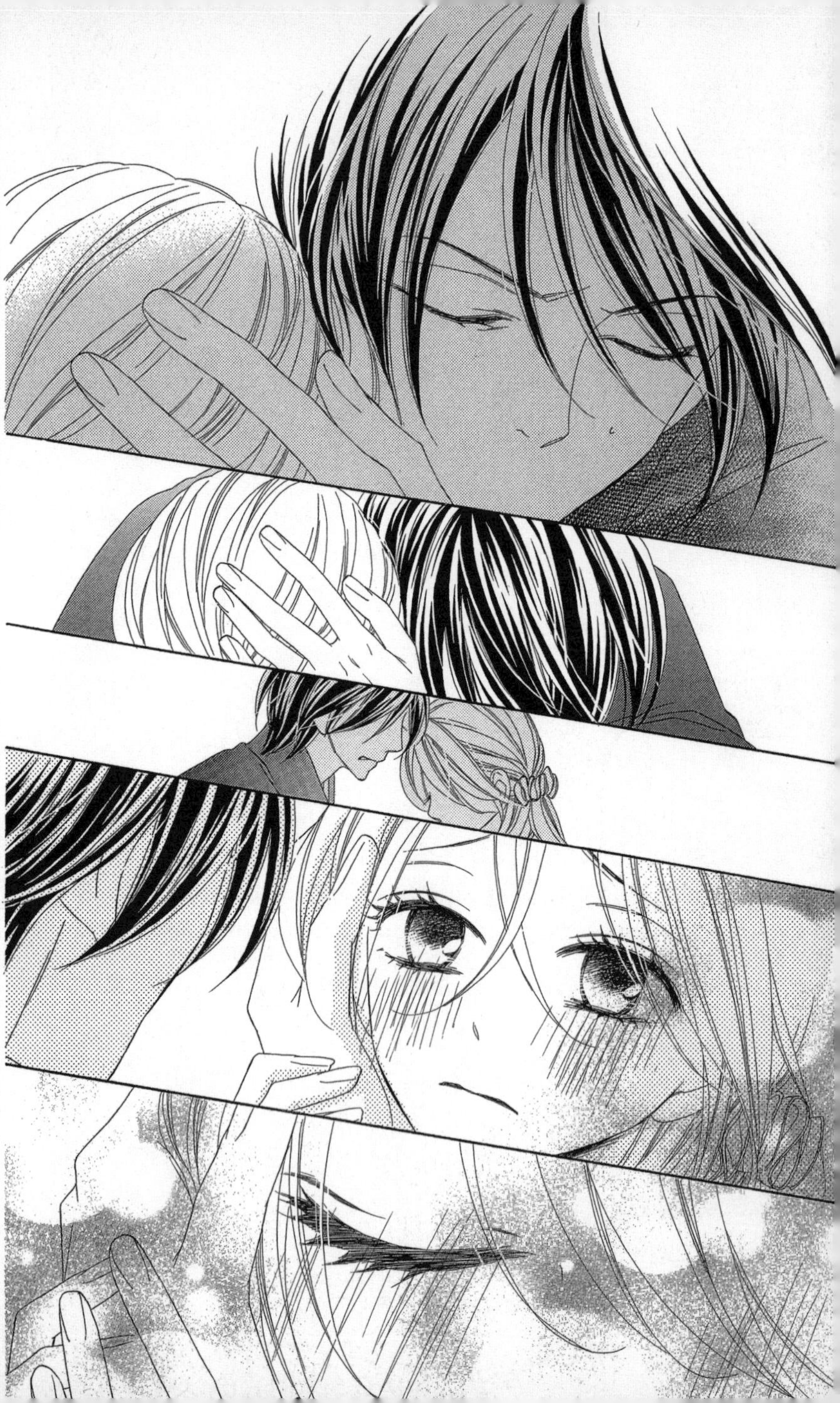

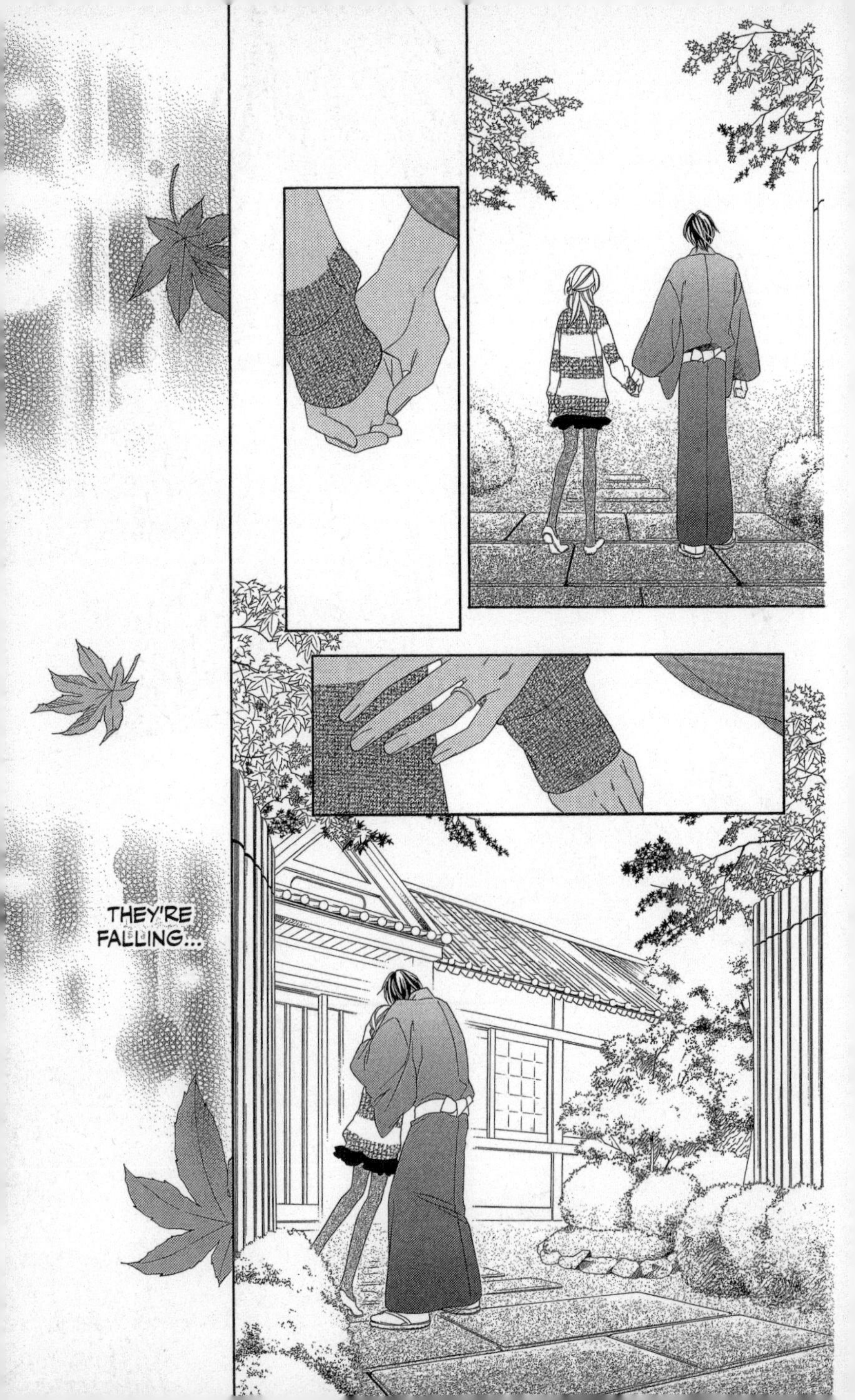
THEY'RE FALLING...

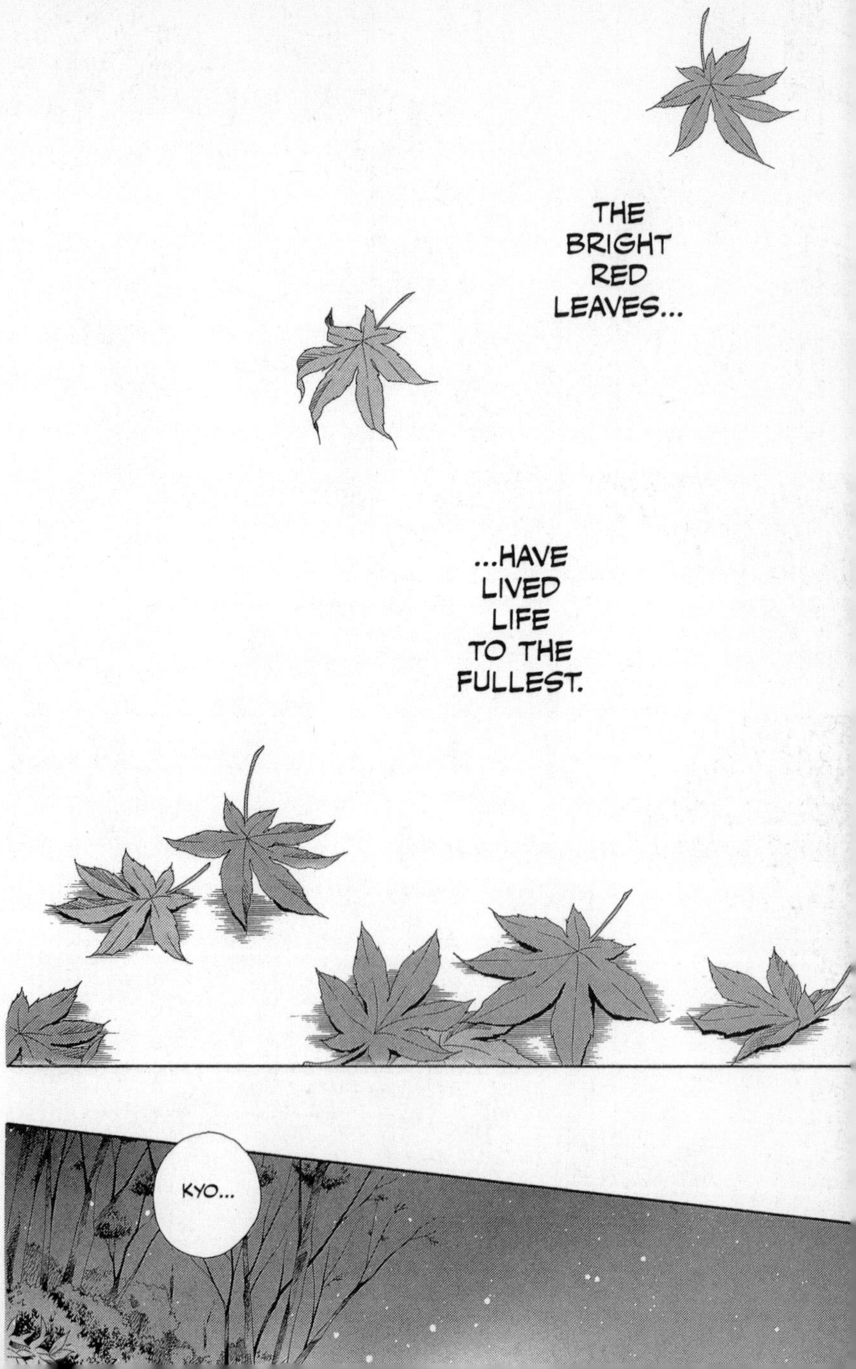
THE BRIGHT RED LEAVES...
...HAVE LIVED LIFE TO THE FULLEST.
KYO...

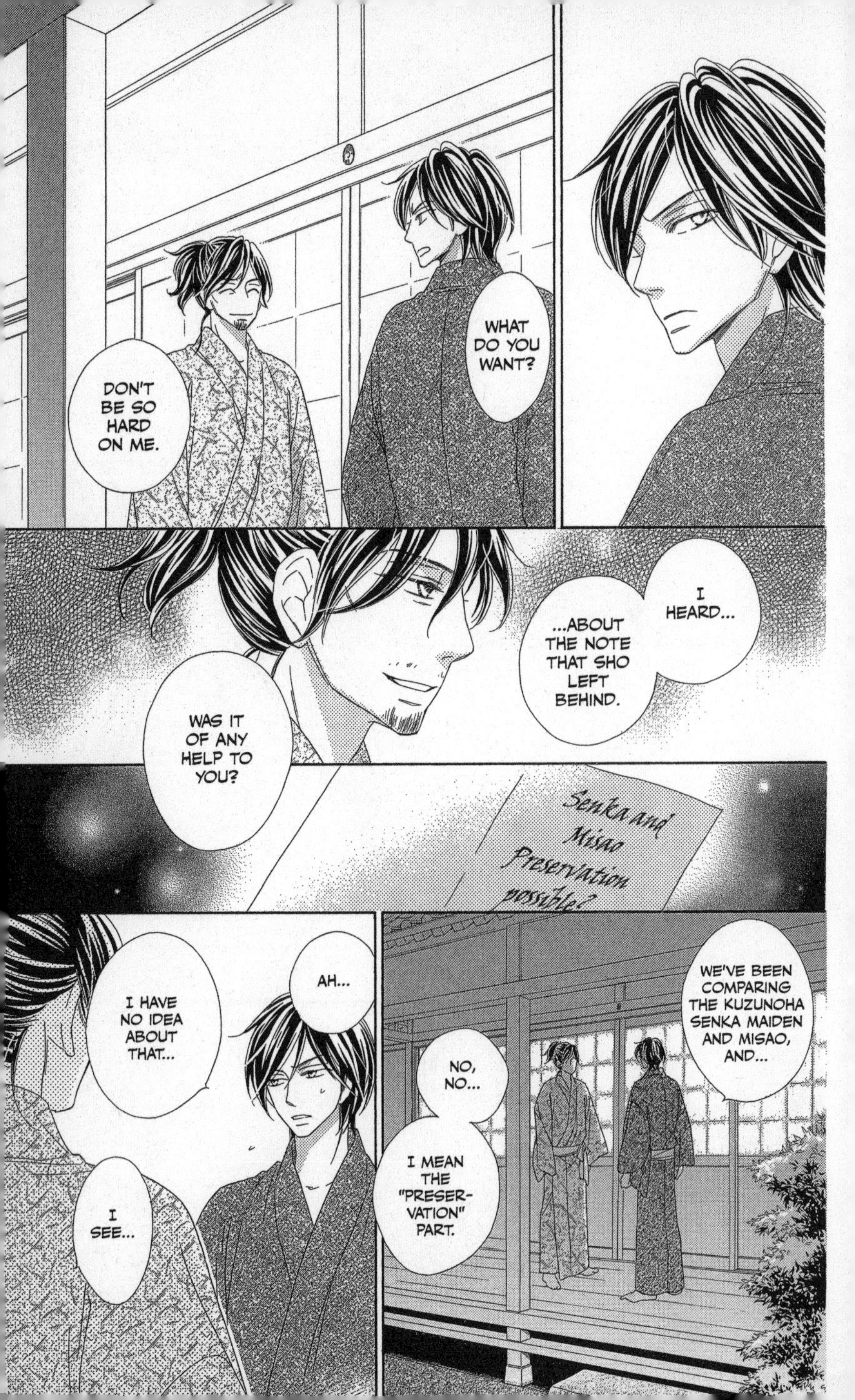
WHAT DO YOU WANT?
DON'T BE SO HARD ON ME.
I HEARD...
...ABOUT THE NOTE THAT SHO LEFT BEHIND.
WAS IT OF ANY HELP TO YOU?
Senka and Misao Preservation possible?
WE'VE BEEN COMPARING THE KUZUNOHA SENKA MAIDEN AND MISAO, AND...
NO, NO...
I MEAN THE "PRESER-VATION" PART.
AH...
I HAVE NO IDEA ABOUT THAT...
I SEE...

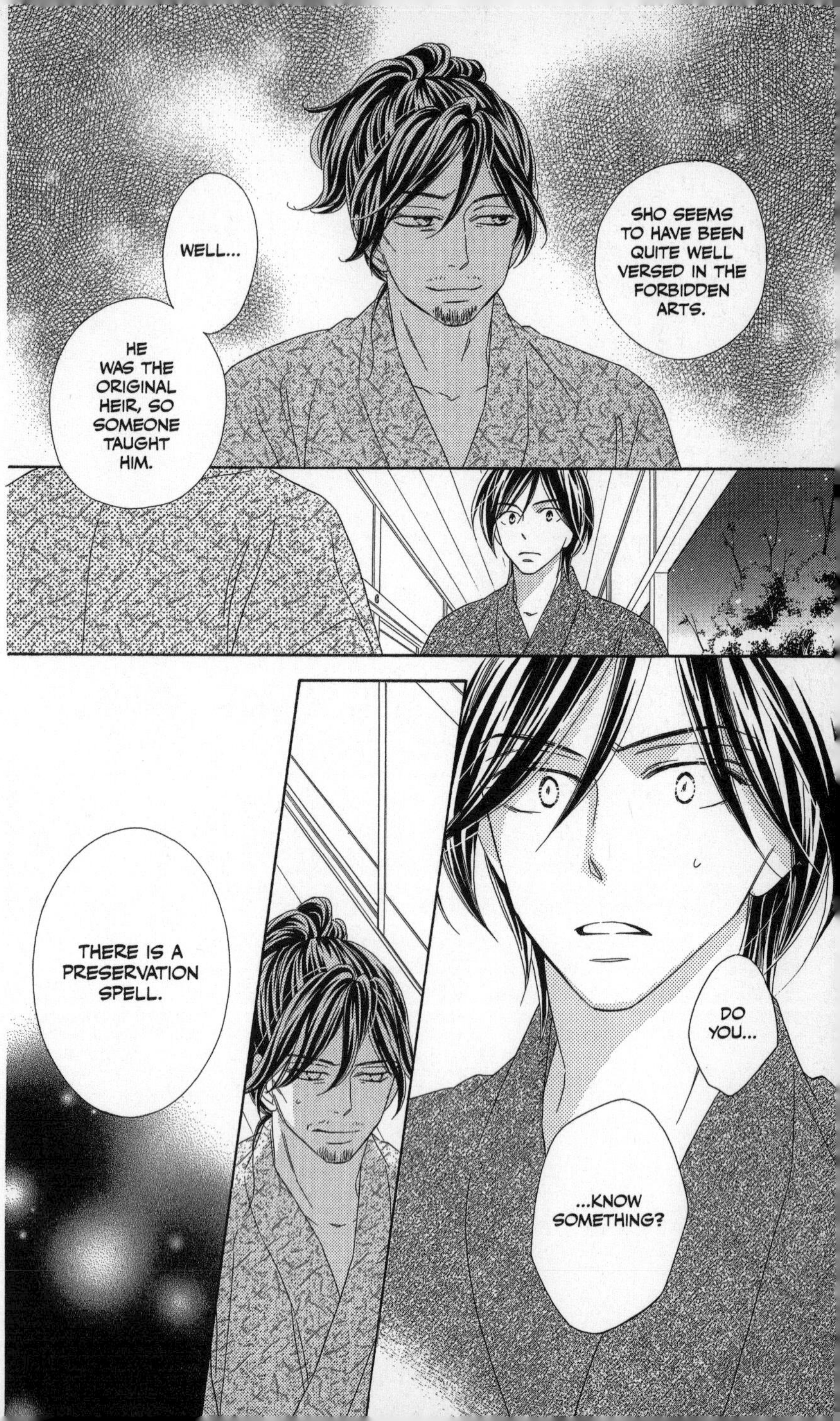
SHO SEEMS TO HAVE BEEN QUITE WELL VERSED IN THE FORBIDDEN ARTS.
WELL...
HE WAS THE ORIGINAL HEIR, SO SOMEONE TAUGHT HIM.
DO YOU...
...KNOW SOMETHING?
THERE IS A PRESERVATION SPELL.

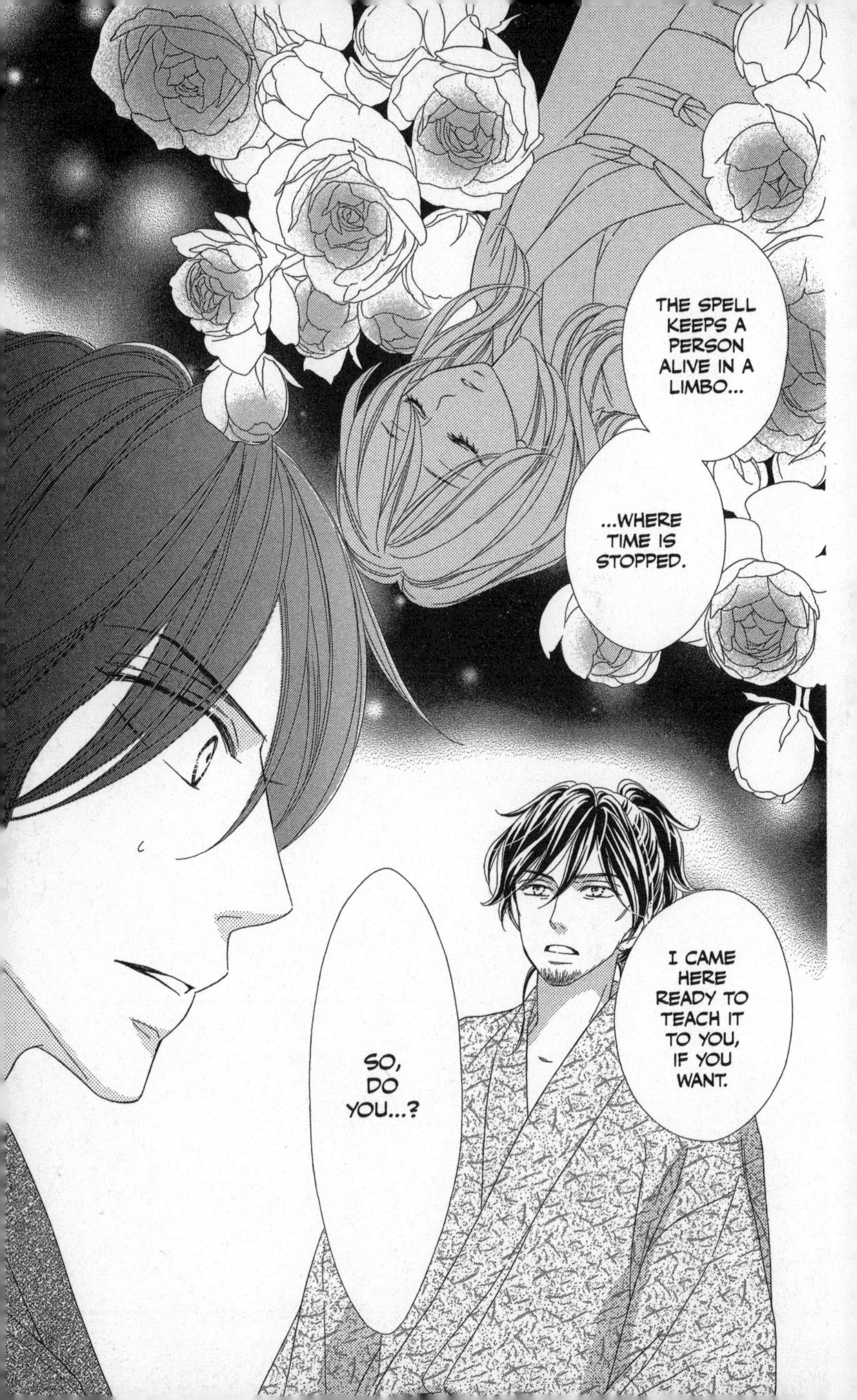
THE SPELL KEEPS A PERSON ALIVE IN A LIMBO...
...WHERE TIME IS STOPPED.
I CAME HERE READY TO TEACH IT TO YOU, IF YOU WANT.
SO, DO YOU...?

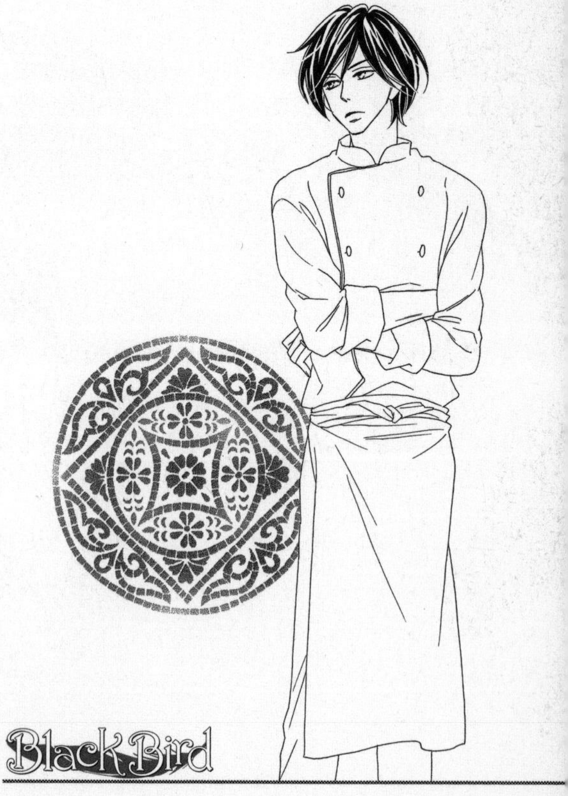
Black Bird

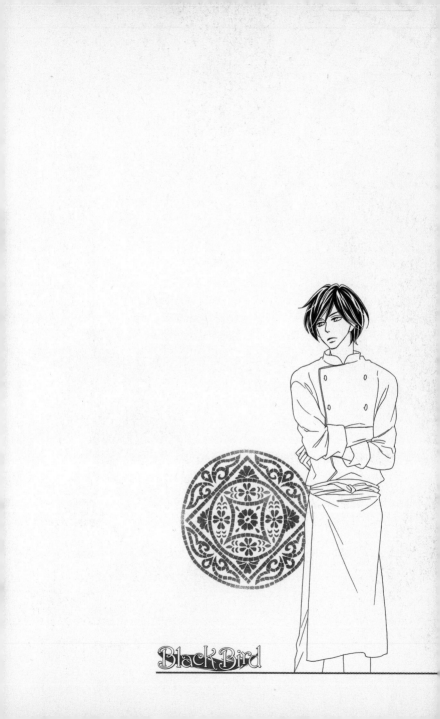

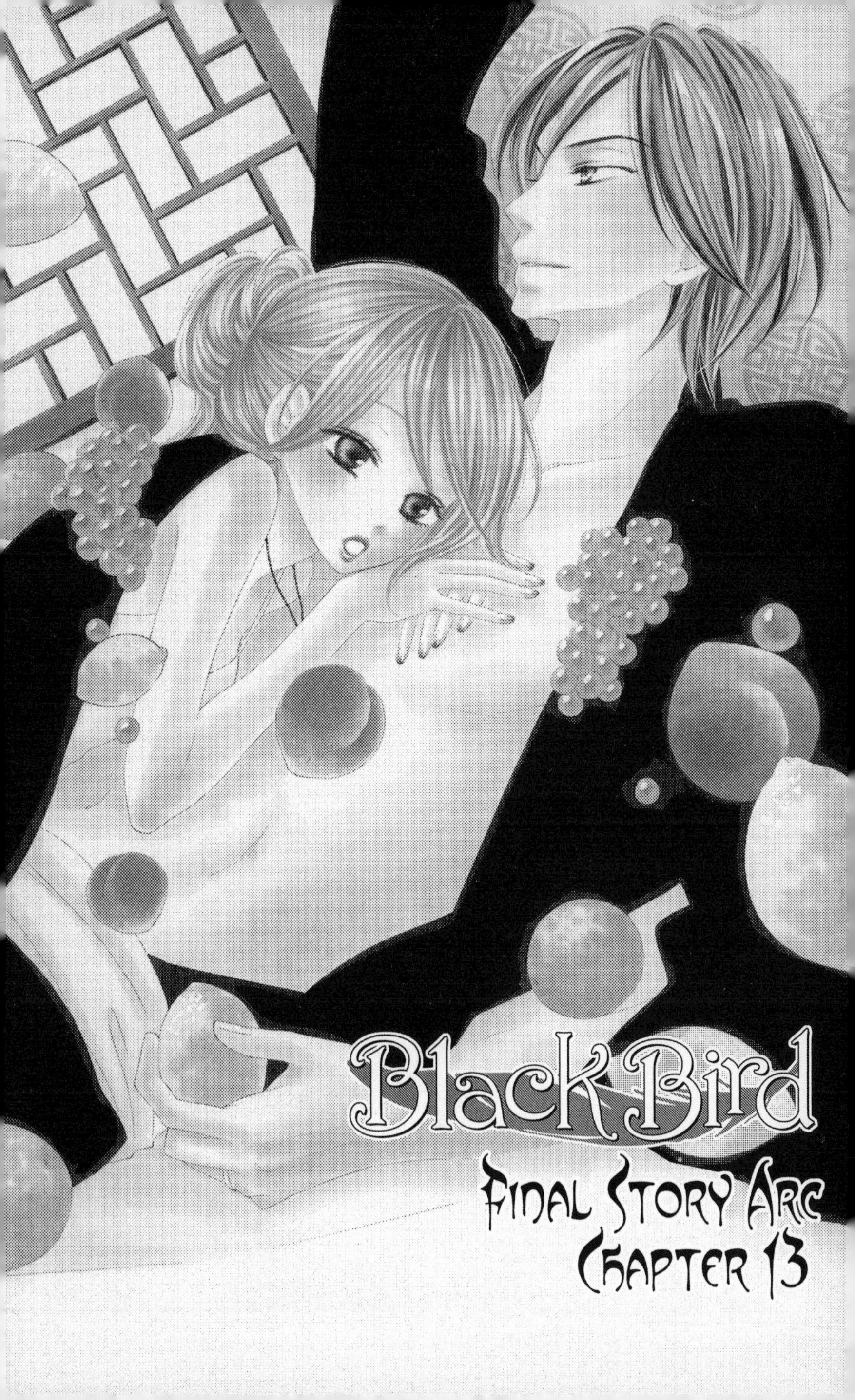
Black Bird
Final Story Arc
Chapter 13

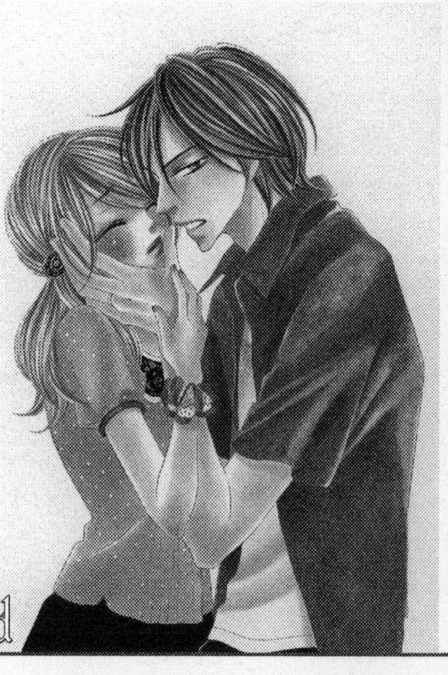

Black Bird

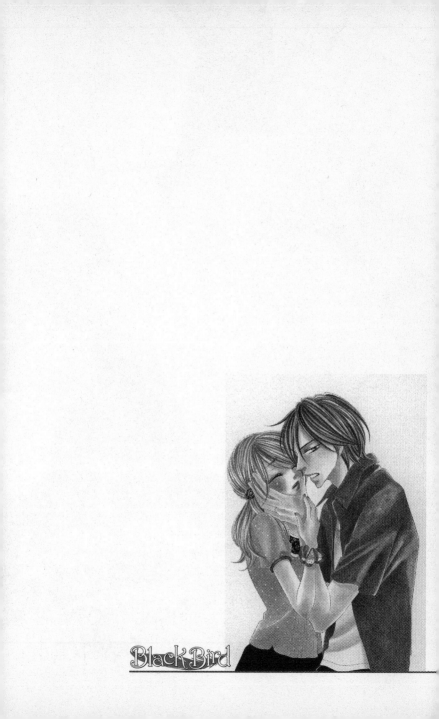

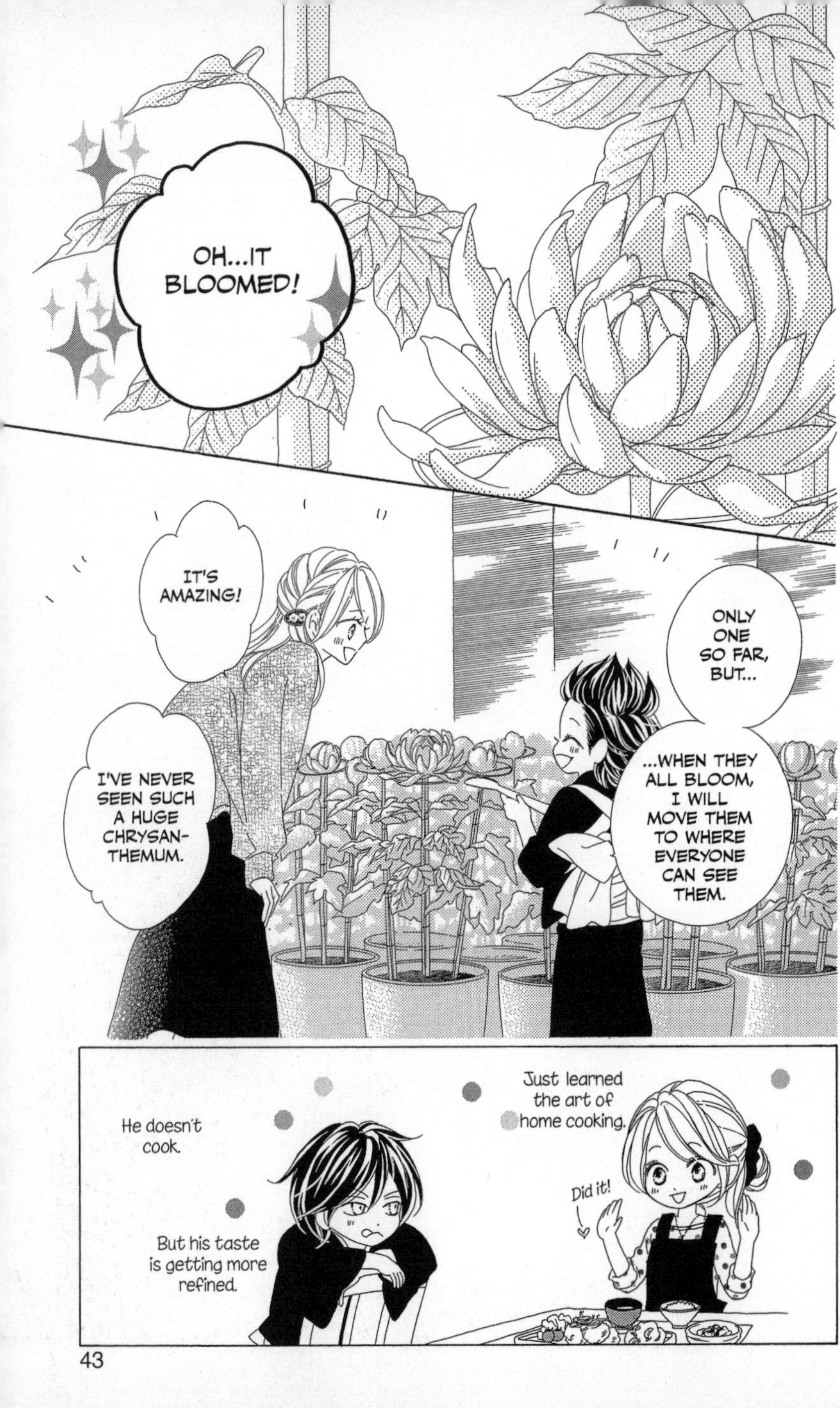
OH...IT BLOOMED!
IT'S AMAZING!
I'VE NEVER SEEN SUCH A HUGE CHRYSANTHEMUM.
ONLY ONE SO FAR, BUT...
...WHEN THEY ALL BLOOM, I WILL MOVE THEM TO WHERE EVERYONE CAN SEE THEM.
Just learned the art of home cooking.
Did it!
He doesn't cook.
But his taste is getting more refined.

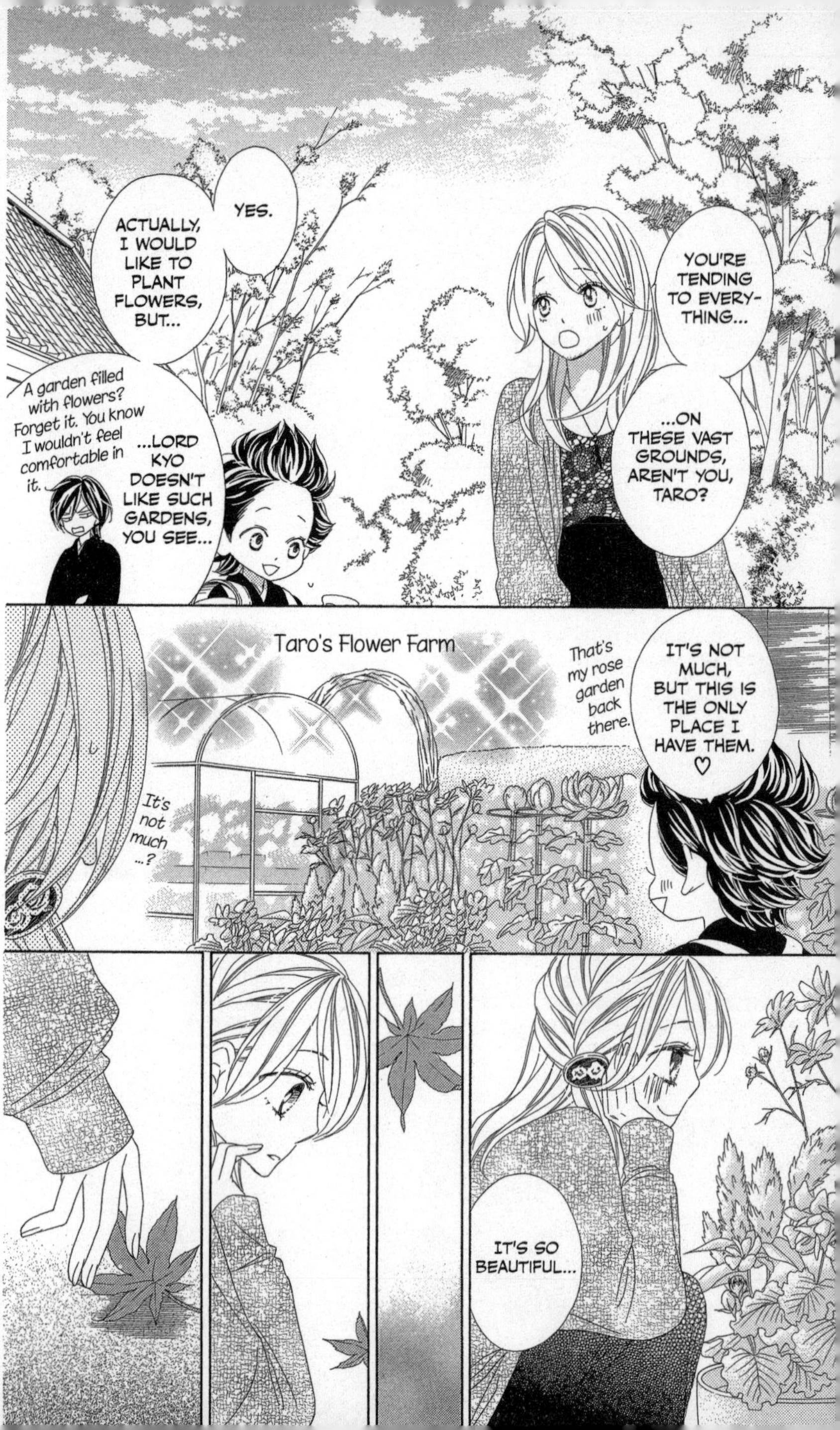
YOU'RE TENDING TO EVERY-THING...
...ON THESE VAST GROUNDS, AREN'T YOU, TARO?
YES.
ACTUALLY, I WOULD LIKE TO PLANT FLOWERS, BUT...
...LORD KYO DOESN'T LIKE SUCH GARDENS, YOU SEE...
A garden filled with flowers? Forget it. You know I wouldn't feel comfortable in it.
IT'S NOT MUCH, BUT THIS IS THE ONLY PLACE I HAVE THEM. ♡
That's my rose garden back there.
Taro's Flower Farm
It's not much ...?
IT'S SO BEAUTIFUL...

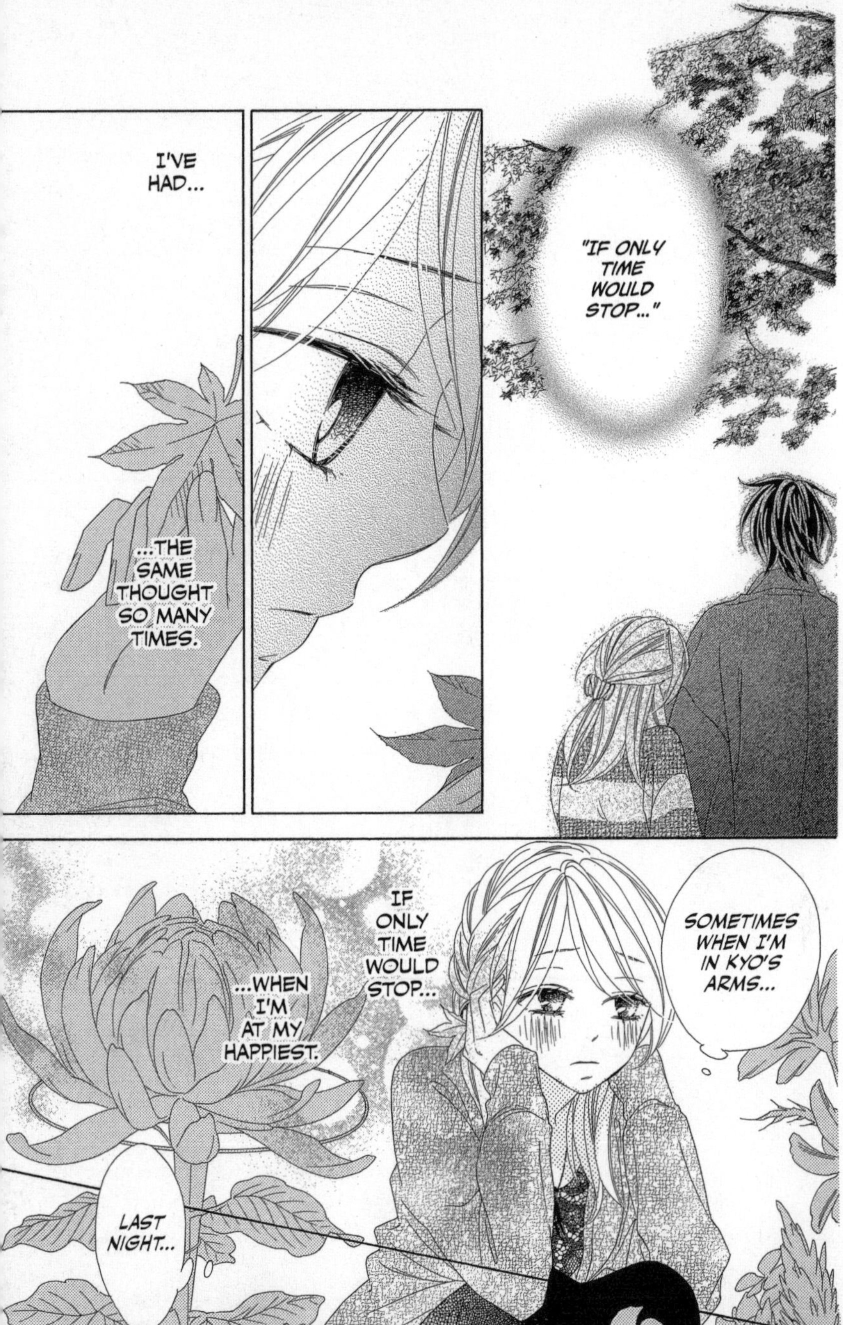
"IF ONLY TIME WOULD STOP..."
I'VE HAD...
...THE SAME THOUGHT SO MANY TIMES.
SOMETIMES WHEN I'M IN KYO'S ARMS...
IF ONLY TIME WOULD STOP...
...WHEN I'M AT MY HAPPIEST.
LAST NIGHT...

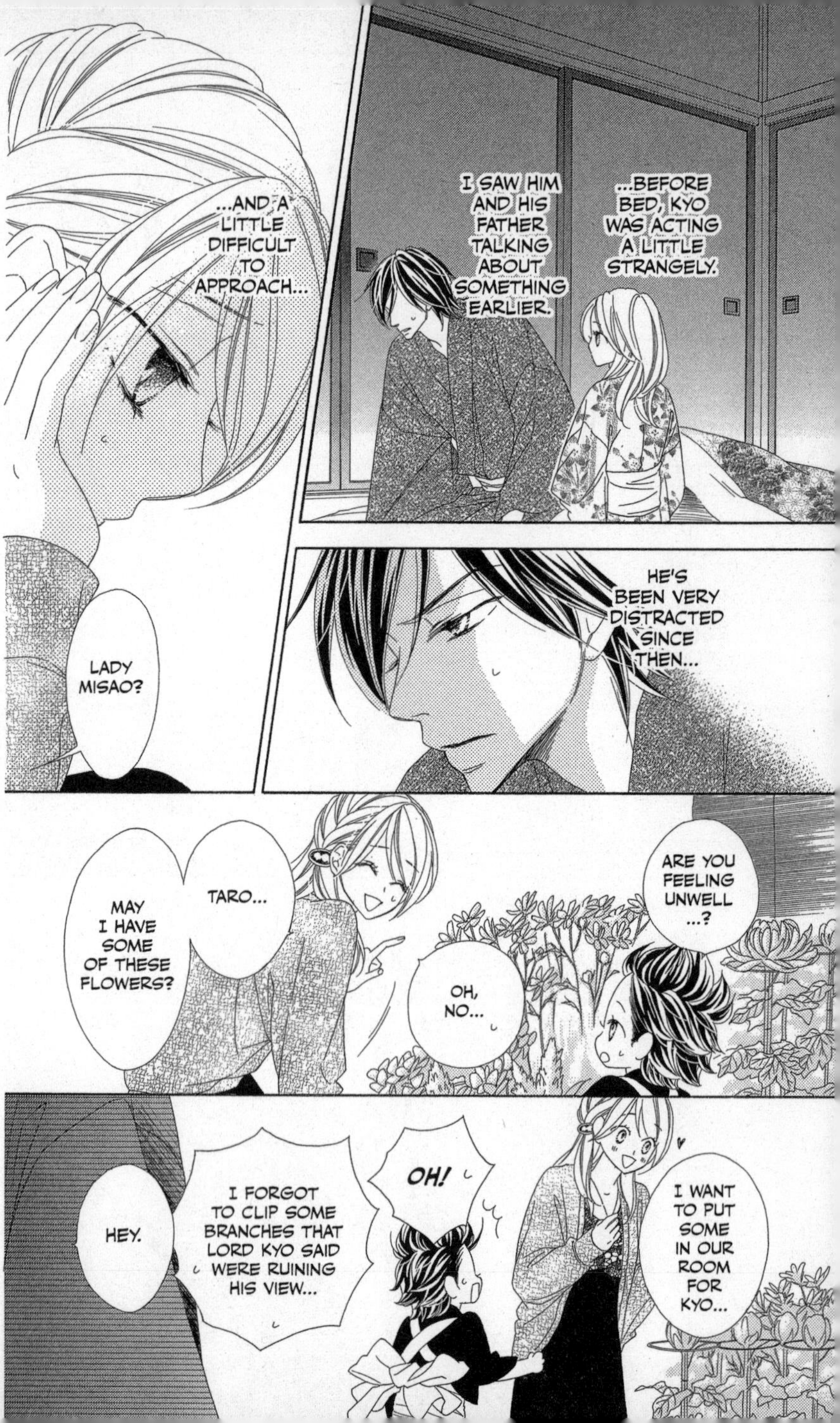
...BEFORE BED, KYO WAS ACTING A LITTLE STRANGELY.
I SAW HIM AND HIS FATHER TALKING ABOUT SOMETHING EARLIER.
HE'S BEEN VERY DISTRACTED SINCE THEN...
...AND A LITTLE DIFFICULT TO APPROACH...
LADY MISAO?
ARE YOU FEELING UNWELL ...?
OH, NO...
TARO...
MAY I HAVE SOME OF THESE FLOWERS?
I WANT TO PUT SOME IN OUR ROOM FOR KYO...
OH!
I FORGOT TO CLIP SOME BRANCHES THAT LORD KYO SAID WERE RUINING HIS VIEW...
HEY.

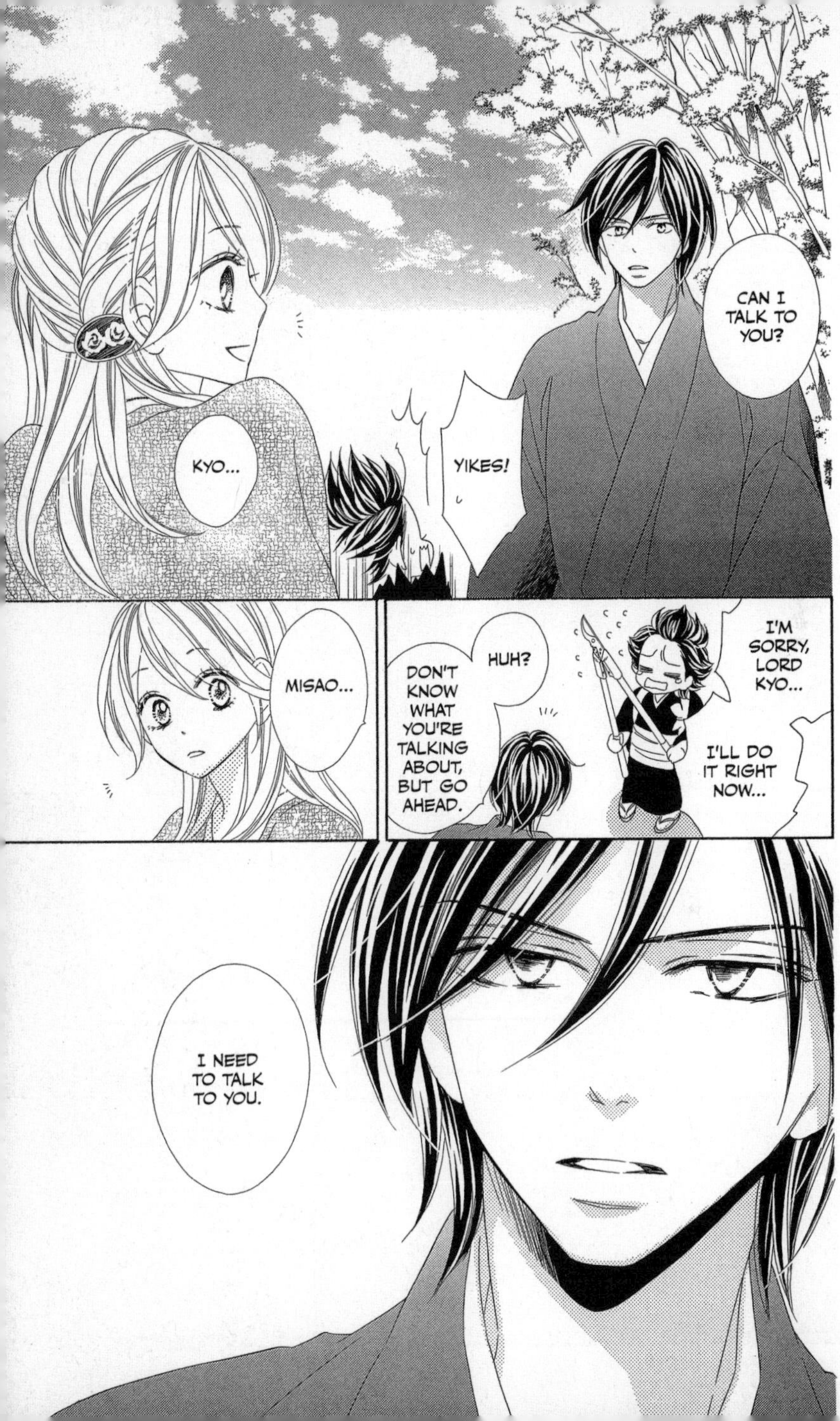
CAN I TALK TO YOU?
YIKES!
KYO...
I'M SORRY, LORD KYO...
I'LL DO IT RIGHT NOW...
HUH?
DON'T KNOW WHAT YOU'RE TALKING ABOUT, BUT GO AHEAD.
MISAO...
I NEED TO TALK TO YOU.

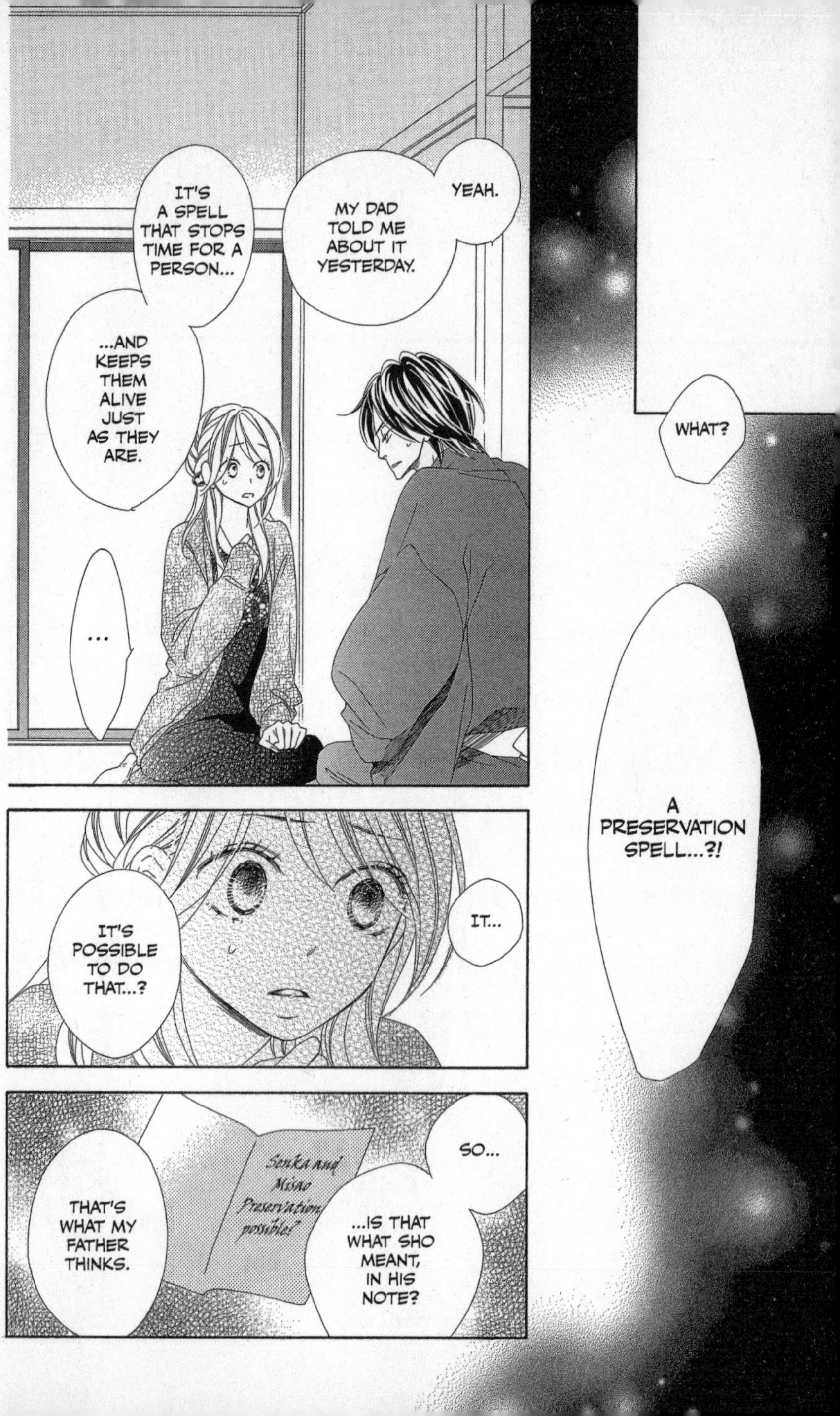
WHAT?
A PRESERVATION SPELL...?!
YEAH.
MY DAD TOLD ME ABOUT IT YESTERDAY.
IT'S A SPELL THAT STOPS TIME FOR A PERSON...
...AND KEEPS THEM ALIVE JUST AS THEY ARE.
...
IT...
IT'S POSSIBLE TO DO THAT...?
SO...
Senka and Misao Preservation possible?
...IS THAT WHAT SHO MEANT, IN HIS NOTE?
THAT'S WHAT MY FATHER THINKS.

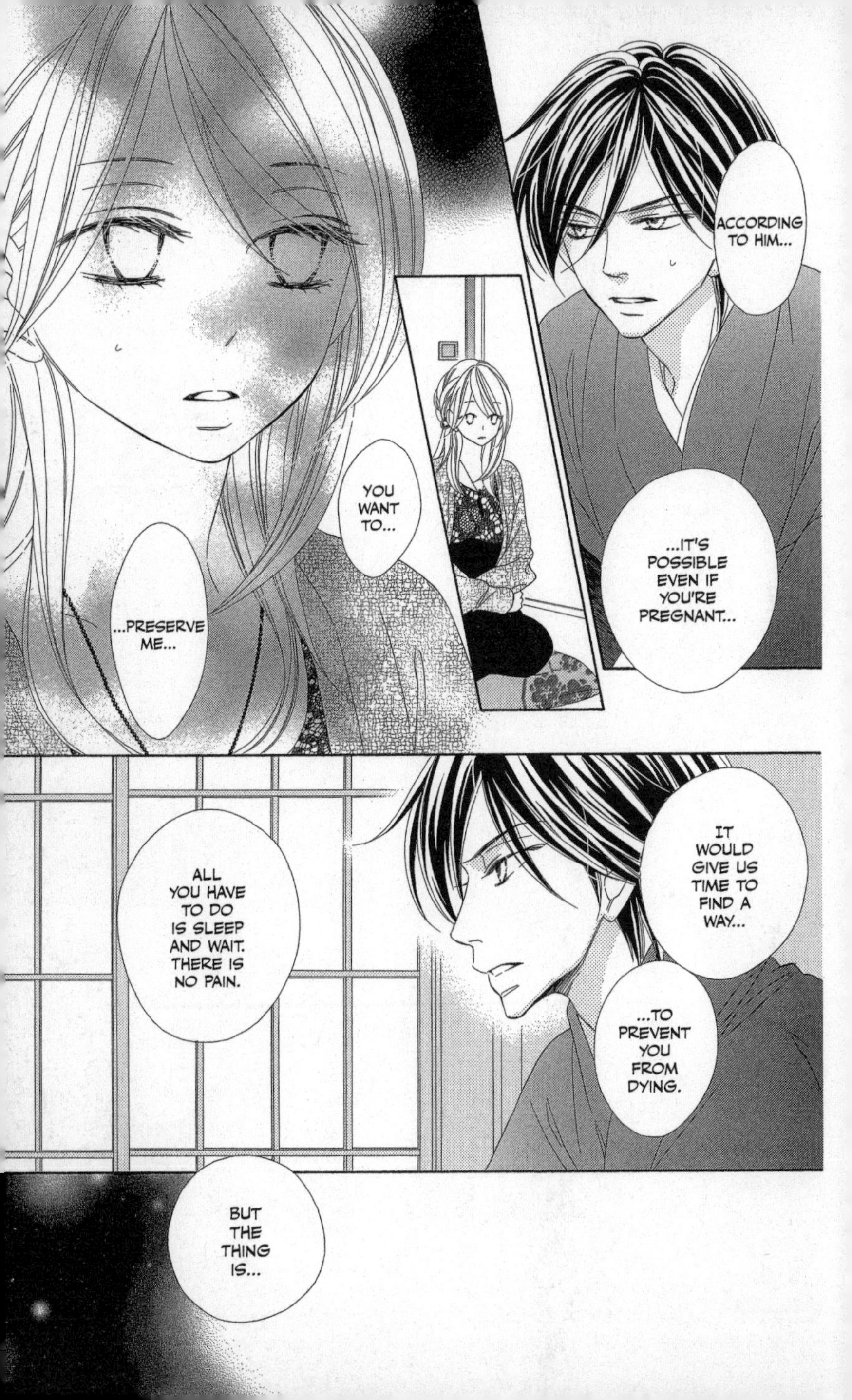
ACCORDING TO HIM...
...IT'S POSSIBLE EVEN IF YOU'RE PREGNANT...
YOU WANT TO...
...PRESERVE ME...
IT WOULD GIVE US TIME TO FIND A WAY...
...TO PREVENT YOU FROM DYING.
ALL YOU HAVE TO DO IS SLEEP AND WAIT. THERE IS NO PAIN.
BUT THE THING IS...

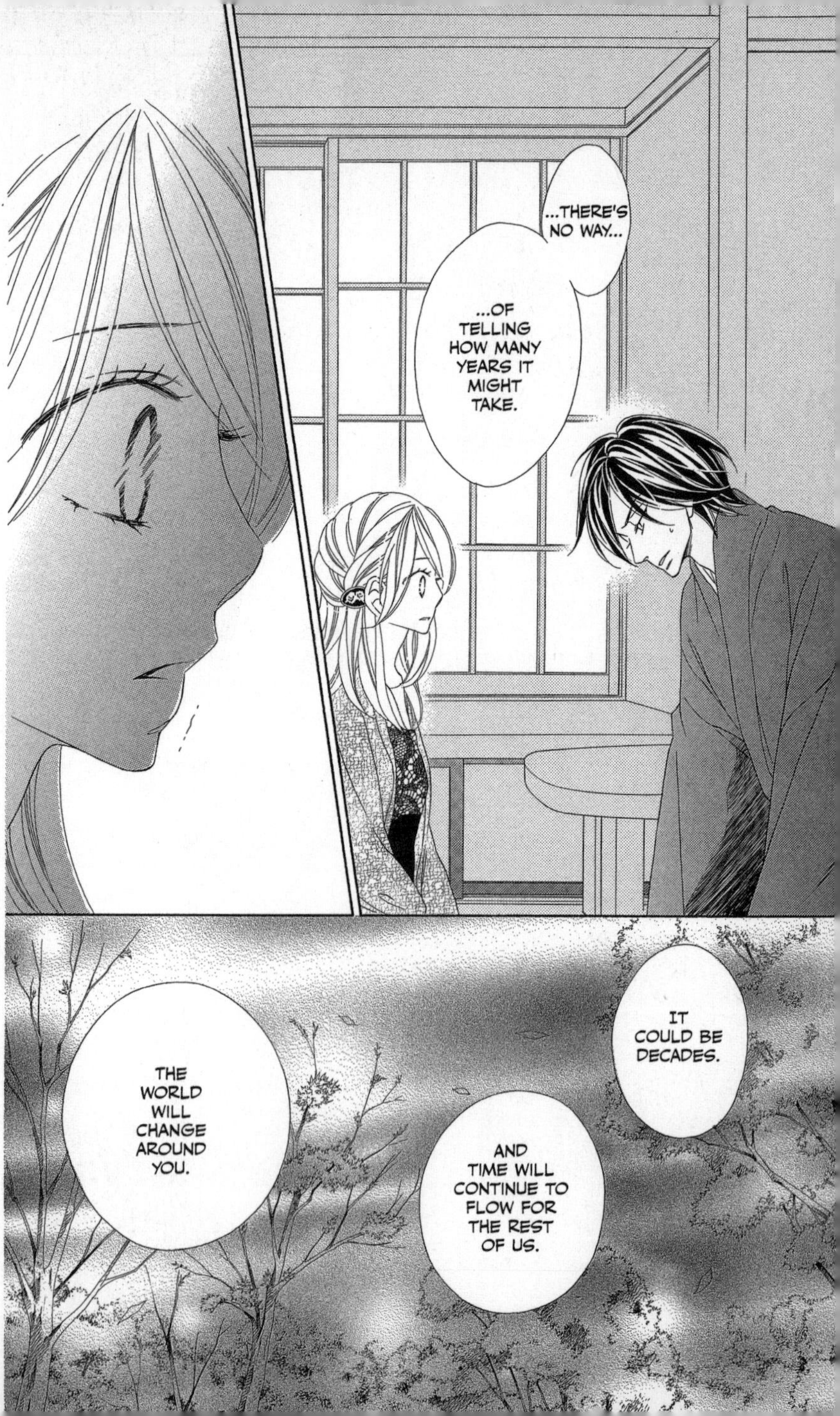
...THERE'S NO WAY...
...OF TELLING HOW MANY YEARS IT MIGHT TAKE.
IT COULD BE DECADES.
AND TIME WILL CONTINUE TO FLOW FOR THE REST OF US.
THE WORLD WILL CHANGE AROUND YOU.

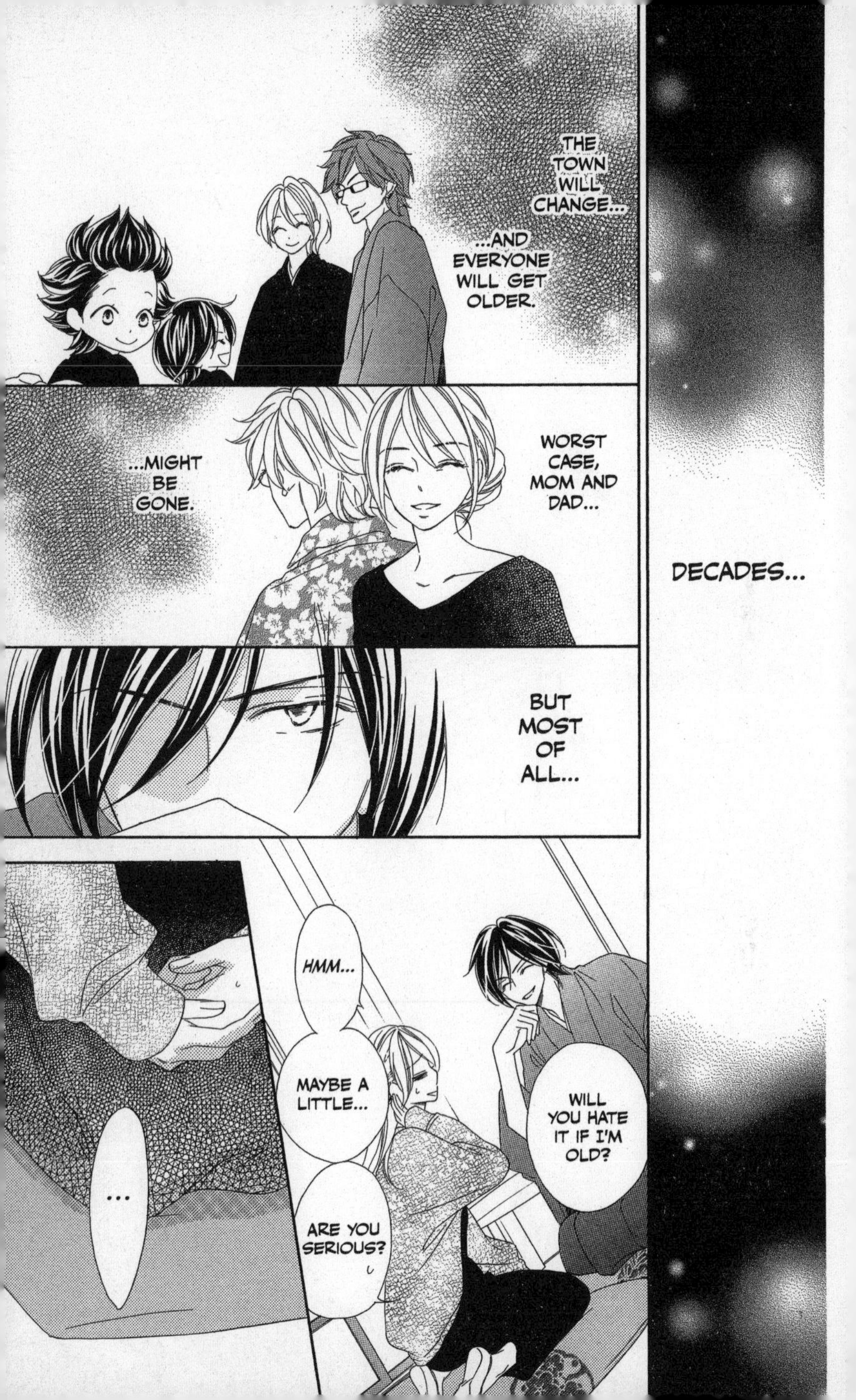
DECADES...
THE TOWN WILL CHANGE...
...AND EVERYONE WILL GET OLDER.
WORST CASE, MOM AND DAD...
...MIGHT BE GONE.
BUT MOST OF ALL...
WILL YOU HATE IT IF I'M OLD?
HMM...
MAYBE A LITTLE...
ARE YOU SERIOUS?
...

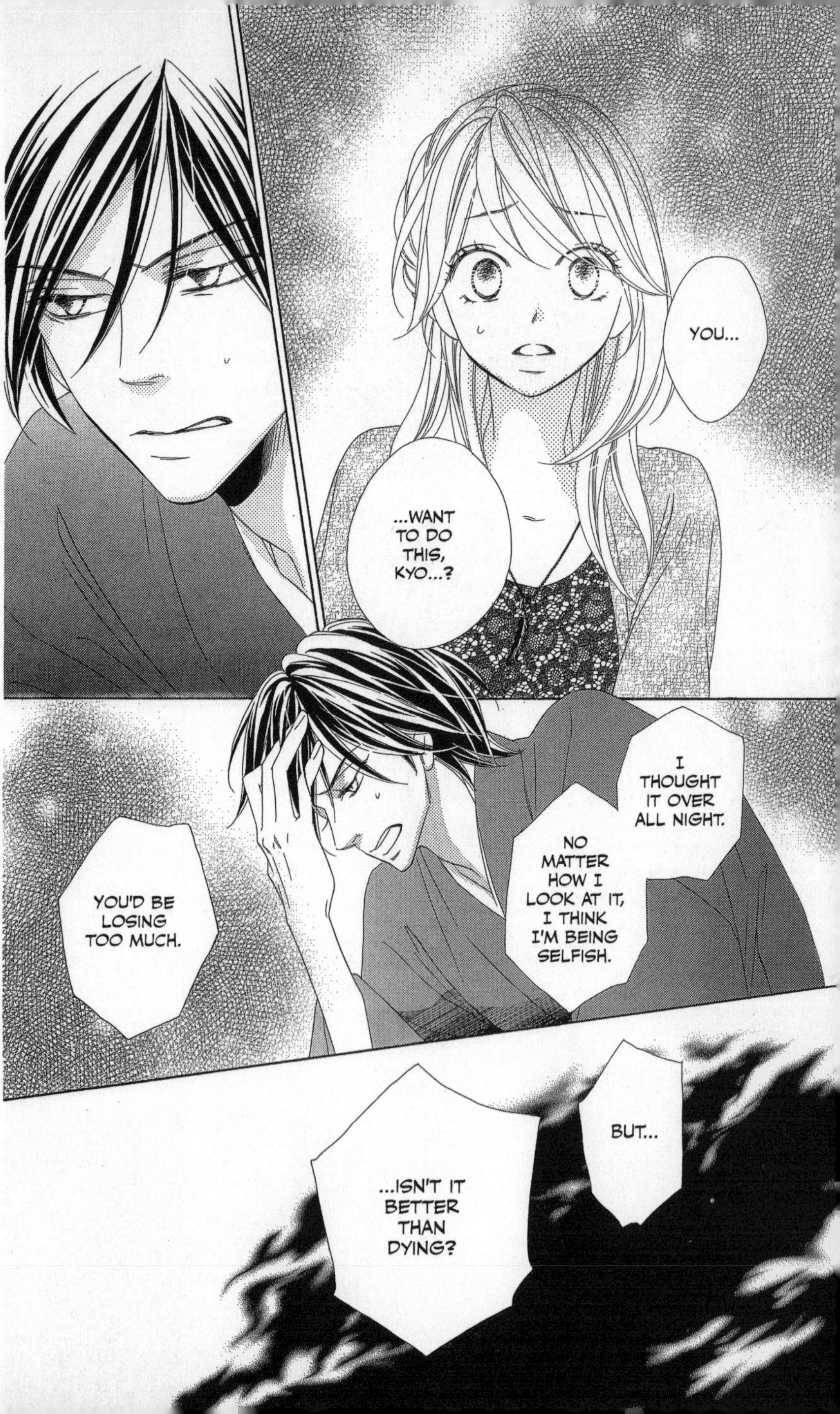
YOU...
...WANT TO DO THIS, KYO...?
I THOUGHT IT OVER ALL NIGHT.
NO MATTER HOW I LOOK AT IT, I THINK I'M BEING SELFISH.
YOU'D BE LOSING TOO MUCH.
BUT...
...ISN'T IT BETTER THAN DYING?

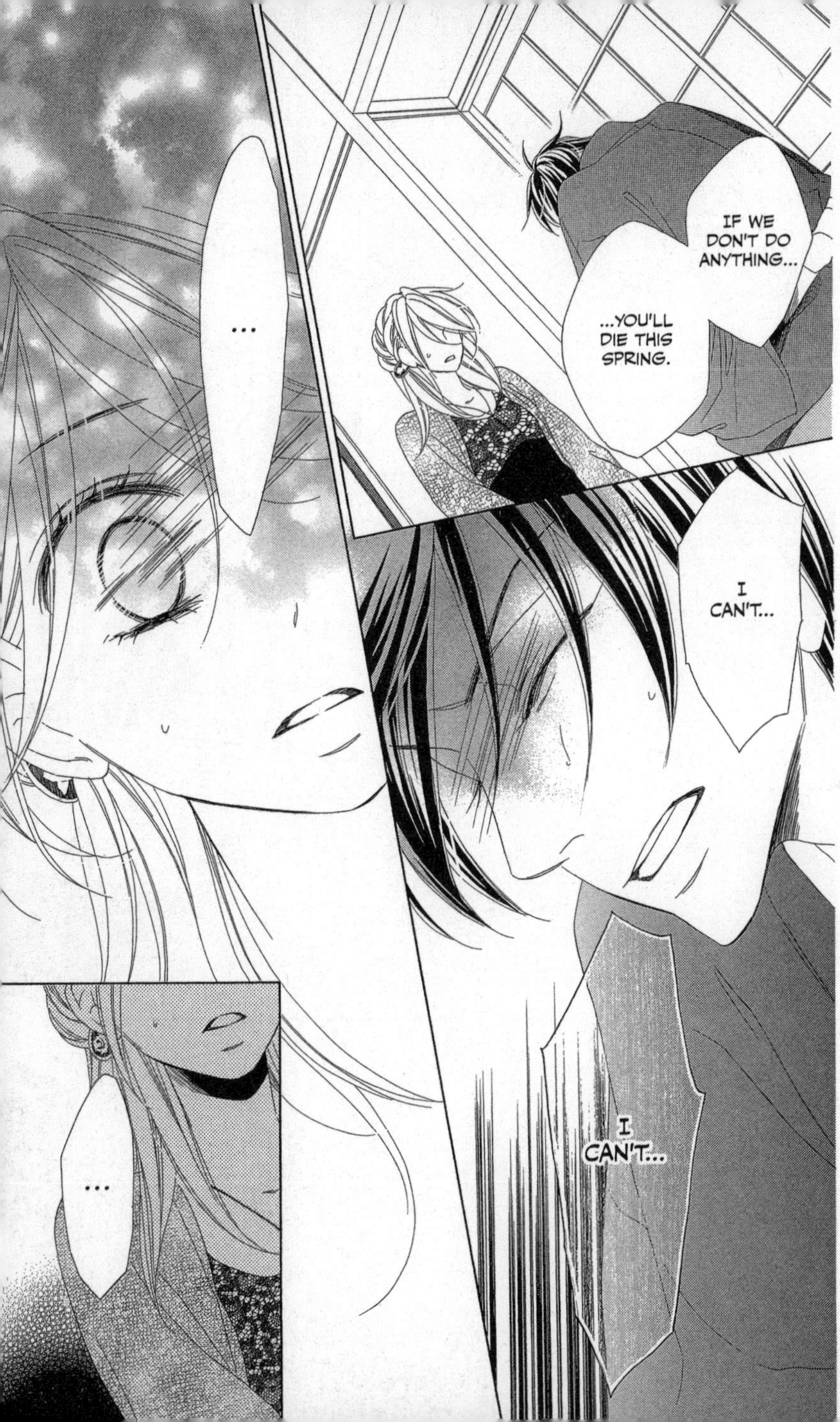
IF WE DON'T DO ANYTHING...
...YOU'LL DIE THIS SPRING.
...
I CAN'T...
I CAN'T...
...

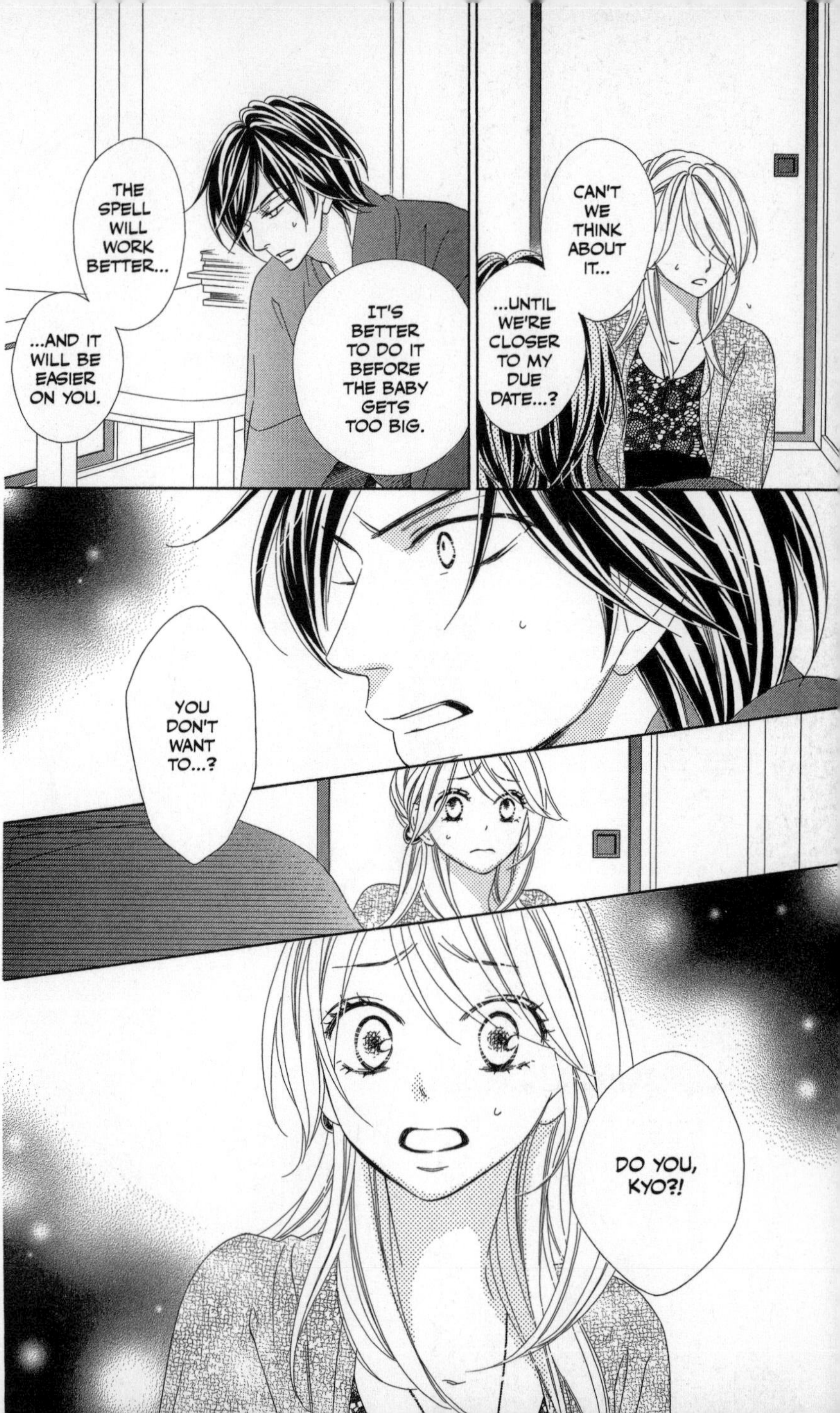
CAN'T WE THINK ABOUT IT...
...UNTIL WE'RE CLOSER TO MY DUE DATE...?
IT'S BETTER TO DO IT BEFORE THE BABY GETS TOO BIG.
THE SPELL WILL WORK BETTER...
...AND IT WILL BE EASIER ON YOU.
YOU DON'T WANT TO...?
DO YOU, KYO?!

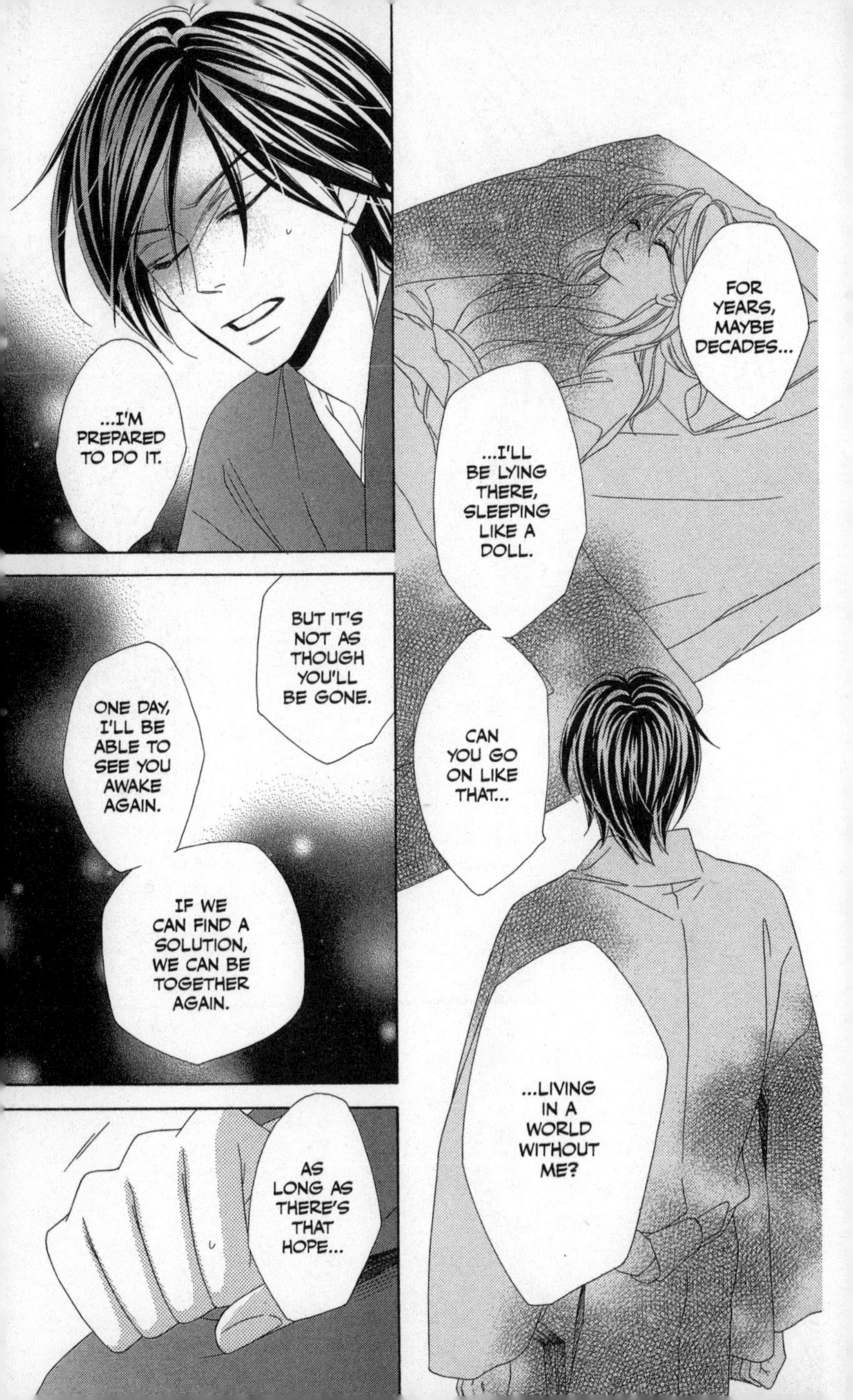
FOR YEARS, MAYBE DECADES...
...I'LL BE LYING THERE, SLEEPING LIKE A DOLL.
CAN YOU GO ON LIKE THAT...
...LIVING IN A WORLD WITHOUT ME?
...I'M PREPARED TO DO IT.
BUT IT'S NOT AS THOUGH YOU'LL BE GONE.
ONE DAY, I'LL BE ABLE TO SEE YOU AWAKE AGAIN.
IF WE CAN FIND A SOLUTION, WE CAN BE TOGETHER AGAIN.
AS LONG AS THERE'S THAT HOPE...

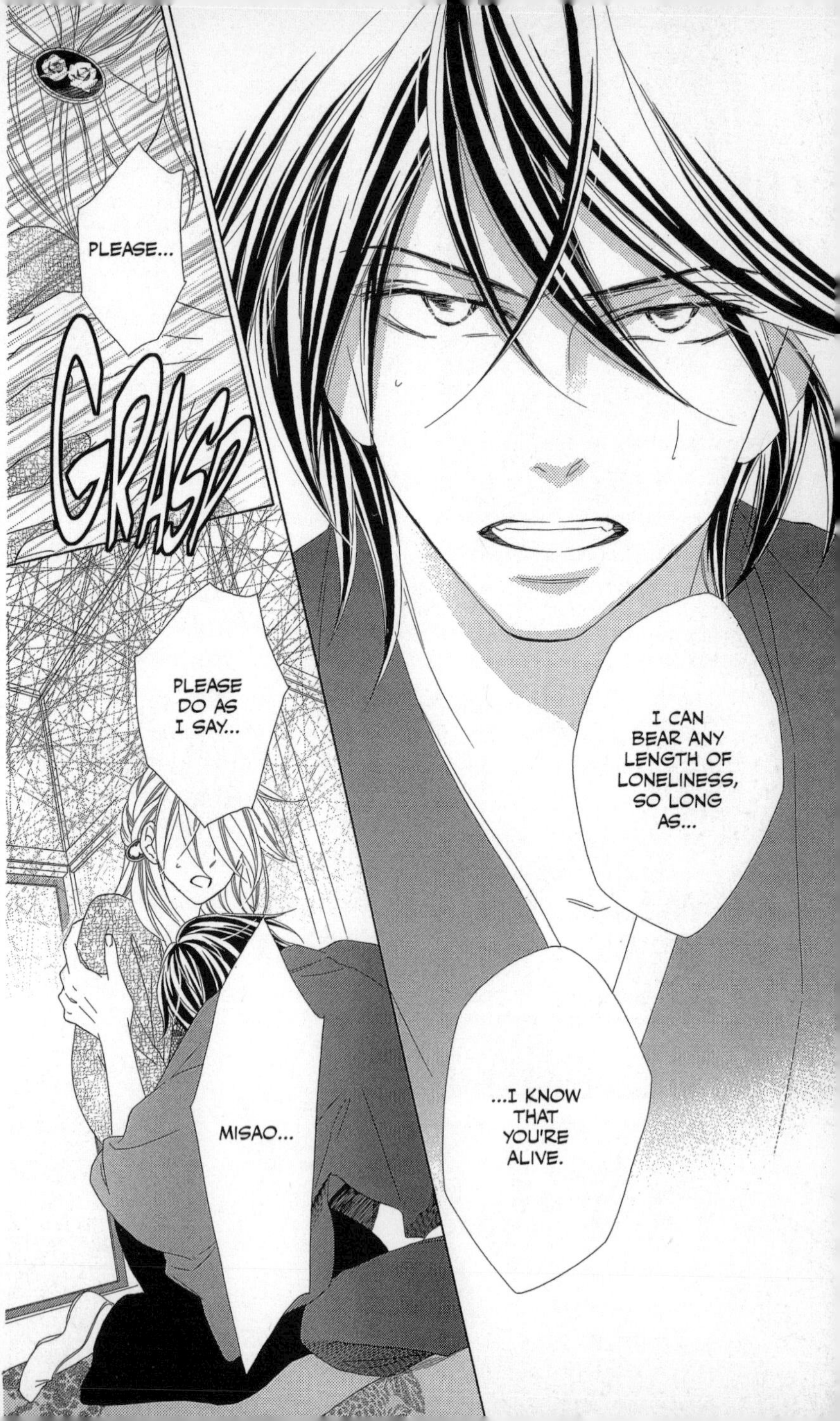
I CAN BEAR ANY LENGTH OF LONELINESS, SO LONG AS...
...I KNOW THAT YOU'RE ALIVE.
PLEASE...
GRASP
PLEASE DO AS I SAY...
MISAO...

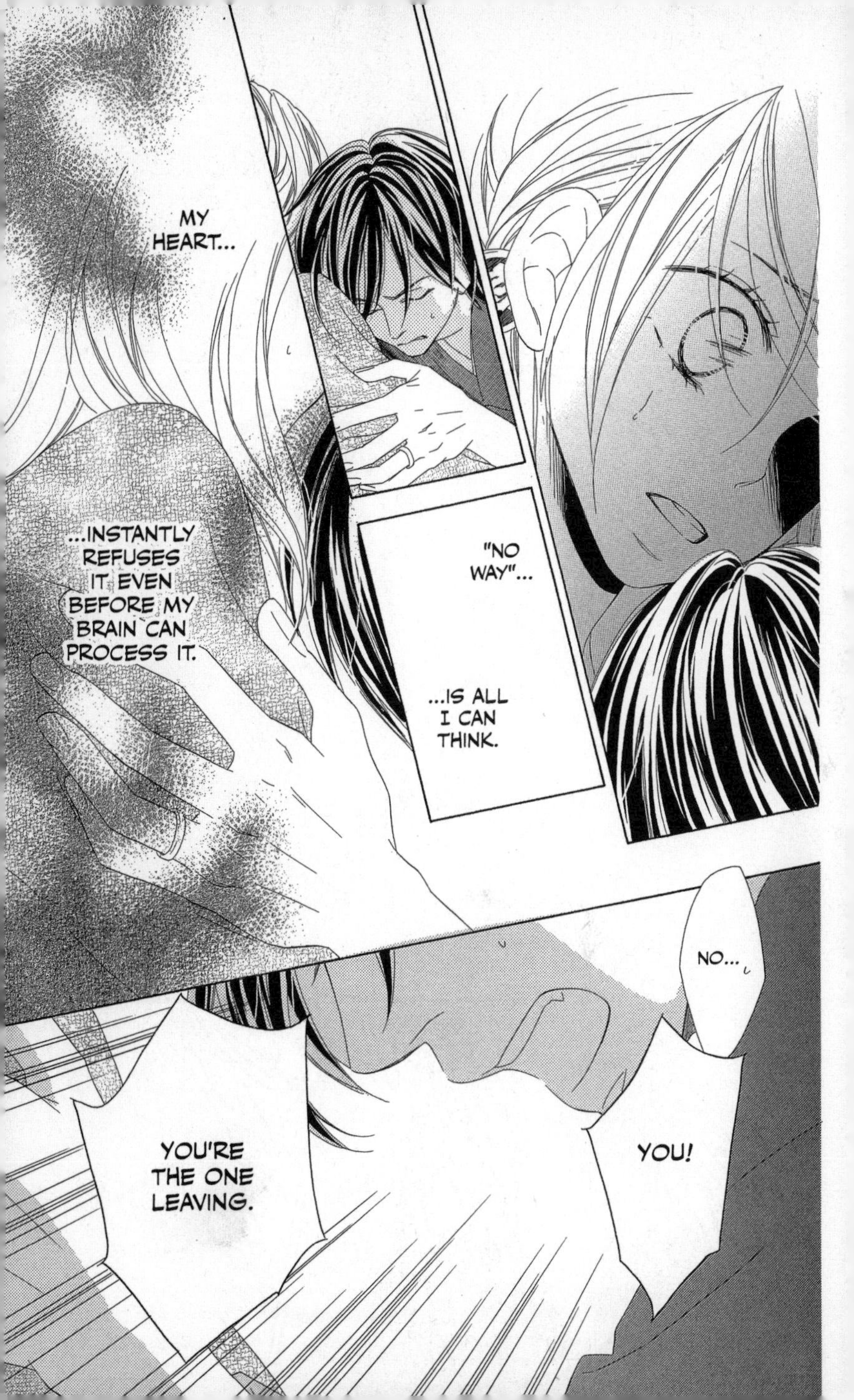
MY HEART...
...INSTANTLY REFUSES IT EVEN BEFORE MY BRAIN CAN PROCESS IT.
"NO WAY"...
...IS ALL I CAN THINK.
NO...
YOU!
YOU'RE THE ONE LEAVING.

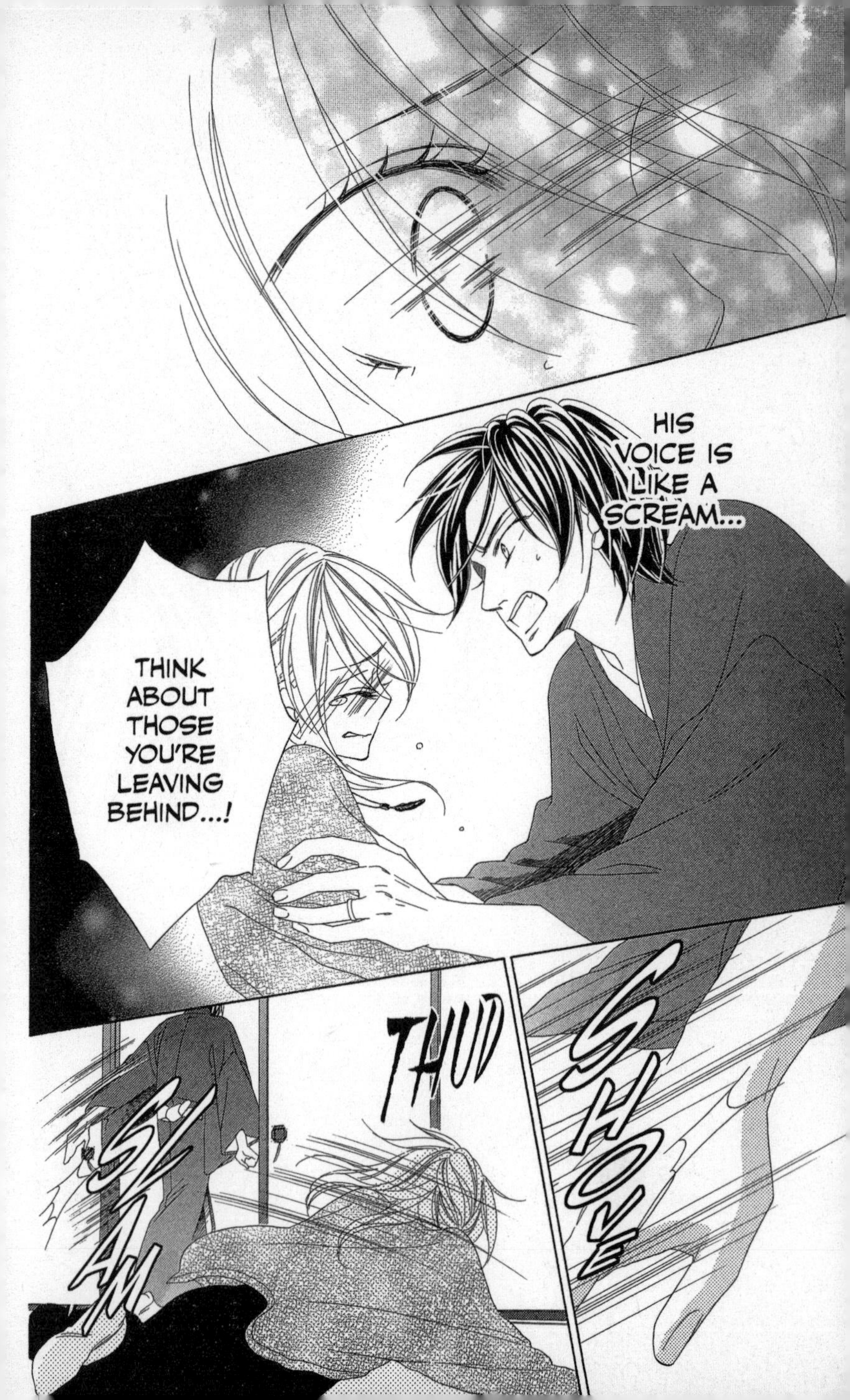
HIS VOICE IS LIKE A SCREAM...
THINK ABOUT THOSE YOU'RE LEAVING BEHIND...!
SHOVE
THUD
SLAM

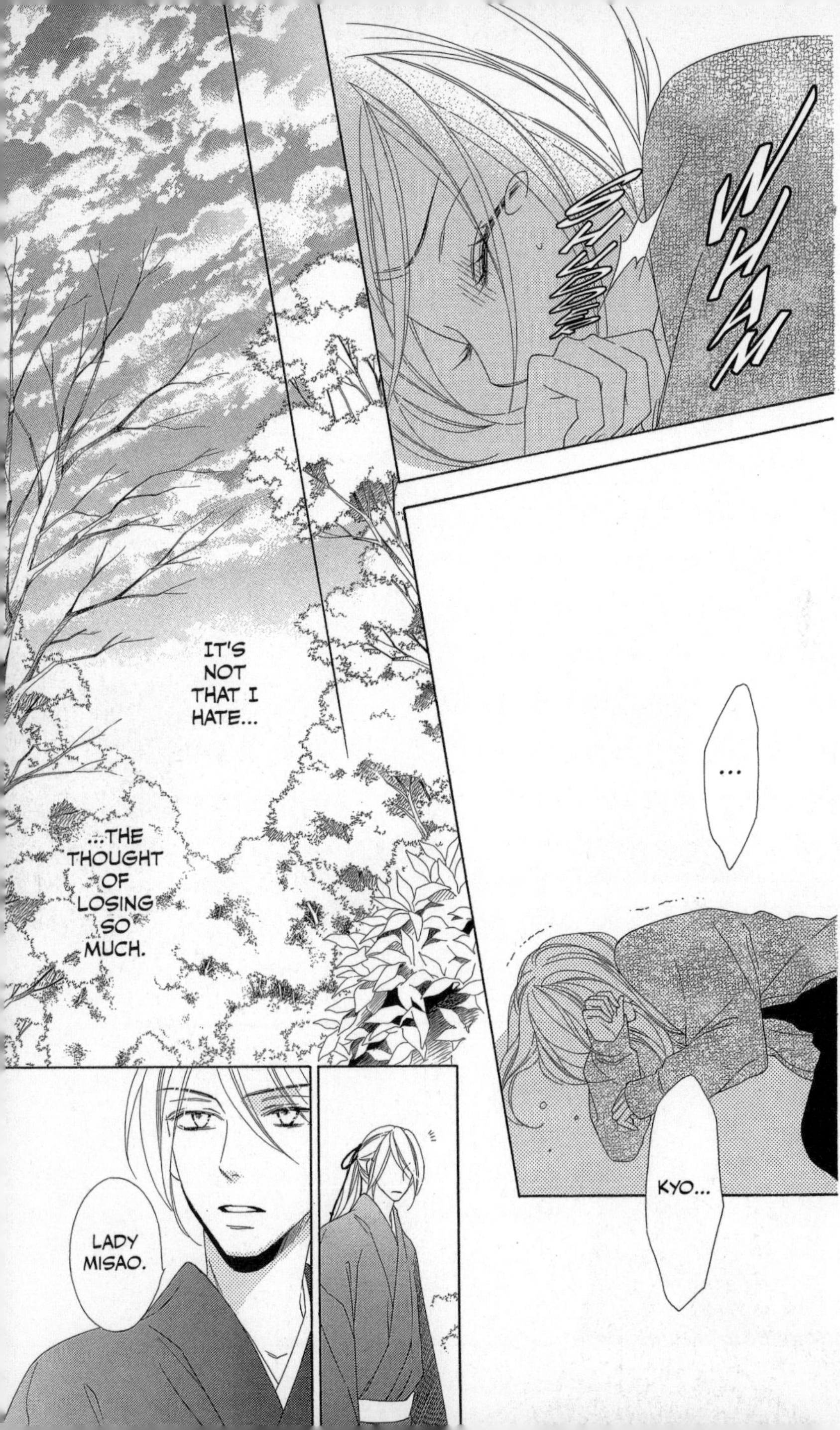
WHAM
...
KYO...
IT'S NOT THAT I HATE...
...THE THOUGHT OF LOSING SO MUCH.
LADY MISAO.

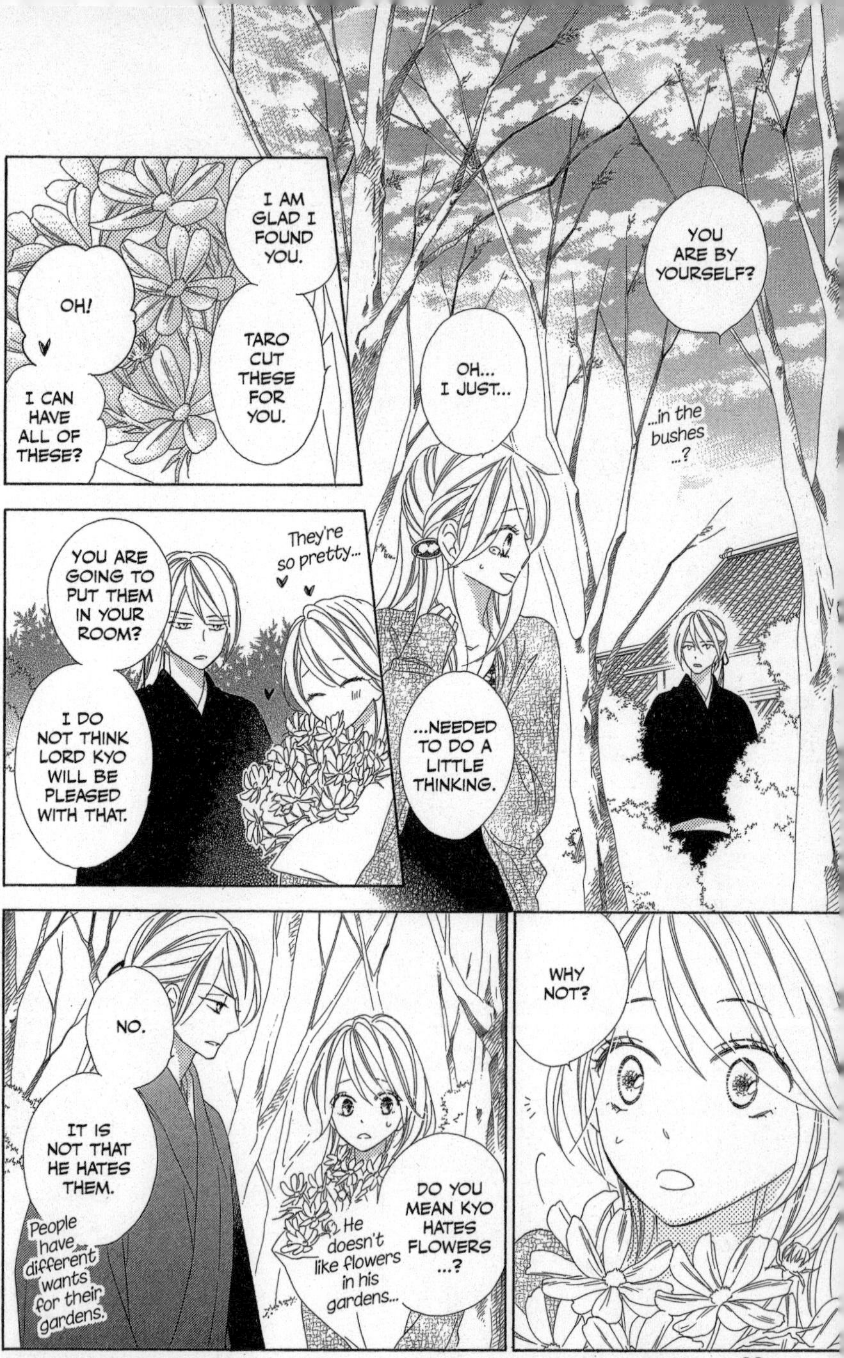
YOU ARE BY YOURSELF?
...in the bushes ...?
OH... I JUST...
...NEEDED TO DO A LITTLE THINKING.
I AM GLAD I FOUND YOU.
TARO CUT THESE FOR YOU.
OH!
I CAN HAVE ALL OF THESE?
They're so pretty...
YOU ARE GOING TO PUT THEM IN YOUR ROOM?
I DO NOT THINK LORD KYO WILL BE PLEASED WITH THAT.
WHY NOT?
DO YOU MEAN KYO HATES FLOWERS ...?
He doesn't like flowers in his gardens...
NO.
IT IS NOT THAT HE HATES THEM.
People have different wants for their gardens.

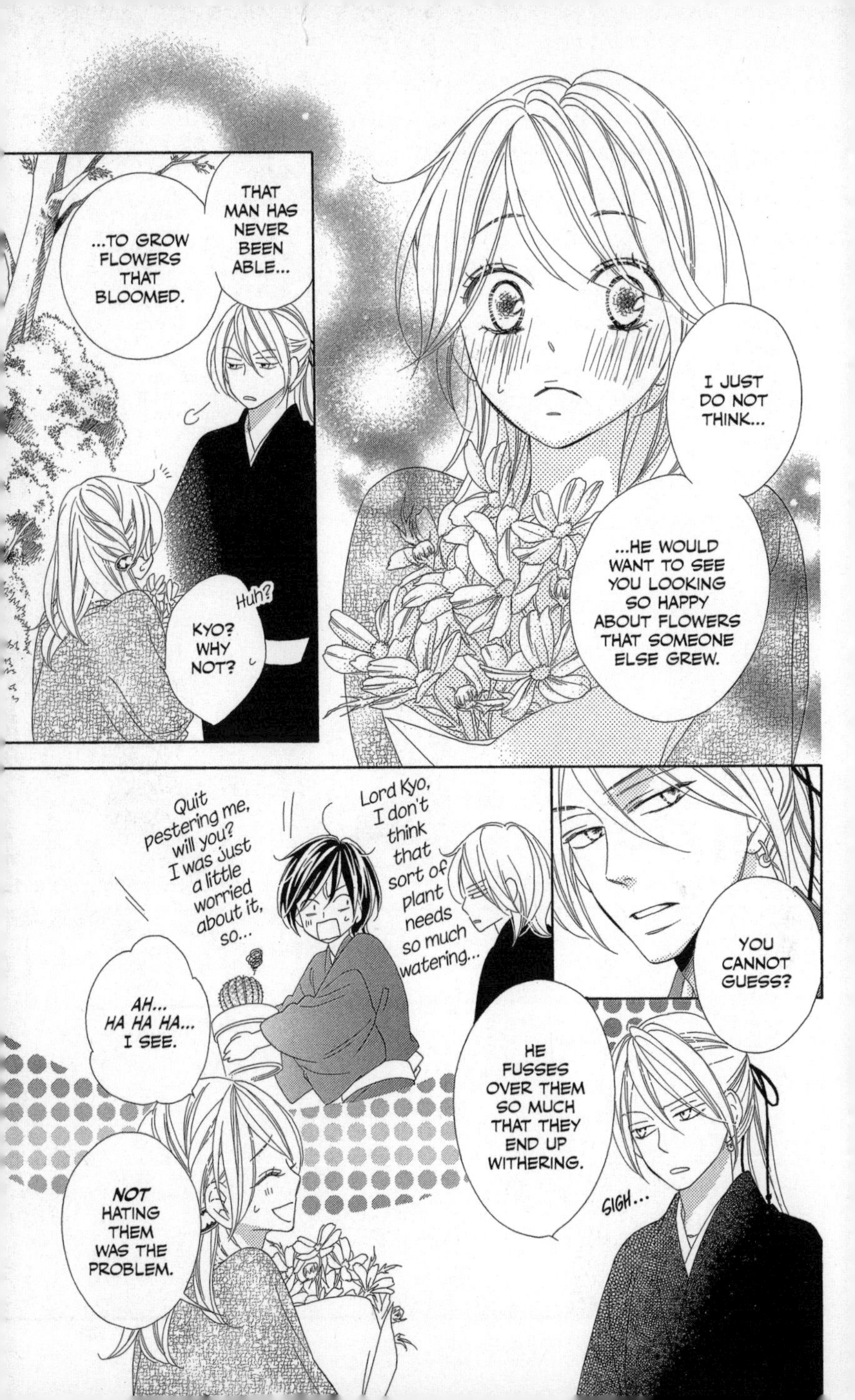
I JUST DO NOT THINK...
...HE WOULD WANT TO SEE YOU LOOKING SO HAPPY ABOUT FLOWERS THAT SOMEONE ELSE GREW.
Huh?
KYO? WHY NOT?
THAT MAN HAS NEVER BEEN ABLE...
...TO GROW FLOWERS THAT BLOOMED.
YOU CANNOT GUESS?
HE FUSSES OVER THEM SO MUCH THAT THEY END UP WITHERING.
SIGH...
Lord Kyo, I don't think that sort of plant needs so much watering...
Quit pestering me, will you? I was just a little worried about it, so...
AH... HA HA HA... I SEE.
*NOT* HATING THEM WAS THE PROBLEM.

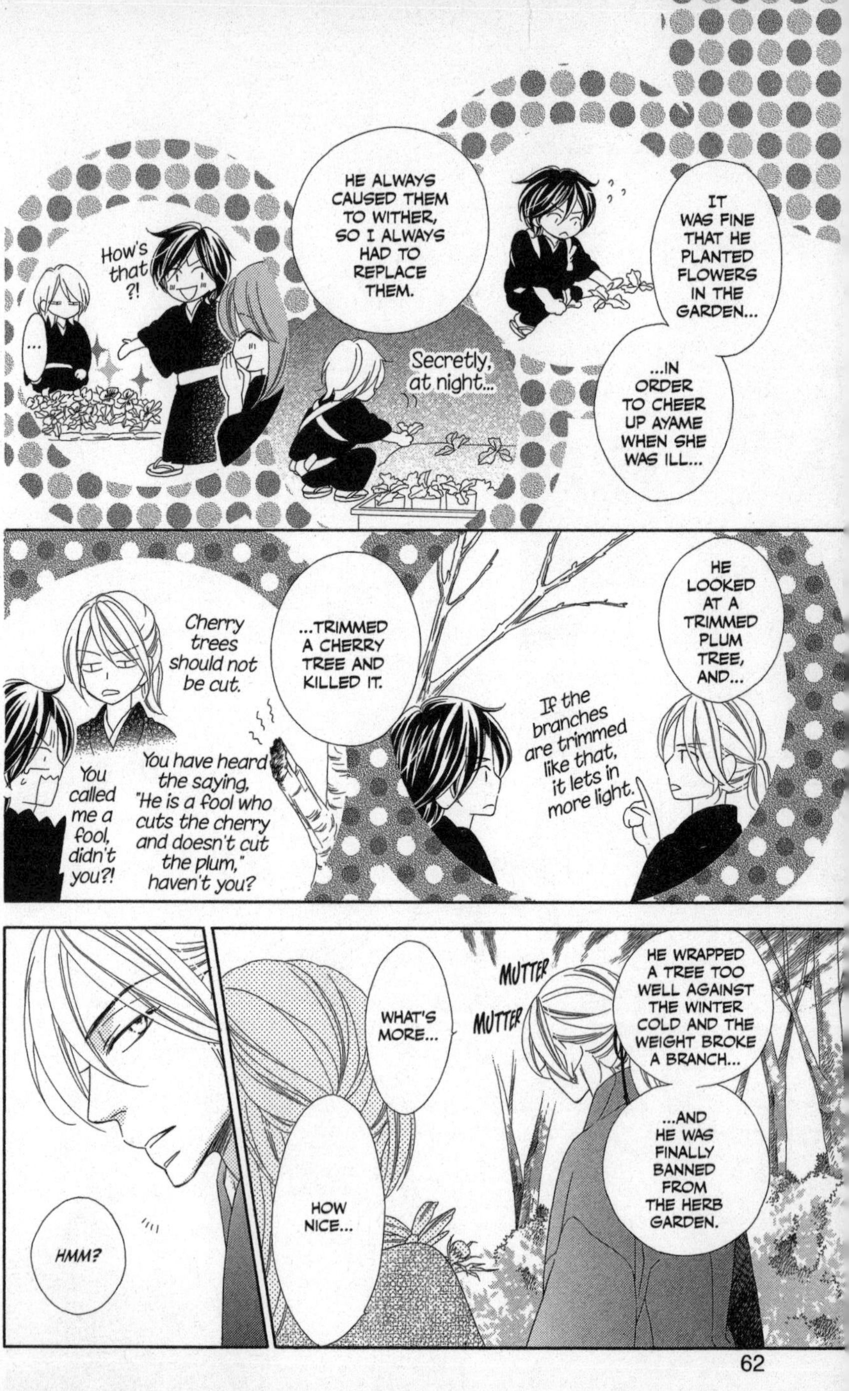
IT WAS FINE THAT HE PLANTED FLOWERS IN THE GARDEN...
...IN ORDER TO CHEER UP AYAME WHEN SHE WAS ILL...
HE ALWAYS CAUSED THEM TO WITHER, SO I ALWAYS HAD TO REPLACE THEM.
Secretly, at night...
How's that?!
...
HE LOOKED AT A TRIMMED PLUM TREE, AND...
If the branches are trimmed like that, it lets in more light.
...TRIMMED A CHERRY TREE AND KILLED IT.
Cherry trees should not be cut.
You have heard the saying, "He is a fool who cuts the cherry and doesn't cut the plum," haven't you?
You called me a fool, didn't you?!
MUTTER
MUTTER
WHAT'S MORE...
HE WRAPPED A TREE TOO WELL AGAINST THE WINTER COLD AND THE WEIGHT BROKE A BRANCH...
...AND HE WAS FINALLY BANNED FROM THE HERB GARDEN.
HOW NICE...
HMM?

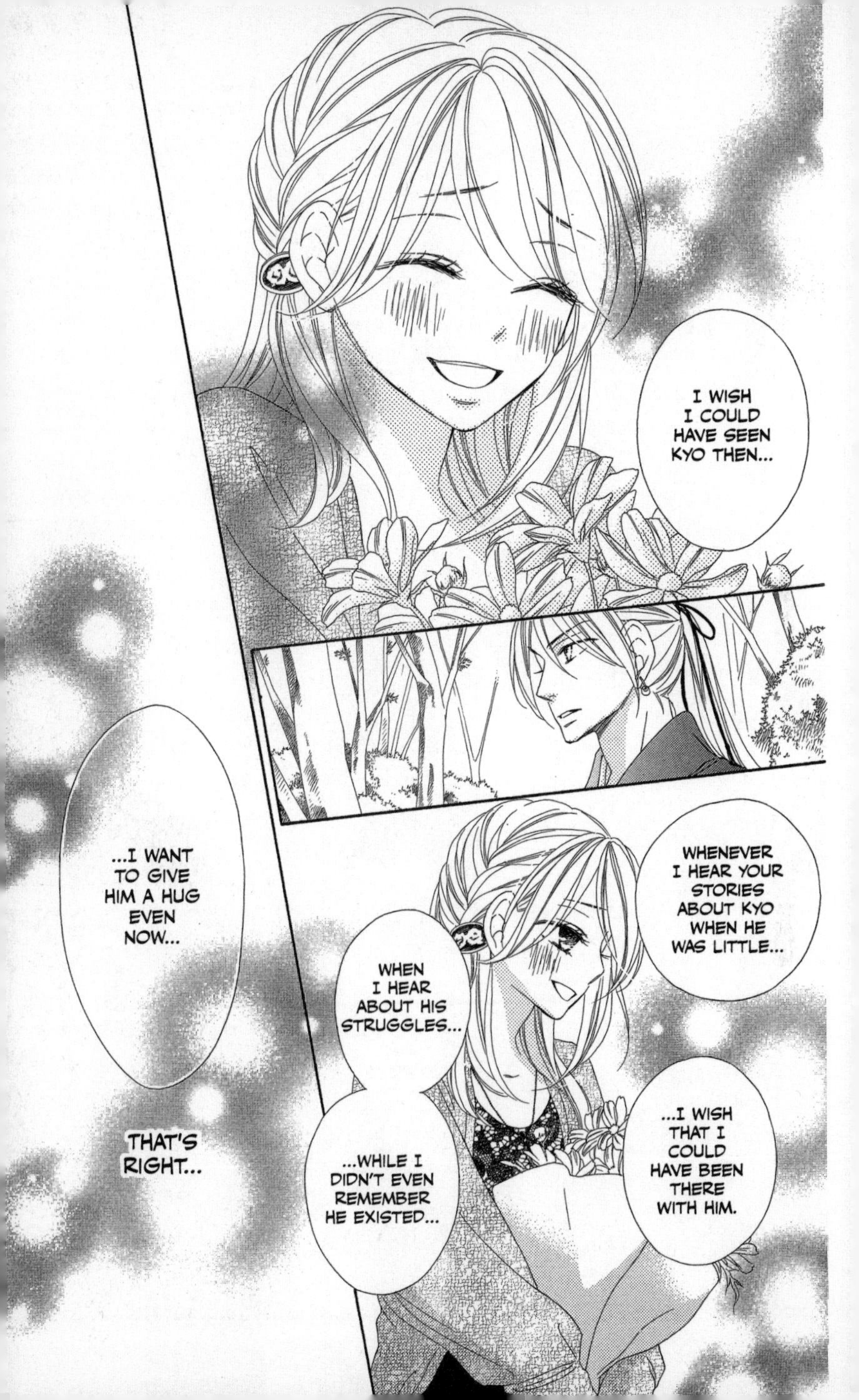
I WISH I COULD HAVE SEEN KYO THEN...
WHENEVER I HEAR YOUR STORIES ABOUT KYO WHEN HE WAS LITTLE...
WHEN I HEAR ABOUT HIS STRUGGLES...
...WHILE I DIDN'T EVEN REMEMBER HE EXISTED...
...I WISH THAT I COULD HAVE BEEN THERE WITH HIM.
...I WANT TO GIVE HIM A HUG EVEN NOW...
THAT'S RIGHT...

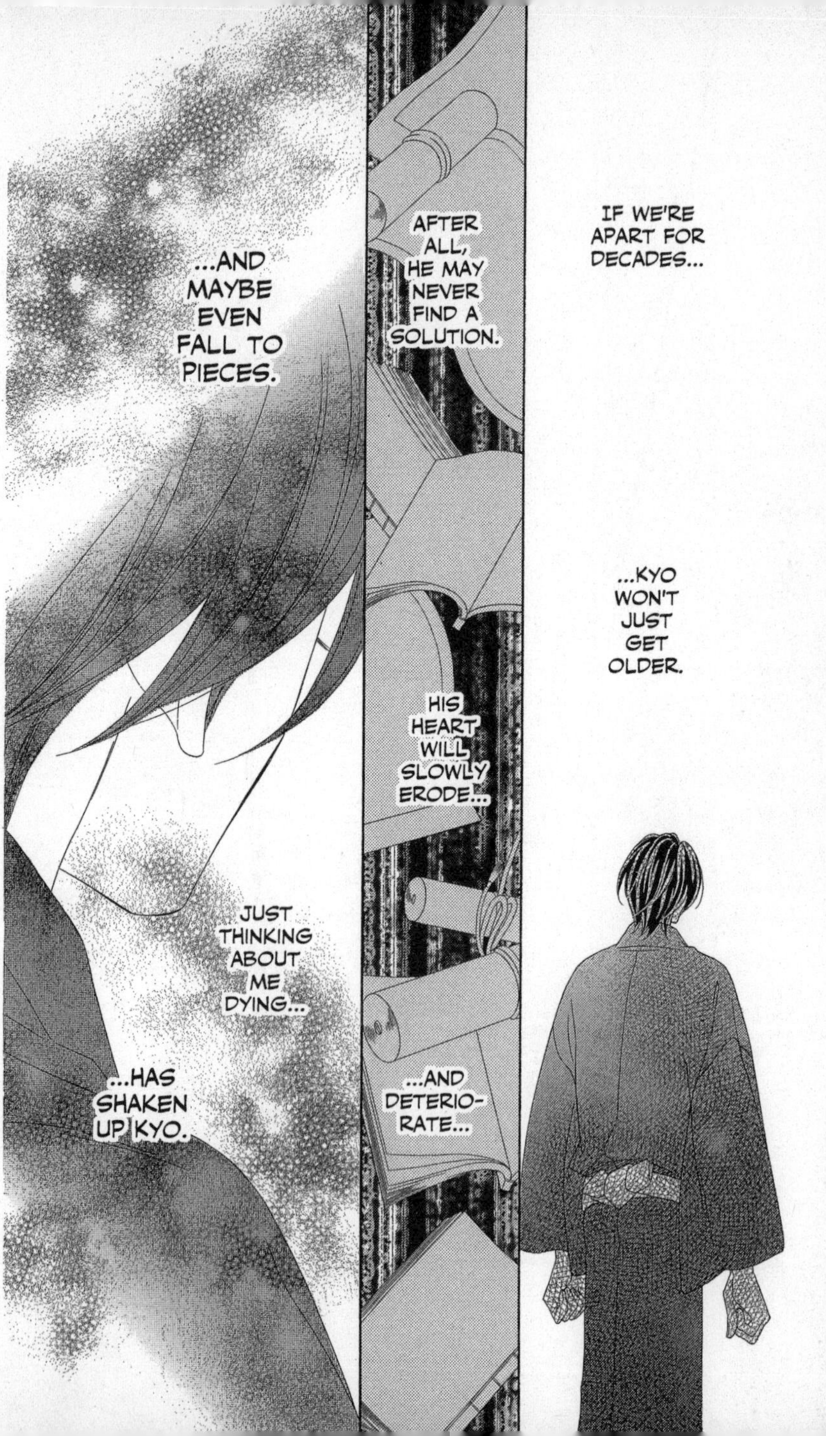
IF WE'RE APART FOR DECADES...
...KYO WON'T JUST GET OLDER.
AFTER ALL, HE MAY NEVER FIND A SOLUTION.
HIS HEART WILL SLOWLY ERODE...
...AND DETERIORATE...
...AND MAYBE EVEN FALL TO PIECES.
JUST THINKING ABOUT ME DYING...
...HAS SHAKEN UP KYO.

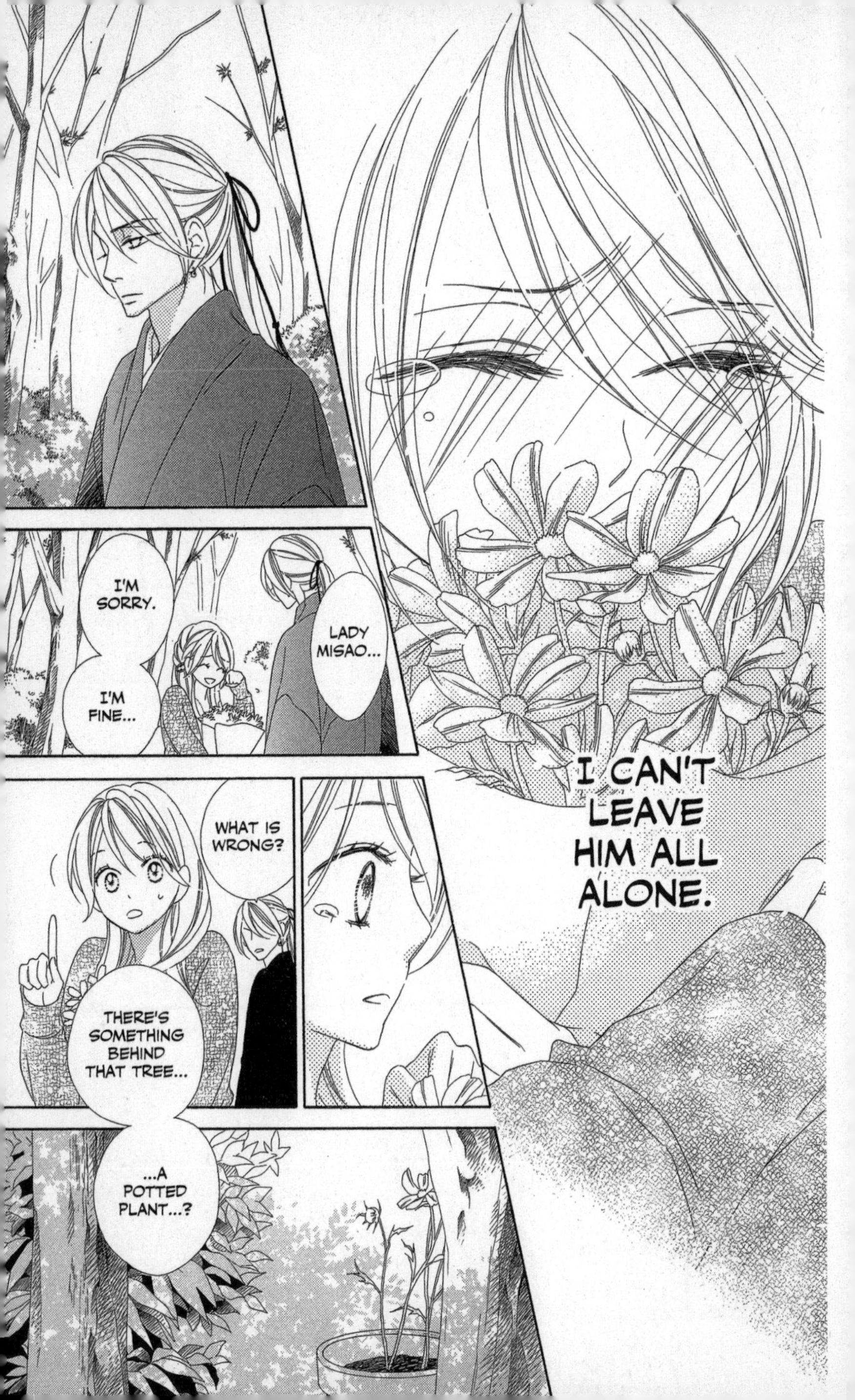
I CAN'T LEAVE HIM ALL ALONE.
LADY MISAO...
I'M SORRY.
I'M FINE...
WHAT IS WRONG?
THERE'S SOMETHING BEHIND THAT TREE...
...A POTTED PLANT...?

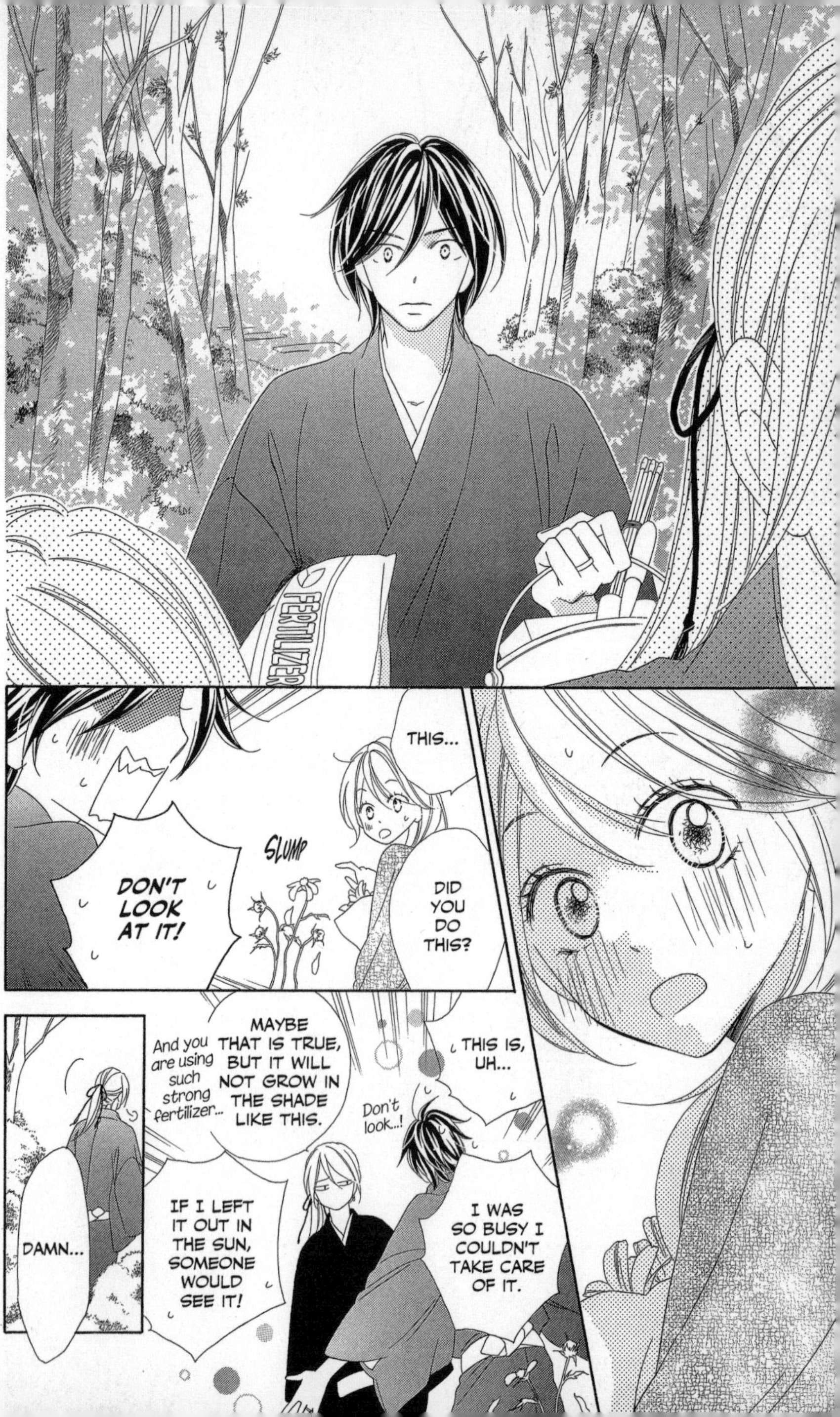
FERTILIZER
FERTILIZER
THIS...
DID YOU DO THIS?
SLUMP
DON'T LOOK AT IT!
THIS IS, UH...
I WAS SO BUSY I COULDN'T TAKE CARE OF IT.
Don't look...!
IF I LEFT IT OUT IN THE SUN, SOMEONE WOULD SEE IT!
MAYBE THAT IS TRUE, BUT IT WILL NOT GROW IN THE SHADE LIKE THIS.
And you are using such strong fertilizer...
DAMN...

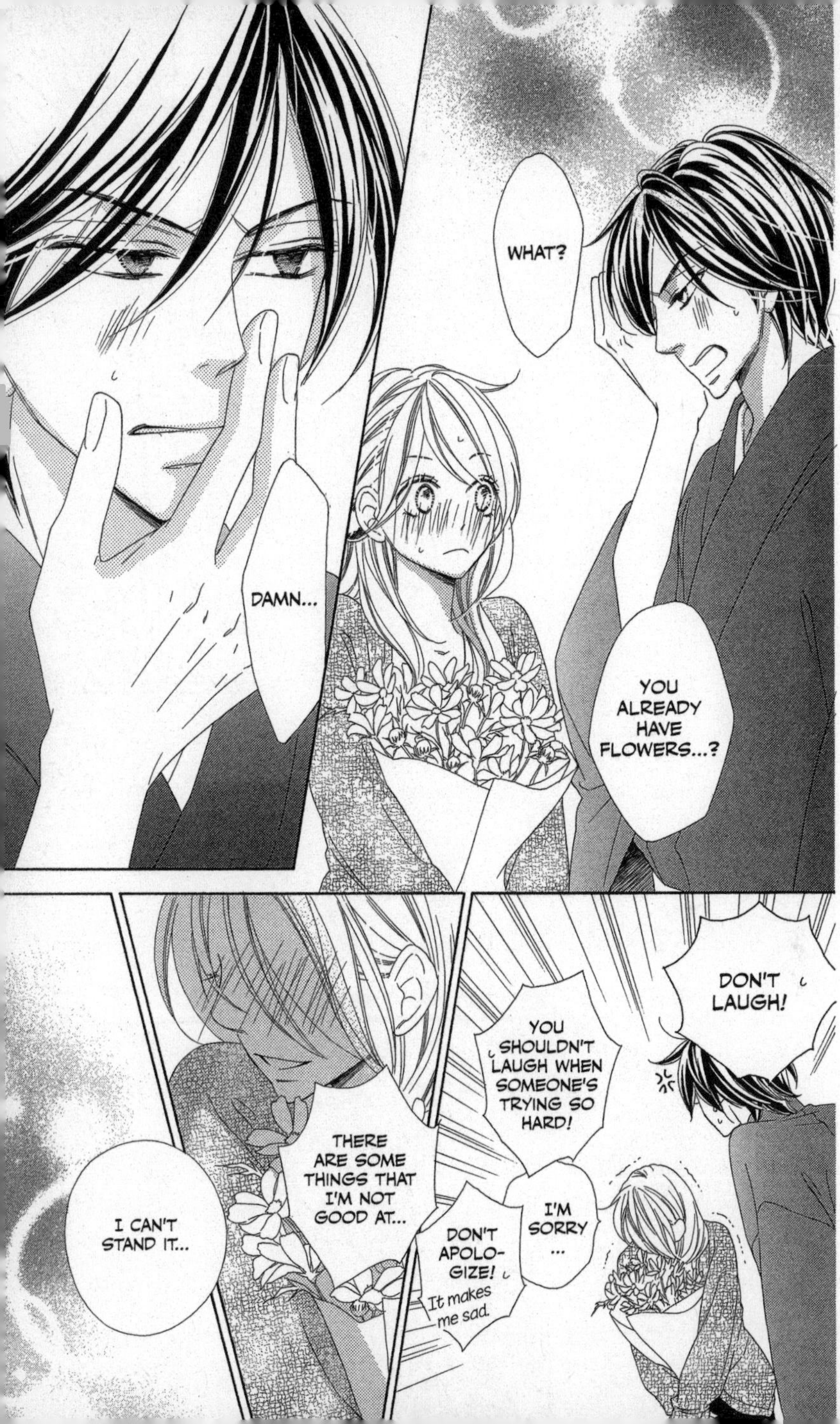
WHAT?
YOU ALREADY HAVE FLOWERS...?
DAMN...
DON'T LAUGH!
YOU SHOULDN'T LAUGH WHEN SOMEONE'S TRYING SO HARD!
I'M SORRY...
DON'T APOLO-GIZE!
It makes me sad.
THERE ARE SOME THINGS THAT I'M NOT GOOD AT...
I CAN'T STAND IT...

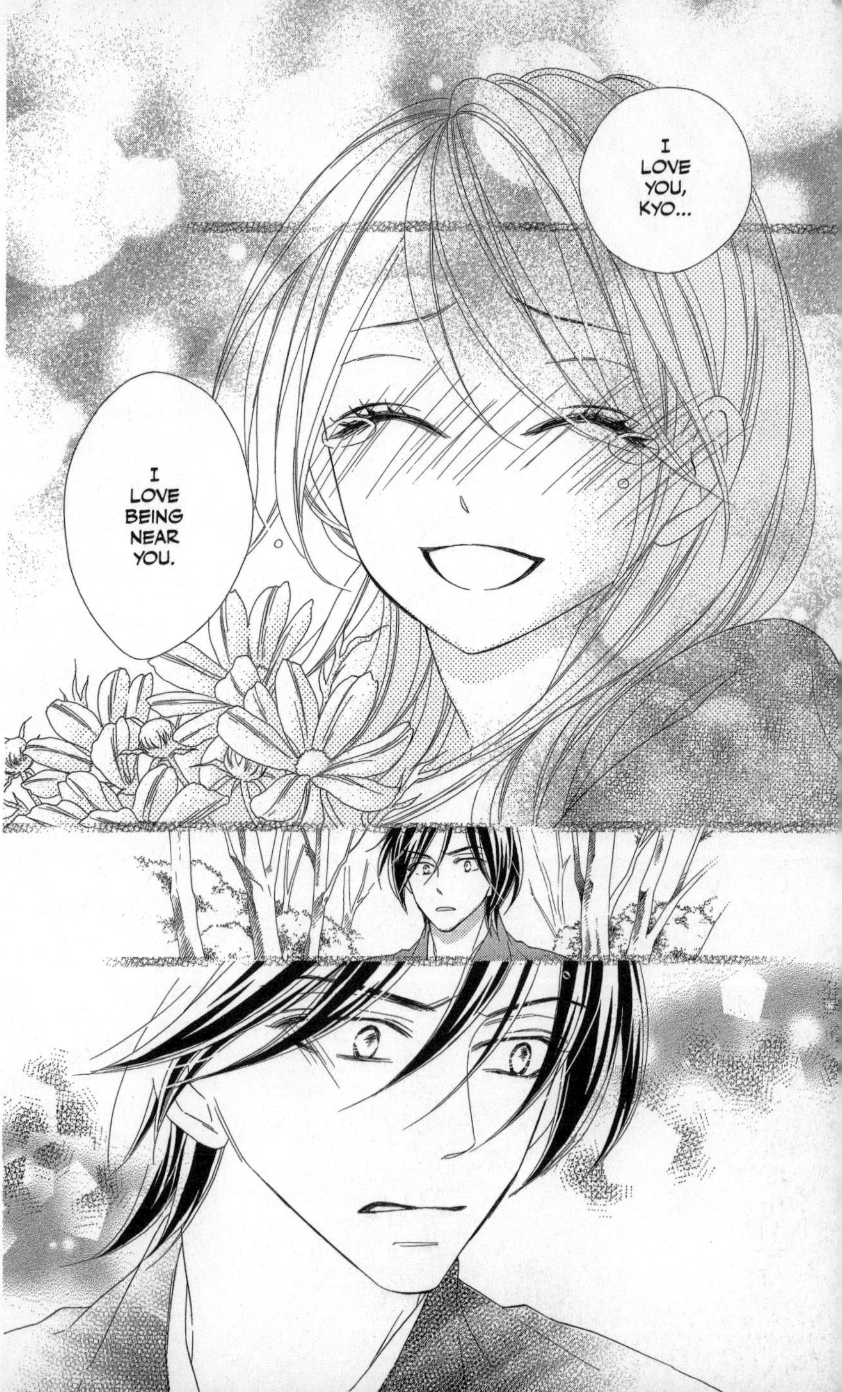
I LOVE YOU, KYO...
I LOVE BEING NEAR YOU.

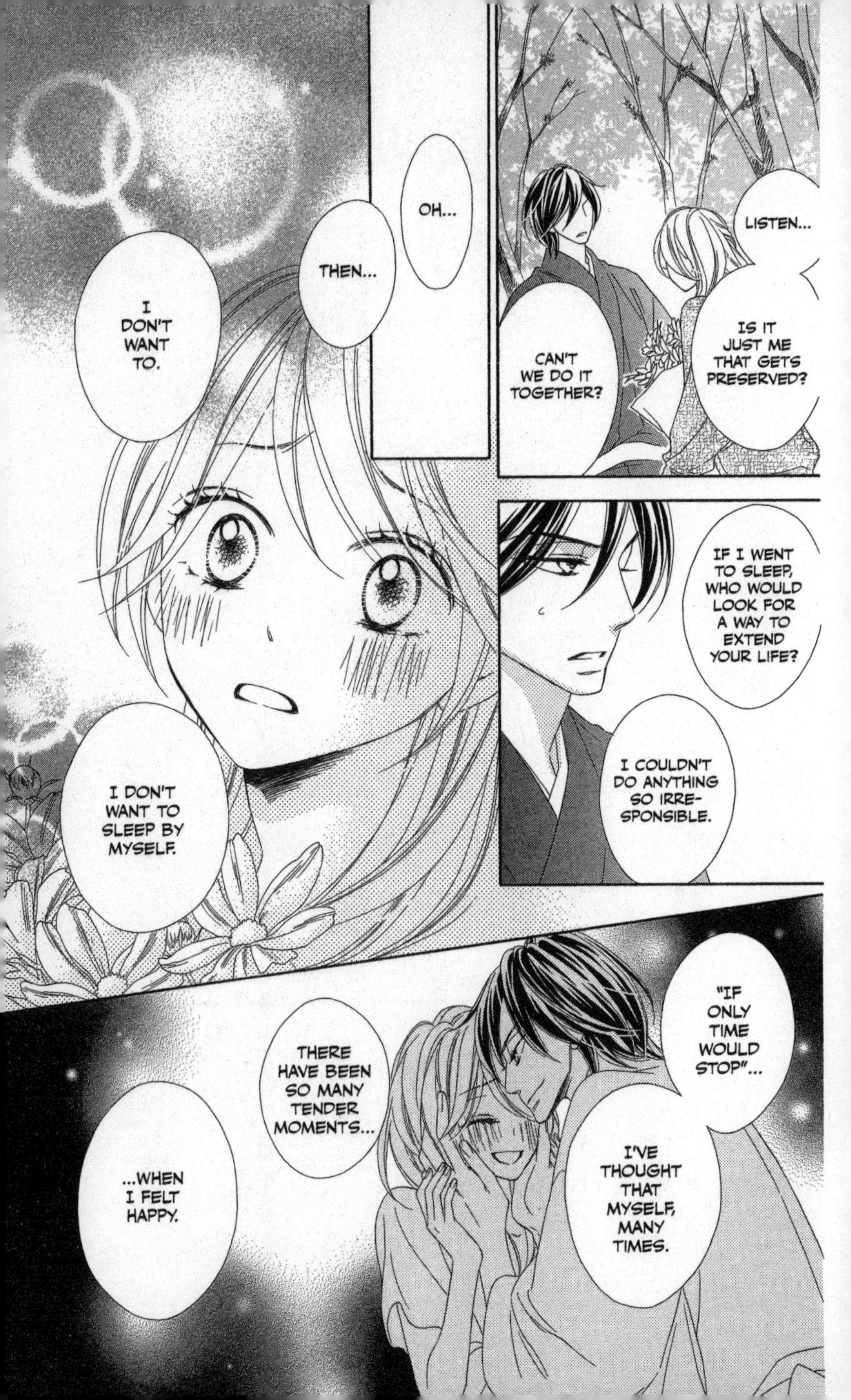
LISTEN...
IS IT JUST ME THAT GETS PRESERVED?
CAN'T WE DO IT TOGETHER?
OH...
IF I WENT TO SLEEP, WHO WOULD LOOK FOR A WAY TO EXTEND YOUR LIFE?
I COULDN'T DO ANYTHING SO IRRE-SPONSIBLE.
THEN...
I DON'T WANT TO.
I DON'T WANT TO SLEEP BY MYSELF.
"IF ONLY TIME WOULD STOP"...
I'VE THOUGHT THAT MYSELF, MANY TIMES.
THERE HAVE BEEN SO MANY TENDER MOMENTS...
...WHEN I FELT HAPPY.

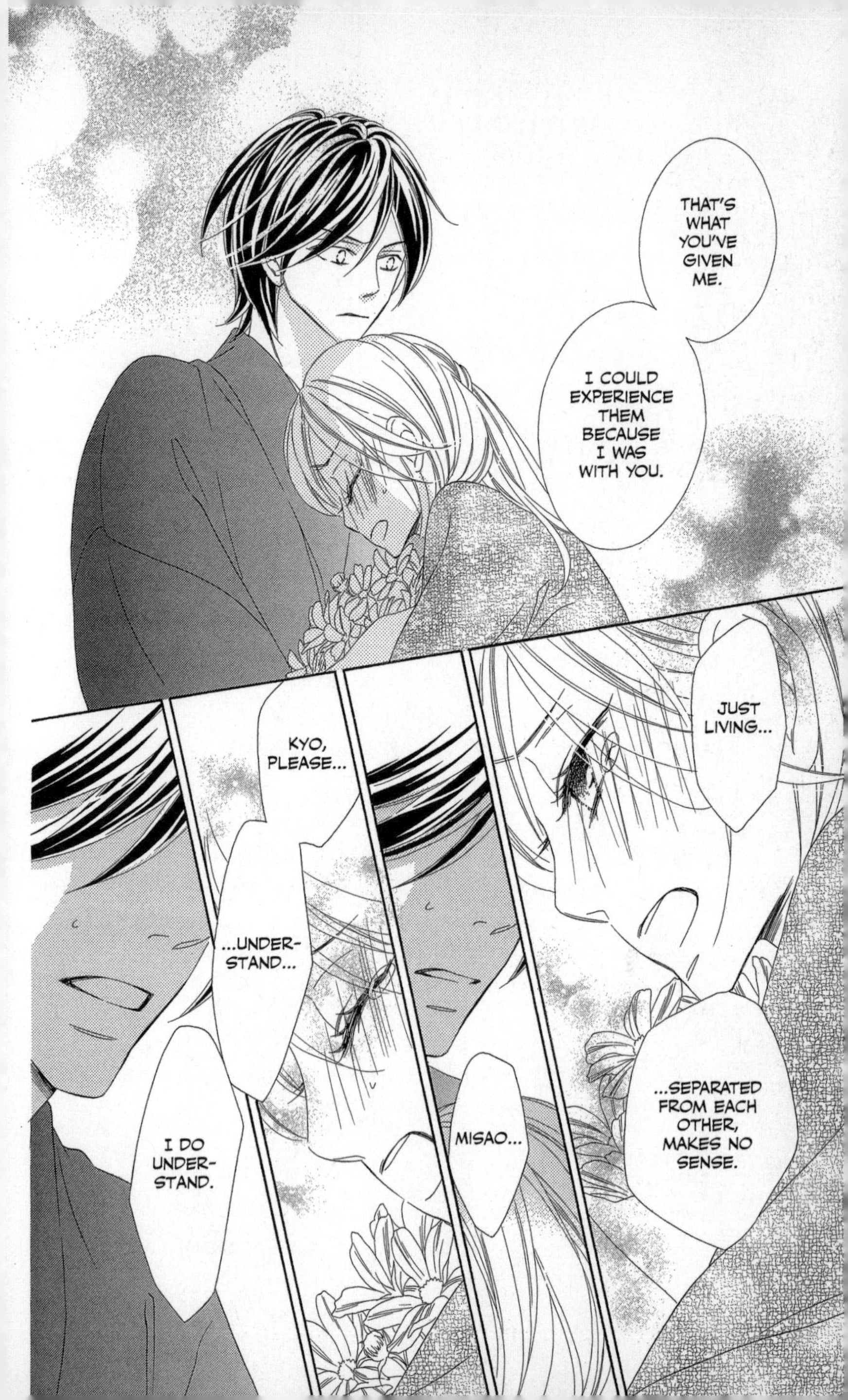
THAT'S WHAT YOU'VE GIVEN ME.
I COULD EXPERIENCE THEM BECAUSE I WAS WITH YOU.
JUST LIVING...
...SEPARATED FROM EACH OTHER, MAKES NO SENSE.
MISAO...
KYO, PLEASE...
...UNDER-STAND...
I DO UNDER-STAND.

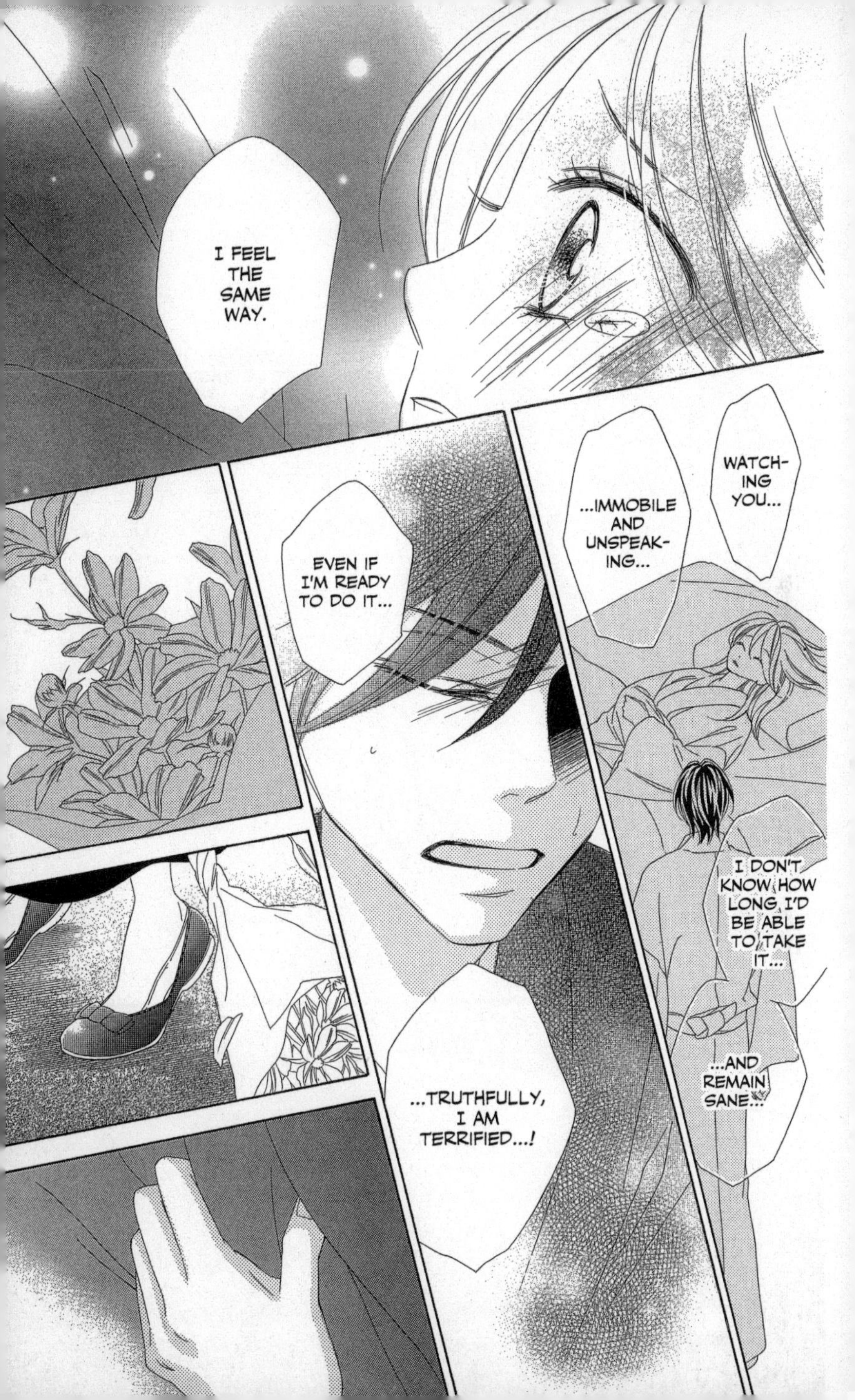
I FEEL THE SAME WAY.
WATCHING YOU...
...IMMOBILE AND UNSPEAKING...
I DON'T KNOW HOW LONG I'D BE ABLE TO TAKE IT...
...AND REMAIN SANE...
EVEN IF I'M READY TO DO IT...
...TRUTHFULLY, I AM TERRIFIED...!

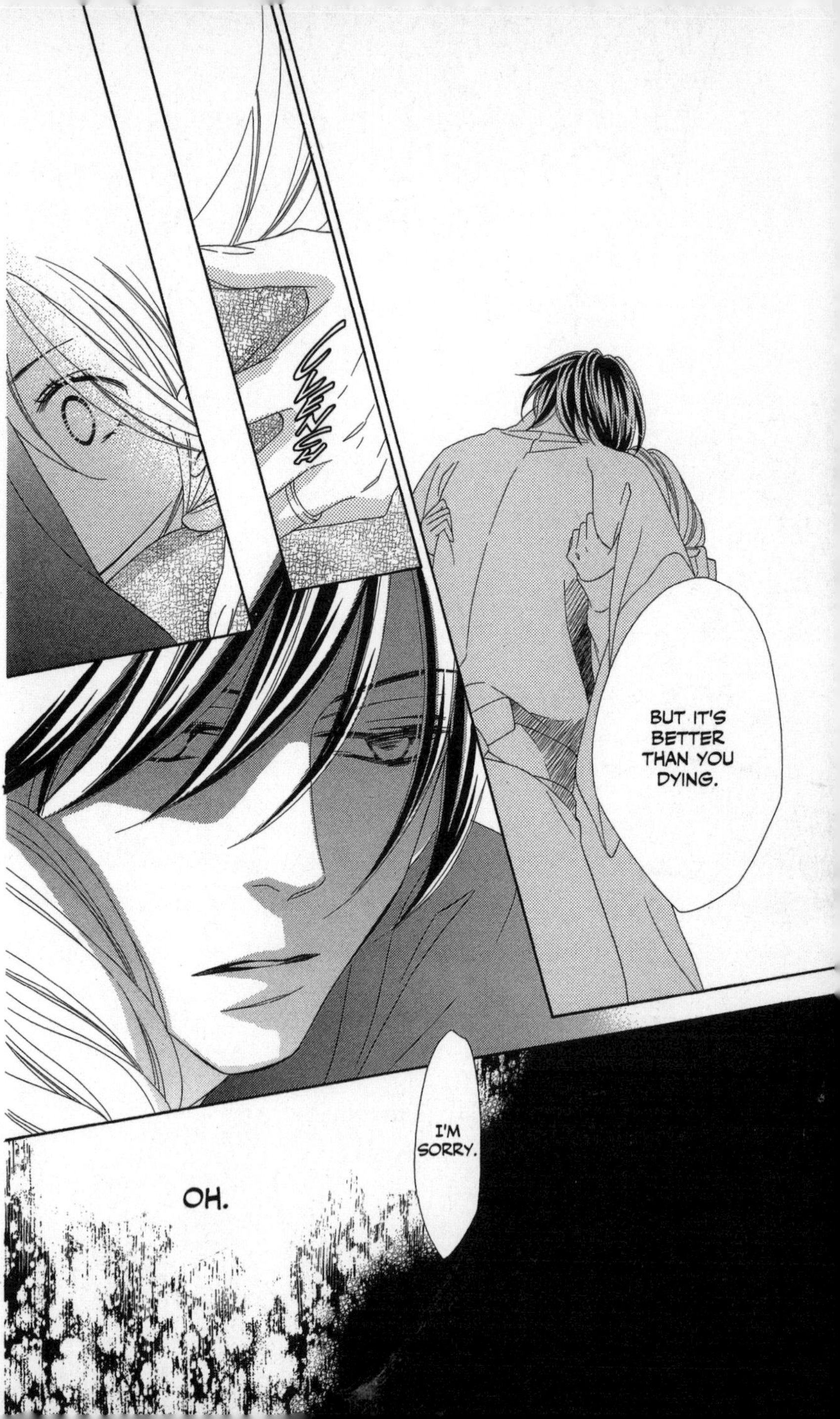
BUT IT'S BETTER THAN YOU DYING.
I'M SORRY.
OH.

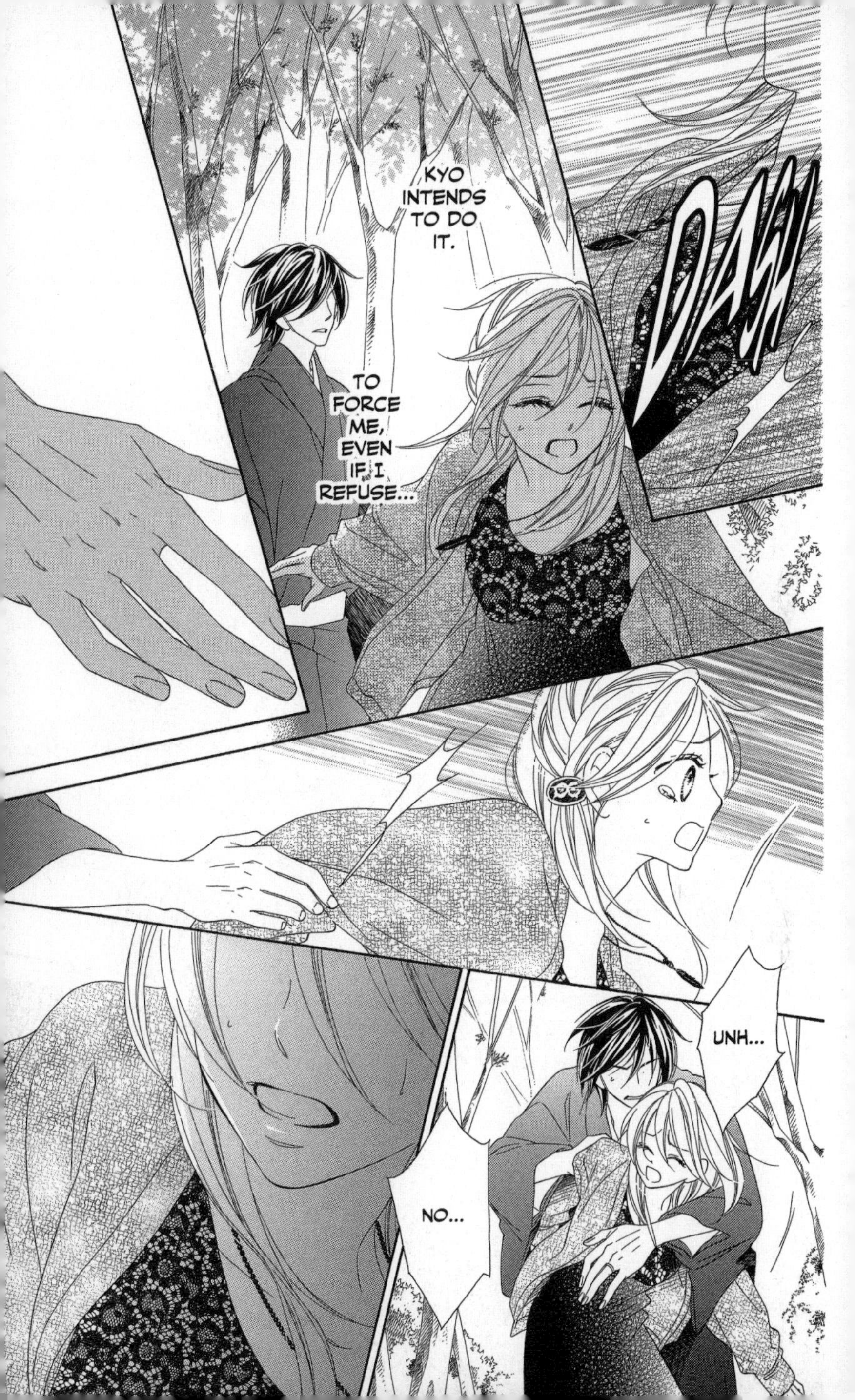
DASH!
KYO INTENDS TO DO IT.
TO FORCE ME, EVEN IF I REFUSE...
UNH...
NO...

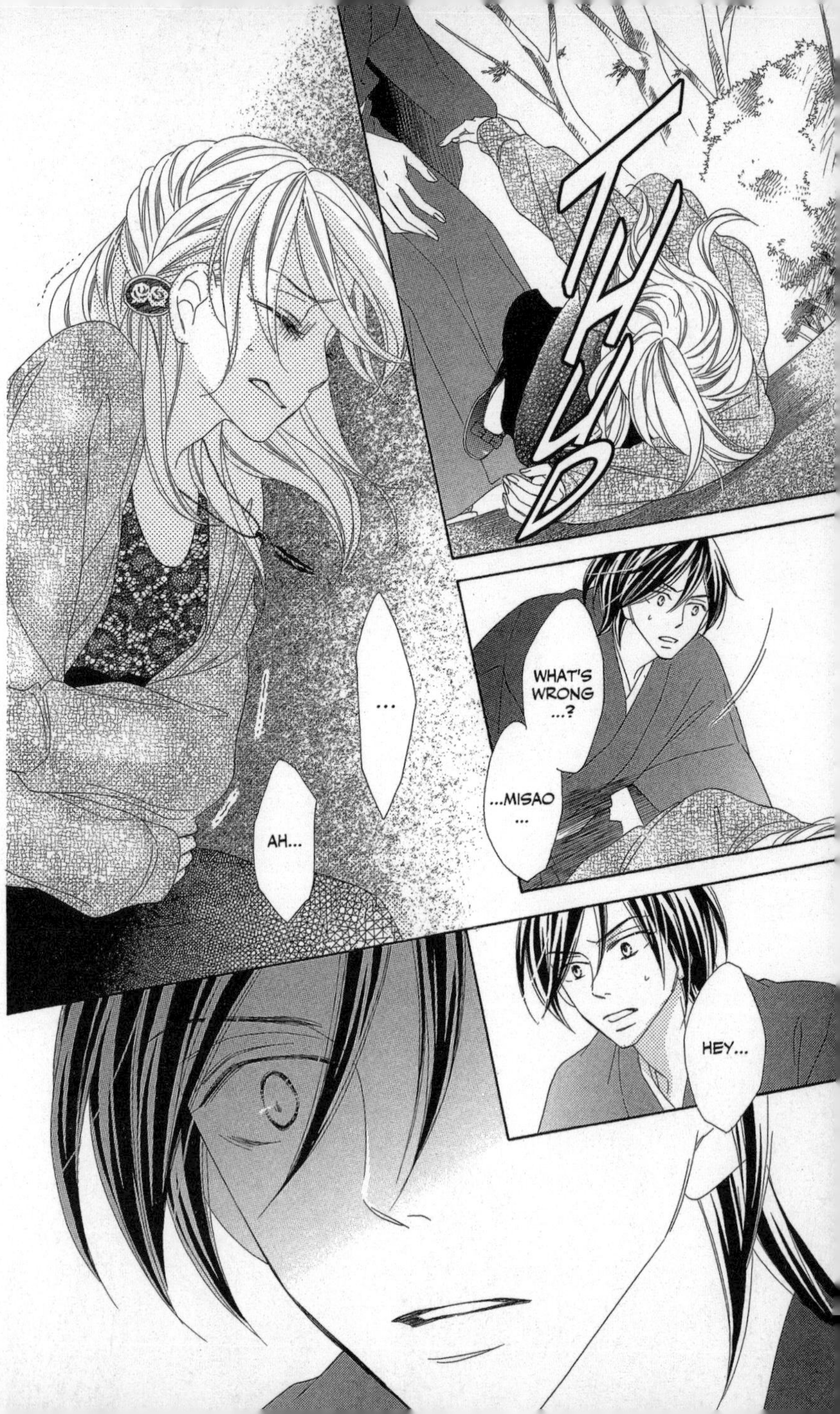
THUD
WHAT'S WRONG ...?
...MISAO ...
...
AH...
HEY...

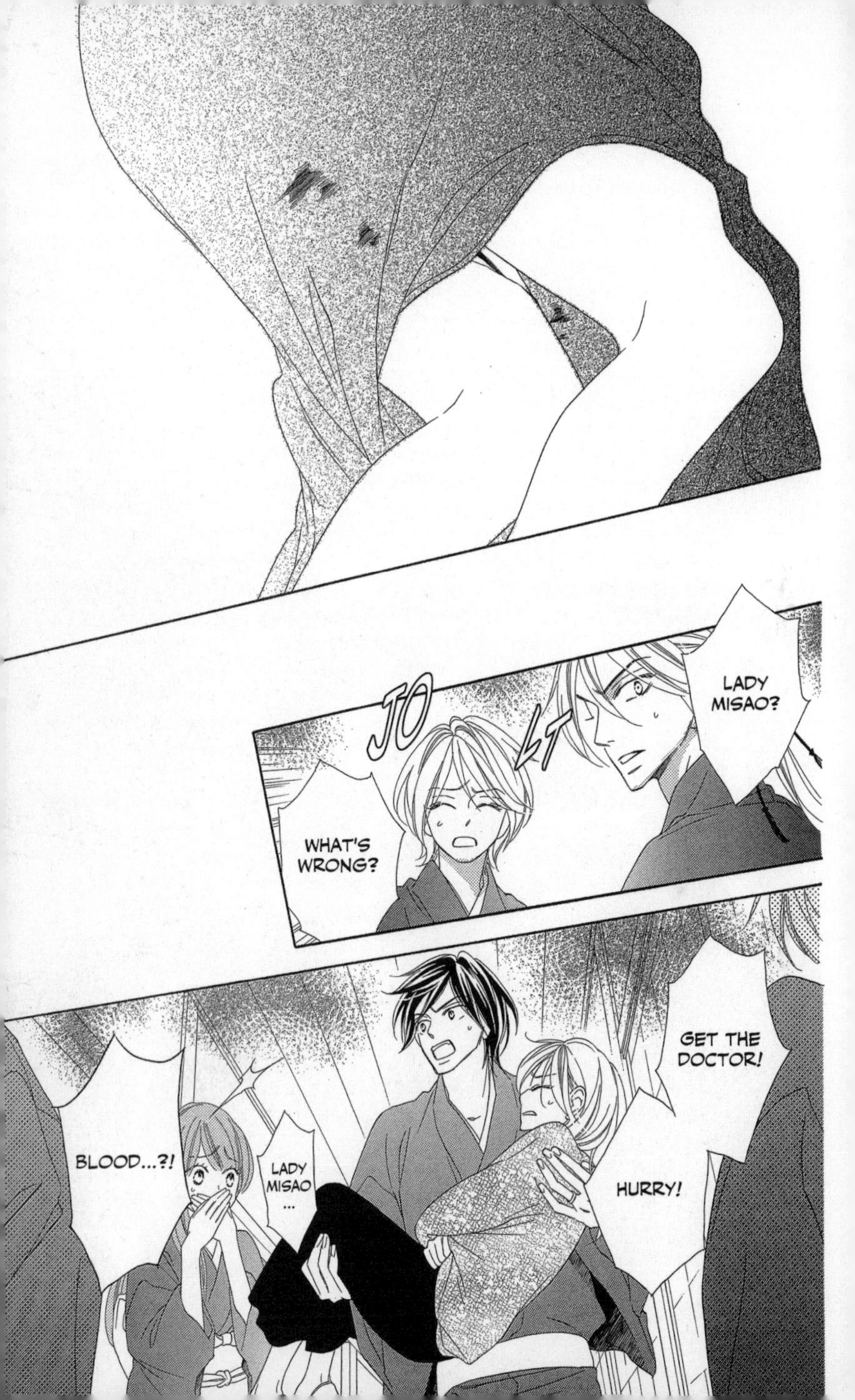
JOLT
LADY MISAO?
WHAT'S WRONG?
GET THE DOCTOR!
HURRY!
LADY MISAO ...
BLOOD...?!

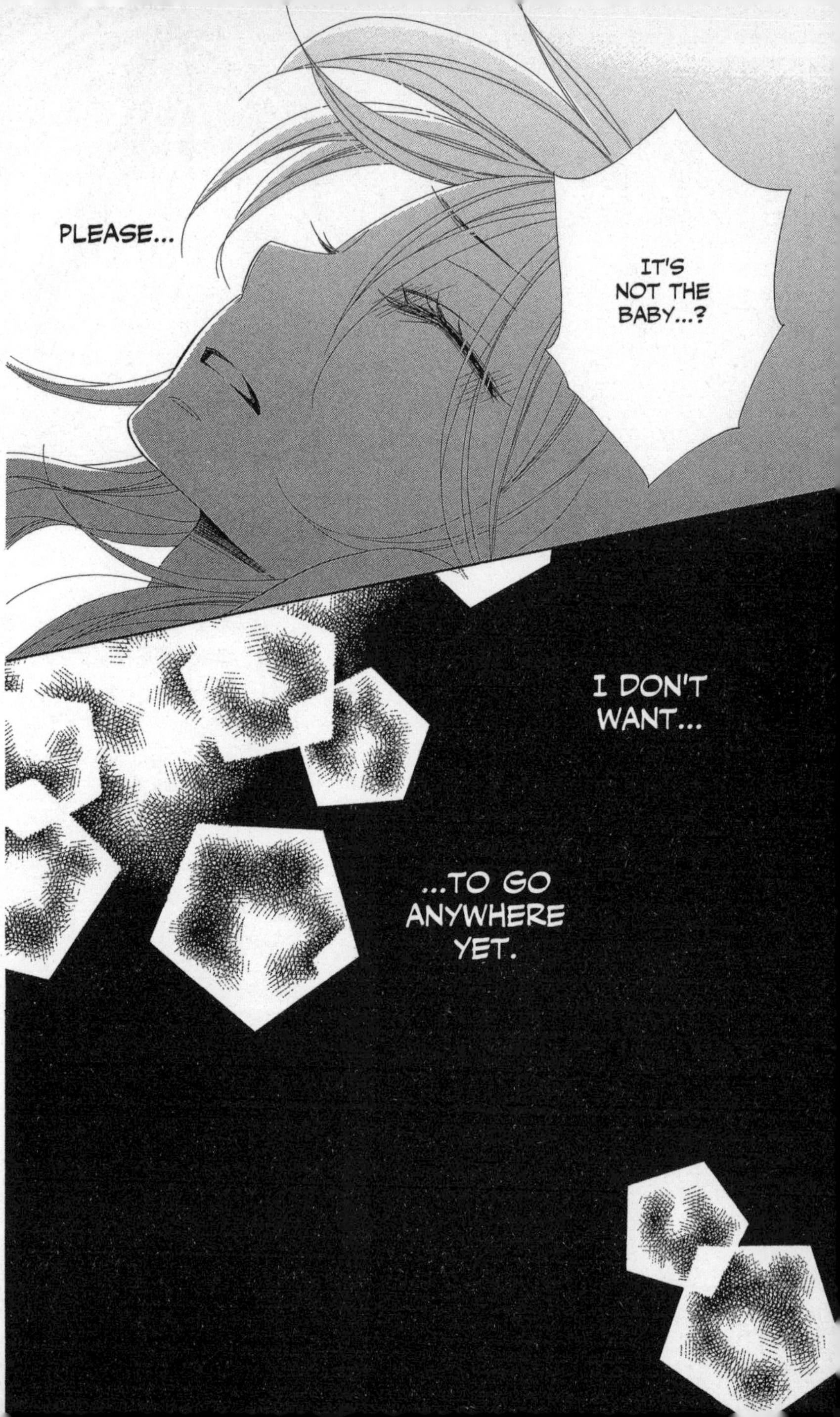
IT'S NOT THE BABY...?
PLEASE...
I DON'T WANT...
...TO GO ANYWHERE YET.

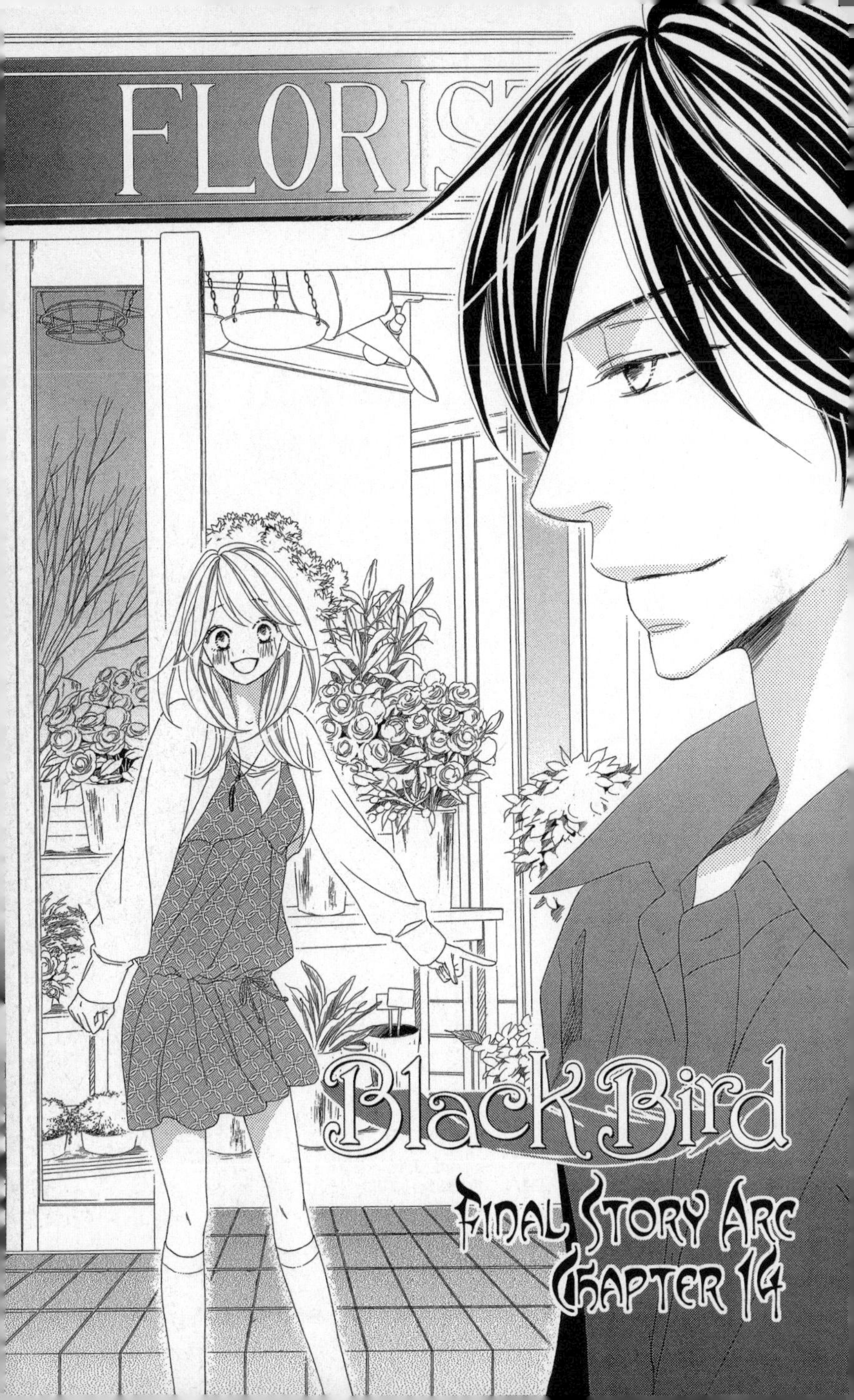
FLORIST
Black Bird
Final Story Arc
Chapter 14

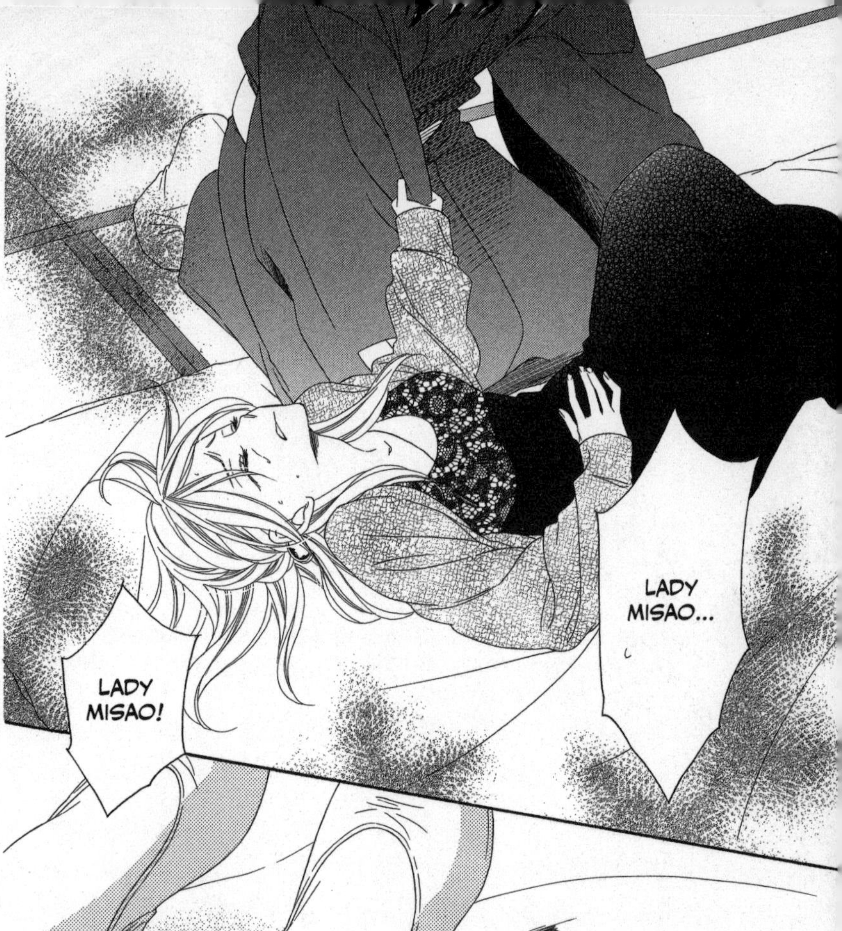
LADY MISAO...
LADY MISAO!

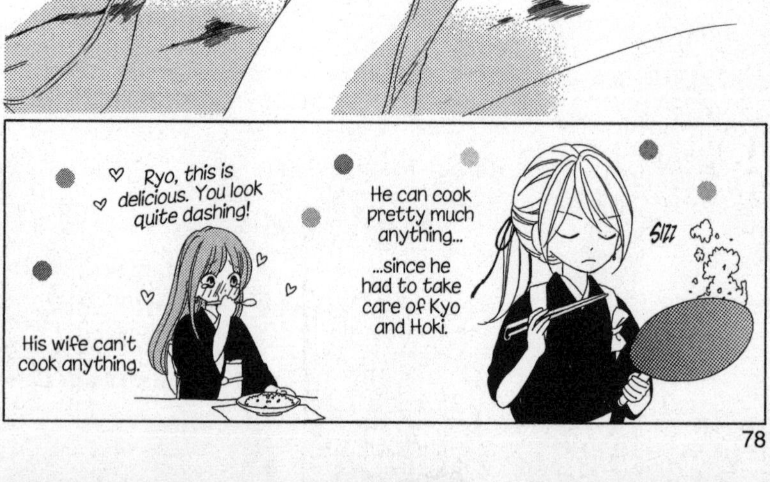
SIZZ
He can cook pretty much anything...
...since he had to take care of Kyo and Hoki.
Ryo, this is delicious. You look quite dashing!
His wife can't cook anything.

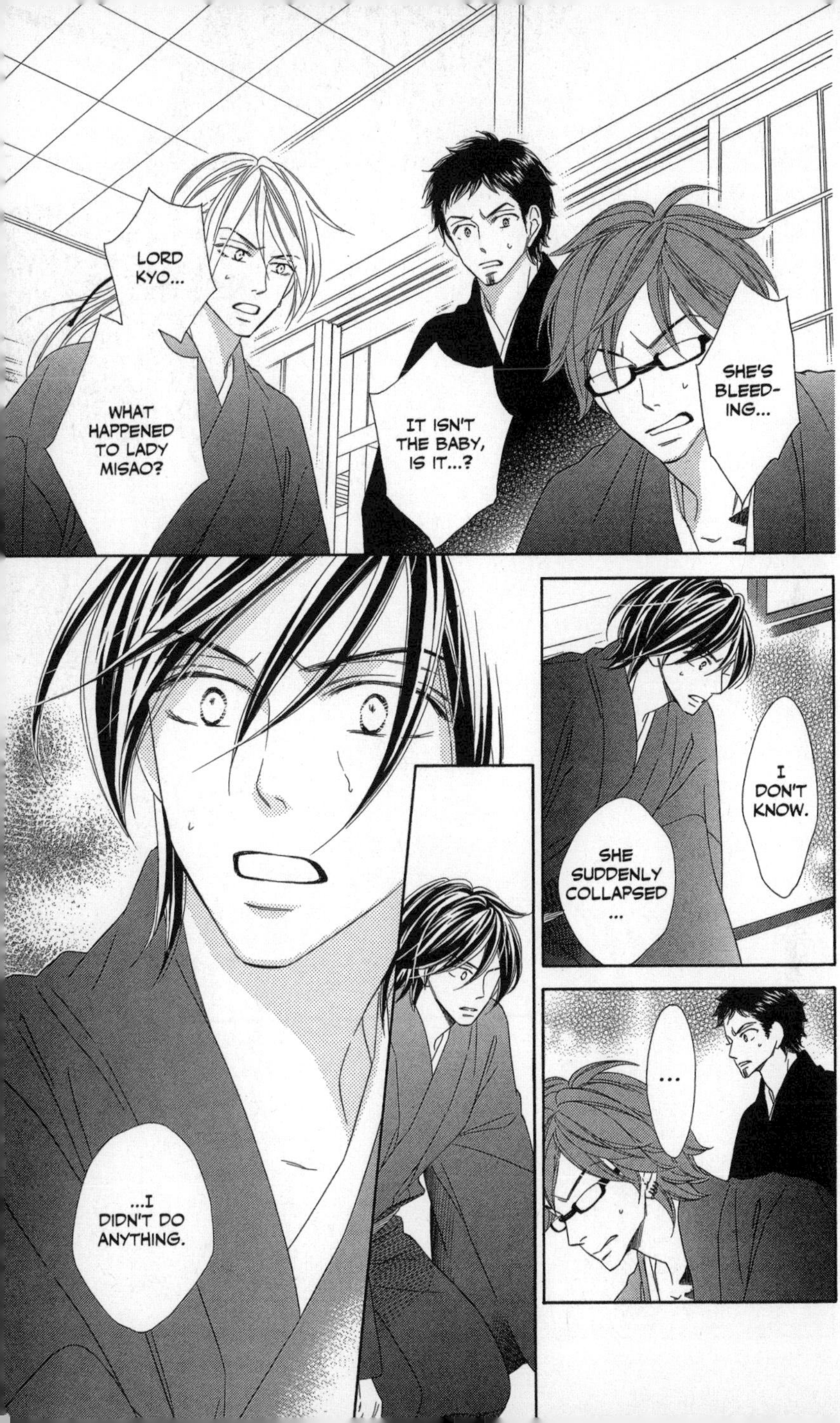
SHE'S BLEED-ING...
IT ISN'T THE BABY, IS IT...?
LORD KYO...
WHAT HAPPENED TO LADY MISAO?
I DON'T KNOW.
SHE SUDDENLY COLLAPSED ...
...
...I DIDN'T DO ANYTHING.

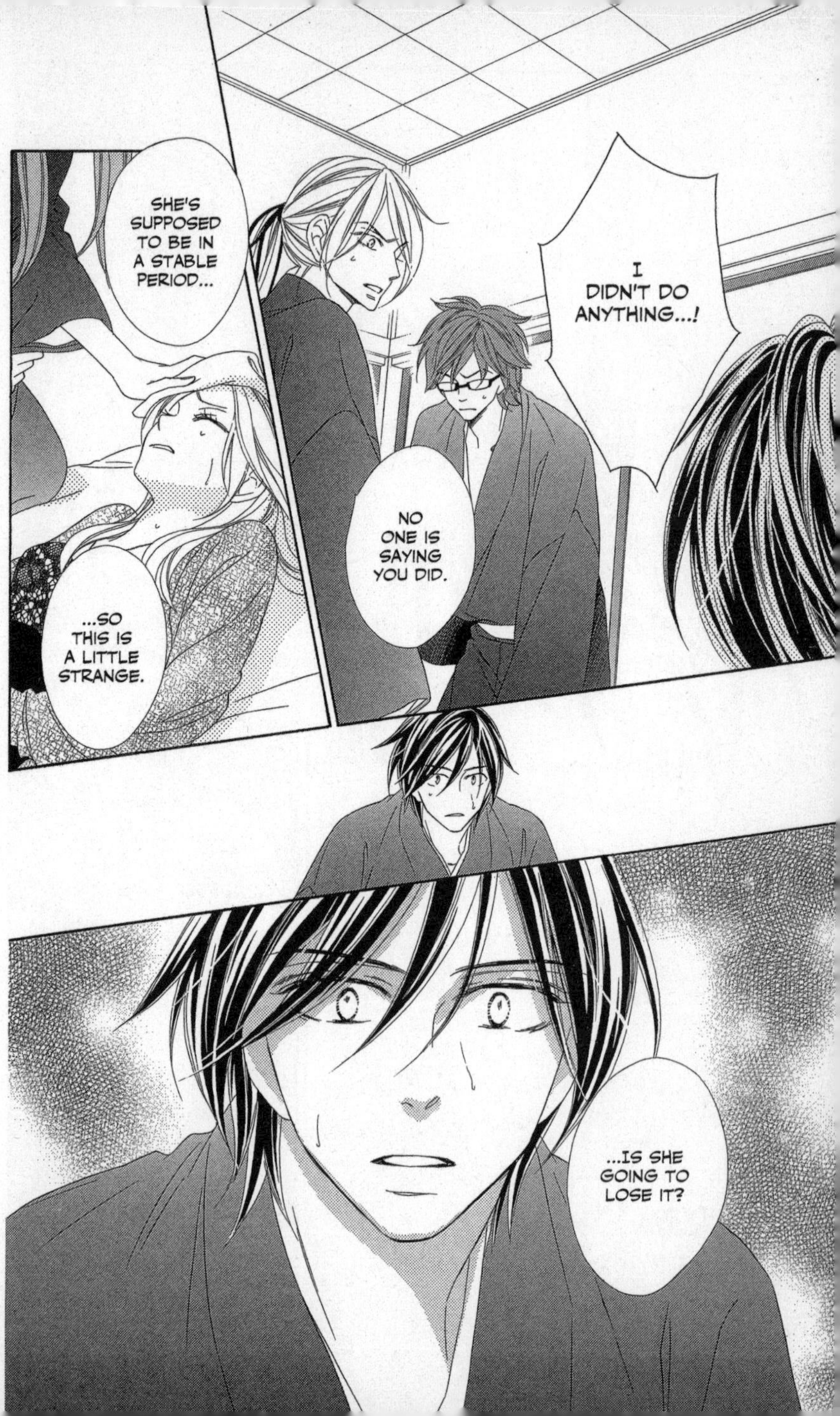
I DIDN'T DO ANYTHING...!
NO ONE IS SAYING YOU DID.
SHE'S SUPPOSED TO BE IN A STABLE PERIOD...
...SO THIS IS A LITTLE STRANGE.
...IS SHE GOING TO LOSE IT?

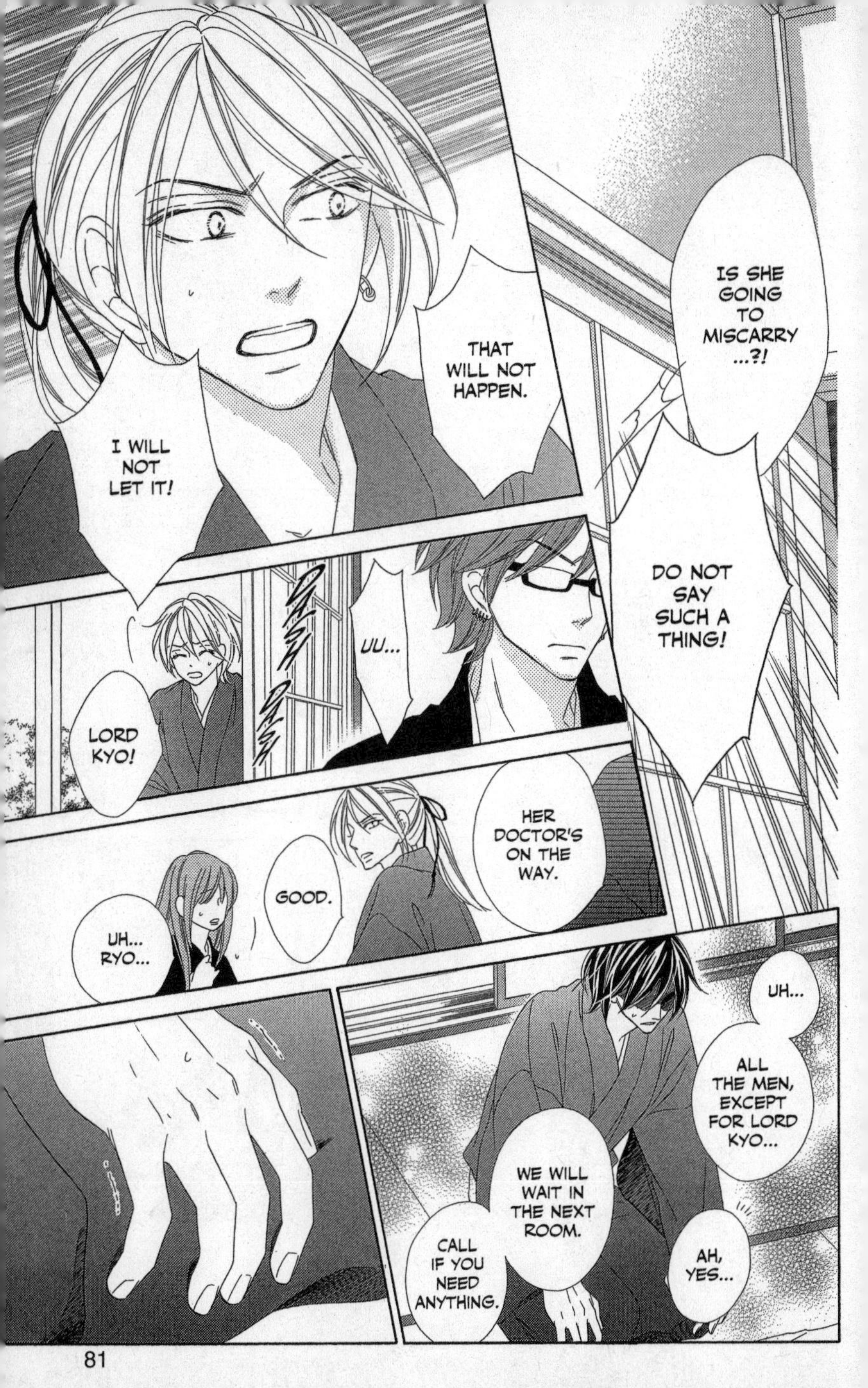
IS SHE GOING TO MISCARRY ...?!
DO NOT SAY SUCH A THING!
THAT WILL NOT HAPPEN.
I WILL NOT LET IT!
UU...
LORD KYO!
HER DOCTOR'S ON THE WAY.
GOOD.
UH... RYO...
UH...
ALL THE MEN, EXCEPT FOR LORD KYO...
WE WILL WAIT IN THE NEXT ROOM.
AH, YES...
CALL IF YOU NEED ANYTHING.

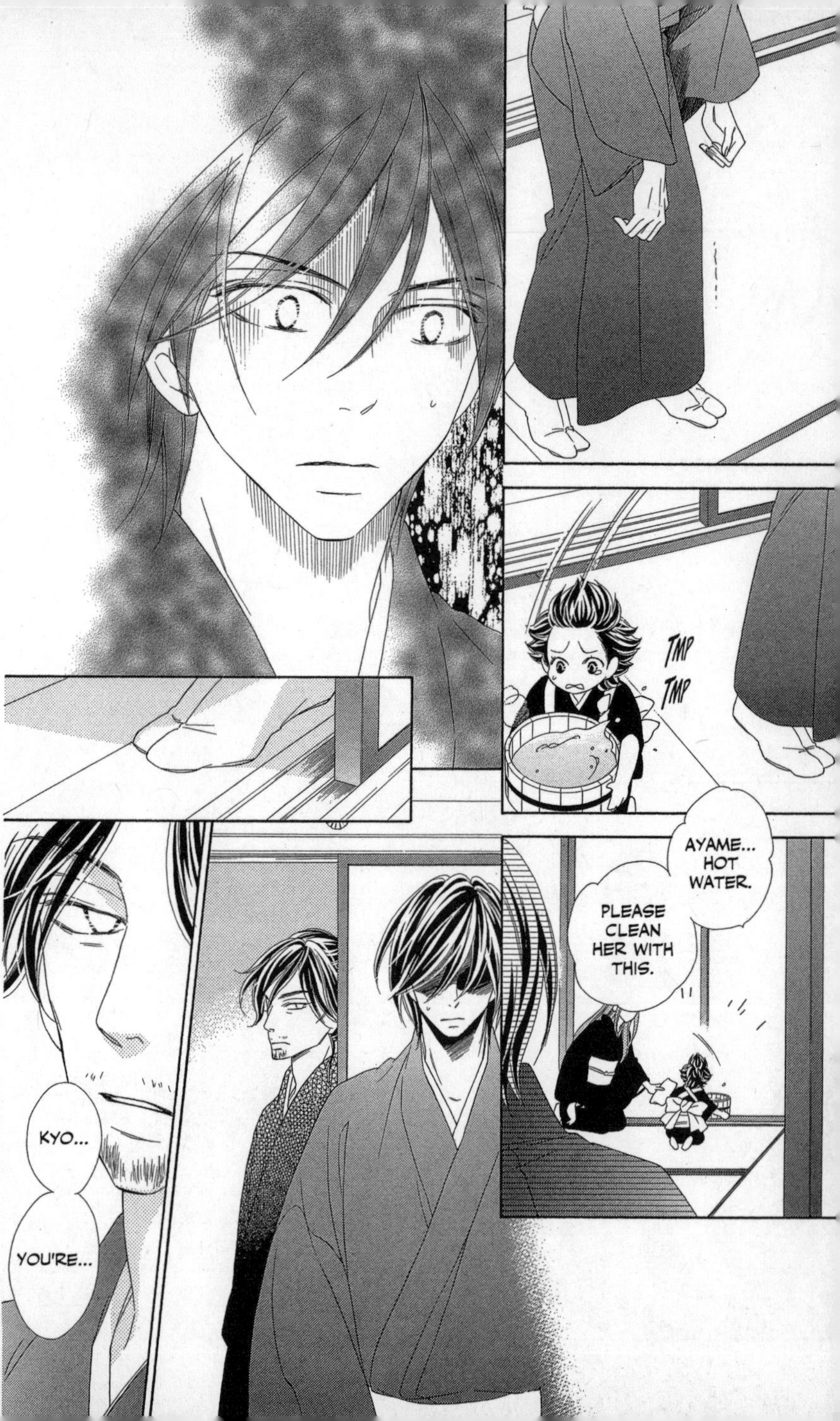
TMP
TMP
AYAME... HOT WATER.
PLEASE CLEAN HER WITH THIS.
KYO...
YOU'RE...

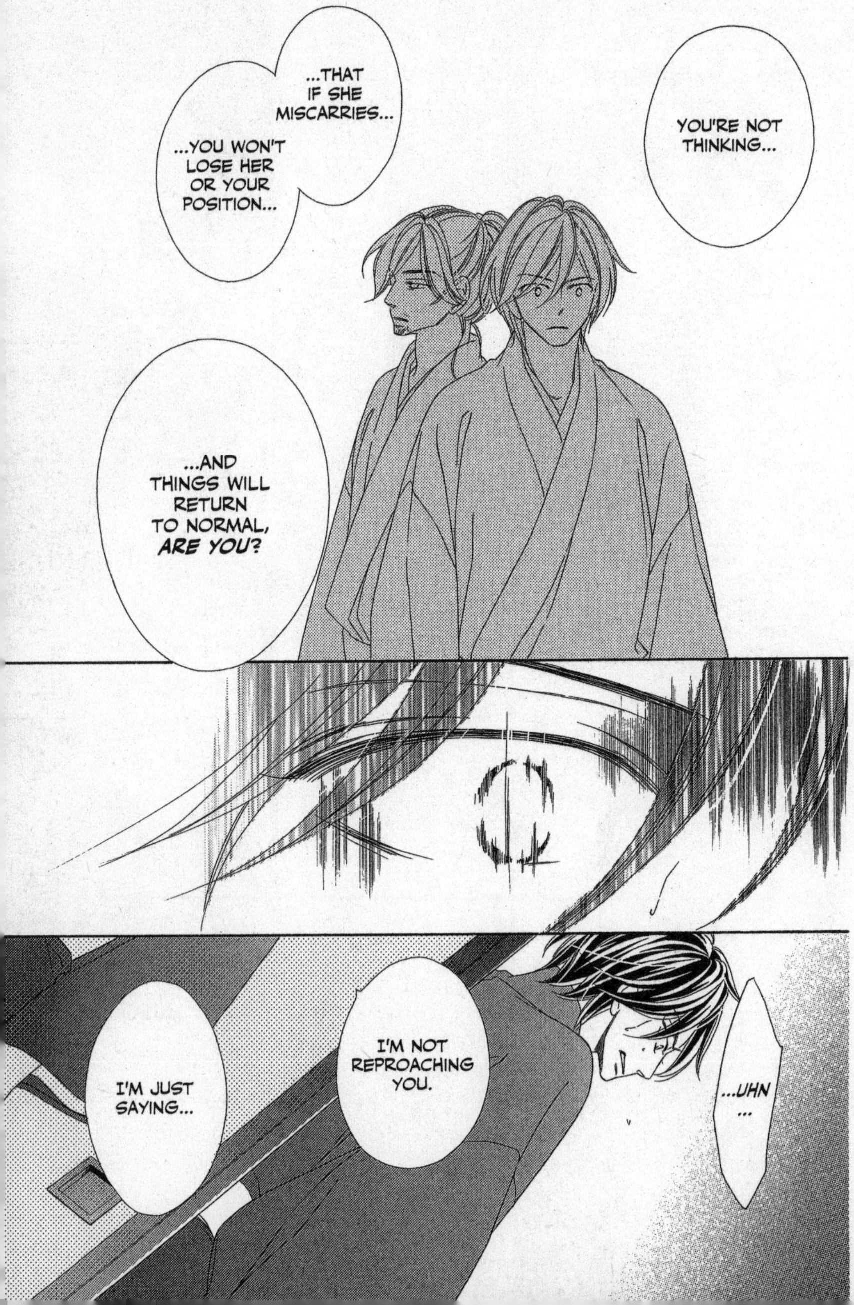
YOU'RE NOT THINKING...
...THAT IF SHE MISCARRIES...
...YOU WON'T LOSE HER OR YOUR POSITION...
...AND THINGS WILL RETURN TO NORMAL, *ARE YOU*?
...UHN ...
I'M NOT REPROACHING YOU.
I'M JUST SAYING...

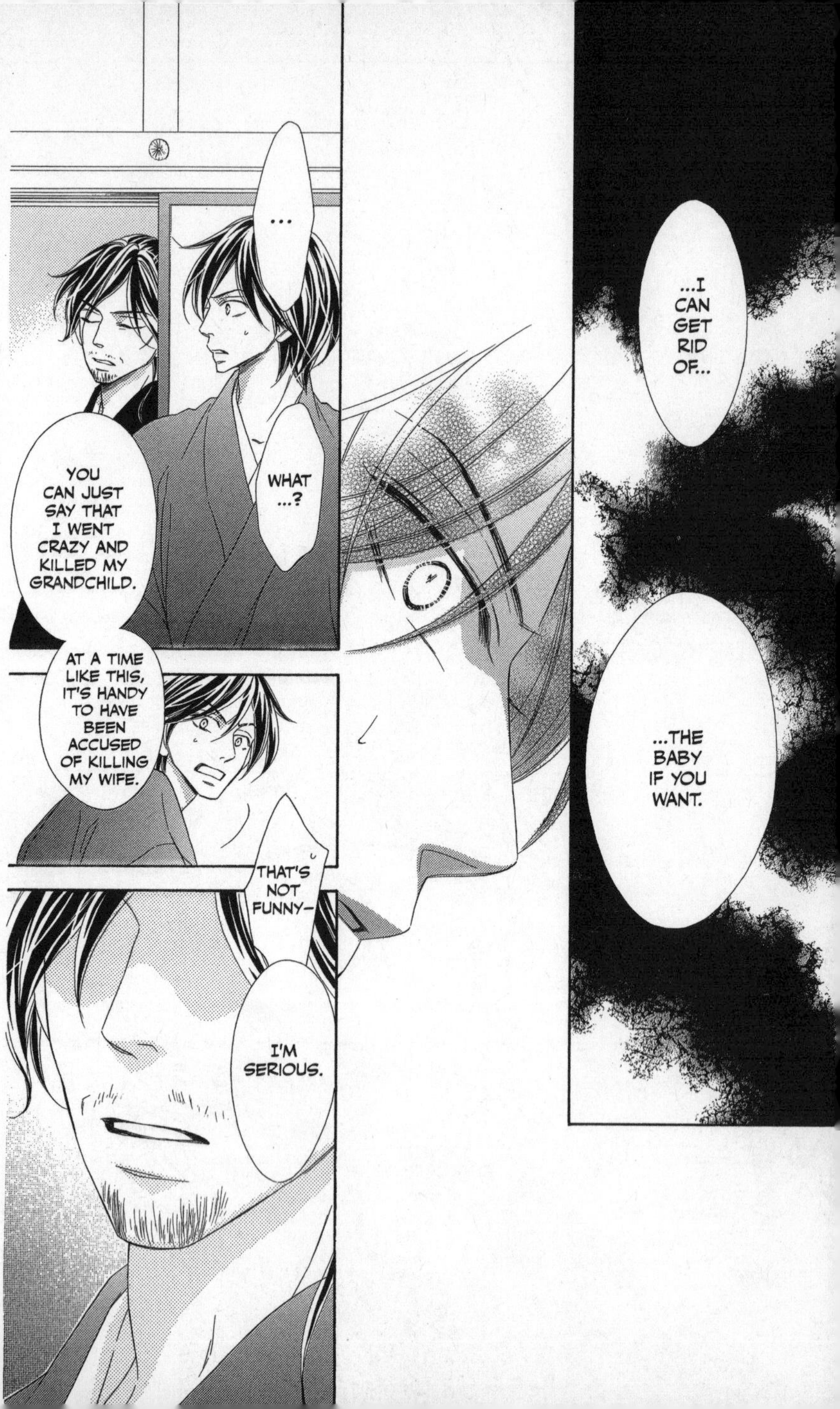
...I CAN GET RID OF...
...THE BABY IF YOU WANT.
...
WHAT ...?
YOU CAN JUST SAY THAT I WENT CRAZY AND KILLED MY GRANDCHILD.
AT A TIME LIKE THIS, IT'S HANDY TO HAVE BEEN ACCUSED OF KILLING MY WIFE.
THAT'S NOT FUNNY—
I'M SERIOUS.

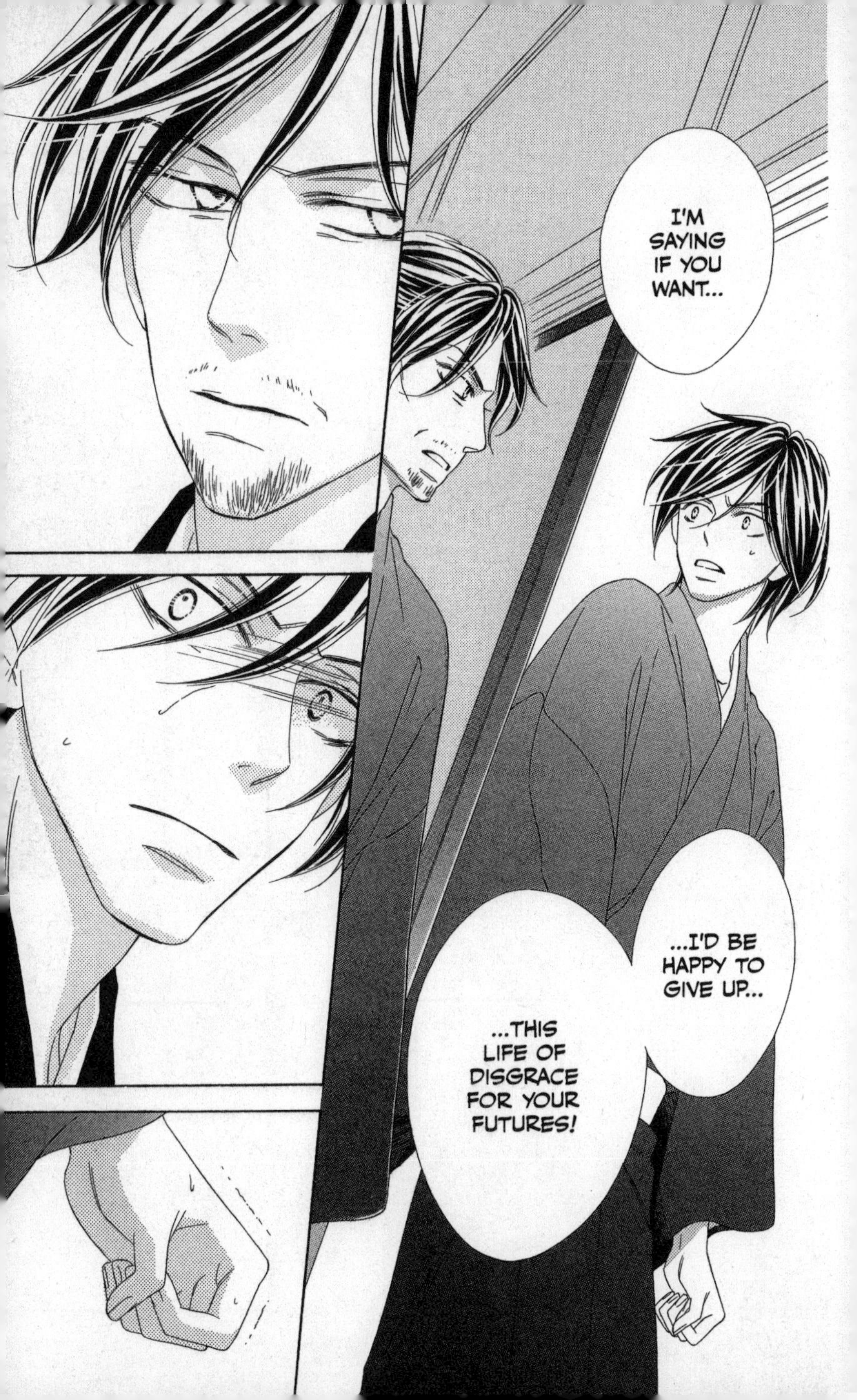
I'M SAYING IF YOU WANT...
...I'D BE HAPPY TO GIVE UP...
...THIS LIFE OF DISGRACE FOR YOUR FUTURES!

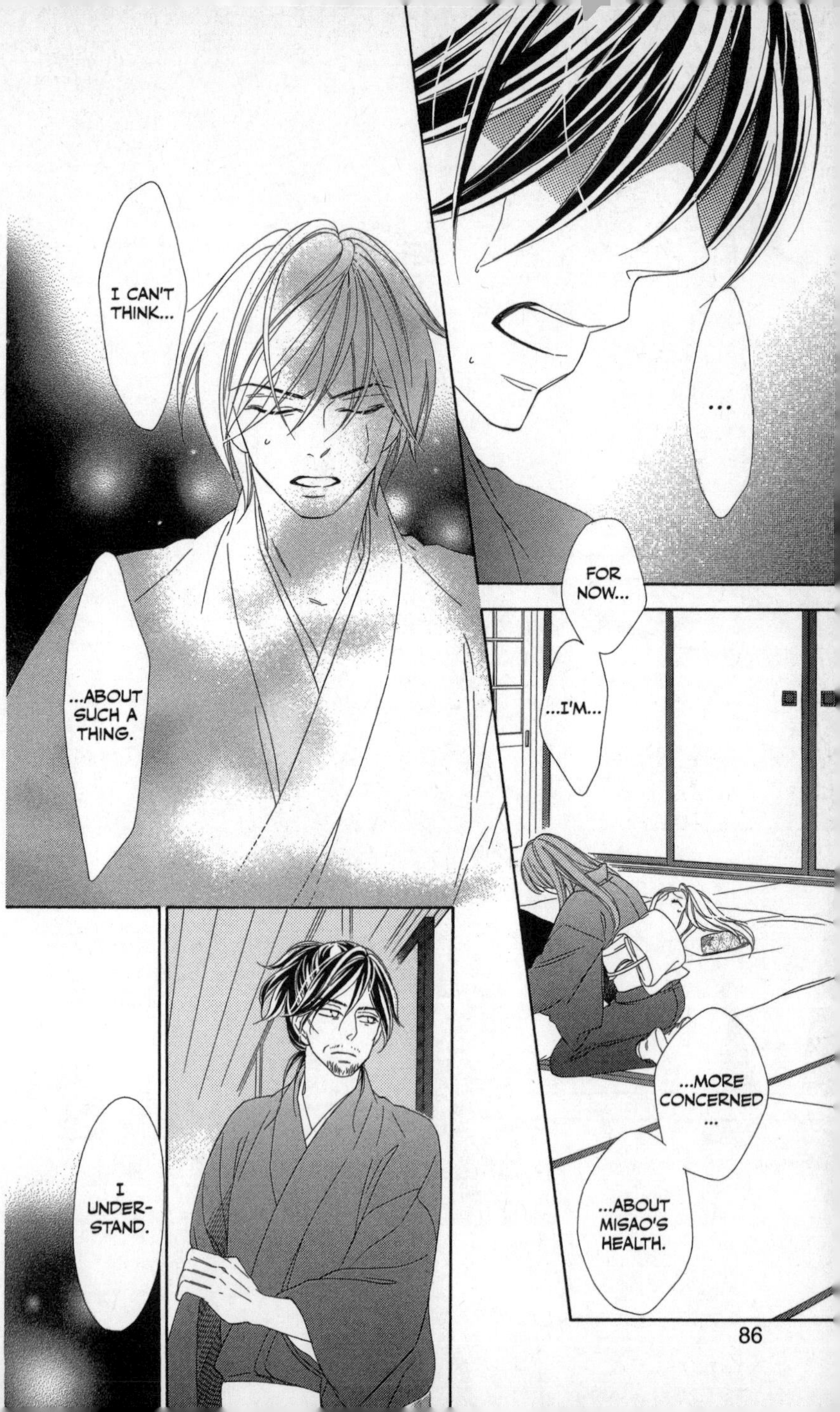
...
FOR NOW...
...I'M...
...MORE CONCERNED ...
...ABOUT MISAO'S HEALTH.
I CAN'T THINK...
...ABOUT SUCH A THING.
I UNDER-STAND.

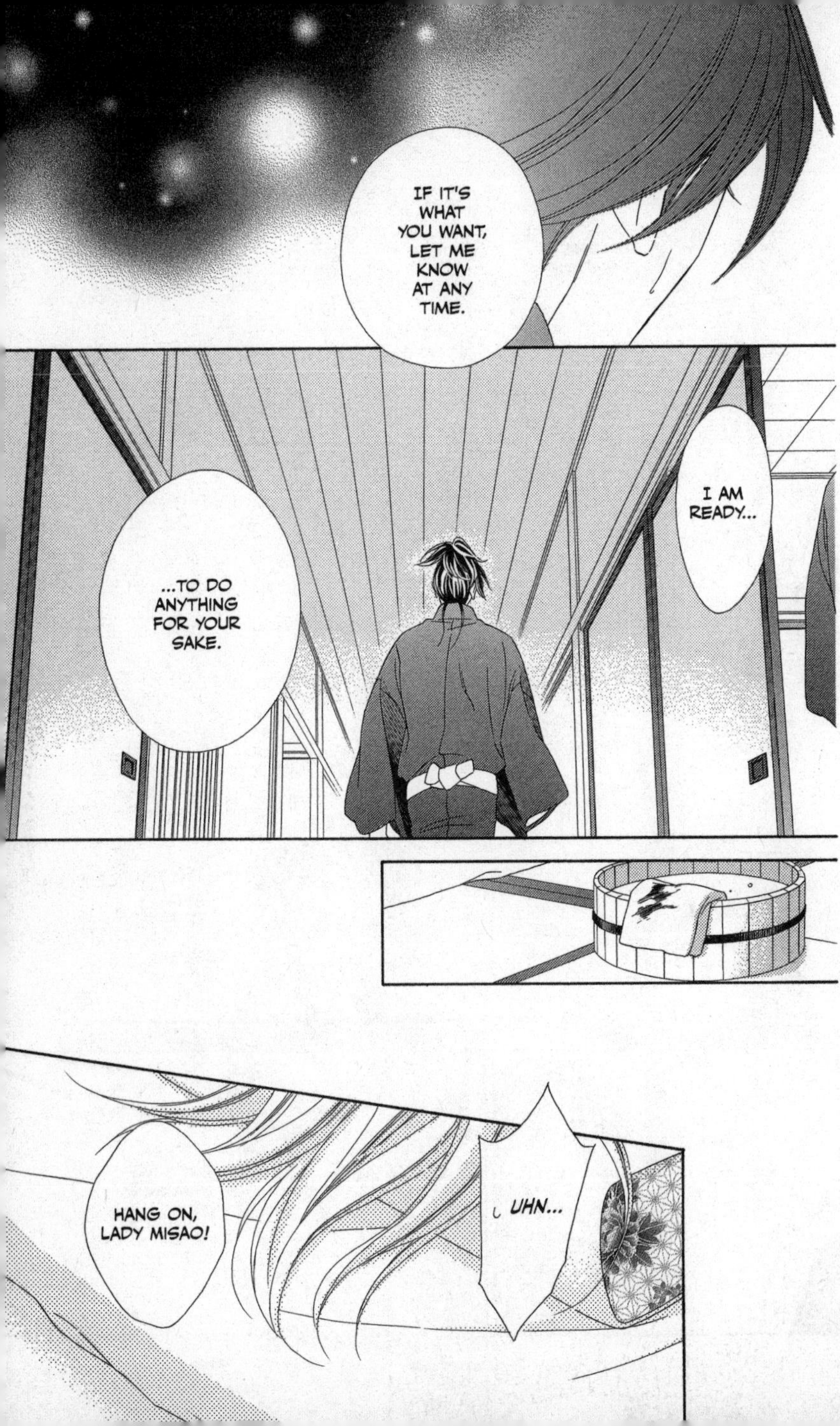
IF IT'S WHAT YOU WANT, LET ME KNOW AT ANY TIME.
I AM READY...
...TO DO ANYTHING FOR YOUR SAKE.
UHN...
HANG ON, LADY MISAO!

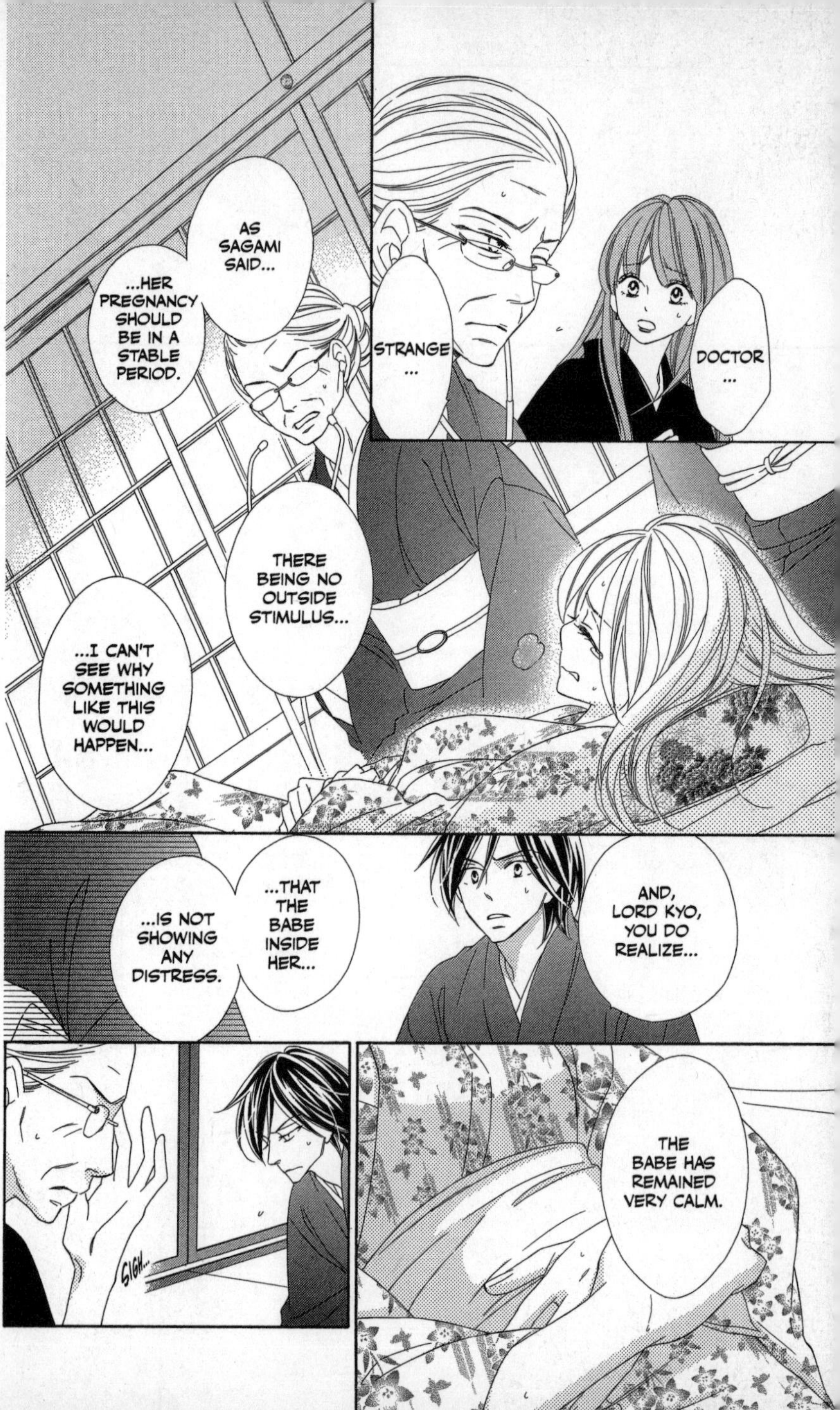
DOCTOR...
STRANGE...
AS SAGAMI SAID...
...HER PREGNANCY SHOULD BE IN A STABLE PERIOD.
THERE BEING NO OUTSIDE STIMULUS...
...I CAN'T SEE WHY SOMETHING LIKE THIS WOULD HAPPEN...
AND, LORD KYO, YOU DO REALIZE...
...THAT THE BABE INSIDE HER...
...IS NOT SHOWING ANY DISTRESS.
THE BABE HAS REMAINED VERY CALM.
SIGH...

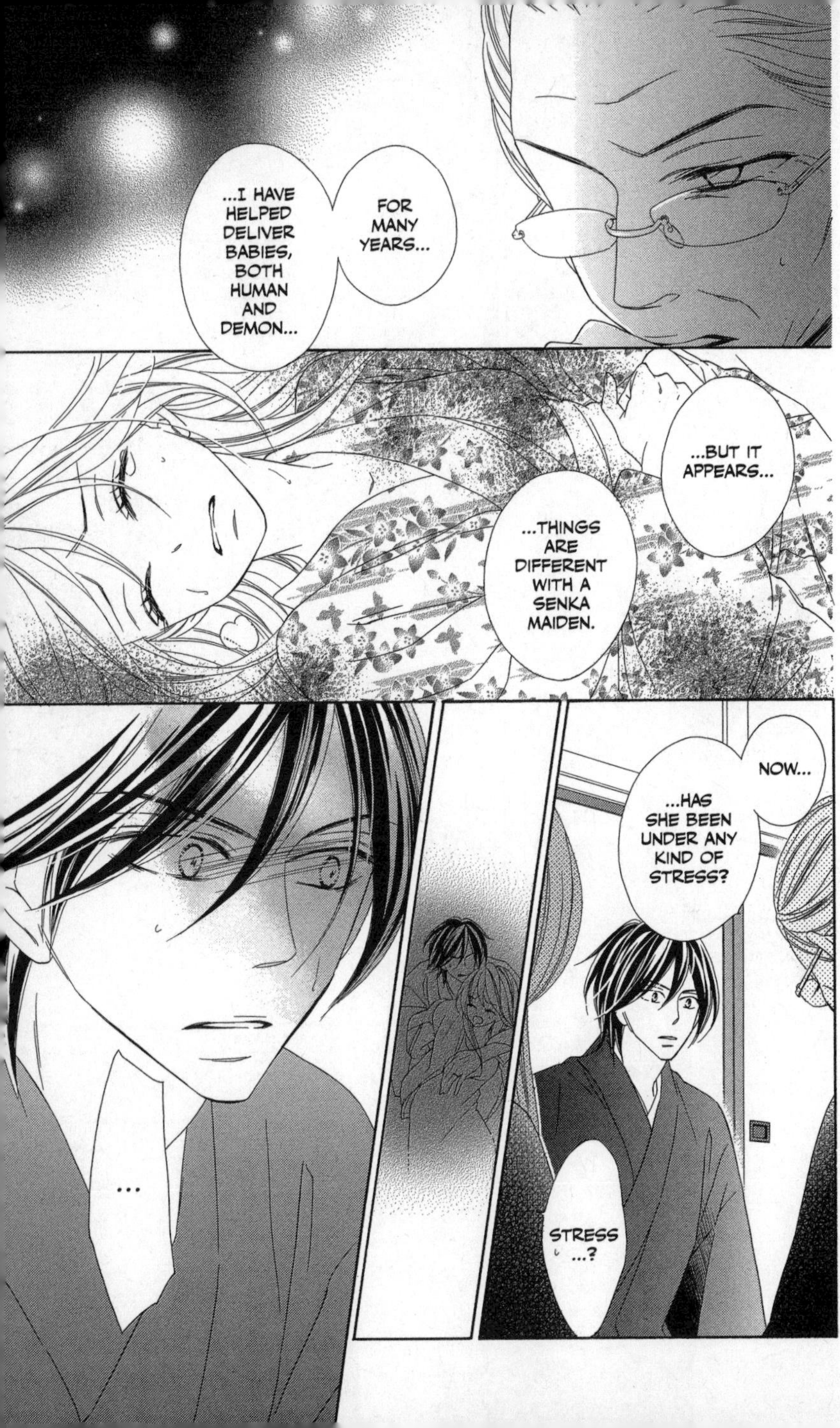
FOR MANY YEARS...
...I HAVE HELPED DELIVER BABIES, BOTH HUMAN AND DEMON...
...BUT IT APPEARS...
...THINGS ARE DIFFERENT WITH A SENKA MAIDEN.
NOW...
...HAS SHE BEEN UNDER ANY KIND OF STRESS?
STRESS ...?
...

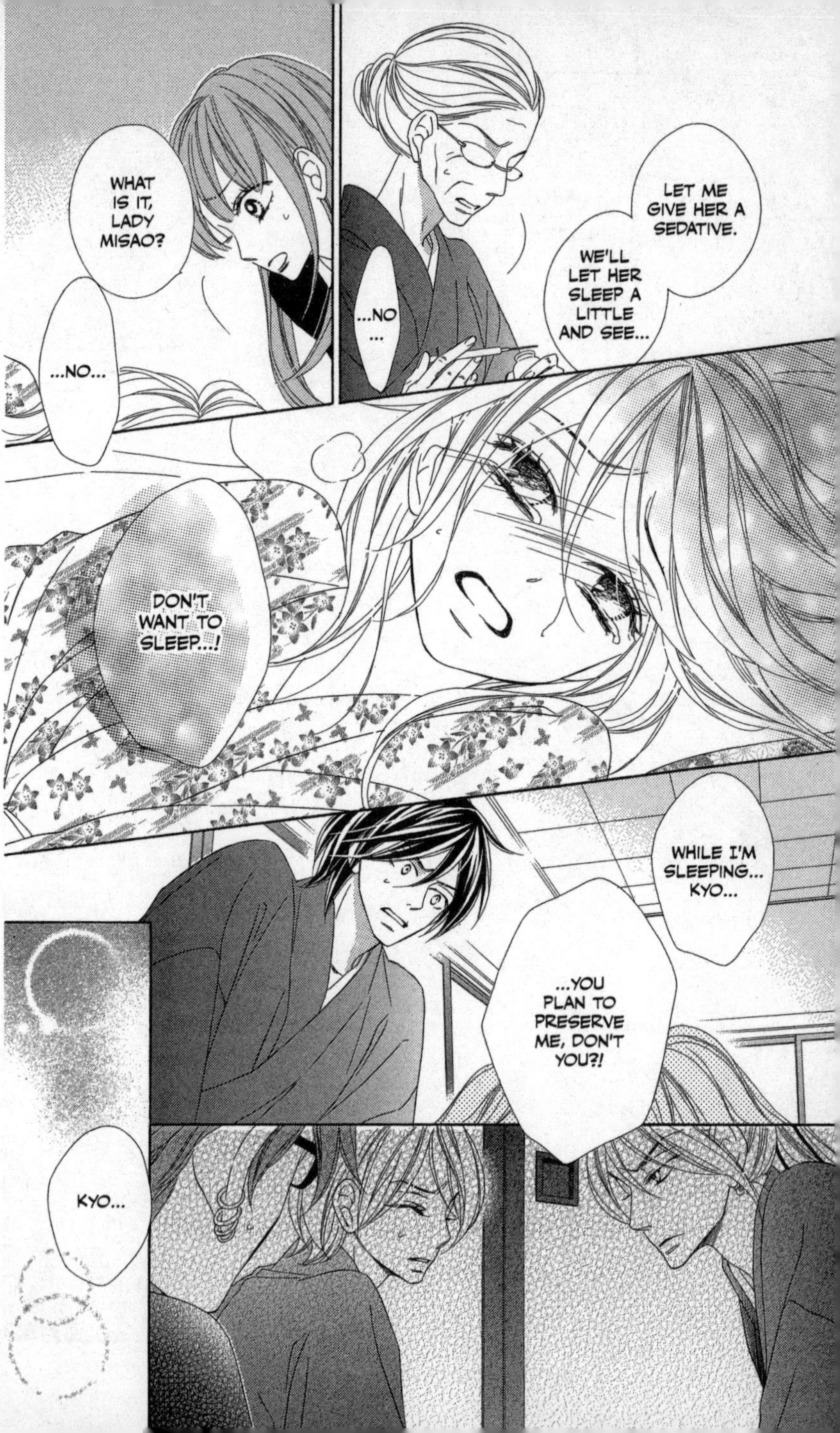
LET ME GIVE HER A SEDATIVE.
WE'LL LET HER SLEEP A LITTLE AND SEE...
...NO ...
WHAT IS IT, LADY MISAO?
...NO...
DON'T WANT TO SLEEP...!
WHILE I'M SLEEPING... KYO...
...YOU PLAN TO PRESERVE ME, DON'T YOU?!
KYO...

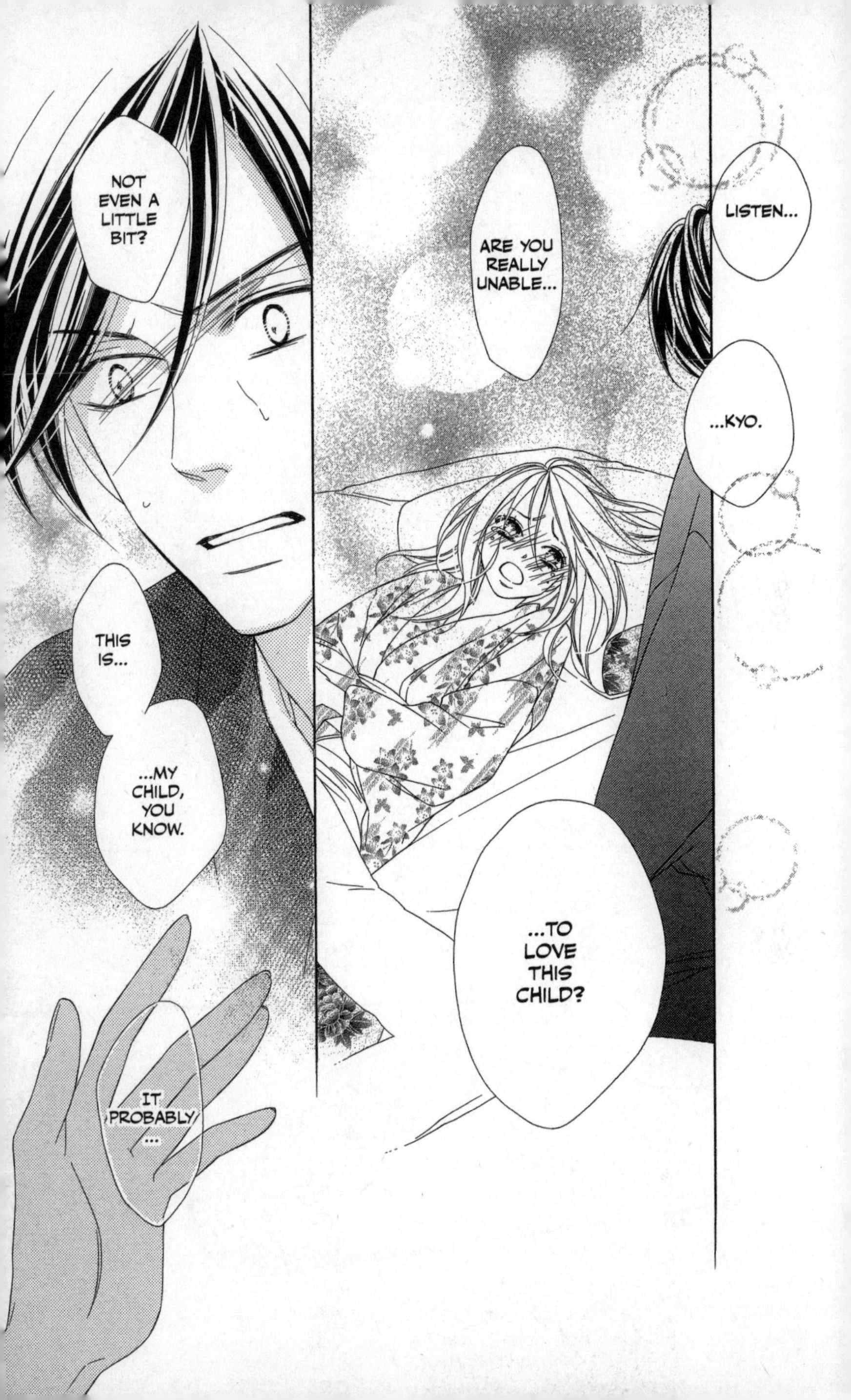
LISTEN...
...KYO.
ARE YOU REALLY UNABLE...
...TO LOVE THIS CHILD?
NOT EVEN A LITTLE BIT?
THIS IS...
...MY CHILD, YOU KNOW.
IT PROBABLY...

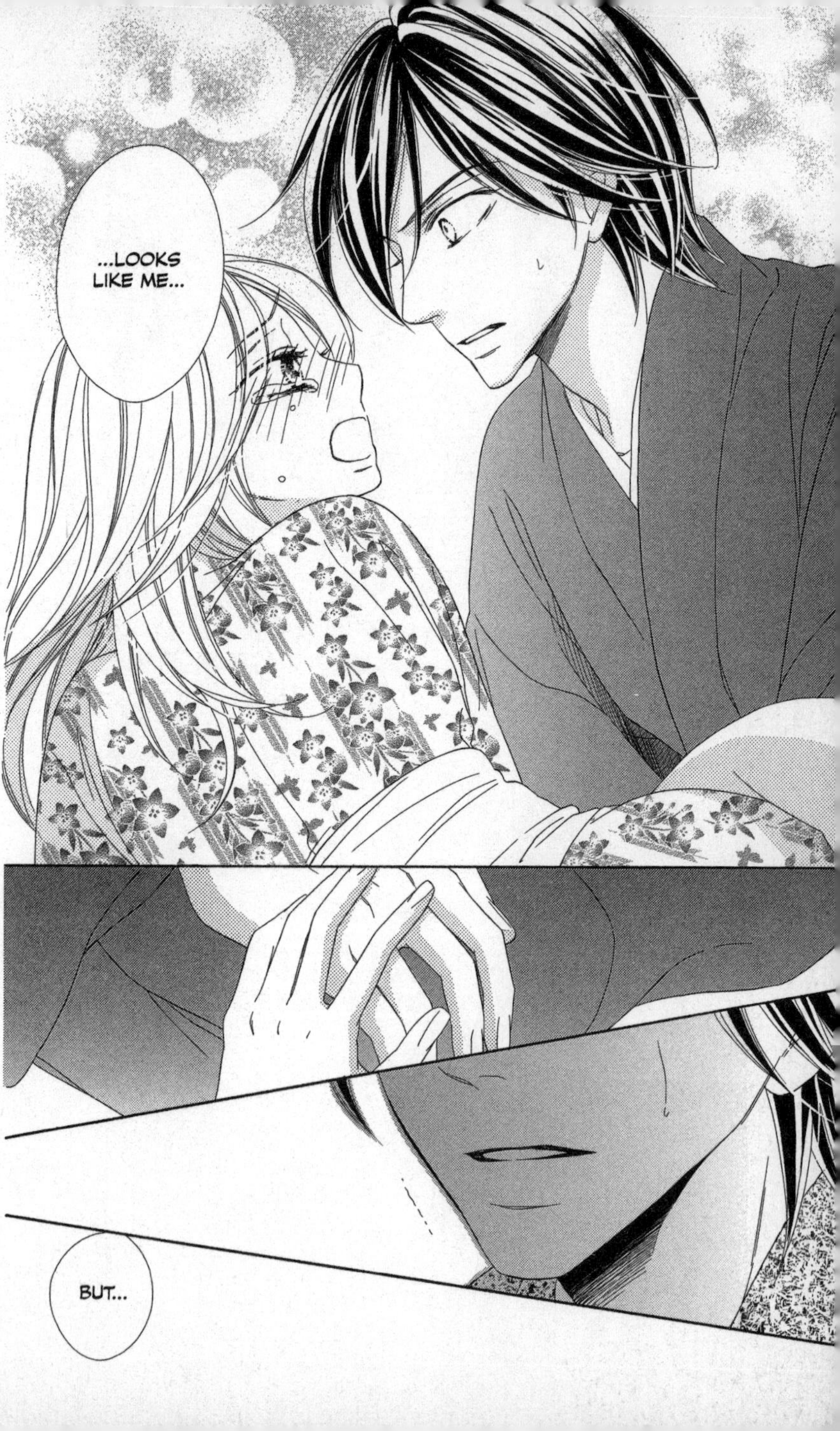
...LOOKS LIKE ME...
BUT...

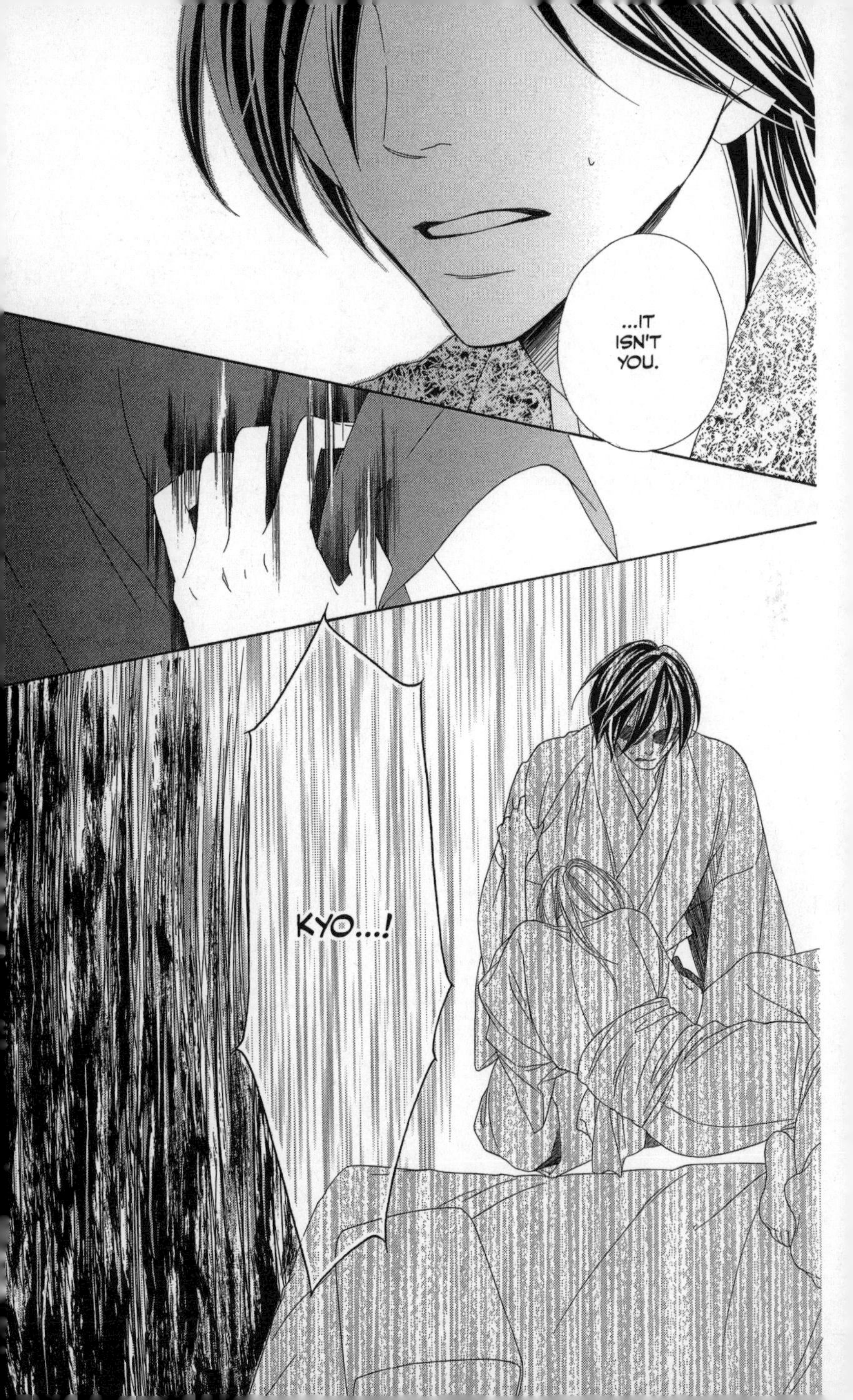
...IT ISN'T YOU.
KYO...!

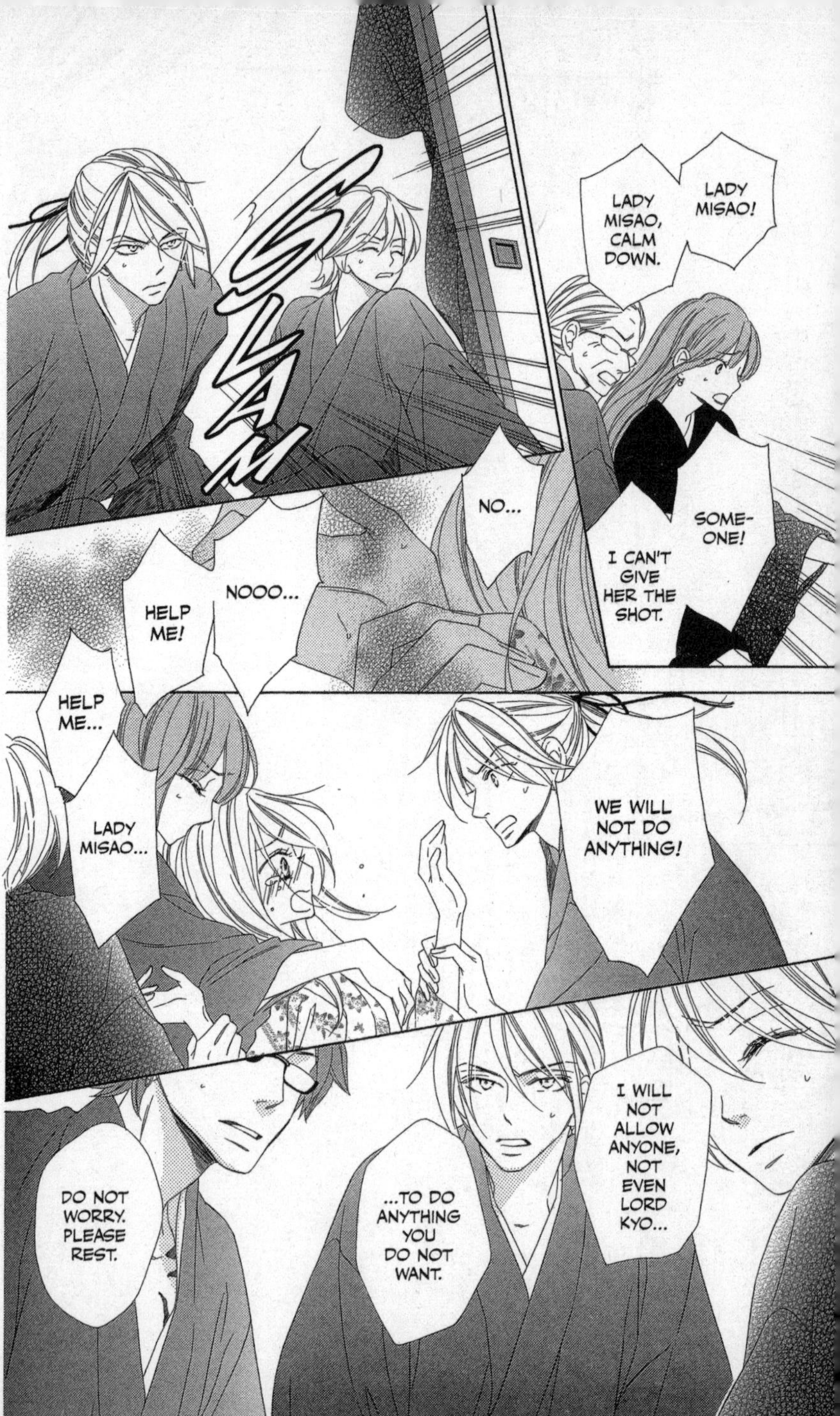
LADY MISAO!
LADY MISAO, CALM DOWN.
SLAM
SOME-ONE!
I CAN'T GIVE HER THE SHOT.
NO...
NOOO...
HELP ME!
WE WILL NOT DO ANYTHING!
HELP ME...
LADY MISAO...
I WILL NOT ALLOW ANYONE, NOT EVEN LORD KYO...
...TO DO ANYTHING YOU DO NOT WANT.
DO NOT WORRY. PLEASE REST.

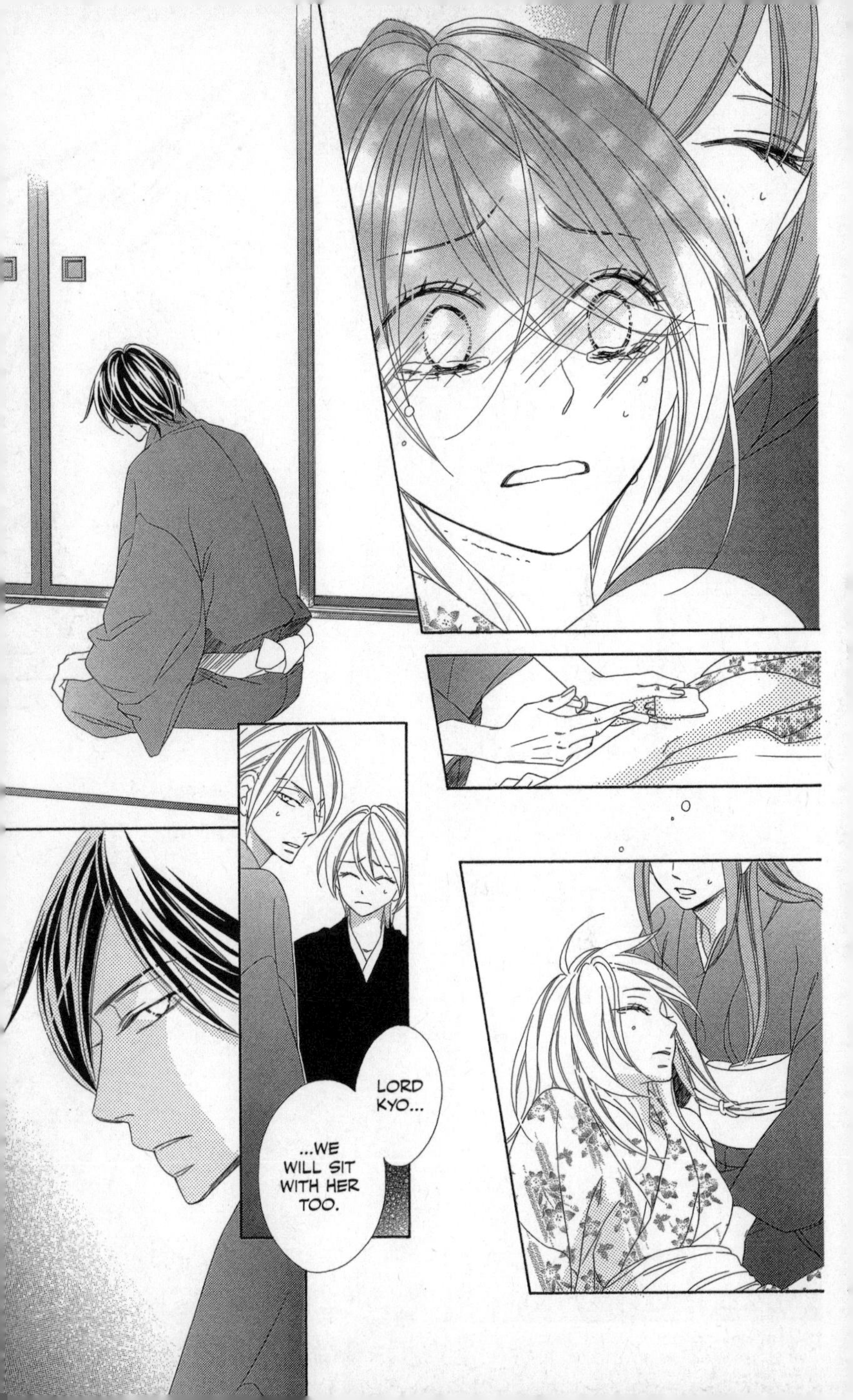
LORD KYO...
...WE WILL SIT WITH HER TOO.

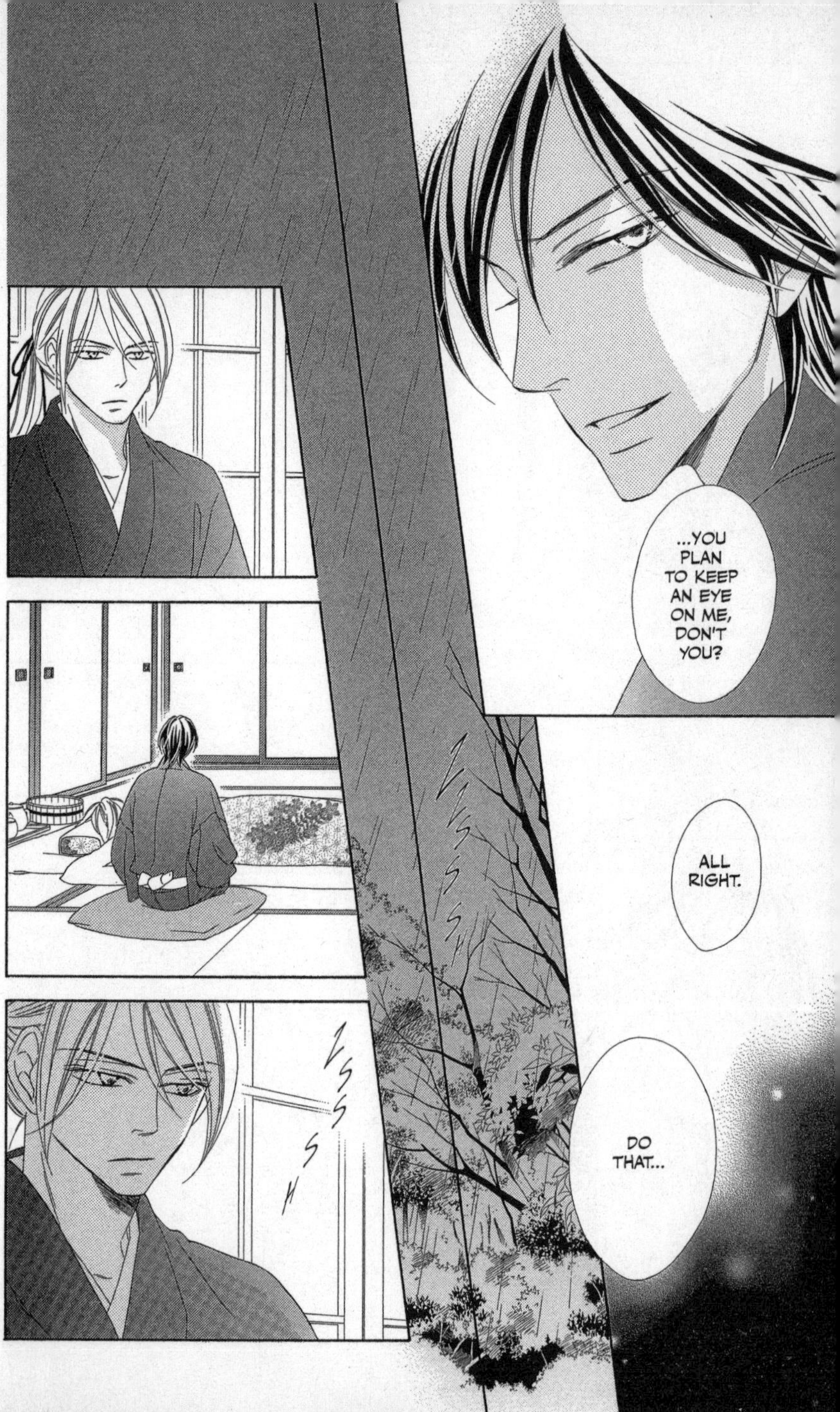
...YOU PLAN TO KEEP AN EYE ON ME, DON'T YOU?
ZSSSH
ALL RIGHT.
DO THAT...
ZSSSH

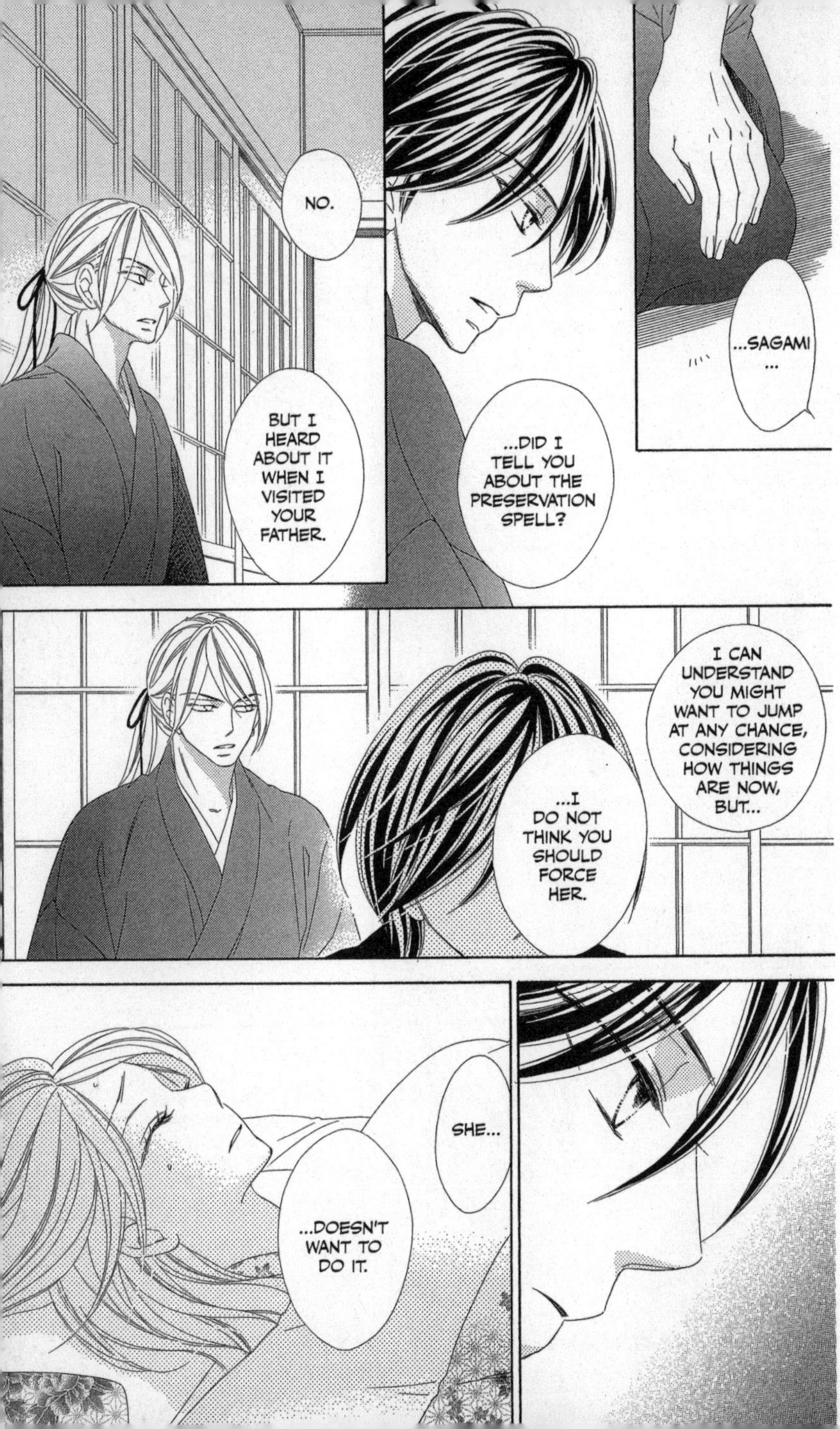
...SAGAMI ...
...DID I TELL YOU ABOUT THE PRESERVATION SPELL?
NO.
BUT I HEARD ABOUT IT WHEN I VISITED YOUR FATHER.
I CAN UNDERSTAND YOU MIGHT WANT TO JUMP AT ANY CHANCE, CONSIDERING HOW THINGS ARE NOW, BUT...
...I DO NOT THINK YOU SHOULD FORCE HER.
SHE...
...DOESN'T WANT TO DO IT.

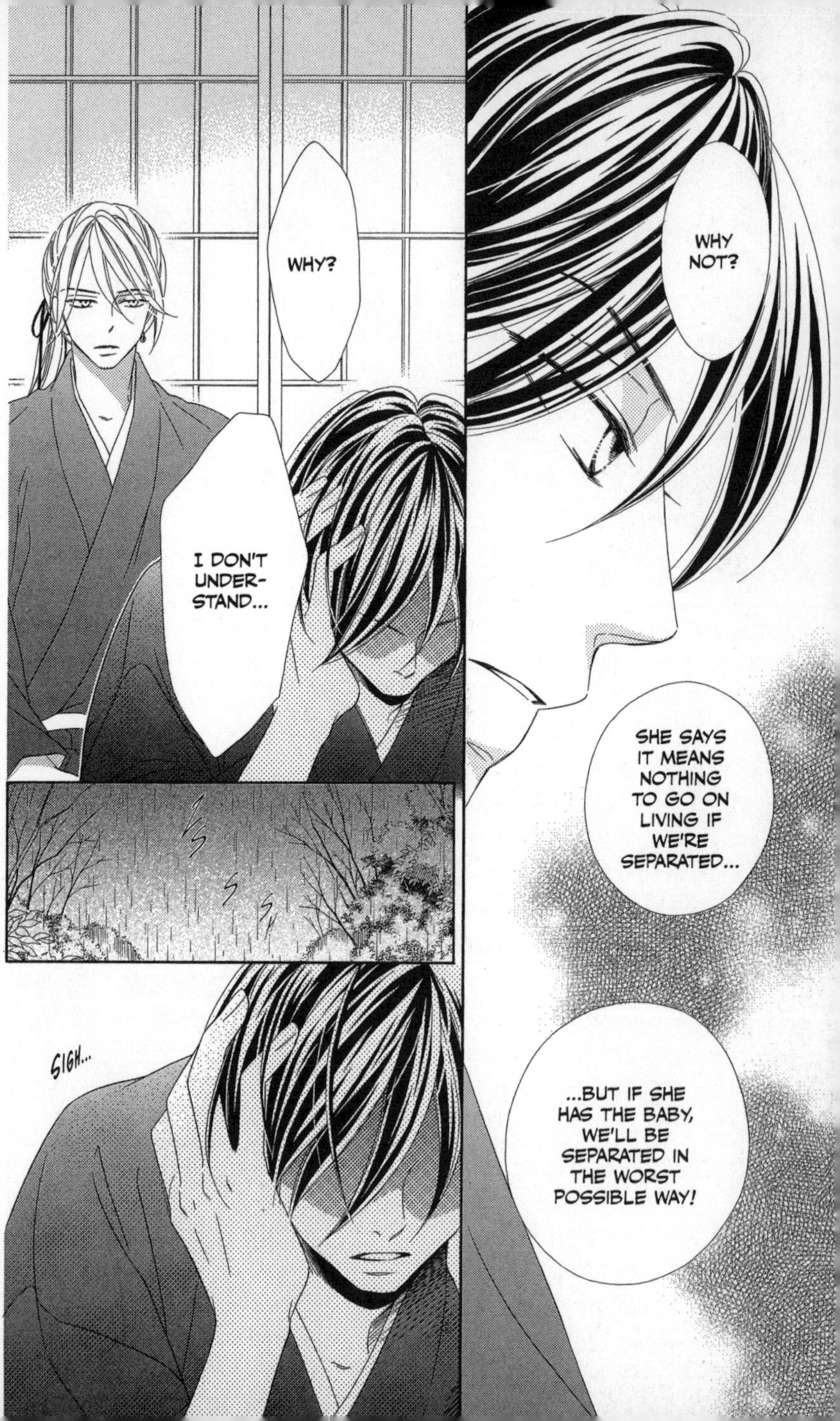
WHY NOT?
SHE SAYS IT MEANS NOTHING TO GO ON LIVING IF WE'RE SEPARATED...
...BUT IF SHE HAS THE BABY, WE'LL BE SEPARATED IN THE WORST POSSIBLE WAY!
WHY?
I DON'T UNDER-STAND...
SIGH...

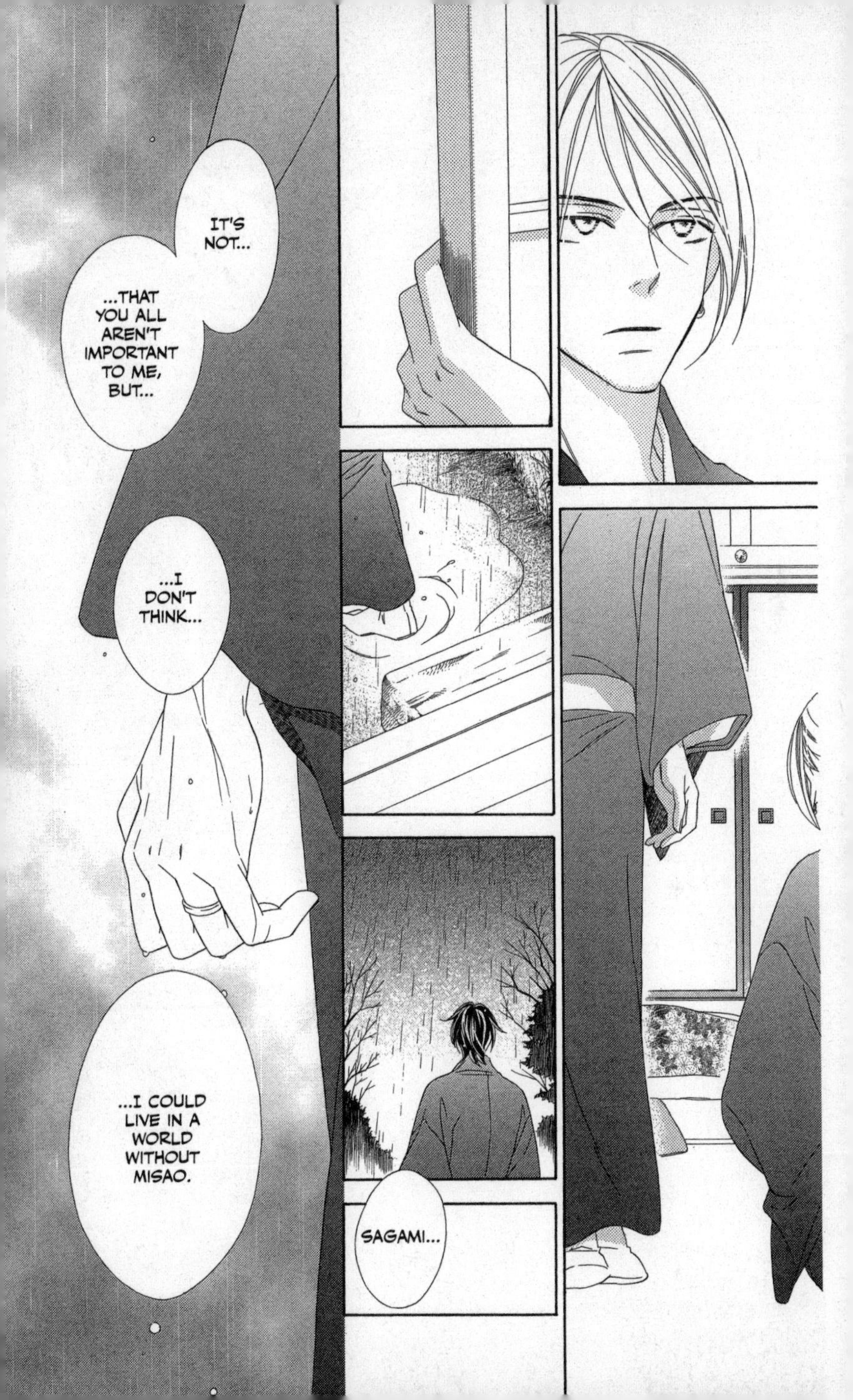
SAGAMI...
IT'S NOT...
...THAT YOU ALL AREN'T IMPORTANT TO ME, BUT...
...I DON'T THINK...
...I COULD LIVE IN A WORLD WITHOUT MISAO.

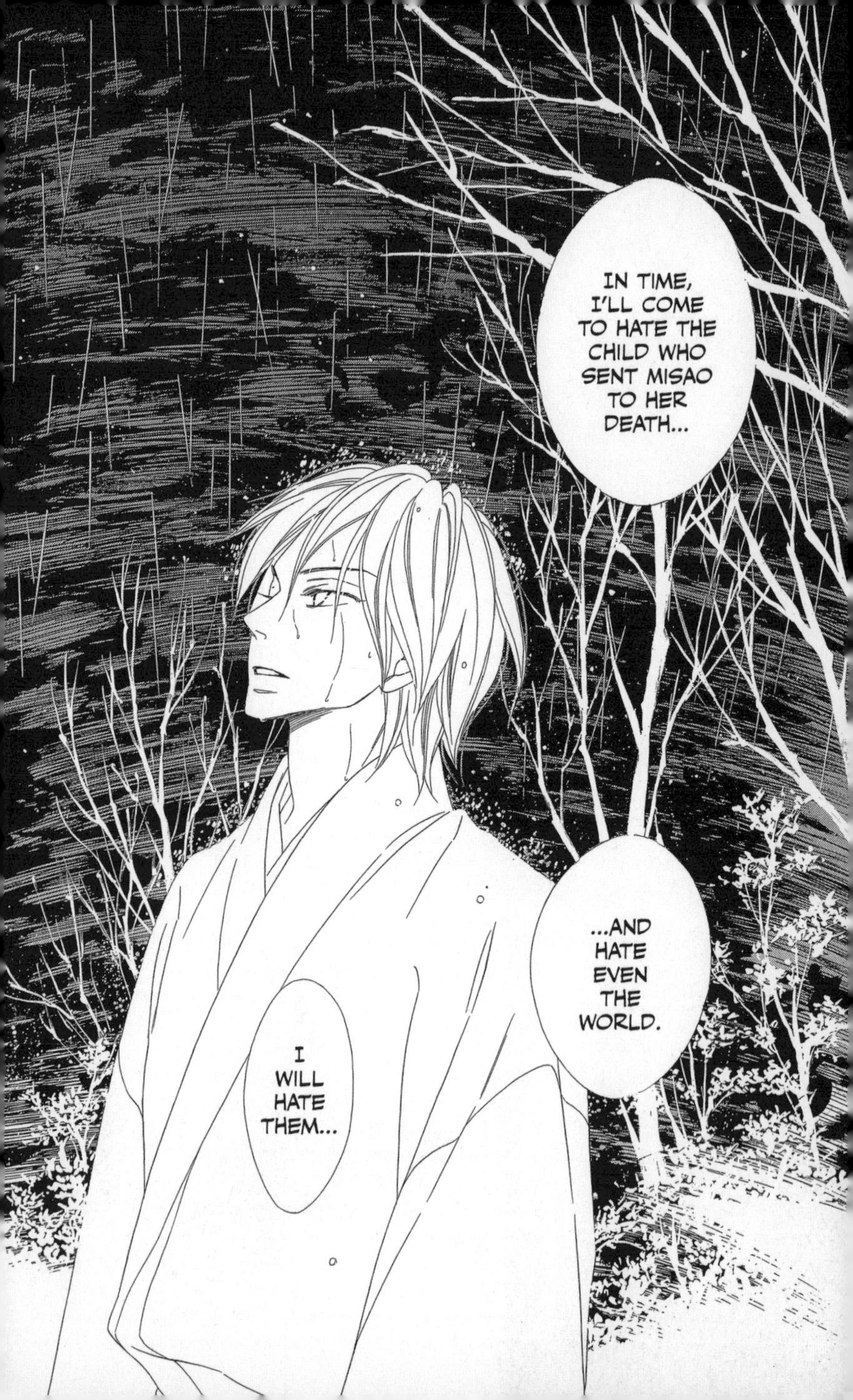
IN TIME, I'LL COME TO HATE THE CHILD WHO SENT MISAO TO HER DEATH...
...AND HATE EVEN THE WORLD.
I WILL HATE THEM...

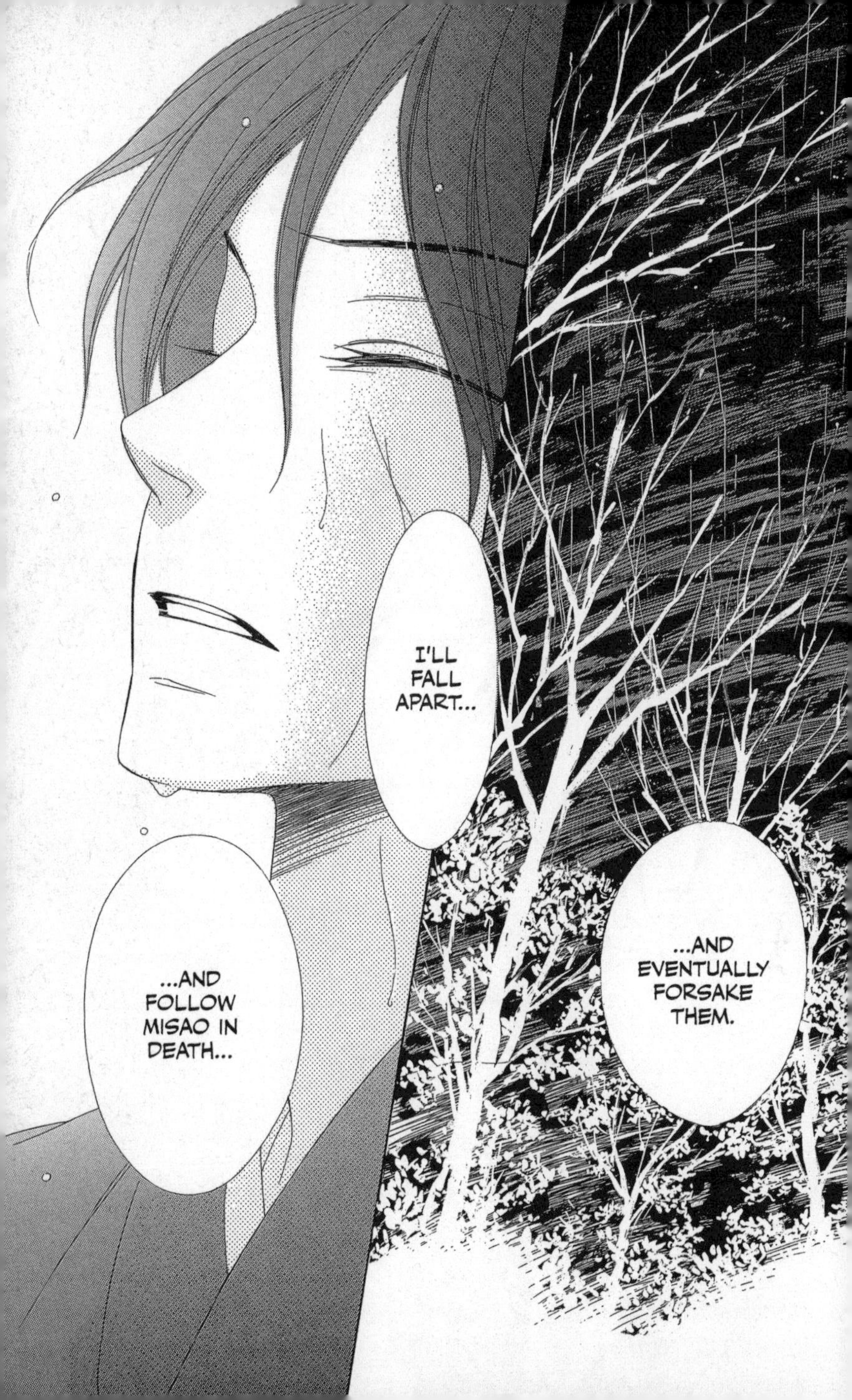
I'LL FALL APART...
...AND EVENTUALLY FORSAKE THEM.
...AND FOLLOW MISAO IN DEATH...

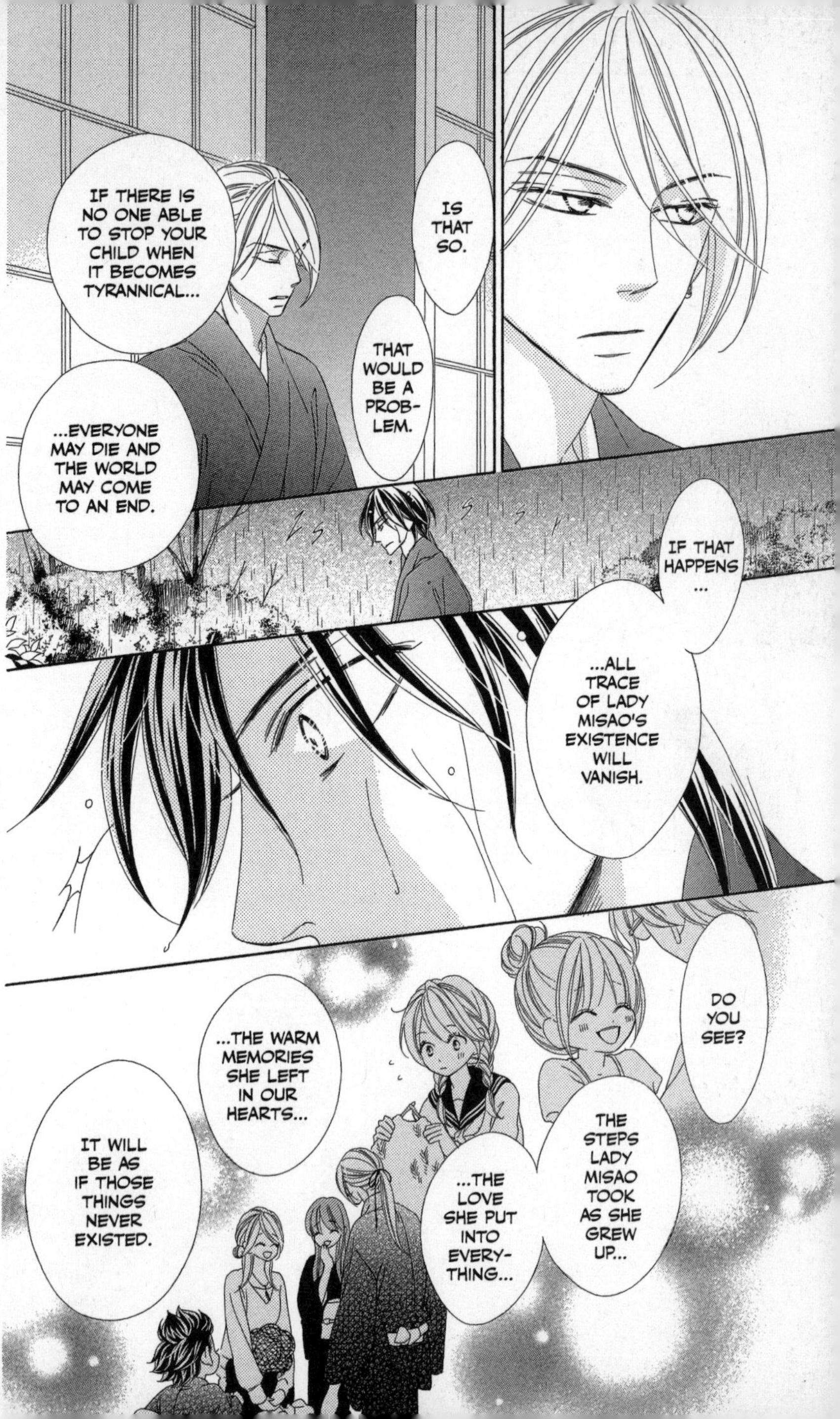
IS THAT SO.
THAT WOULD BE A PROB-LEM.
IF THERE IS NO ONE ABLE TO STOP YOUR CHILD WHEN IT BECOMES TYRANNICAL...
...EVERYONE MAY DIE AND THE WORLD MAY COME TO AN END.
IF THAT HAPPENS...
...ALL TRACE OF LADY MISAO'S EXISTENCE WILL VANISH.
DO YOU SEE?
THE STEPS LADY MISAO TOOK AS SHE GREW UP...
...THE LOVE SHE PUT INTO EVERY-THING...
...THE WARM MEMORIES SHE LEFT IN OUR HEARTS...
IT WILL BE AS IF THOSE THINGS NEVER EXISTED.

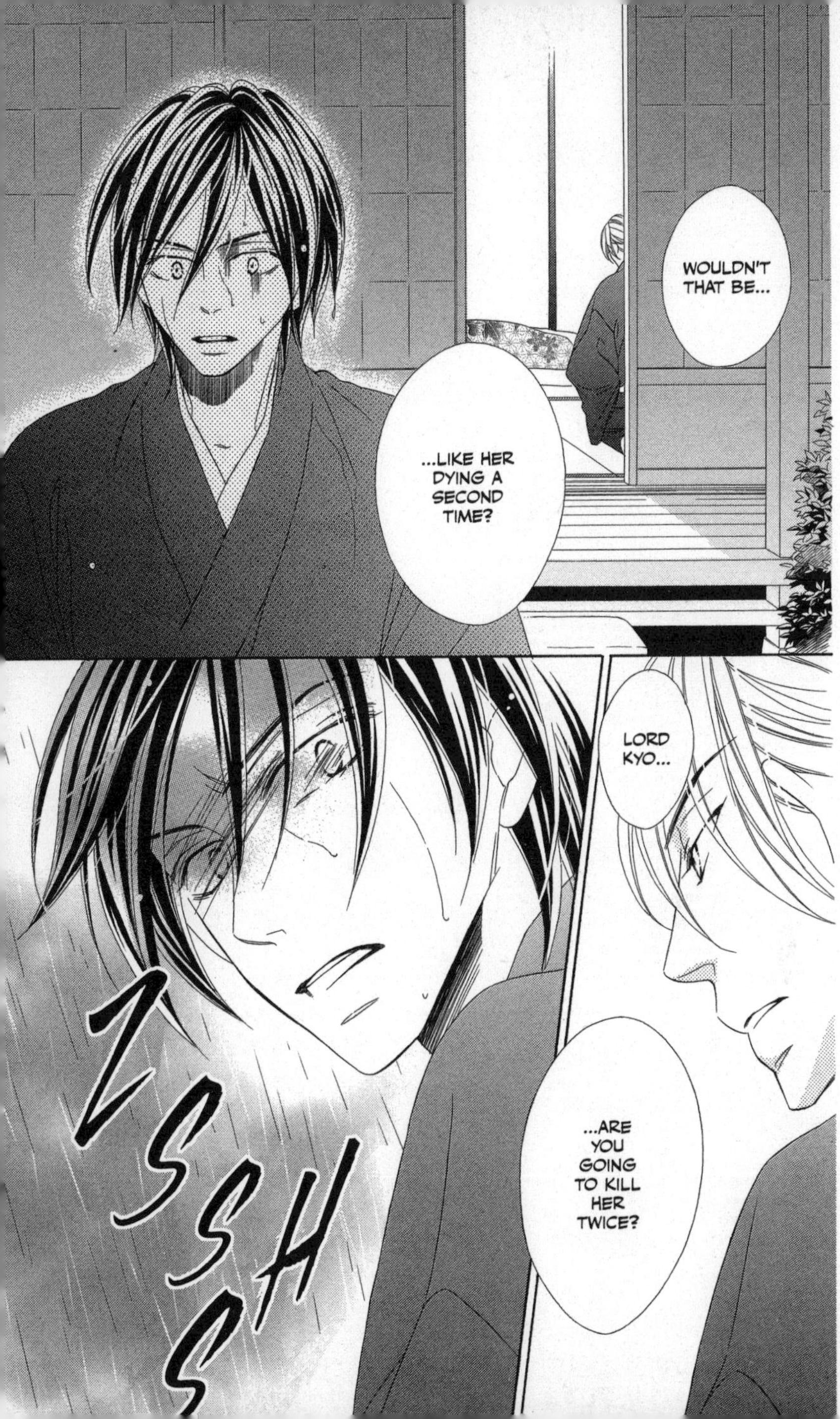
WOULDN'T THAT BE...
...LIKE HER DYING A SECOND TIME?
LORD KYO...
...ARE YOU GOING TO KILL HER TWICE?
ZSSH

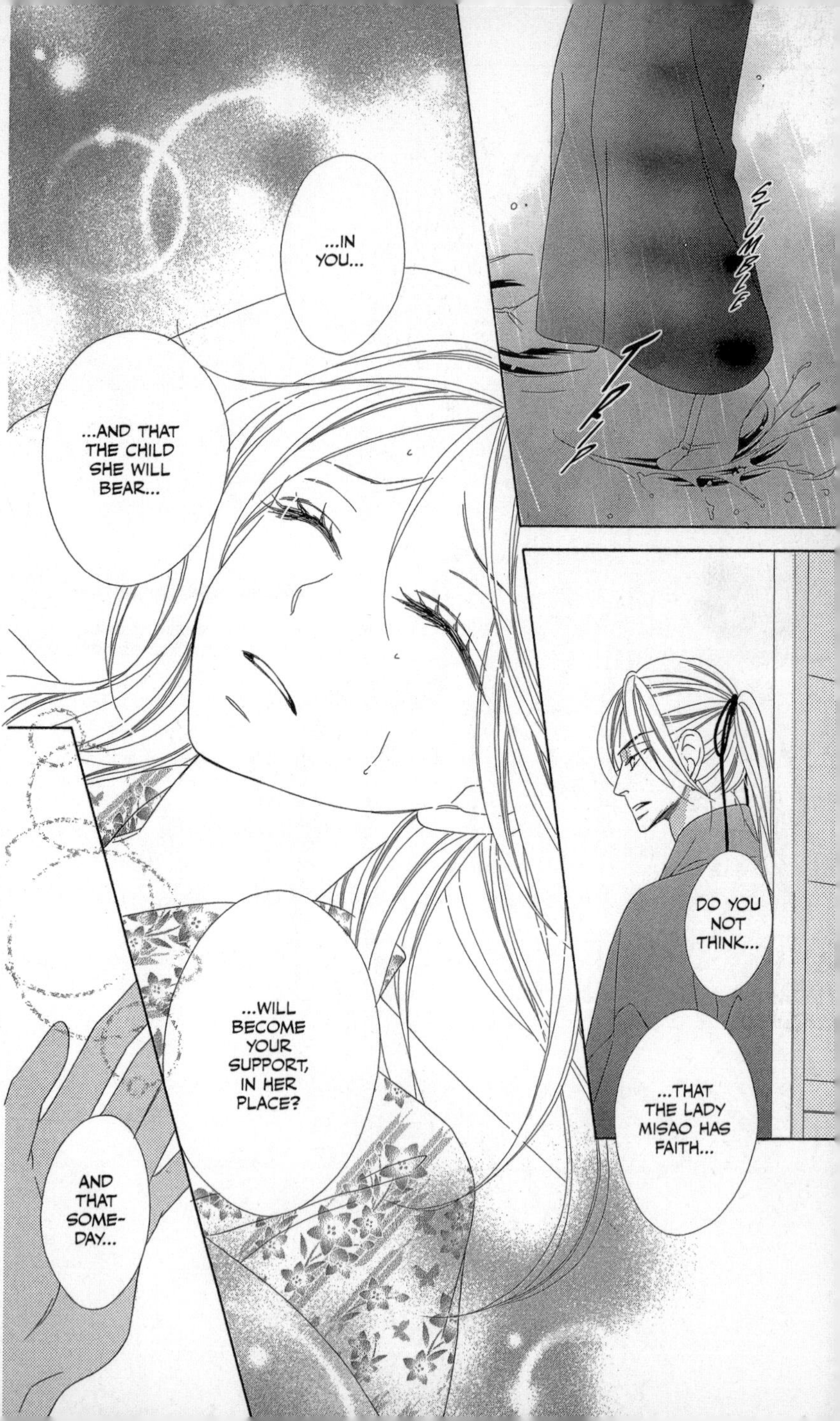
STUMBLE
TRIP
DO YOU NOT THINK...
...THAT THE LADY MISAO HAS FAITH...
...IN YOU...
...AND THAT THE CHILD SHE WILL BEAR...
...WILL BECOME YOUR SUPPORT, IN HER PLACE?
AND THAT SOME-DAY...

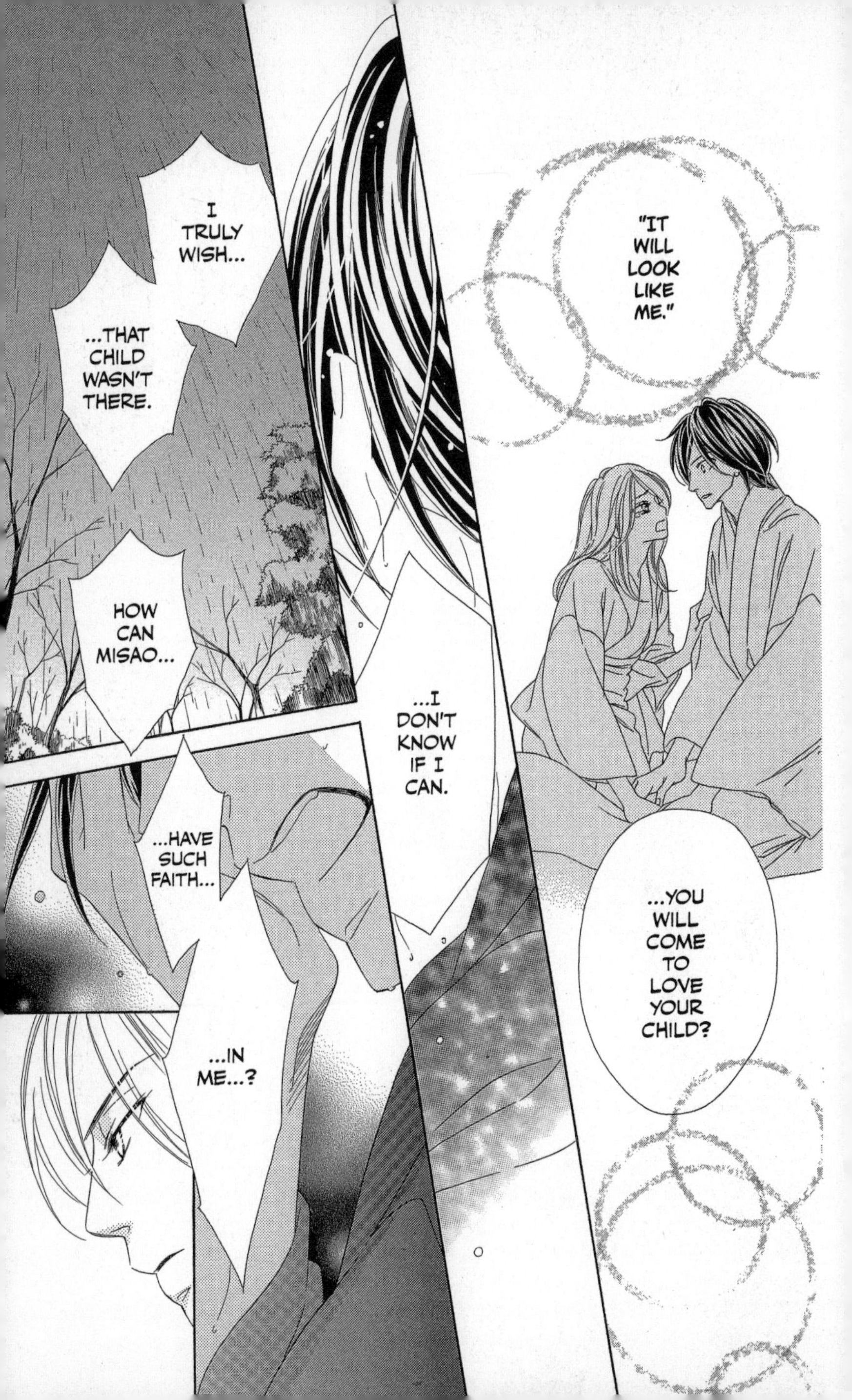
"IT WILL LOOK LIKE ME."
...YOU WILL COME TO LOVE YOUR CHILD?
...I DON'T KNOW IF I CAN.
I TRULY WISH...
...THAT CHILD WASN'T THERE.
HOW CAN MISAO...
...HAVE SUCH FAITH...
...IN ME...?

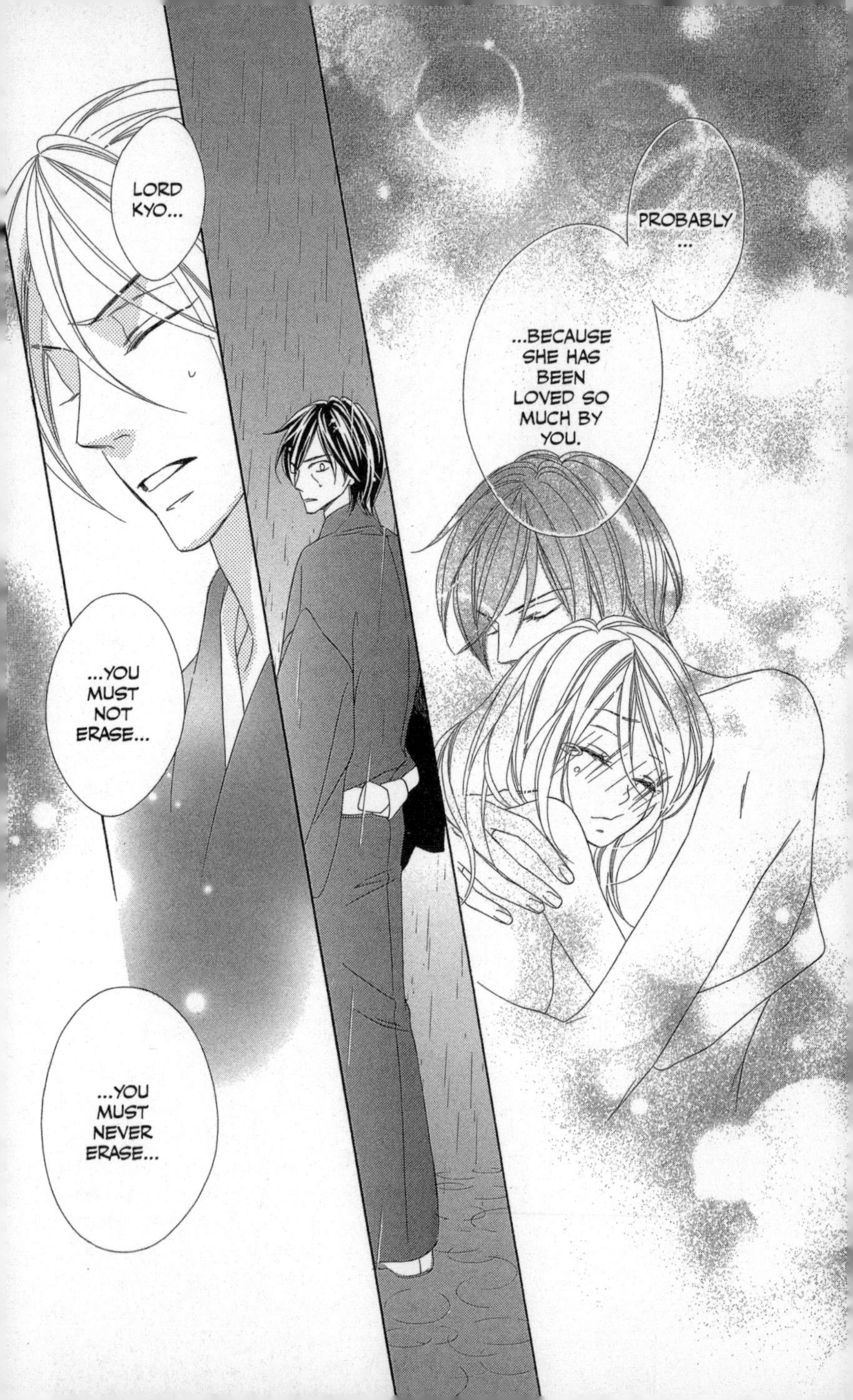
PROBABLY ...
...BECAUSE SHE HAS BEEN LOVED SO MUCH BY YOU.
LORD KYO...
...YOU MUST NOT ERASE...
...YOU MUST NEVER ERASE...

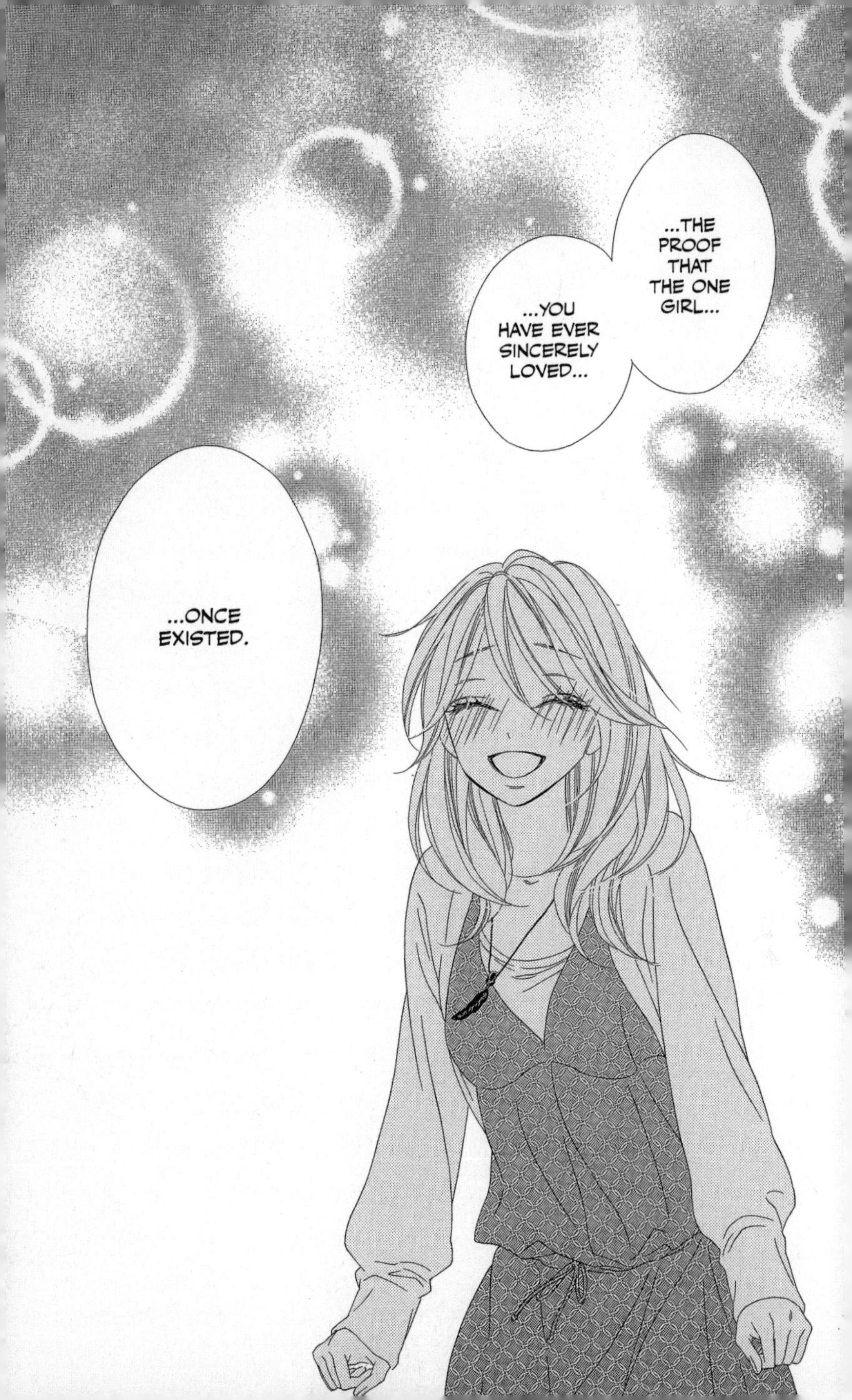
...THE PROOF THAT THE ONE GIRL...
...YOU HAVE EVER SINCERELY LOVED...
...ONCE EXISTED.

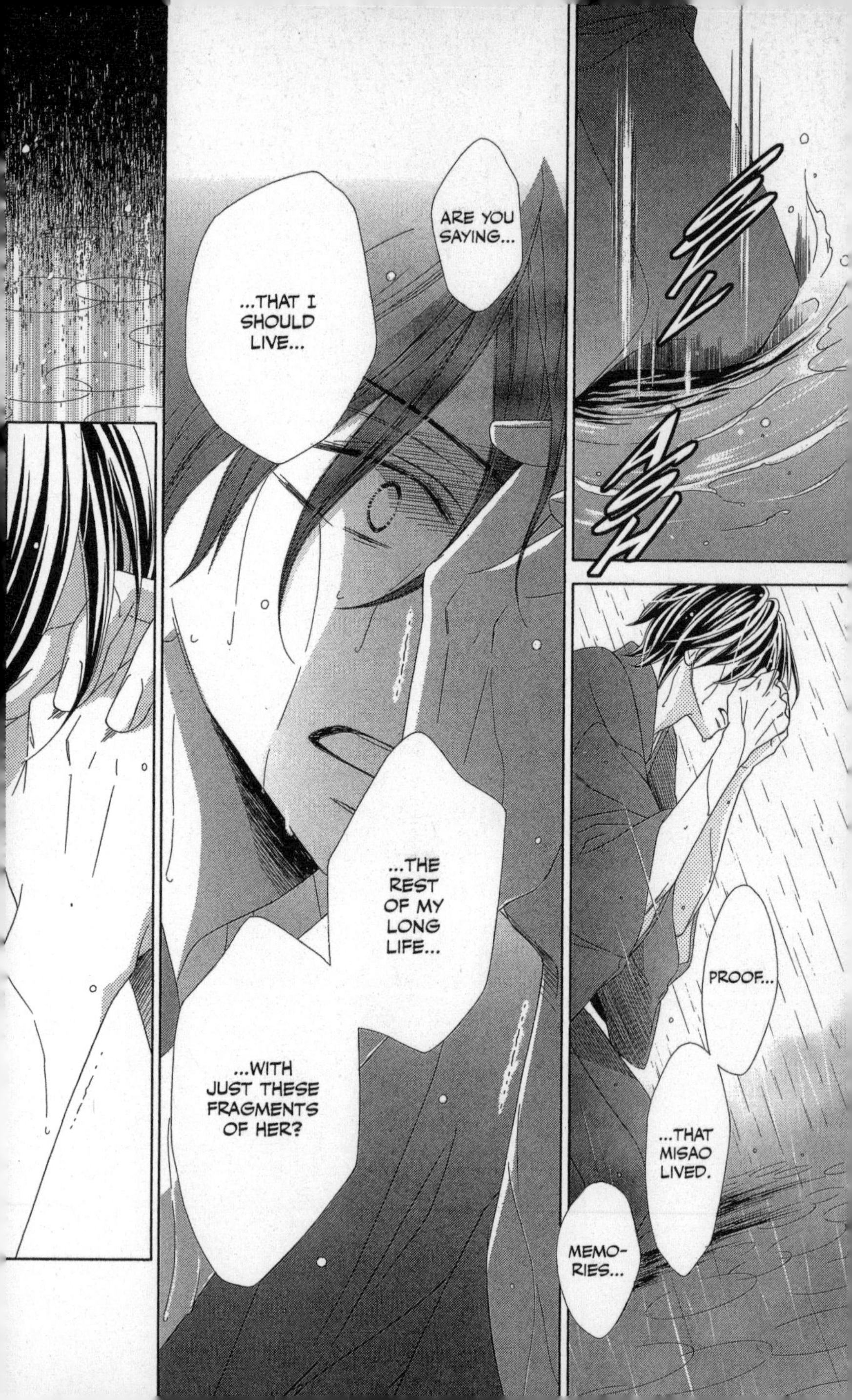
PROOF...
...THAT MISAO LIVED.
MEMORIES...
ARE YOU SAYING...
...THAT I SHOULD LIVE...
...THE REST OF MY LONG LIFE...
...WITH JUST THESE FRAGMENTS OF HER?

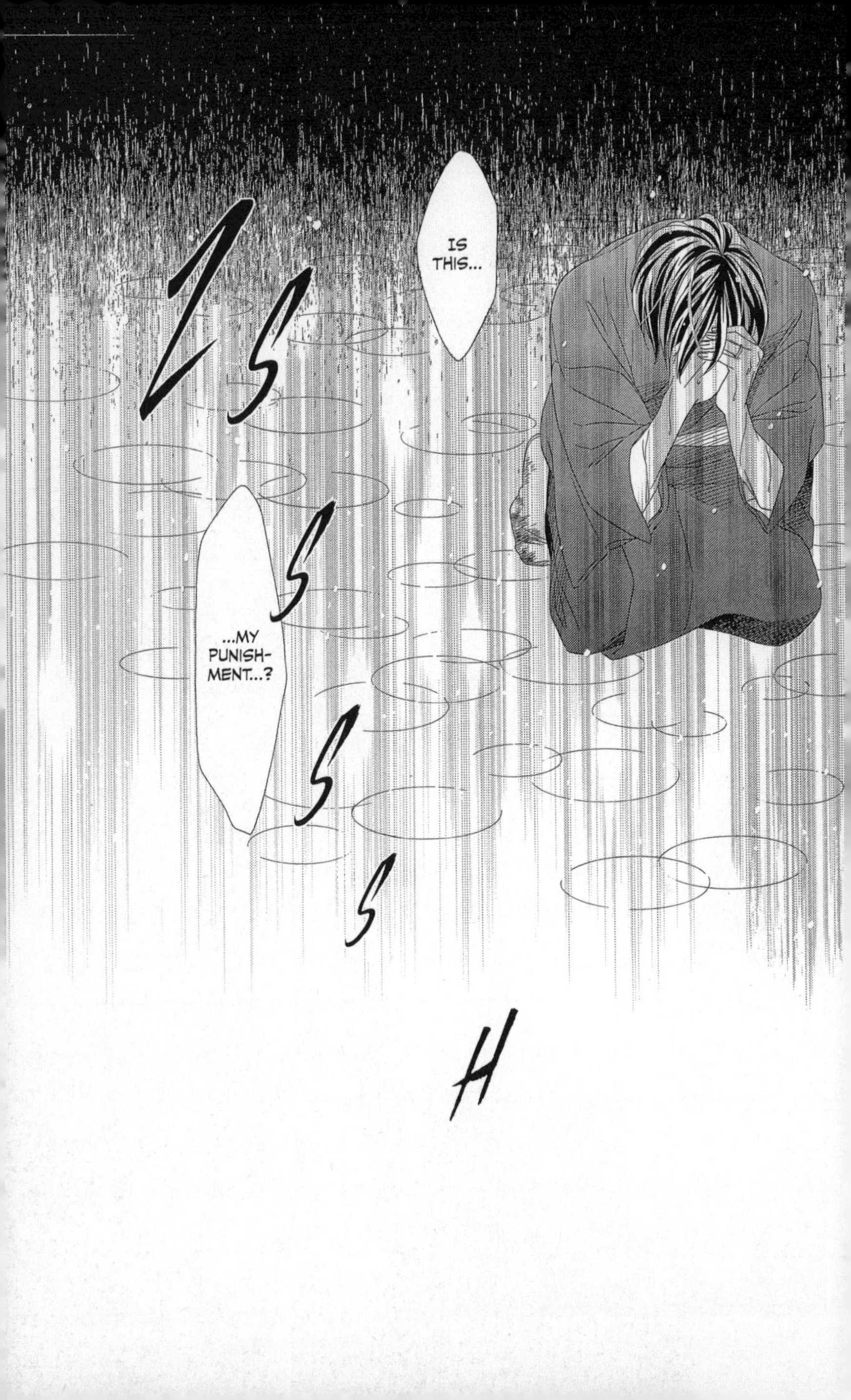
IS THIS...
...MY PUNISH-MENT...?
ZSSSSH

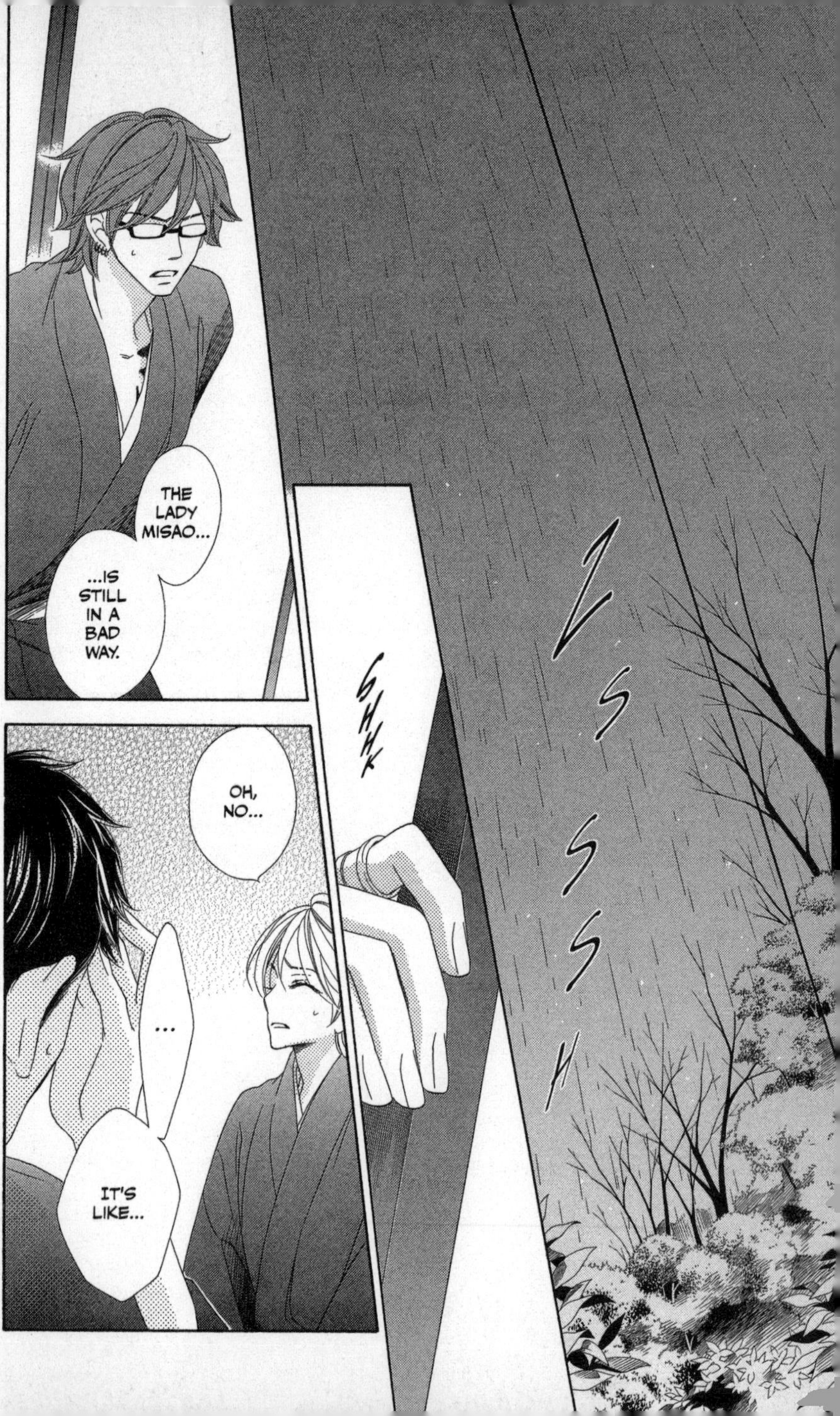
ZSSSSH
SHHH
THE LADY MISAO...
...IS STILL IN A BAD WAY.
OH, NO...
...
IT'S LIKE...

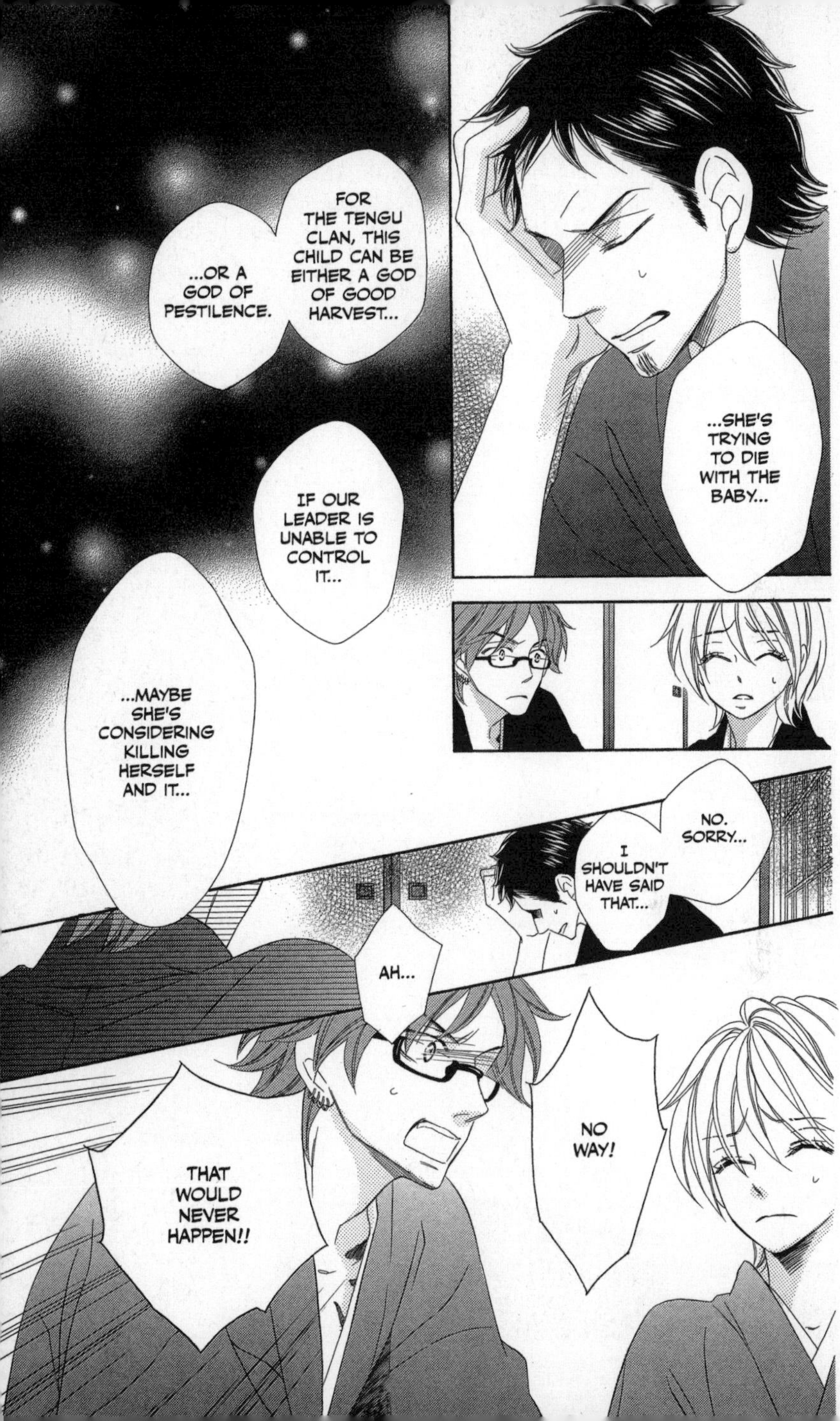
...SHE'S TRYING TO DIE WITH THE BABY...
FOR THE TENGU CLAN, THIS CHILD CAN BE EITHER A GOD OF GOOD HARVEST...
...OR A GOD OF PESTILENCE.
IF OUR LEADER IS UNABLE TO CONTROL IT...
...MAYBE SHE'S CONSIDERING KILLING HERSELF AND IT...
NO. SORRY...
I SHOULDN'T HAVE SAID THAT...
AH...
NO WAY!
THAT WOULD NEVER HAPPEN!!

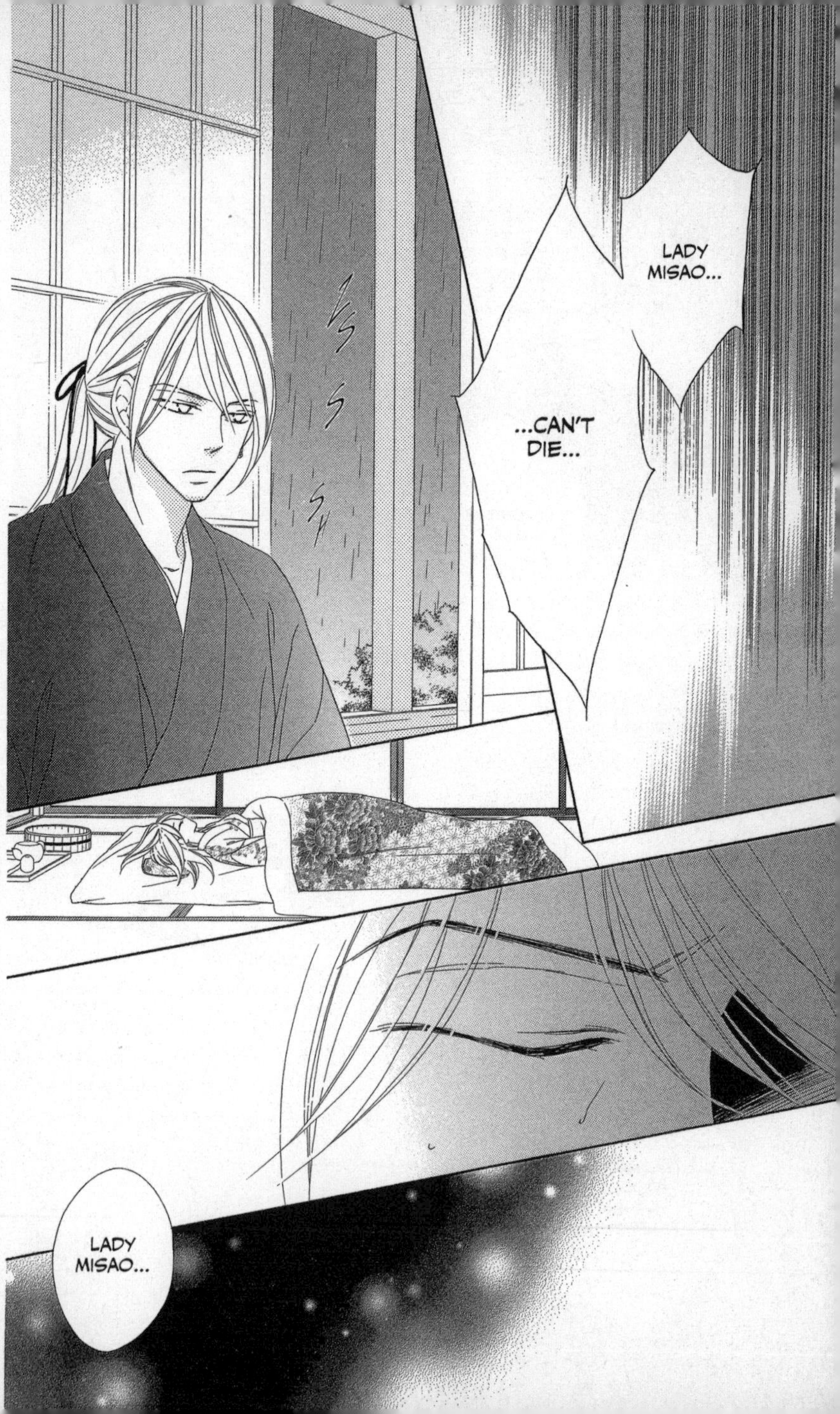
LADY MISAO...
...CAN'T DIE...
LADY MISAO...

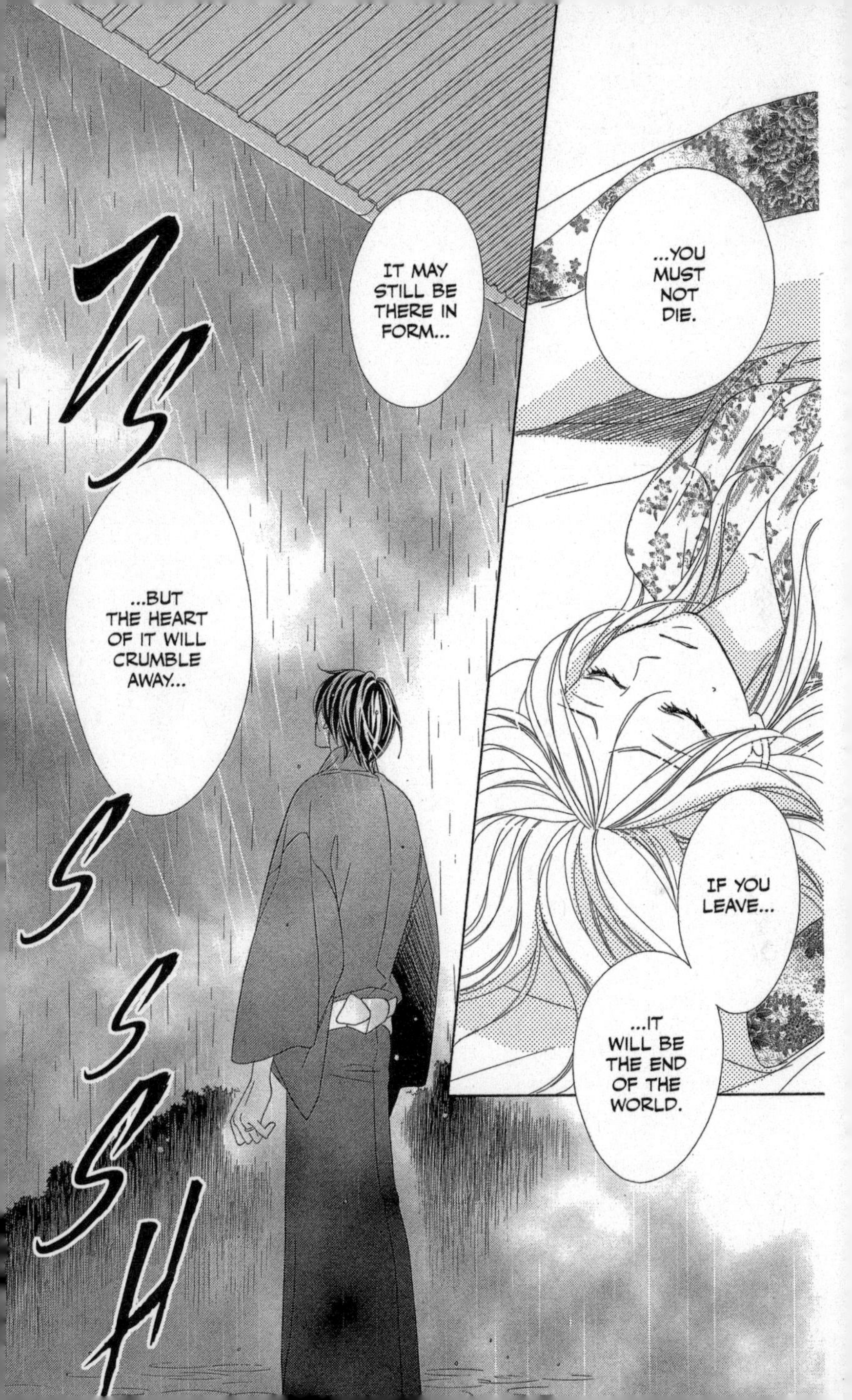
...YOU MUST NOT DIE.
IF YOU LEAVE...
...IT WILL BE THE END OF THE WORLD.
IT MAY STILL BE THERE IN FORM...
...BUT THE HEART OF IT WILL CRUMBLE AWAY...
ZSSSSH

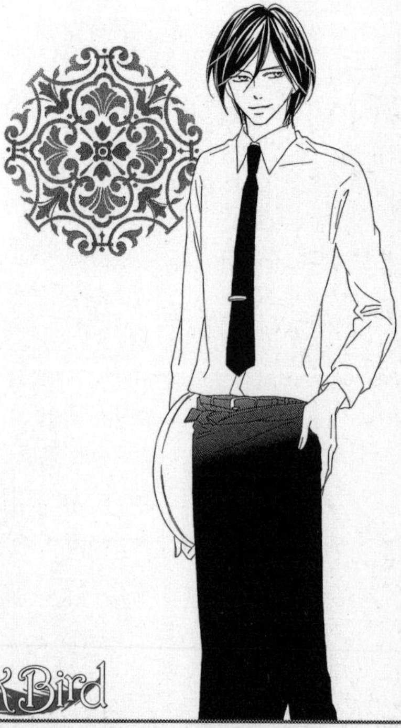

Black Bird

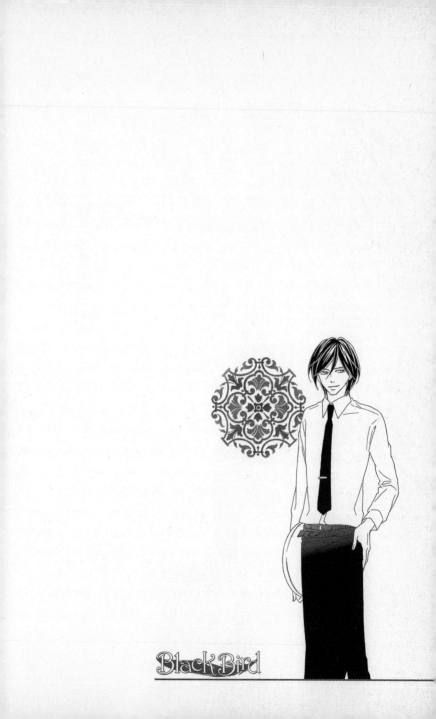

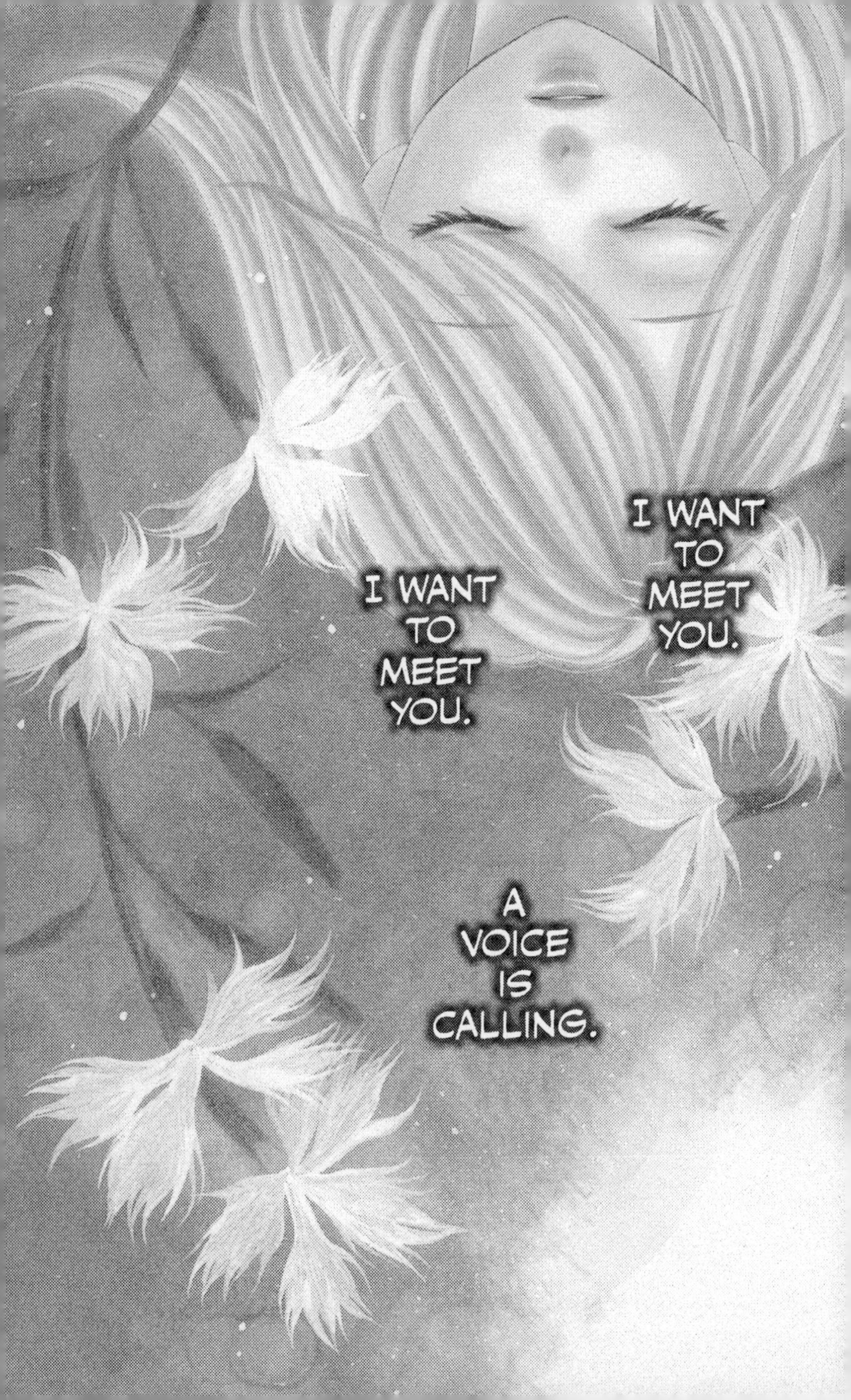
I WANT TO MEET YOU.
I WANT TO MEET YOU.
A VOICE IS CALLING.

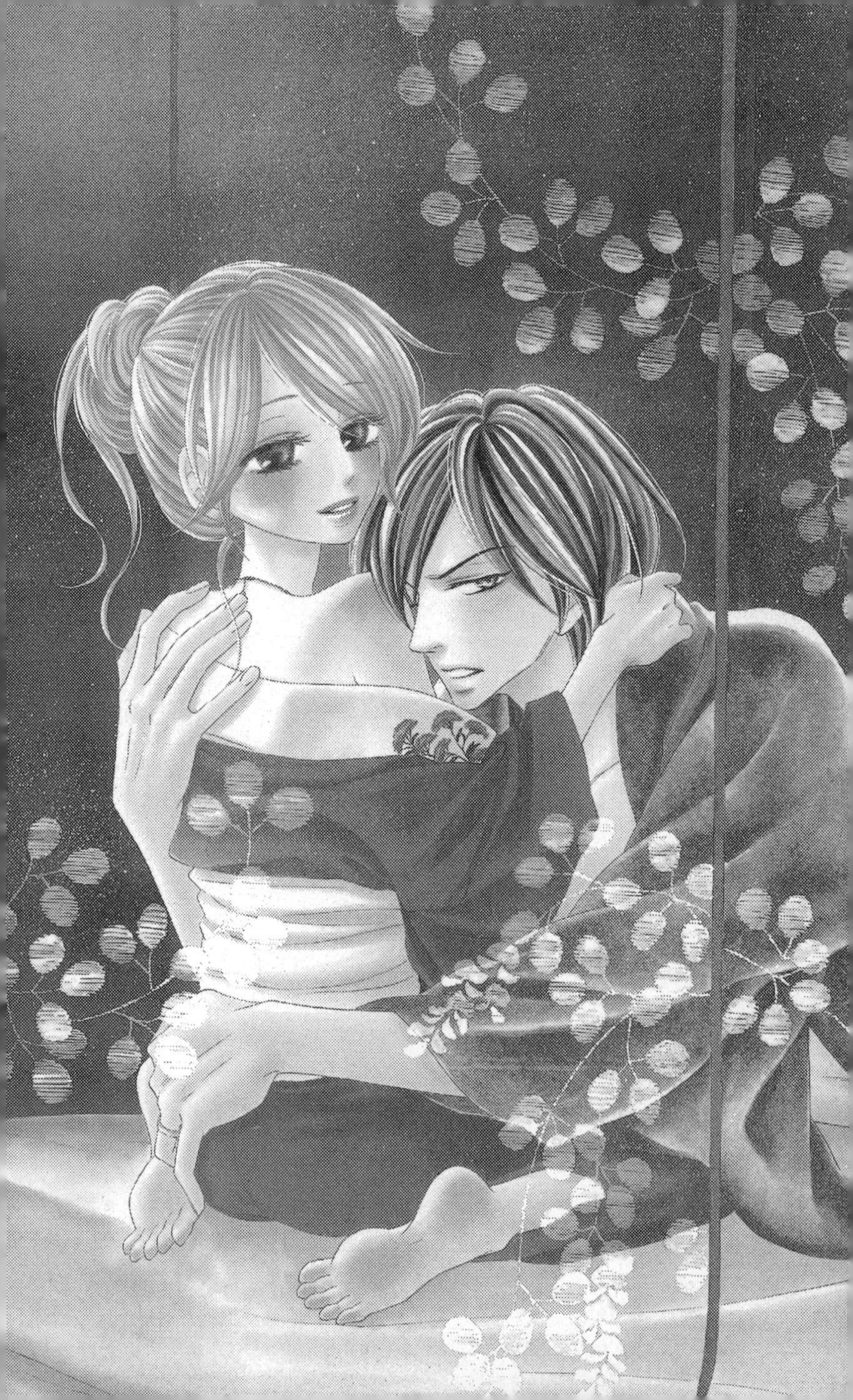

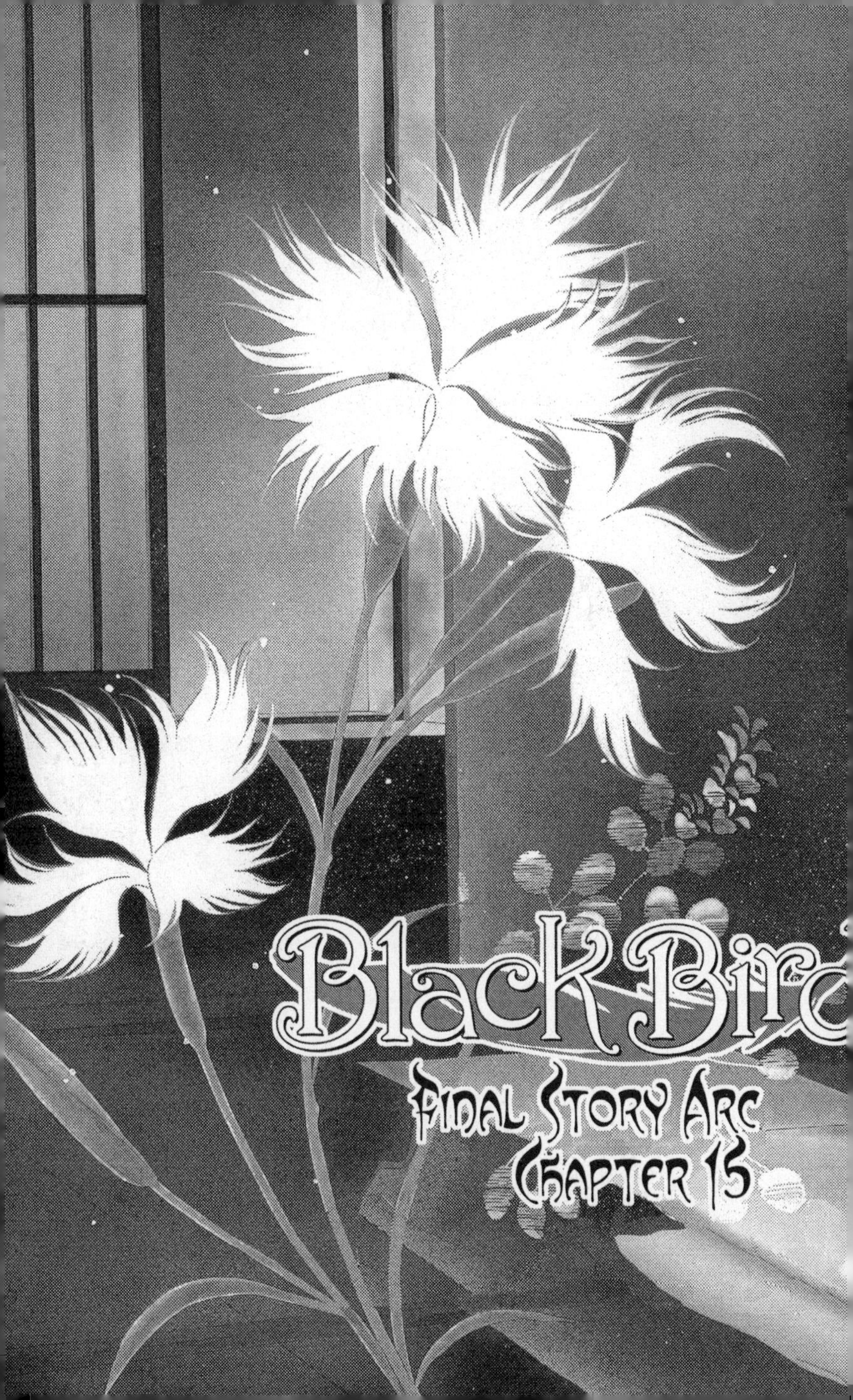
Black Bird
Final Story Arc
Chapter 15

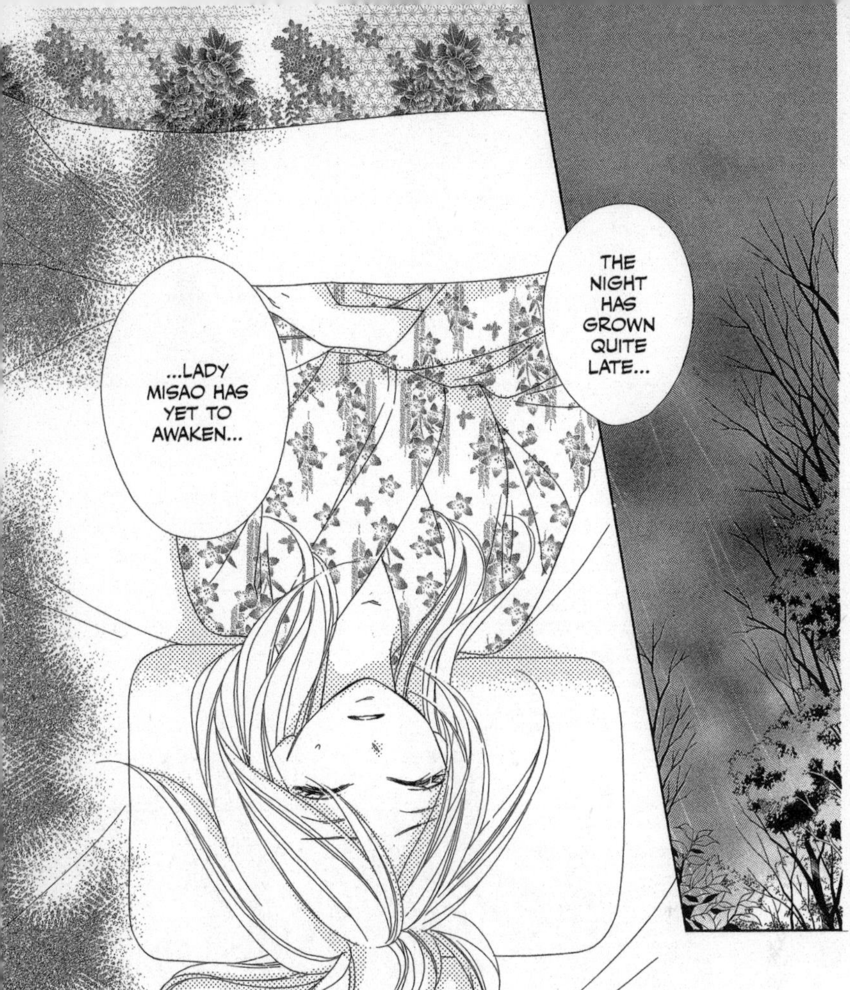
THE NIGHT HAS GROWN QUITE LATE...
...LADY MISAO HAS YET TO AWAKEN...

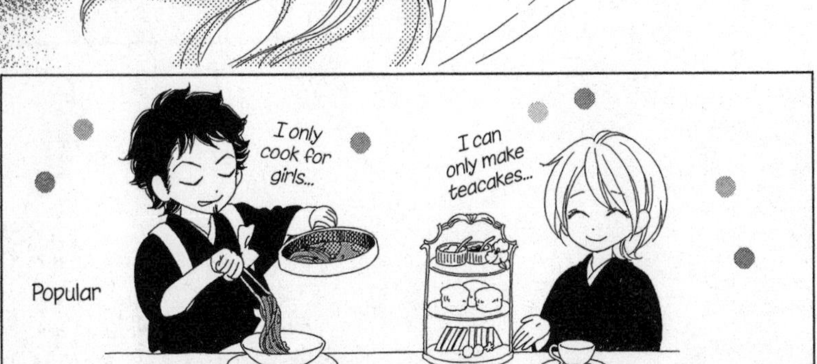
I can only make teacakes...
I only cook for girls...
Popular

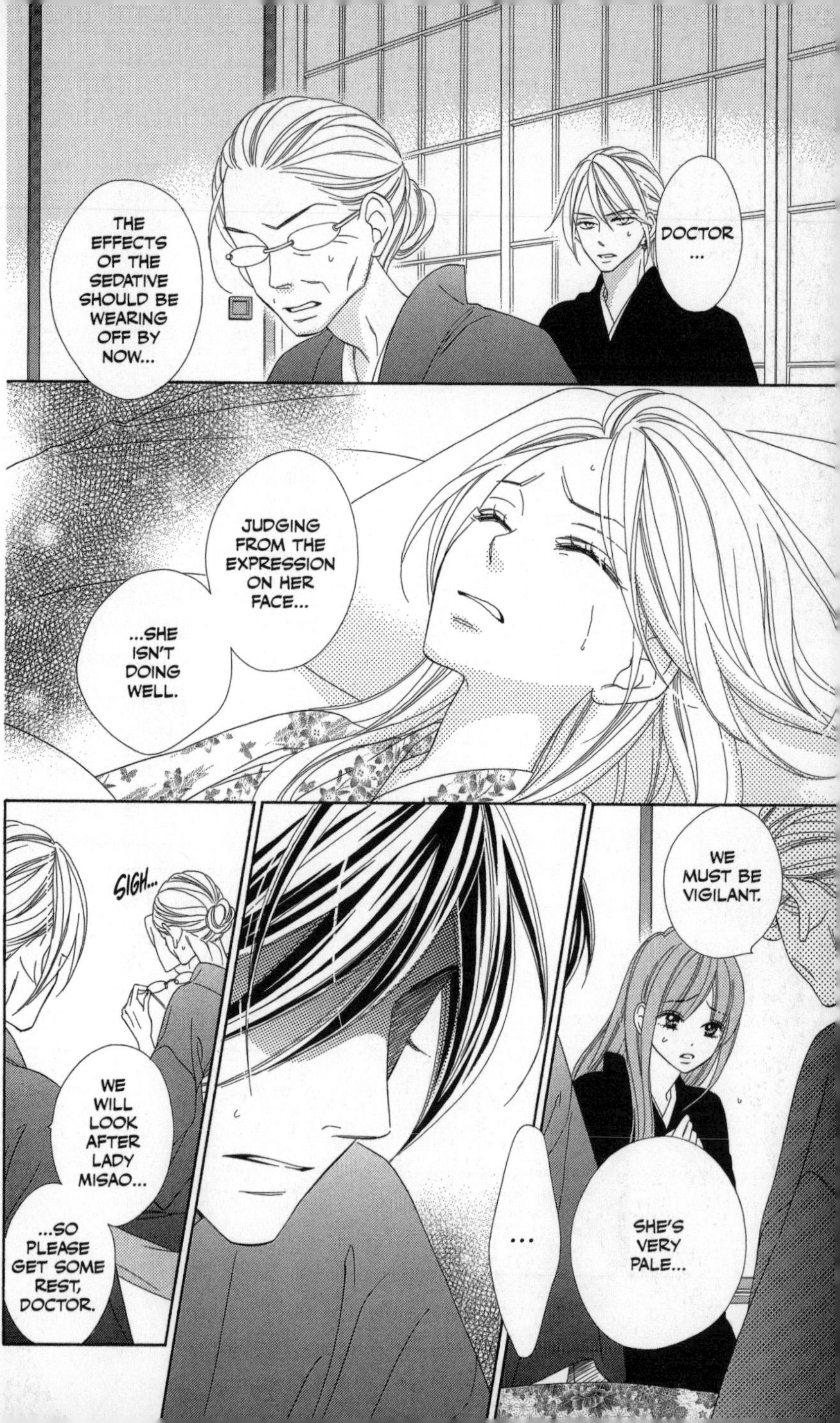
DOCTOR...
THE EFFECTS OF THE SEDATIVE SHOULD BE WEARING OFF BY NOW...
JUDGING FROM THE EXPRESSION ON HER FACE...
...SHE ISN'T DOING WELL.
WE MUST BE VIGILANT.
SHE'S VERY PALE...
...
SIGH...
WE WILL LOOK AFTER LADY MISAO...
...SO PLEASE GET SOME REST, DOCTOR.

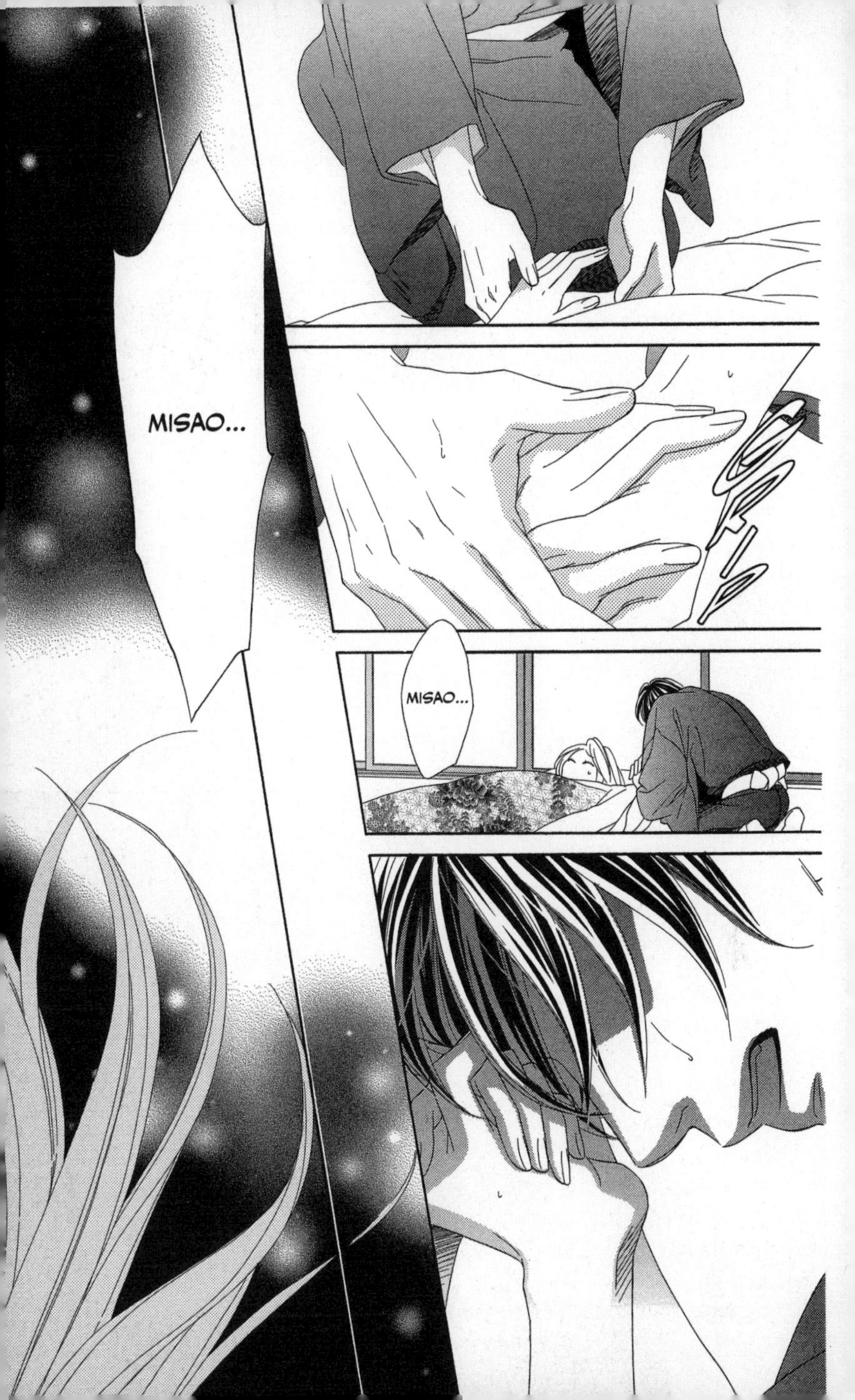
MISAO...
MISAO...

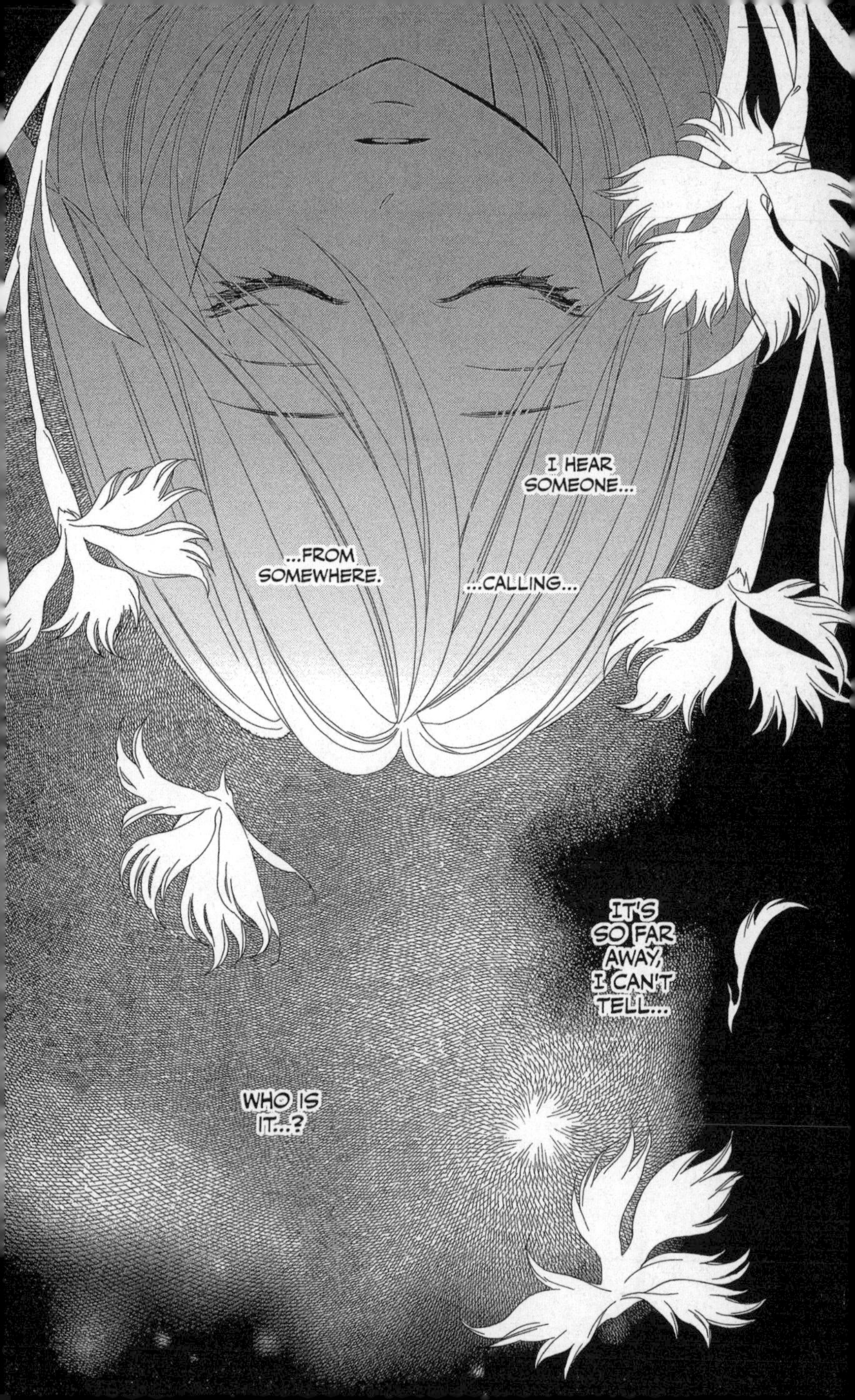
I HEAR SOMEONE...
...CALLING...
...FROM SOMEWHERE.
IT'S SO FAR AWAY, I CAN'T TELL...
WHO IS IT...?

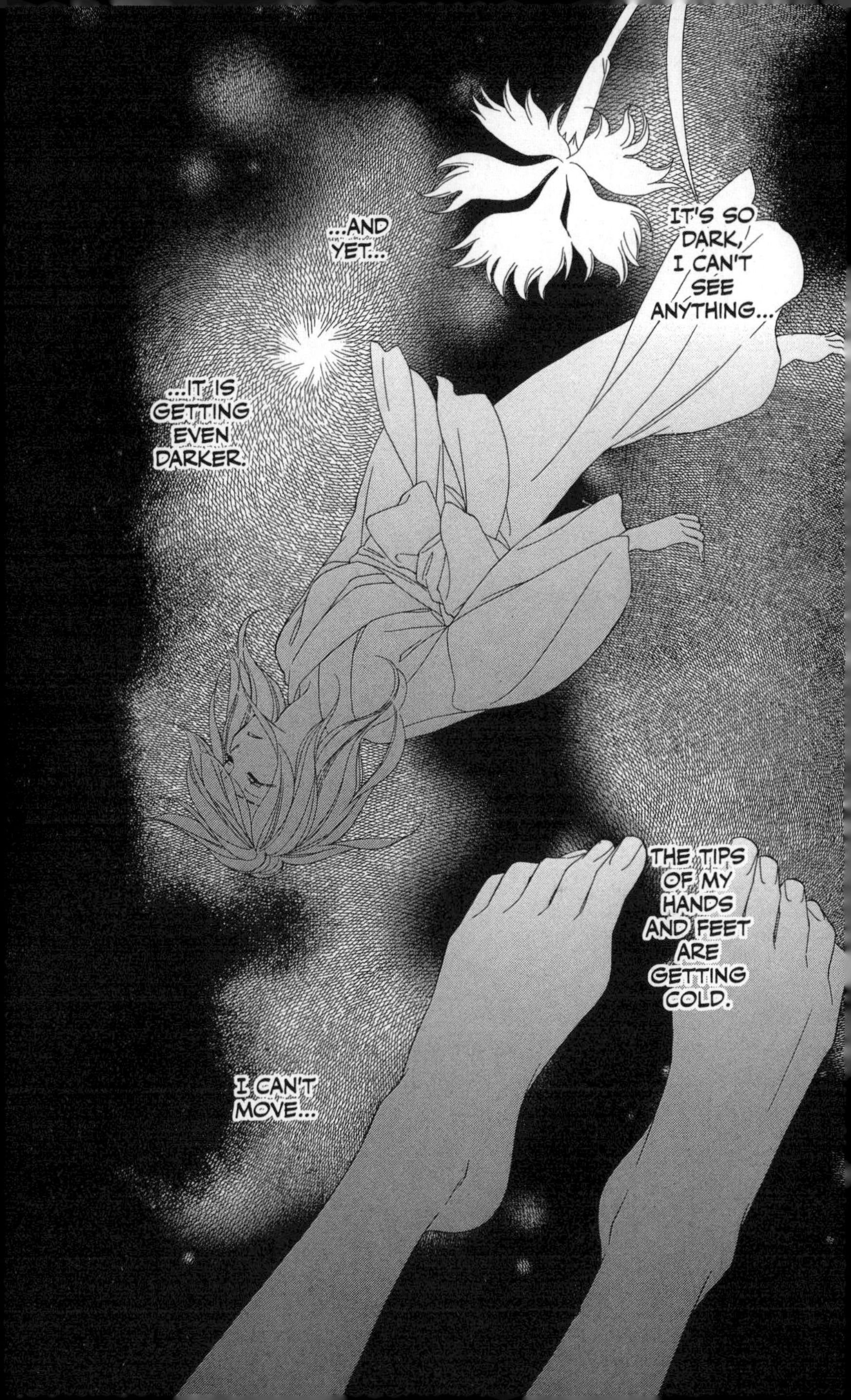
IT'S SO DARK, I CAN'T SEE ANYTHING...
...AND YET...
...IT IS GETTING EVEN DARKER.
THE TIPS OF MY HANDS AND FEET ARE GETTING COLD.
I CAN'T MOVE...

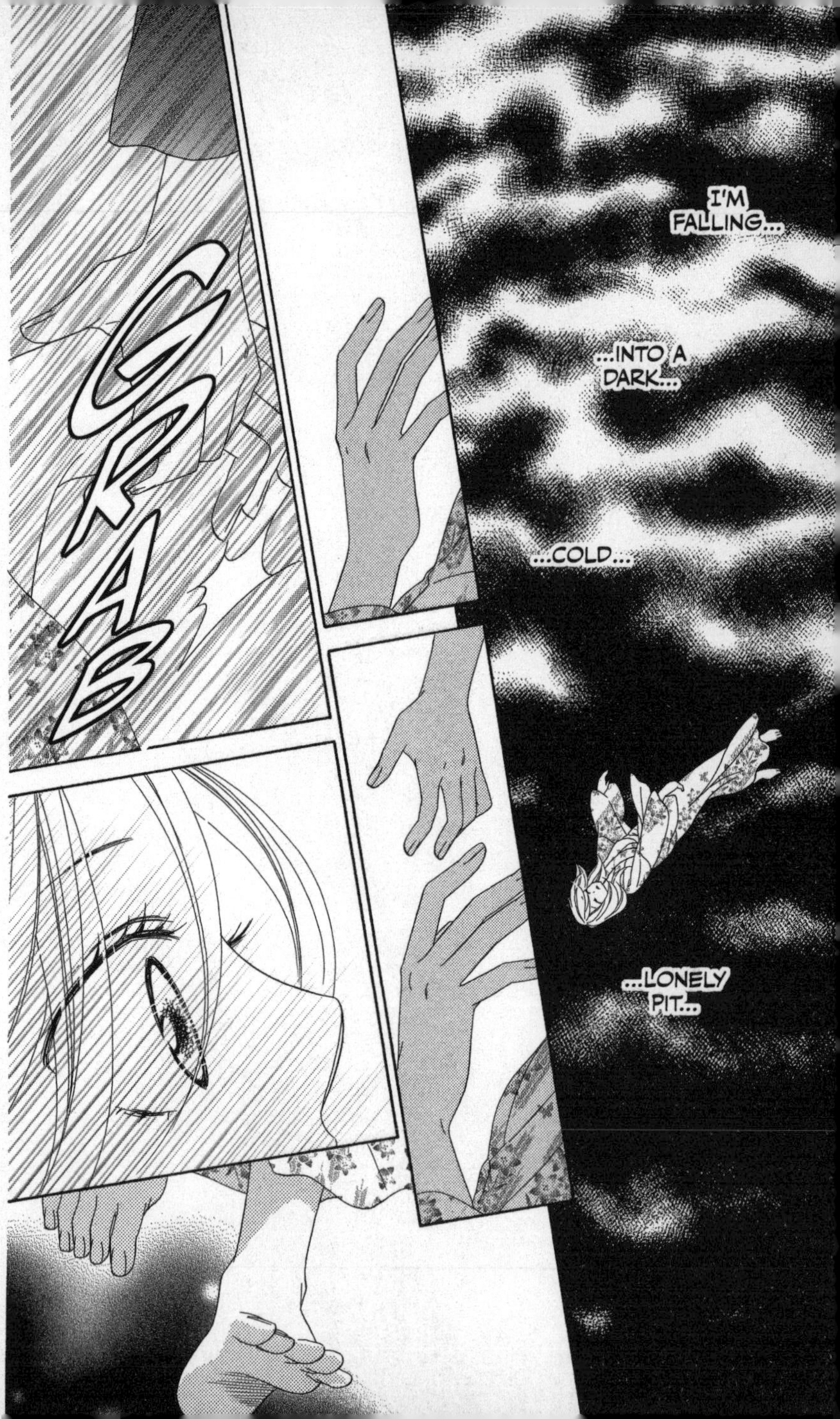
I'M FALLING...
...INTO A DARK...
...COLD...
...LONELY PIT...
GRAB

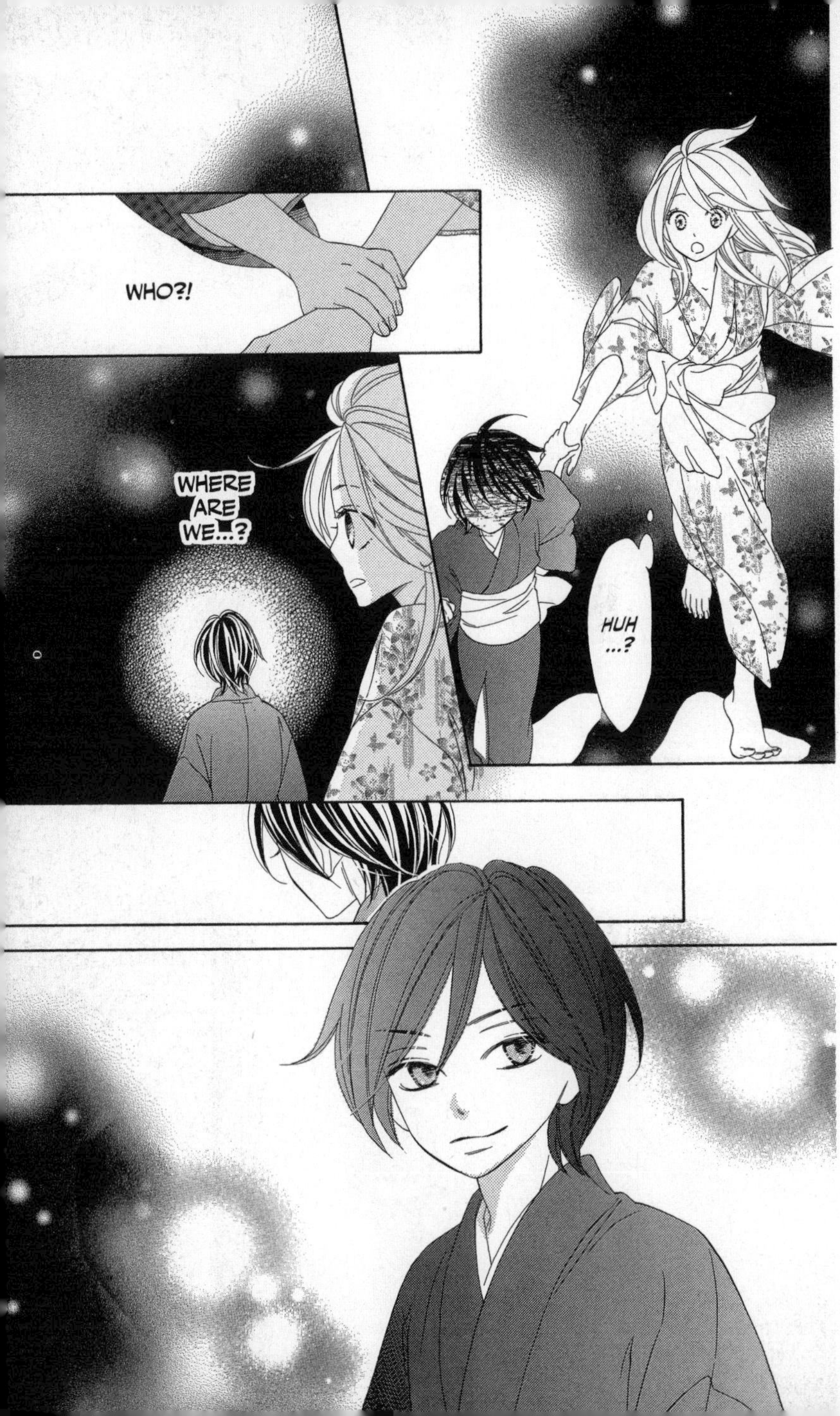
HUH ...?
WHO?!
WHERE ARE WE...?

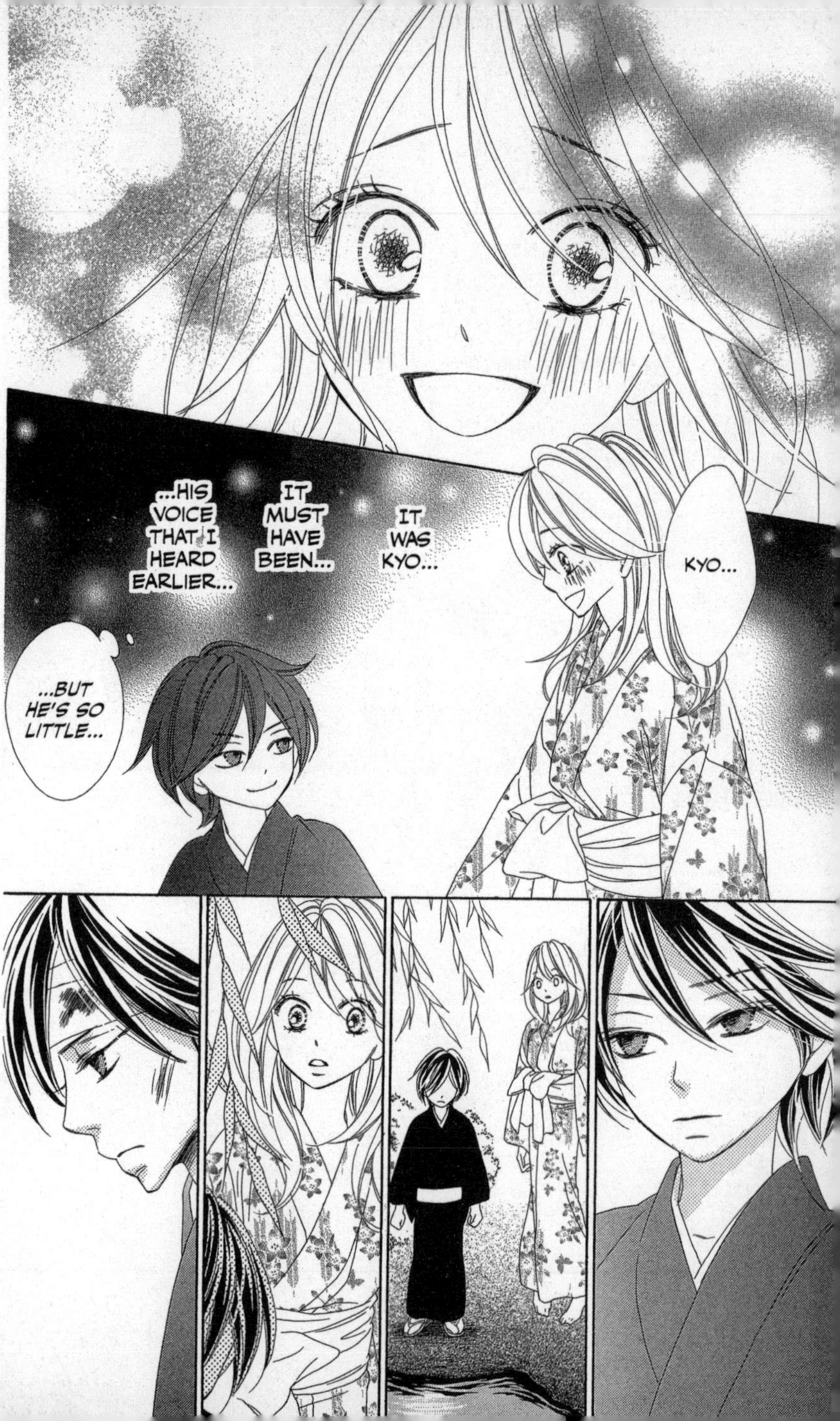
KYO...
IT WAS KYO...
IT MUST HAVE BEEN...
...HIS VOICE THAT I HEARD EARLIER...
...BUT HE'S SO LITTLE...

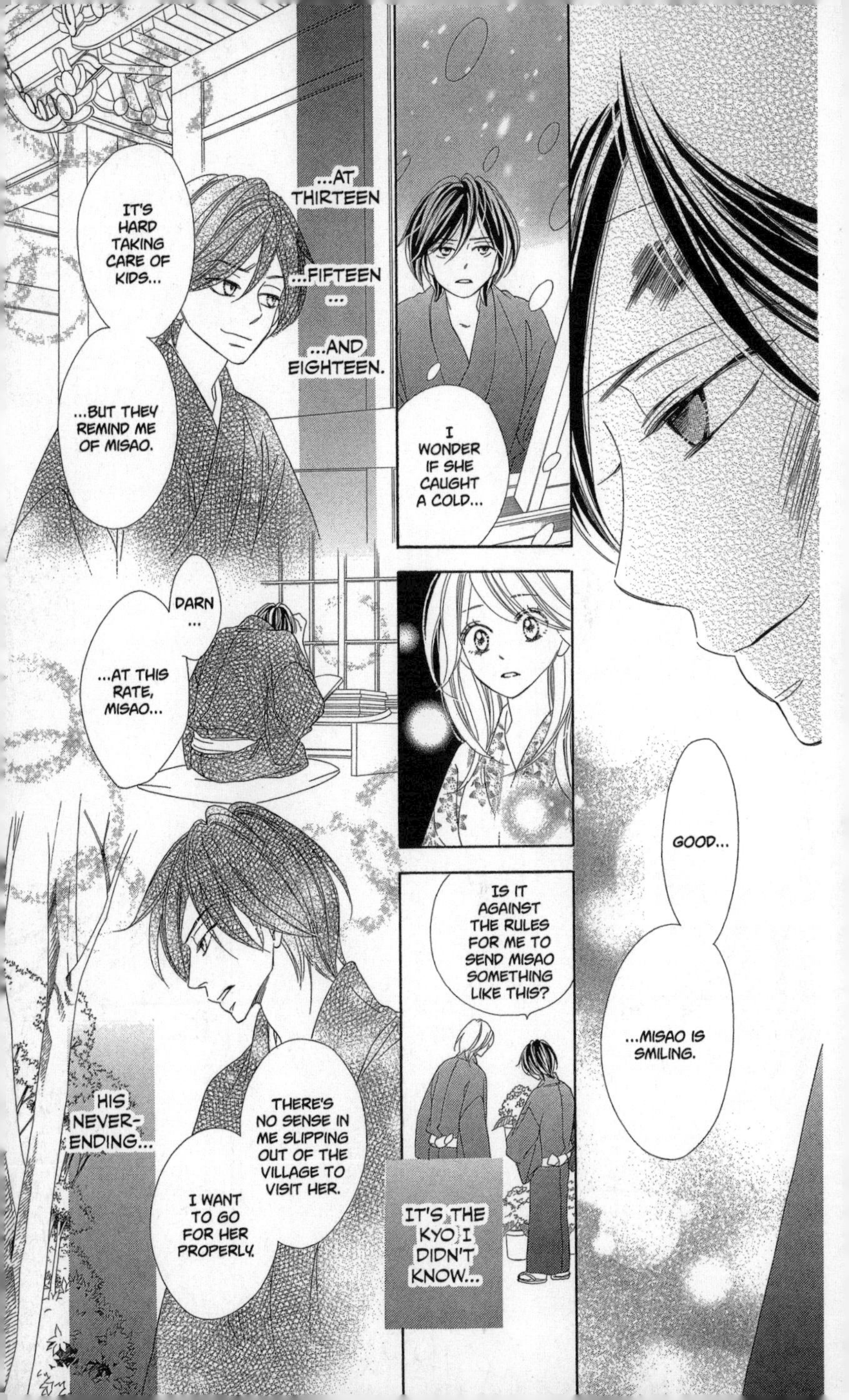

GOOD...
...MISAO IS SMILING.
I WONDER IF SHE CAUGHT A COLD...
...AT THIRTEEN
...FIFTEEN
...
...AND EIGHTEEN.
IS IT AGAINST THE RULES FOR ME TO SEND MISAO SOMETHING LIKE THIS?
IT'S THE KYO I DIDN'T KNOW...
IT'S HARD TAKING CARE OF KIDS...
...BUT THEY REMIND ME OF MISAO.
DARN...
...AT THIS RATE, MISAO...
THERE'S NO SENSE IN ME SLIPPING OUT OF THE VILLAGE TO VISIT HER.
I WANT TO GO FOR HER PROPERLY.
HIS NEVER-ENDING...

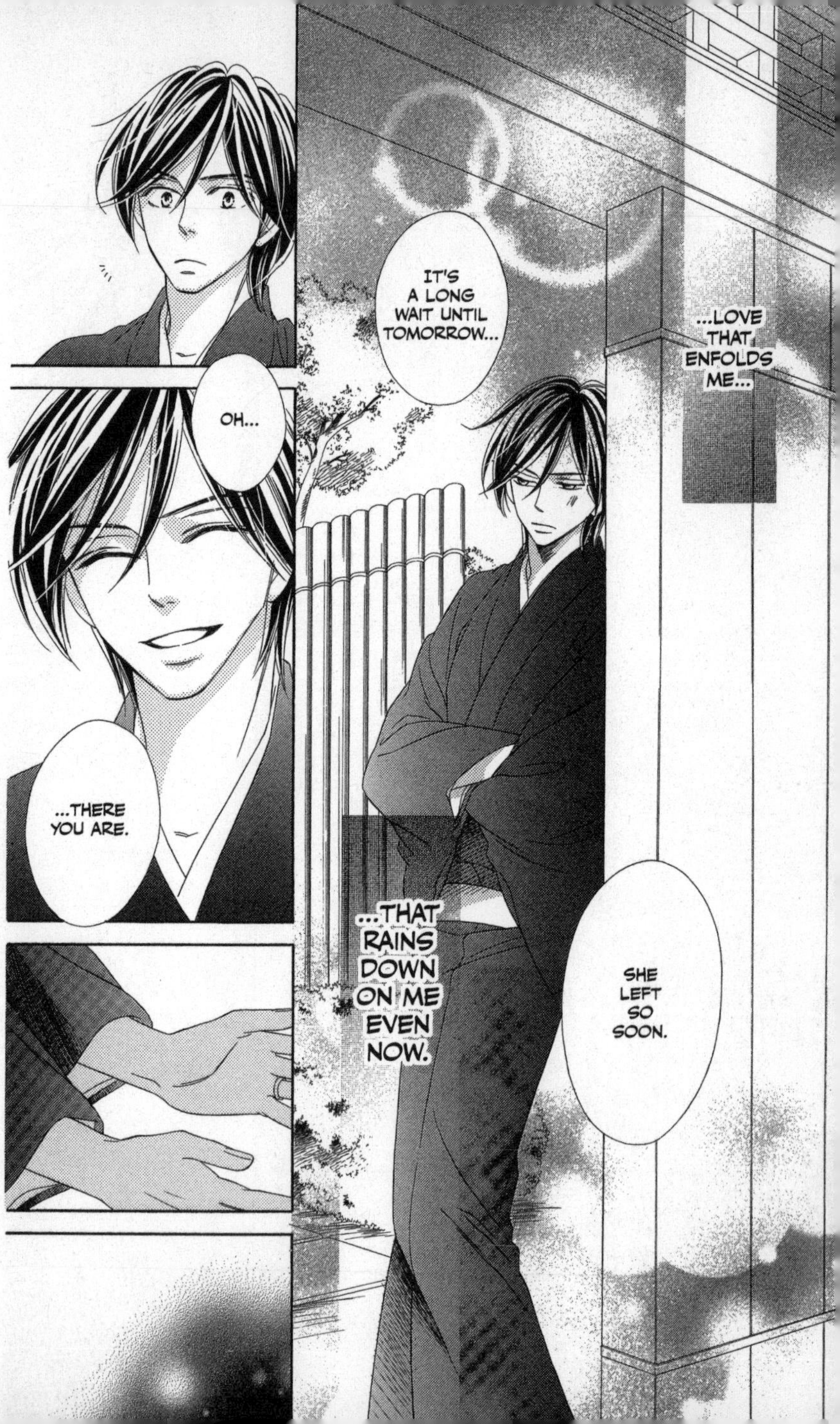
IT'S A LONG WAIT UNTIL TOMORROW...
...LOVE THAT ENFOLDS ME...
SHE LEFT SO SOON.
...THAT RAINS DOWN ON ME EVEN NOW.
OH...
...THERE YOU ARE.

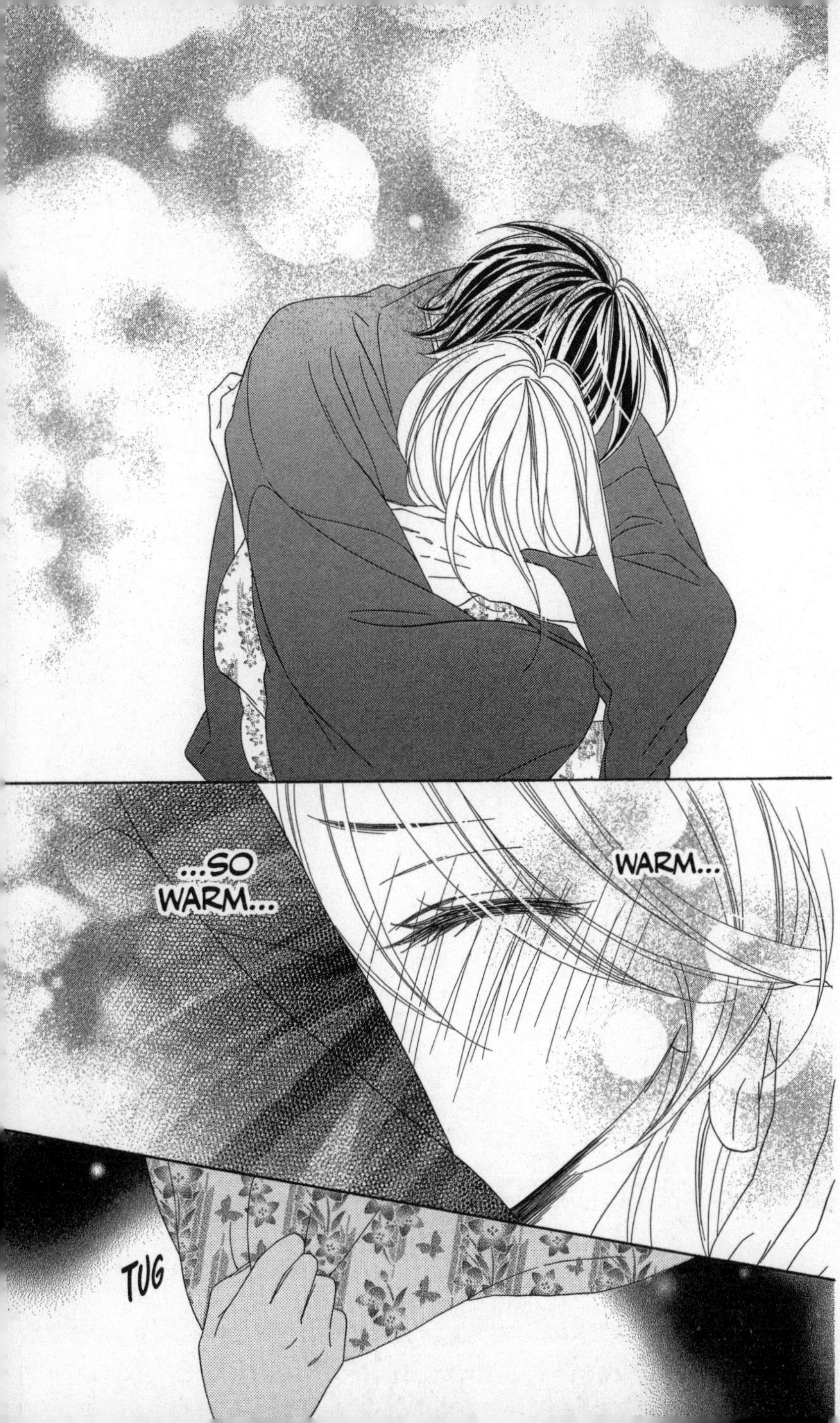
WARM...
...SO WARM...
TUG

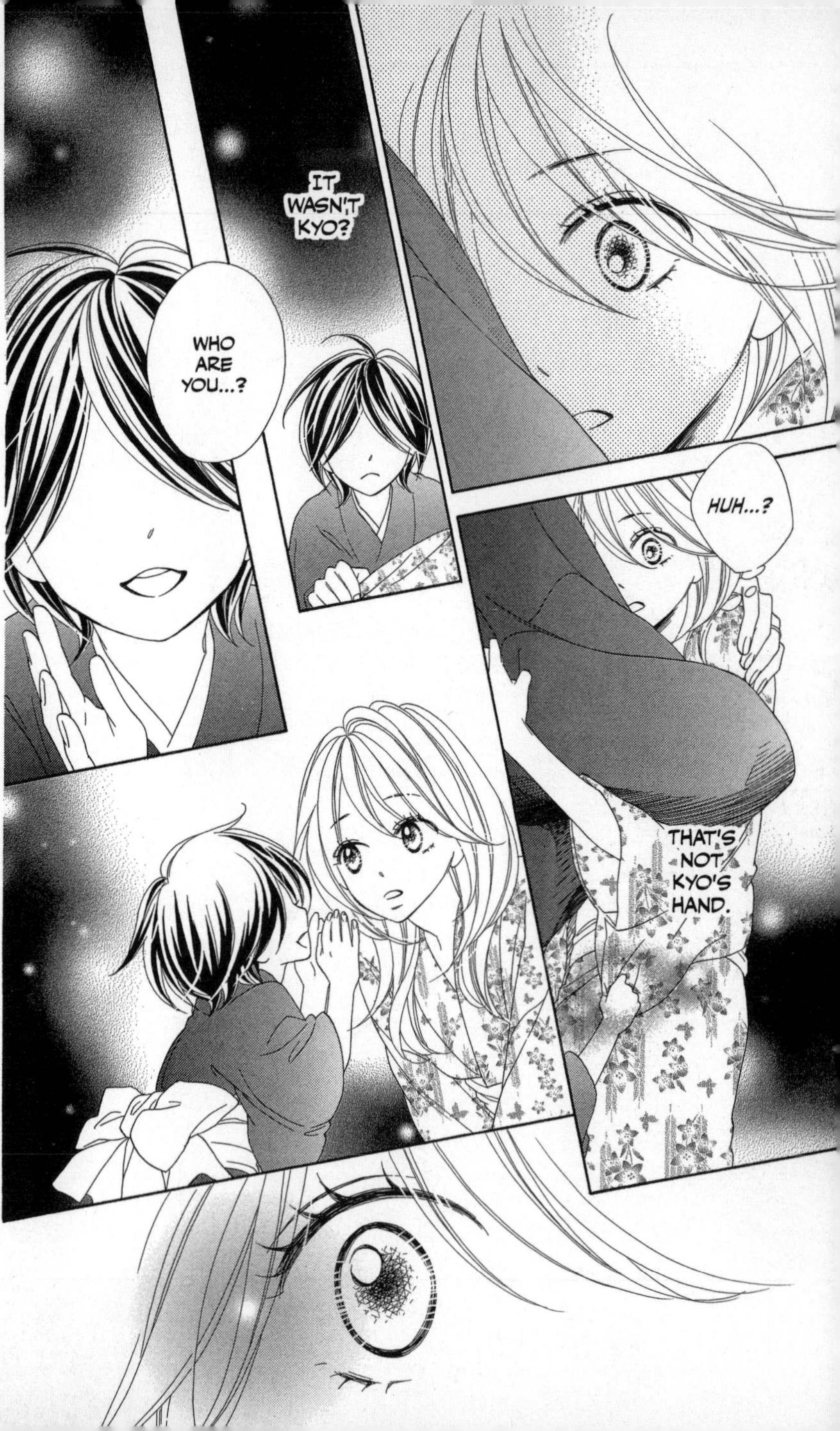
HUH...?
THAT'S NOT KYO'S HAND.
IT WASN'T KYO?
WHO ARE YOU...?

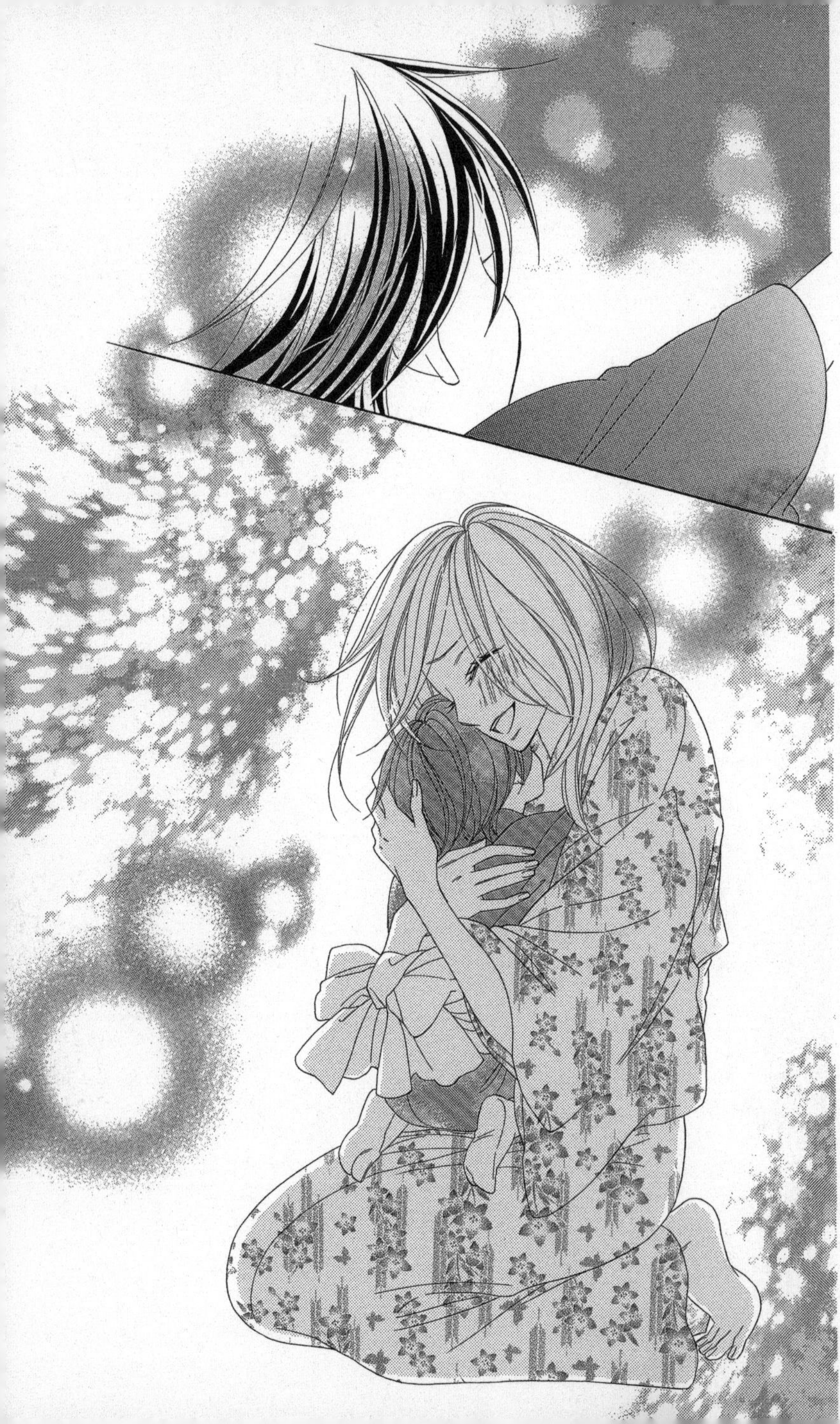

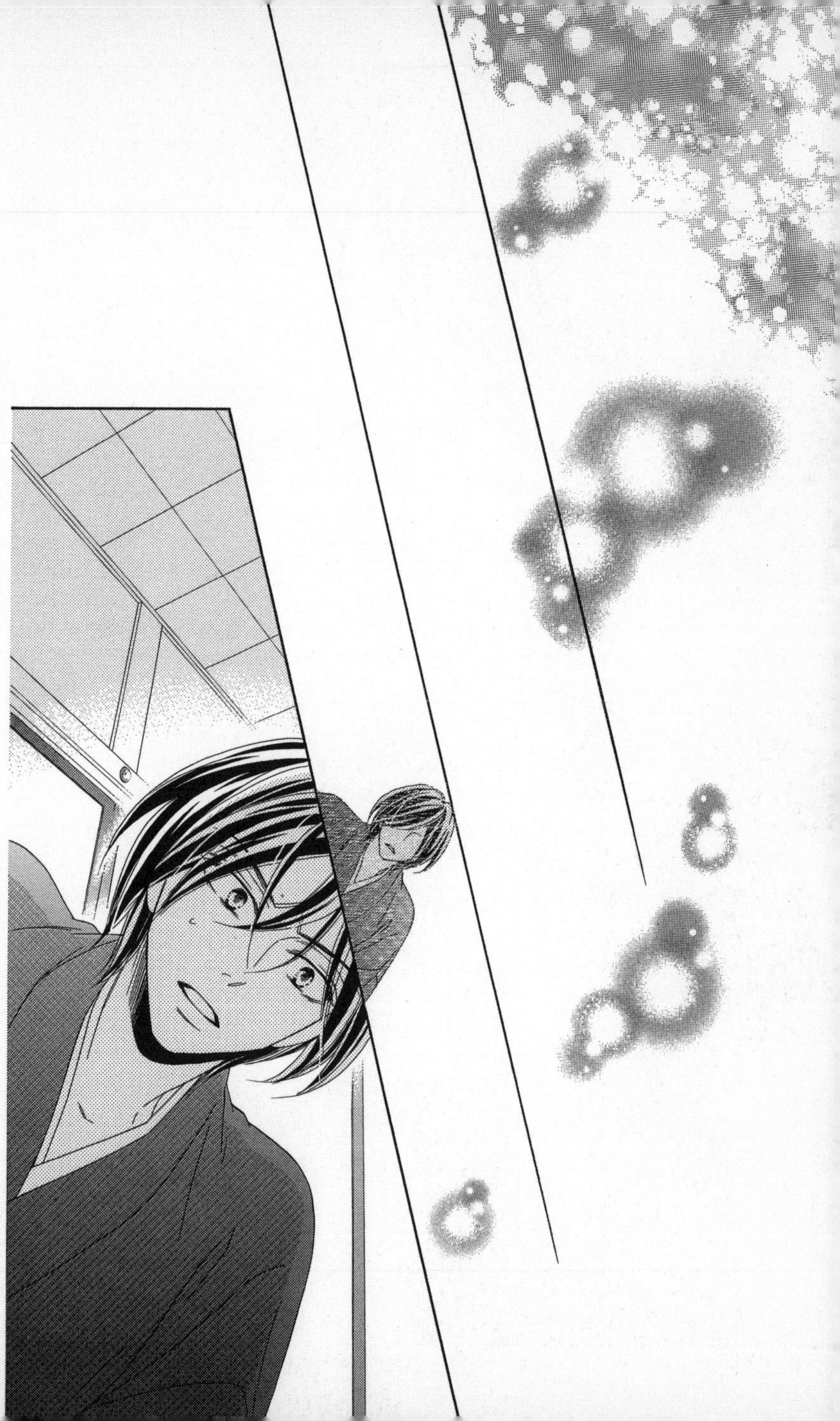

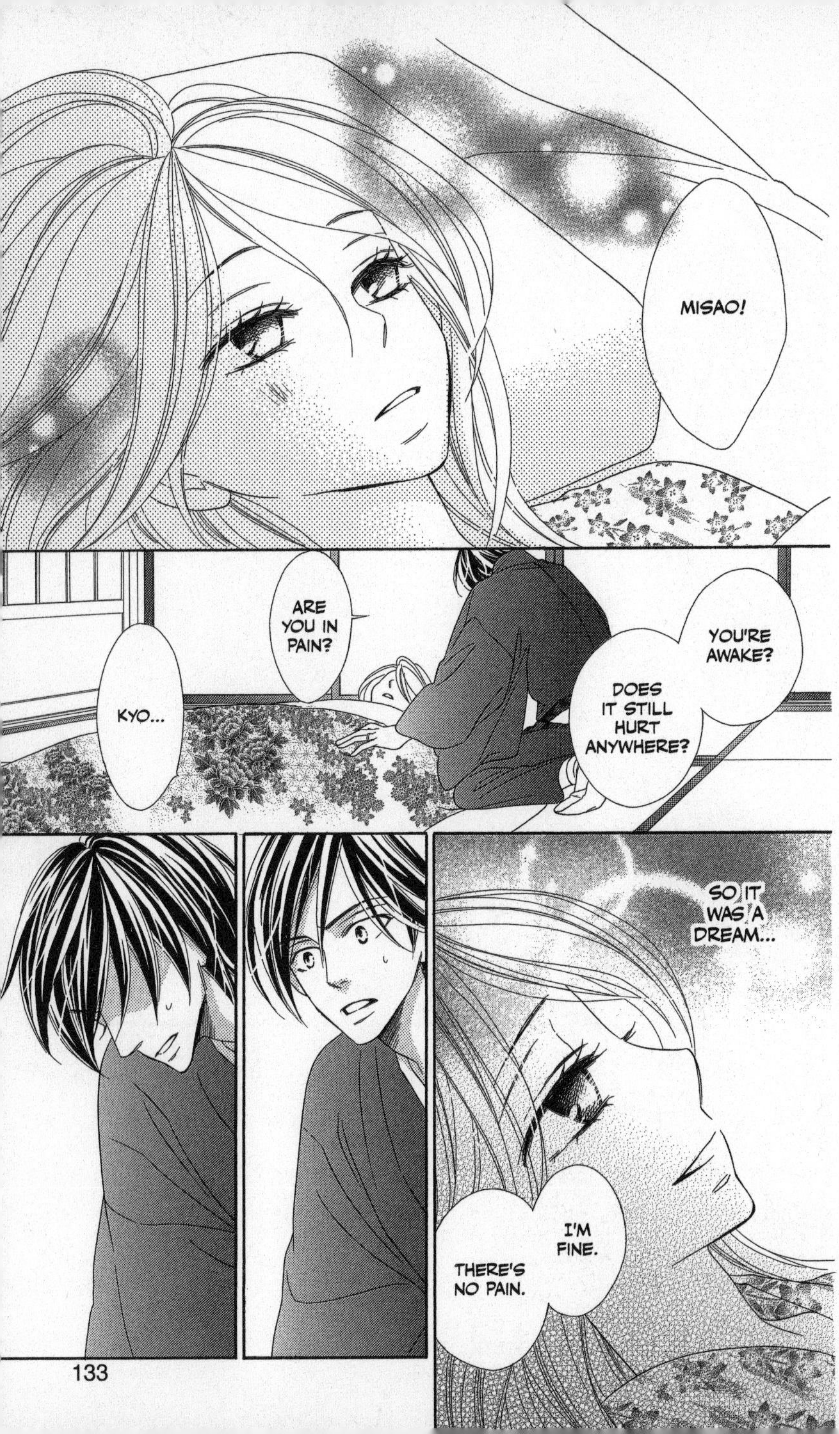
MISAO!
YOU'RE AWAKE?
DOES IT STILL HURT ANYWHERE?
ARE YOU IN PAIN?
KYO...
SO IT WAS A DREAM...
I'M FINE.
THERE'S NO PAIN.

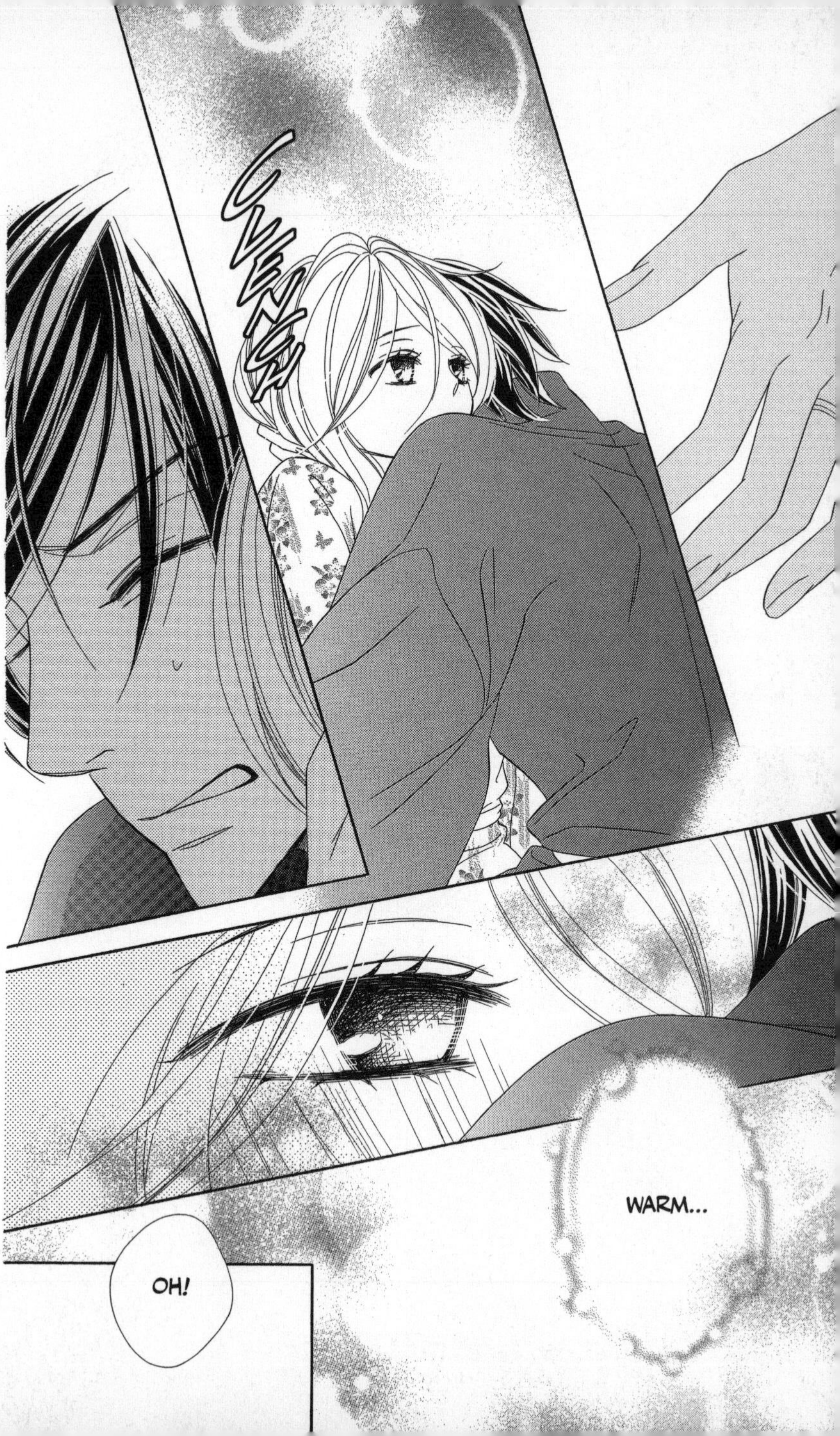
CLENCH
WARM...
OH!

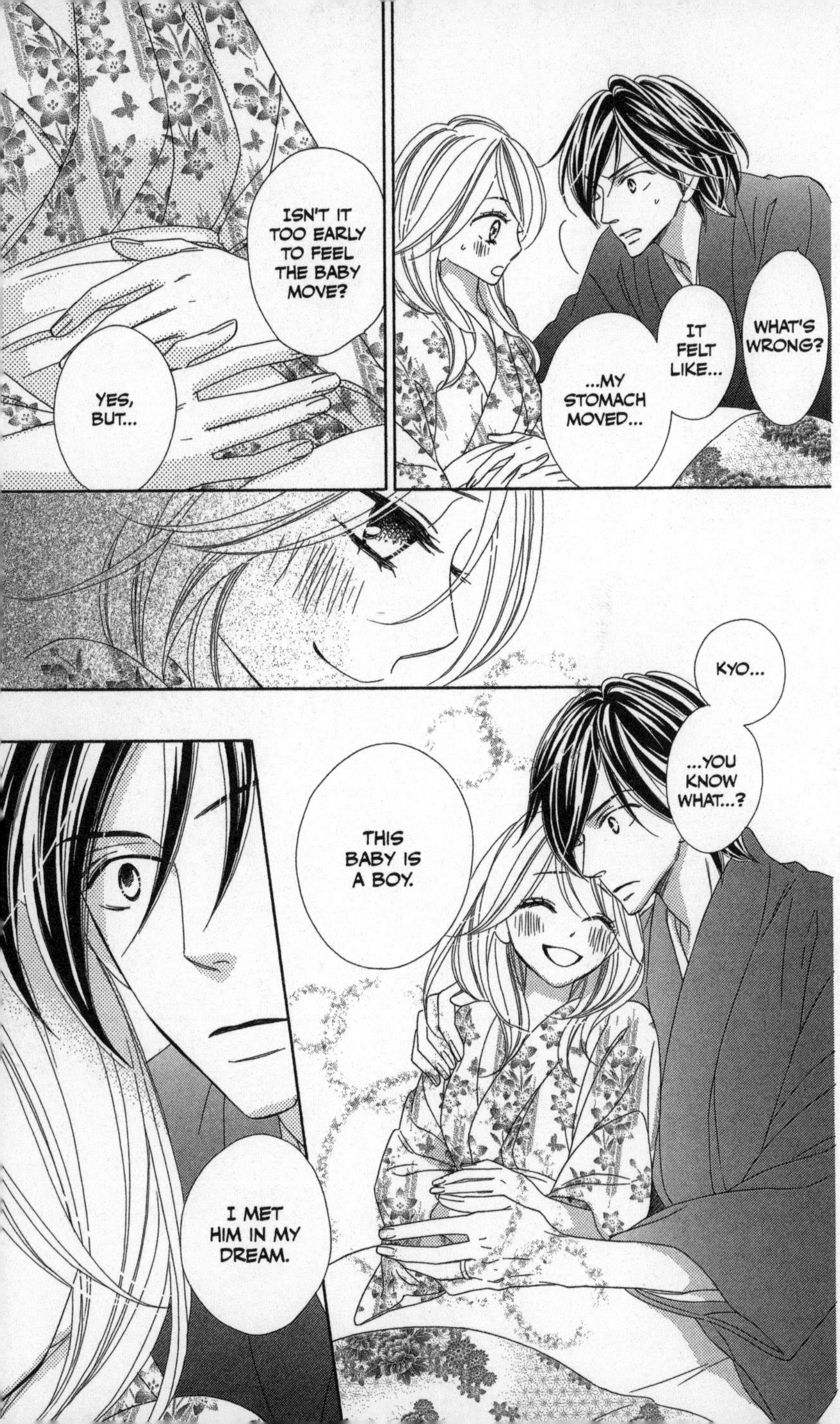
WHAT'S WRONG?
IT FELT LIKE...
...MY STOMACH MOVED...
ISN'T IT TOO EARLY TO FEEL THE BABY MOVE?
YES, BUT...
KYO...
...YOU KNOW WHAT...?
THIS BABY IS A BOY.
I MET HIM IN MY DREAM.

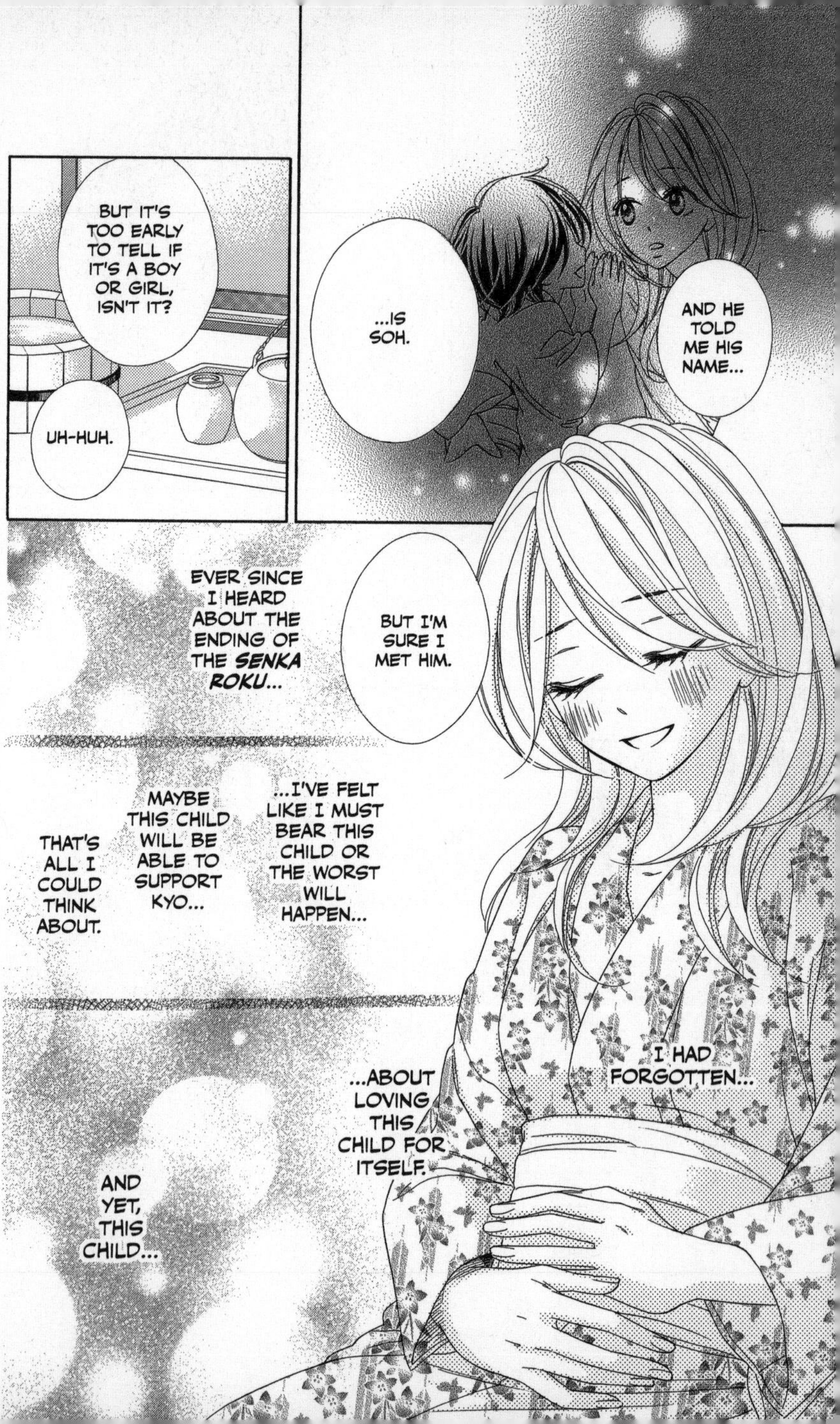
AND HE TOLD ME HIS NAME...
...IS SOH.
BUT IT'S TOO EARLY TO TELL IF IT'S A BOY OR GIRL, ISN'T IT?
UH-HUH.
BUT I'M SURE I MET HIM.
EVER SINCE I HEARD ABOUT THE ENDING OF THE *SENKA ROKU*...
...I'VE FELT LIKE I MUST BEAR THIS CHILD OR THE WORST WILL HAPPEN...
MAYBE THIS CHILD WILL BE ABLE TO SUPPORT KYO...
THAT'S ALL I COULD THINK ABOUT.
I HAD FORGOTTEN...
...ABOUT LOVING THIS CHILD FOR ITSELF.
AND YET, THIS CHILD...

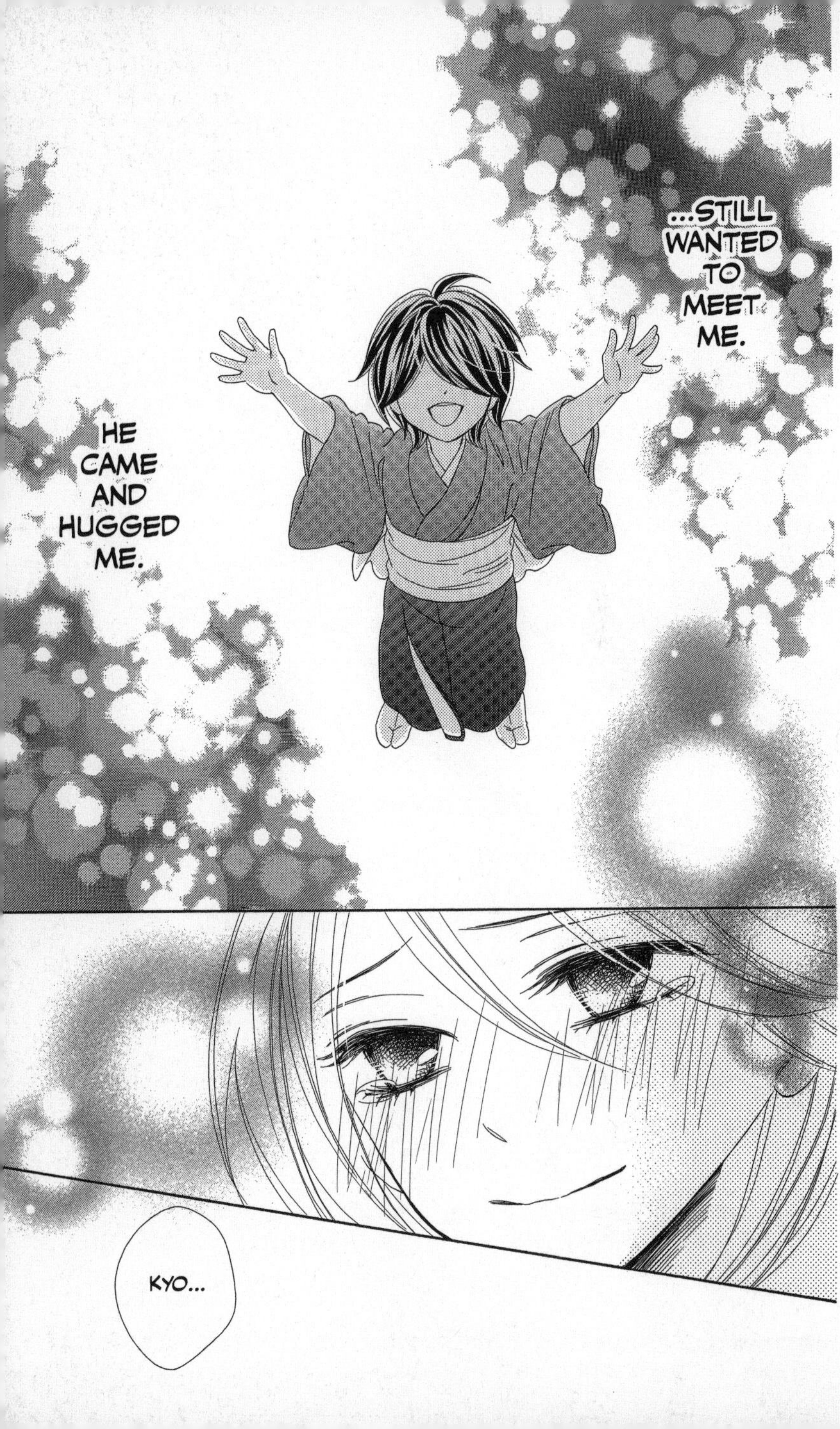
...STILL WANTED TO MEET ME.
HE CAME AND HUGGED ME.
KYO...

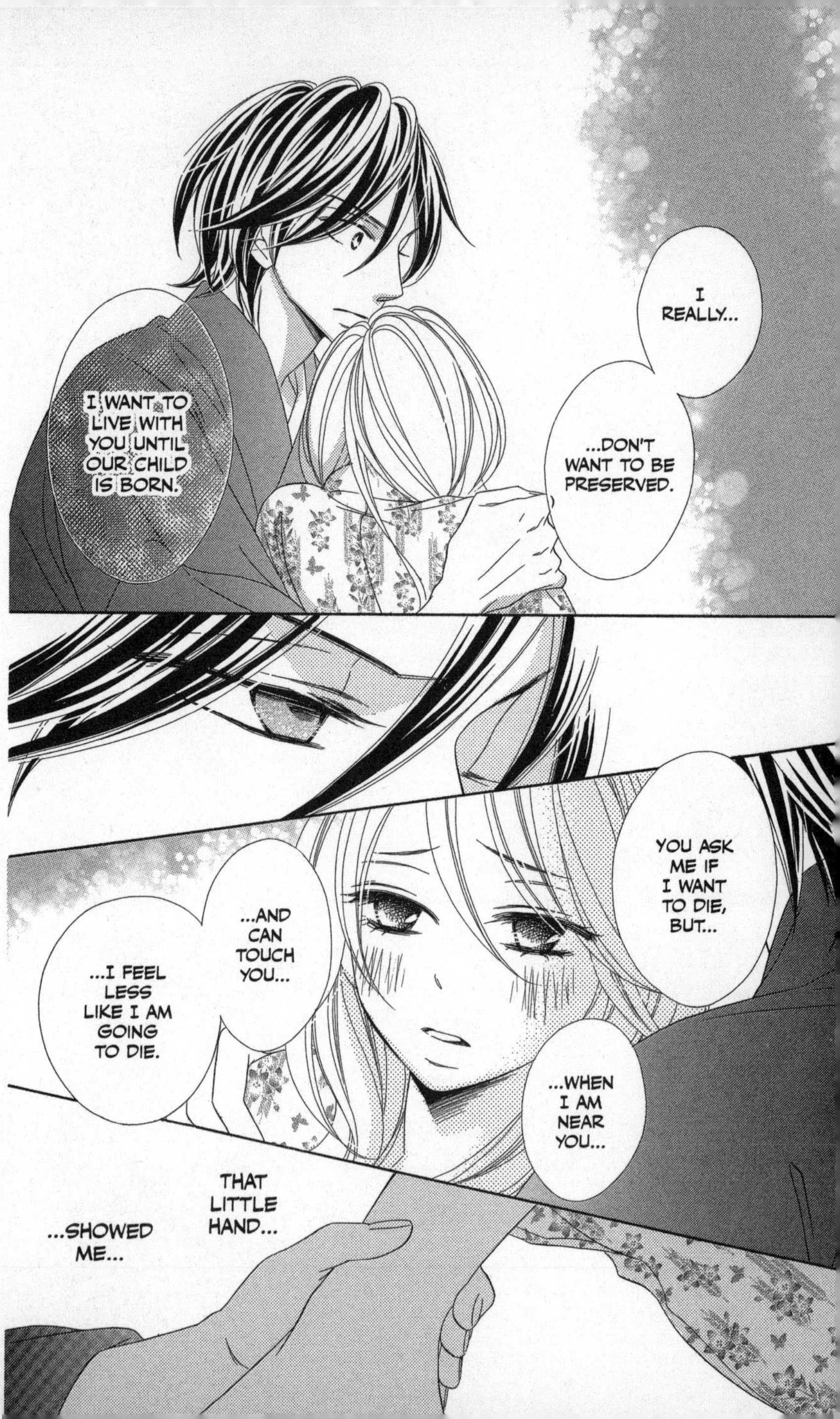
I REALLY...
...DON'T WANT TO BE PRESERVED.
I WANT TO LIVE WITH YOU UNTIL OUR CHILD IS BORN.
YOU ASK ME IF I WANT TO DIE, BUT...
...WHEN I AM NEAR YOU...
...AND CAN TOUCH YOU...
...I FEEL LESS LIKE I AM GOING TO DIE.
THAT LITTLE HAND...
...SHOWED ME...

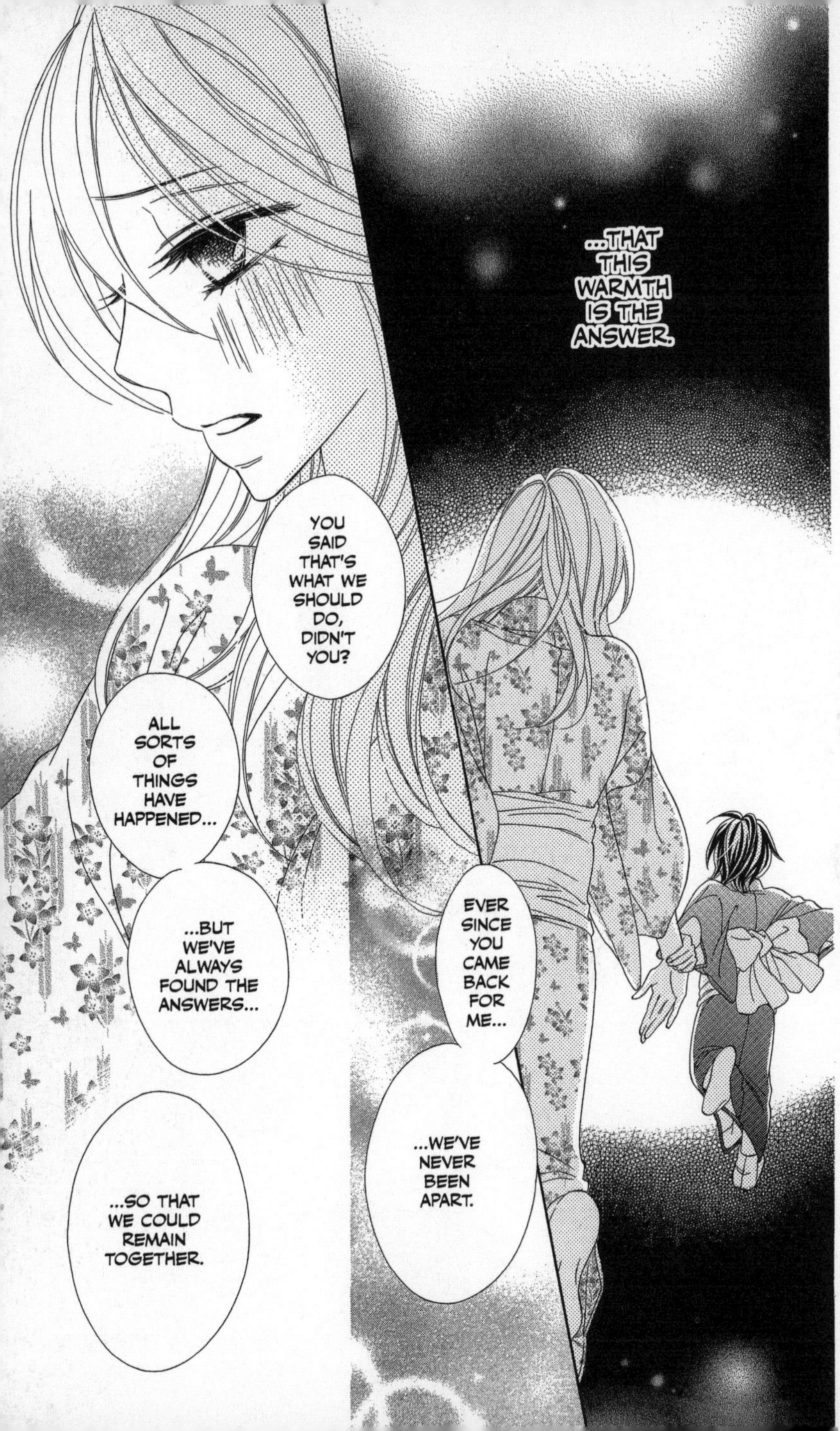
...THAT THIS WARMTH IS THE ANSWER.
EVER SINCE YOU CAME BACK FOR ME...
...WE'VE NEVER BEEN APART.
YOU SAID THAT'S WHAT WE SHOULD DO, DIDN'T YOU?
ALL SORTS OF THINGS HAVE HAPPENED...
...BUT WE'VE ALWAYS FOUND THE ANSWERS...
...SO THAT WE COULD REMAIN TOGETHER.

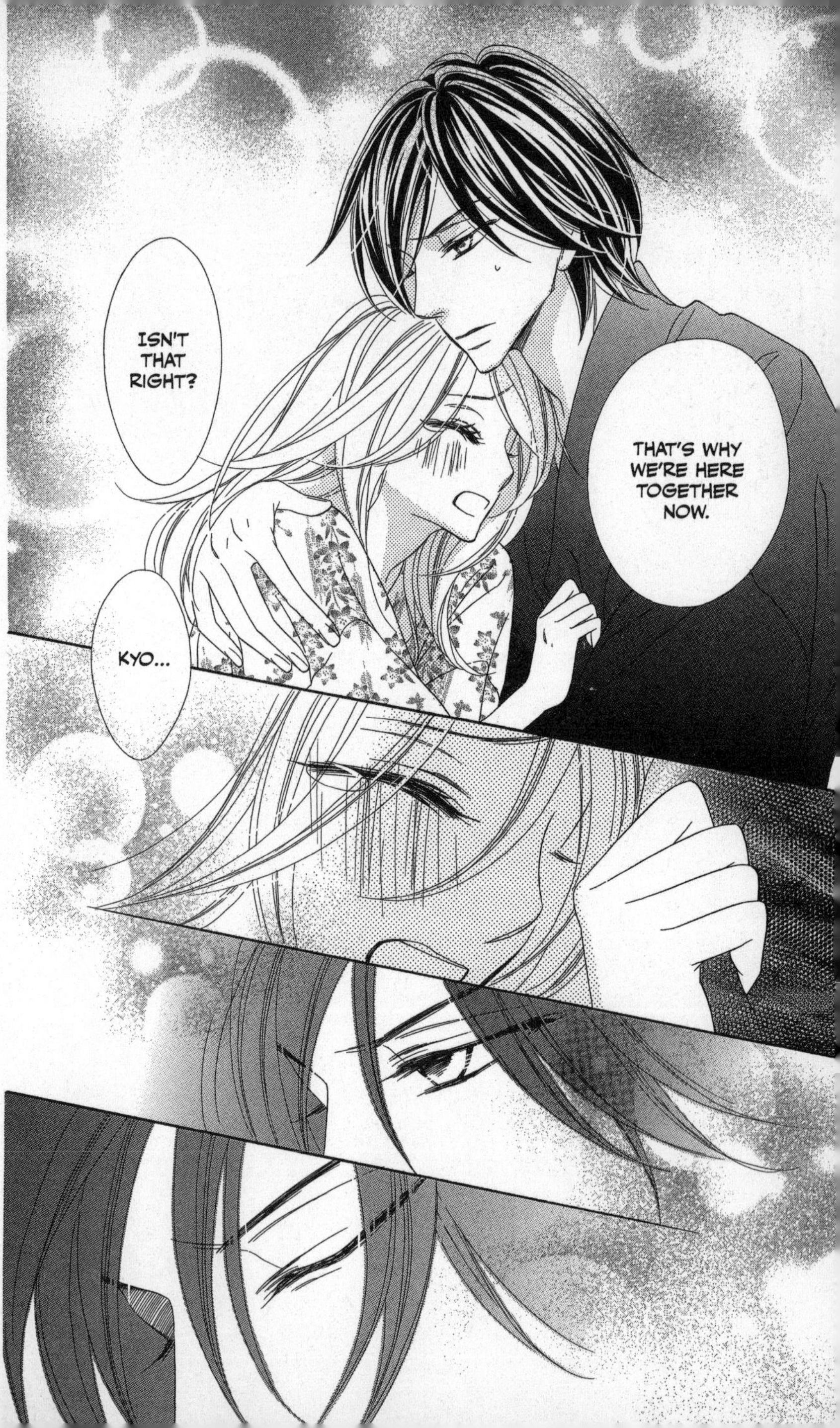

THAT'S WHY WE'RE HERE TOGETHER NOW.
ISN'T THAT RIGHT?
KYO...

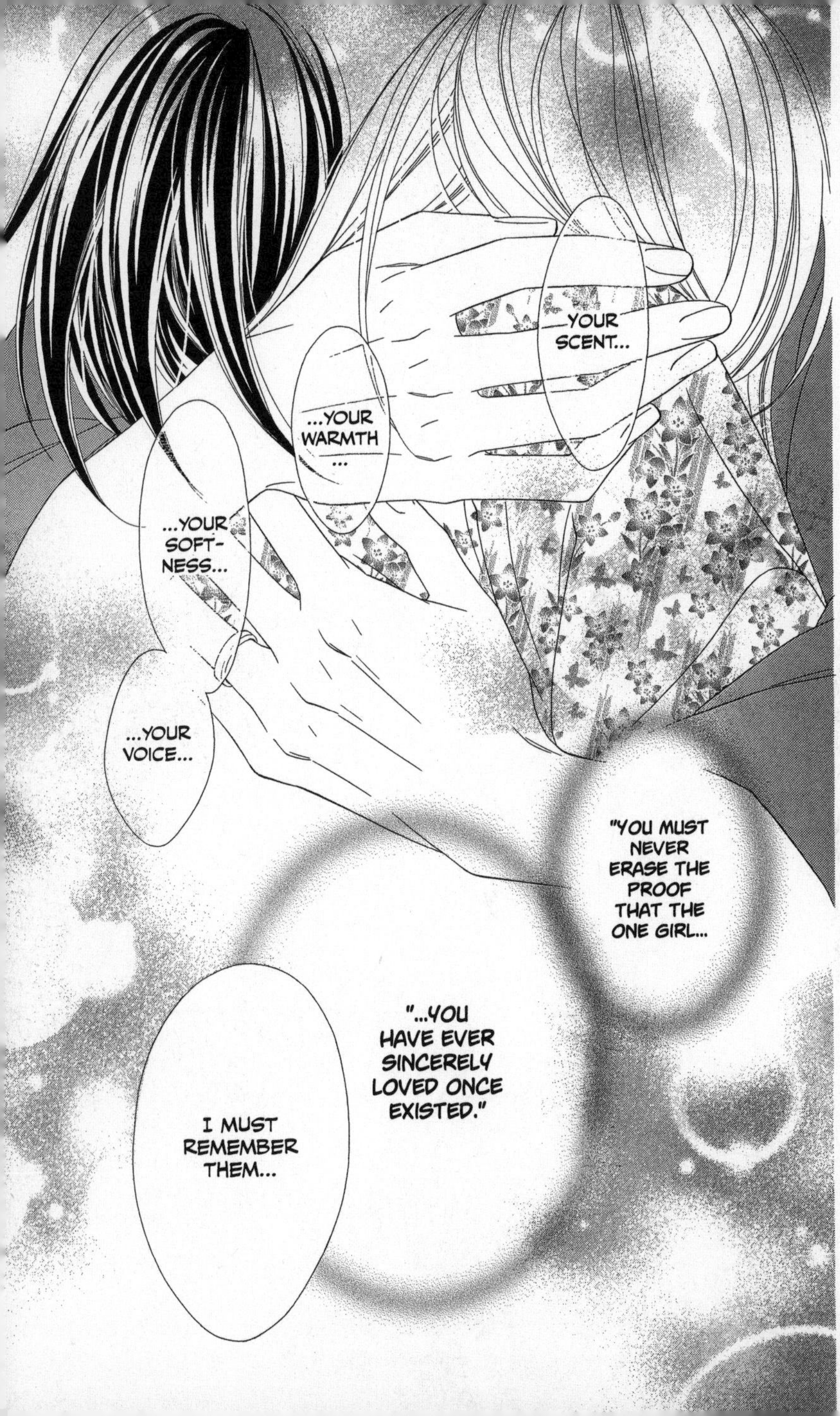
YOUR SCENT...
...YOUR WARMTH ...
...YOUR SOFT-NESS...
...YOUR VOICE...
"YOU MUST NEVER ERASE THE PROOF THAT THE ONE GIRL...
"...YOU HAVE EVER SINCERELY LOVED ONCE EXISTED."
I MUST REMEMBER THEM...

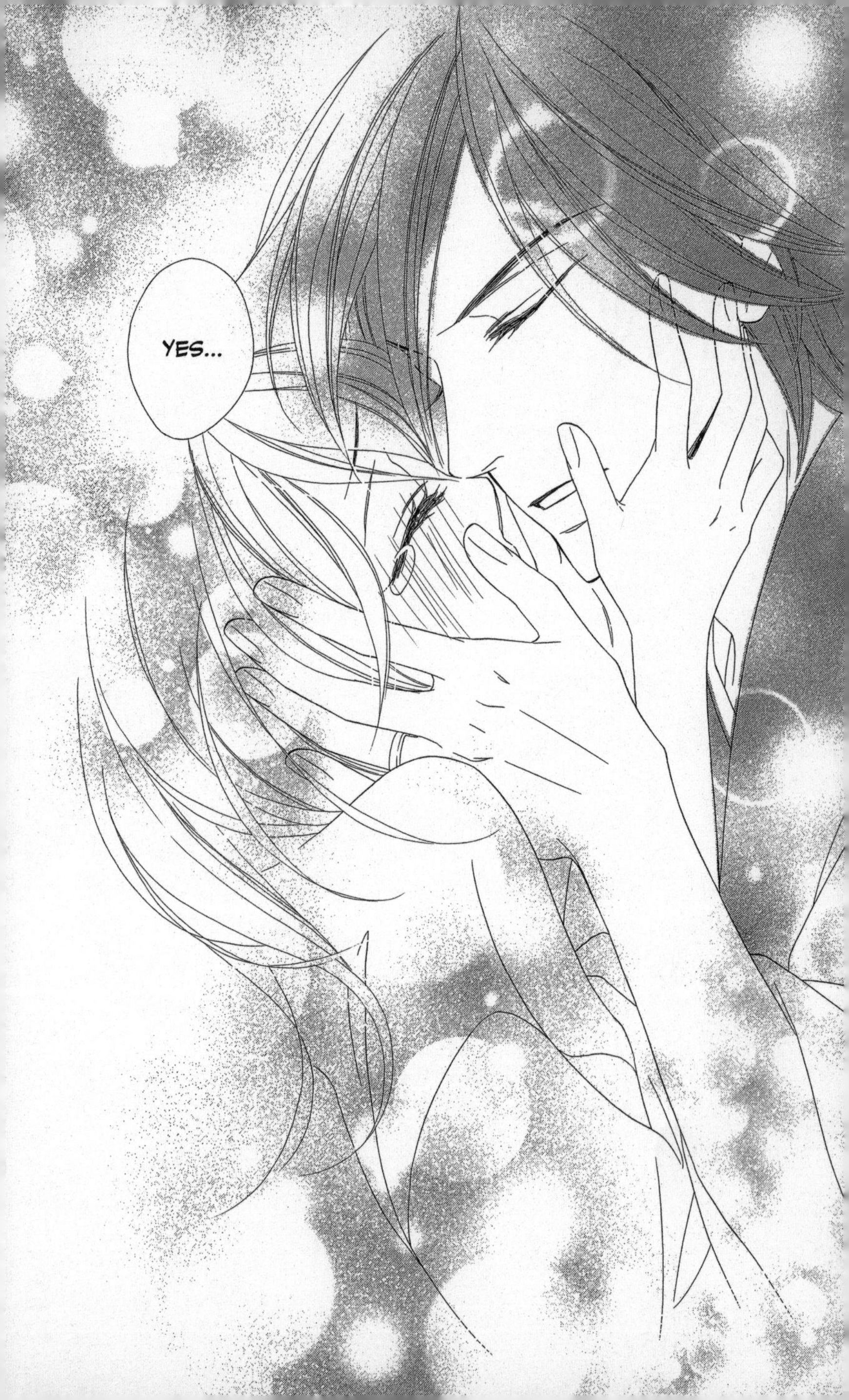
YES...

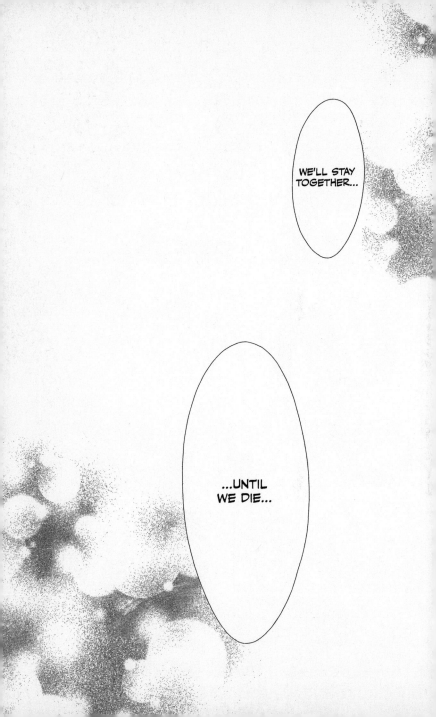

WE'LL STAY
TOGETHER...

...UNTIL
WE DIE...

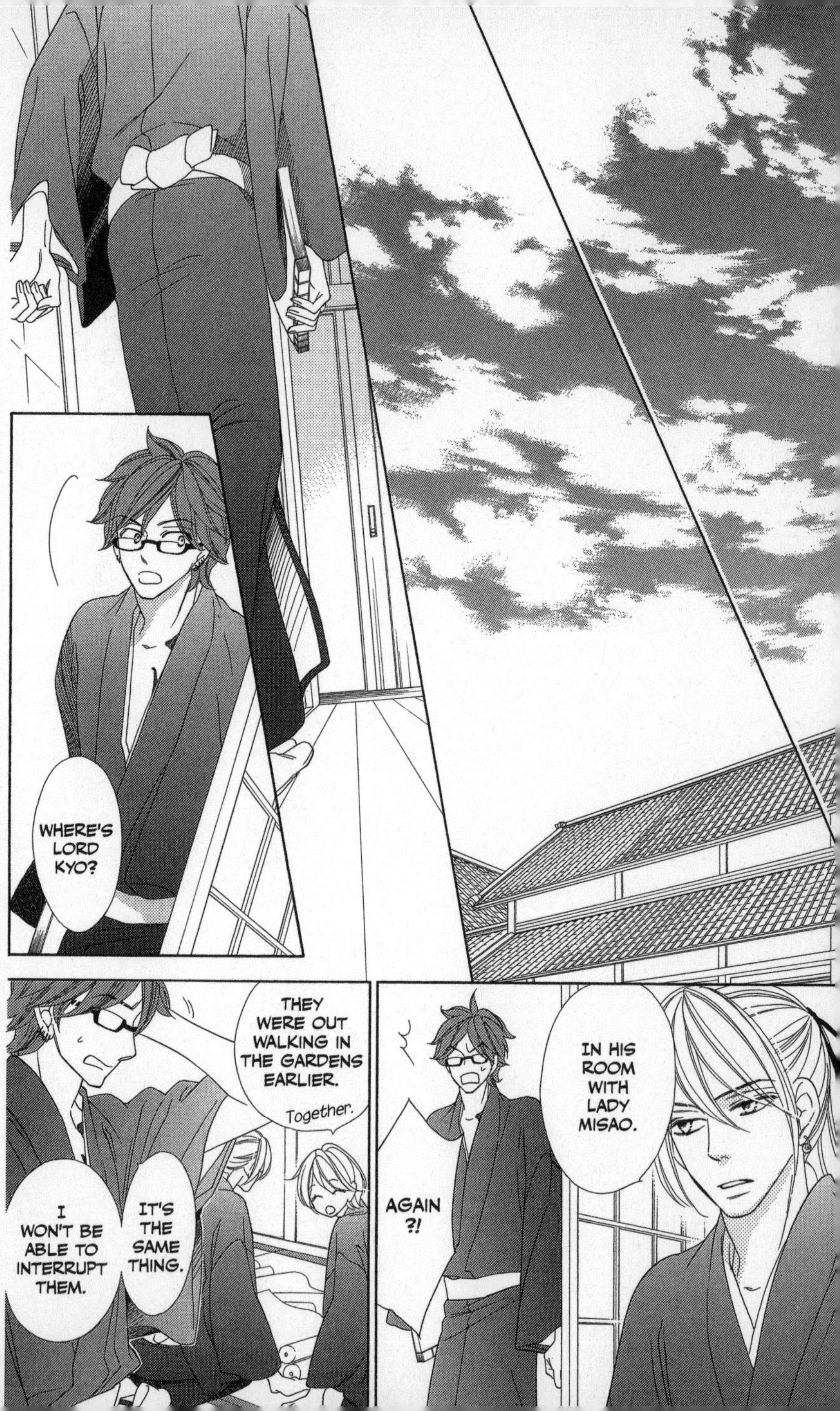
WHERE'S LORD KYO?
IN HIS ROOM WITH LADY MISAO.
AGAIN?!
THEY WERE OUT WALKING IN THE GARDENS EARLIER.
Together.
IT'S THE SAME THING.
I WON'T BE ABLE TO INTERRUPT THEM.

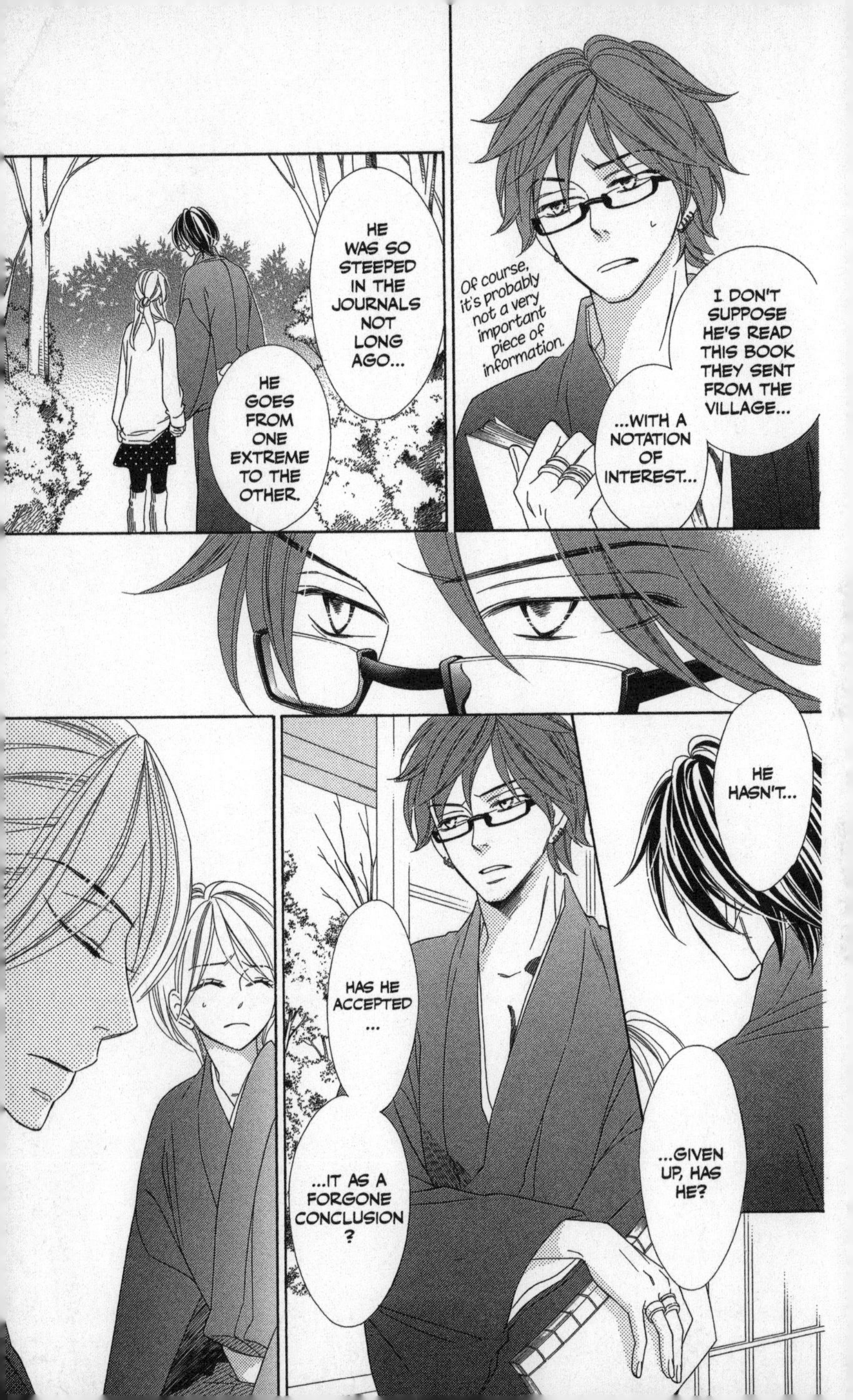
I DON'T SUPPOSE HE'S READ THIS BOOK THEY SENT FROM THE VILLAGE...
...WITH A NOTATION OF INTEREST...
Of course, it's probably not a very important piece of information.
HE WAS SO STEEPED IN THE JOURNALS NOT LONG AGO...
HE GOES FROM ONE EXTREME TO THE OTHER.
HE HASN'T...
...GIVEN UP, HAS HE?
HAS HE ACCEPTED ...
...IT AS A FORGONE CONCLUSION ?

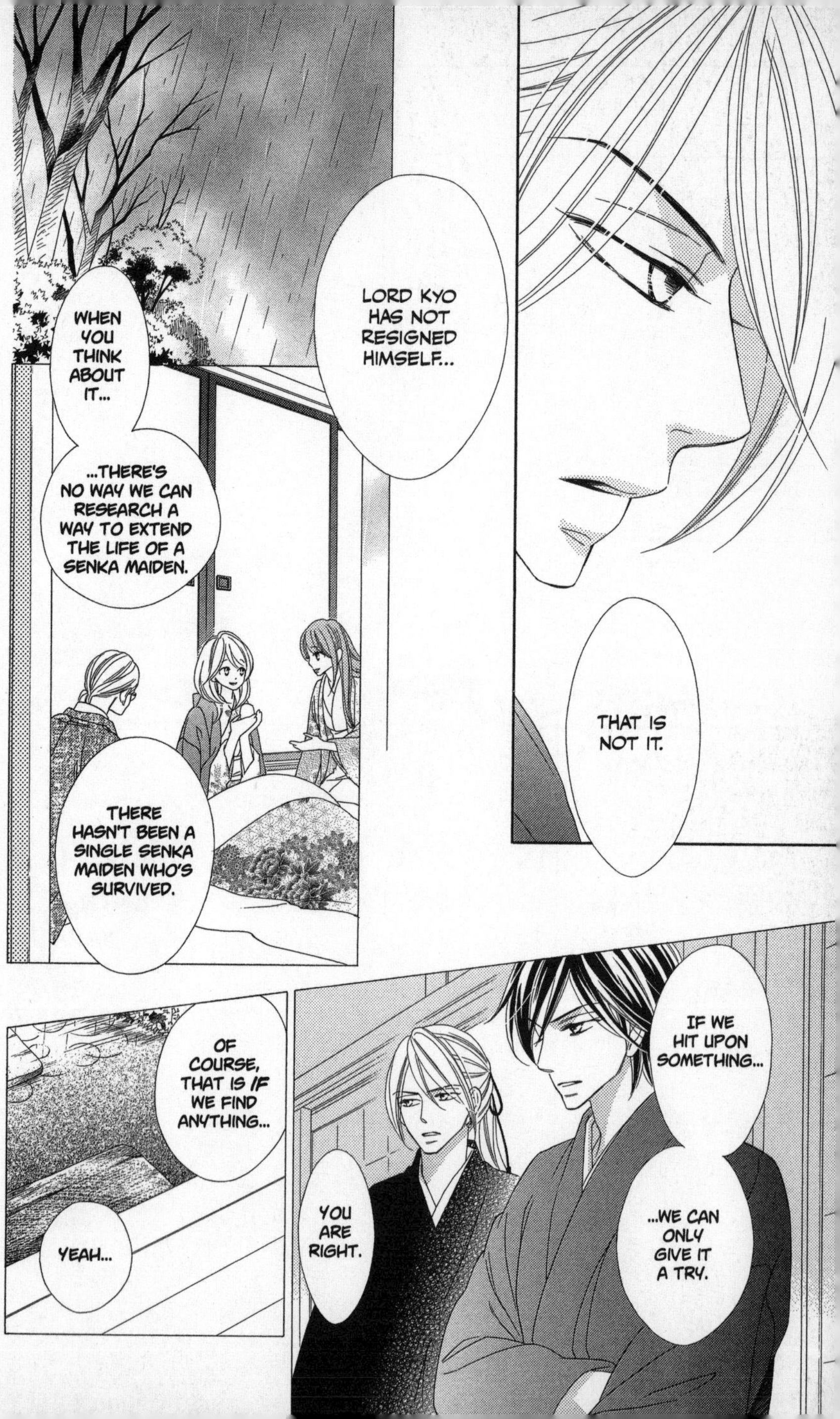
LORD KYO HAS NOT RESIGNED HIMSELF...
THAT IS NOT IT.
WHEN YOU THINK ABOUT IT...
...THERE'S NO WAY WE CAN RESEARCH A WAY TO EXTEND THE LIFE OF A SENKA MAIDEN.
THERE HASN'T BEEN A SINGLE SENKA MAIDEN WHO'S SURVIVED.
IF WE HIT UPON SOMETHING...
...WE CAN ONLY GIVE IT A TRY.
YOU ARE RIGHT.
OF COURSE, THAT IS *IF* WE FIND ANYTHING...
YEAH...

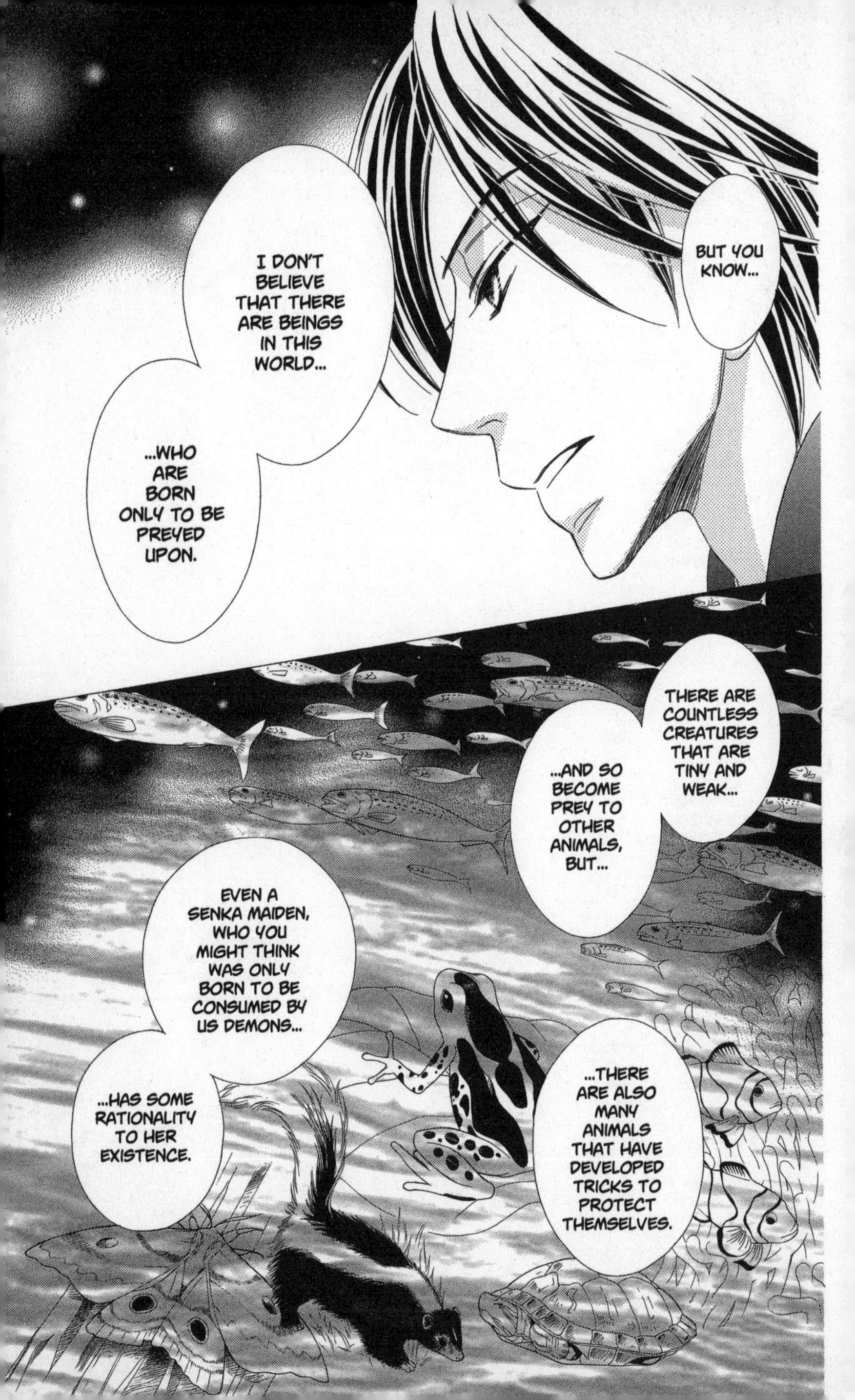
BUT YOU KNOW...
I DON'T BELIEVE THAT THERE ARE BEINGS IN THIS WORLD...
...WHO ARE BORN ONLY TO BE PREYED UPON.
THERE ARE COUNTLESS CREATURES THAT ARE TINY AND WEAK...
...AND SO BECOME PREY TO OTHER ANIMALS, BUT...
...THERE ARE ALSO MANY ANIMALS THAT HAVE DEVELOPED TRICKS TO PROTECT THEMSELVES.
EVEN A SENKA MAIDEN, WHO YOU MIGHT THINK WAS ONLY BORN TO BE CONSUMED BY US DEMONS...
...HAS SOME RATIONALITY TO HER EXISTENCE.

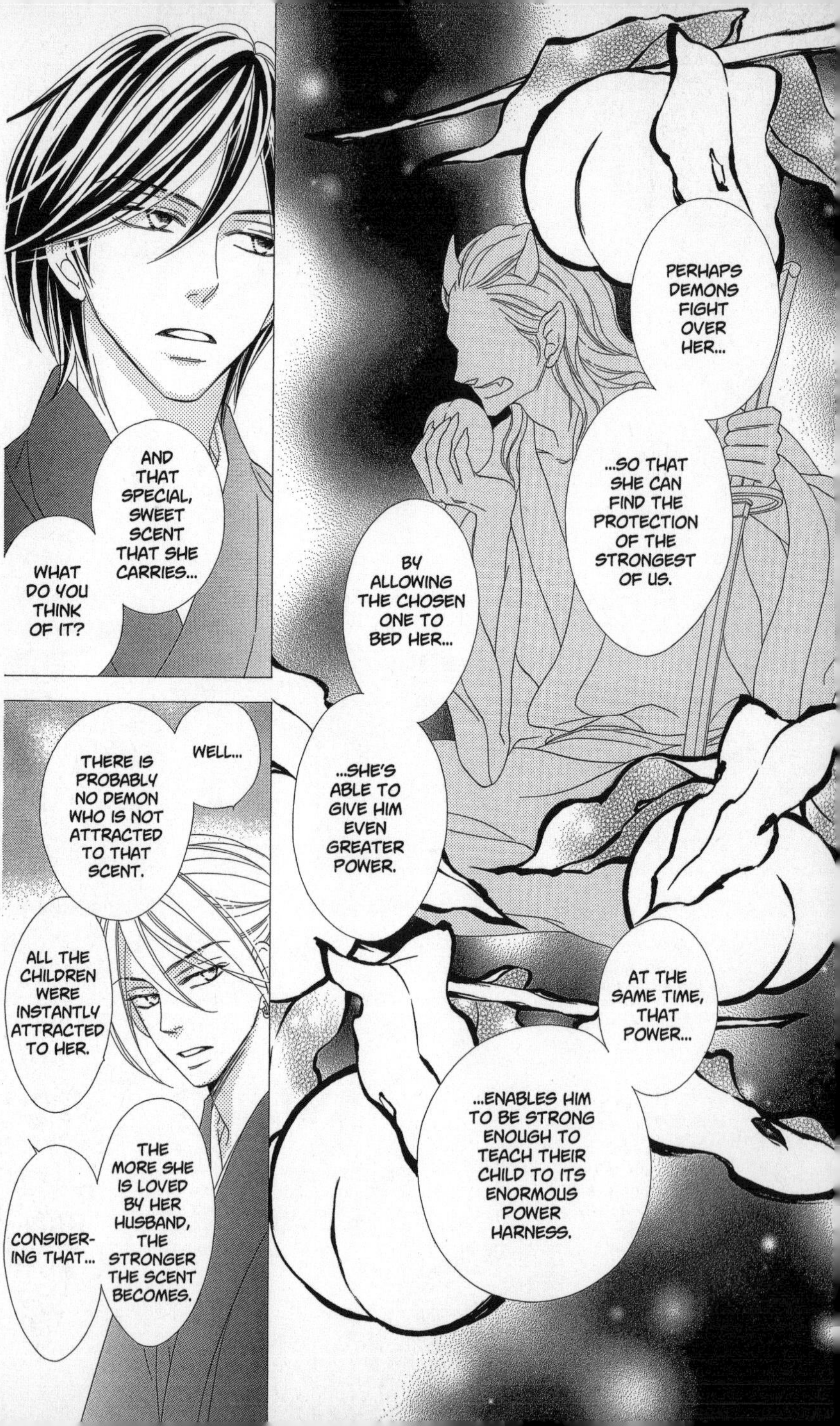
PERHAPS DEMONS FIGHT OVER HER...
...SO THAT SHE CAN FIND THE PROTECTION OF THE STRONGEST OF US.
BY ALLOWING THE CHOSEN ONE TO BED HER...
...SHE'S ABLE TO GIVE HIM EVEN GREATER POWER.
AT THE SAME TIME, THAT POWER...
...ENABLES HIM TO BE STRONG ENOUGH TO TEACH THEIR CHILD TO ITS ENORMOUS POWER HARNESS.
AND THAT SPECIAL, SWEET SCENT THAT SHE CARRIES...
WHAT DO YOU THINK OF IT?
WELL...
THERE IS PROBABLY NO DEMON WHO IS NOT ATTRACTED TO THAT SCENT.
ALL THE CHILDREN WERE INSTANTLY ATTRACTED TO HER.
THE MORE SHE IS LOVED BY HER HUSBAND, THE STRONGER THE SCENT BECOMES.
CONSIDER-ING THAT...

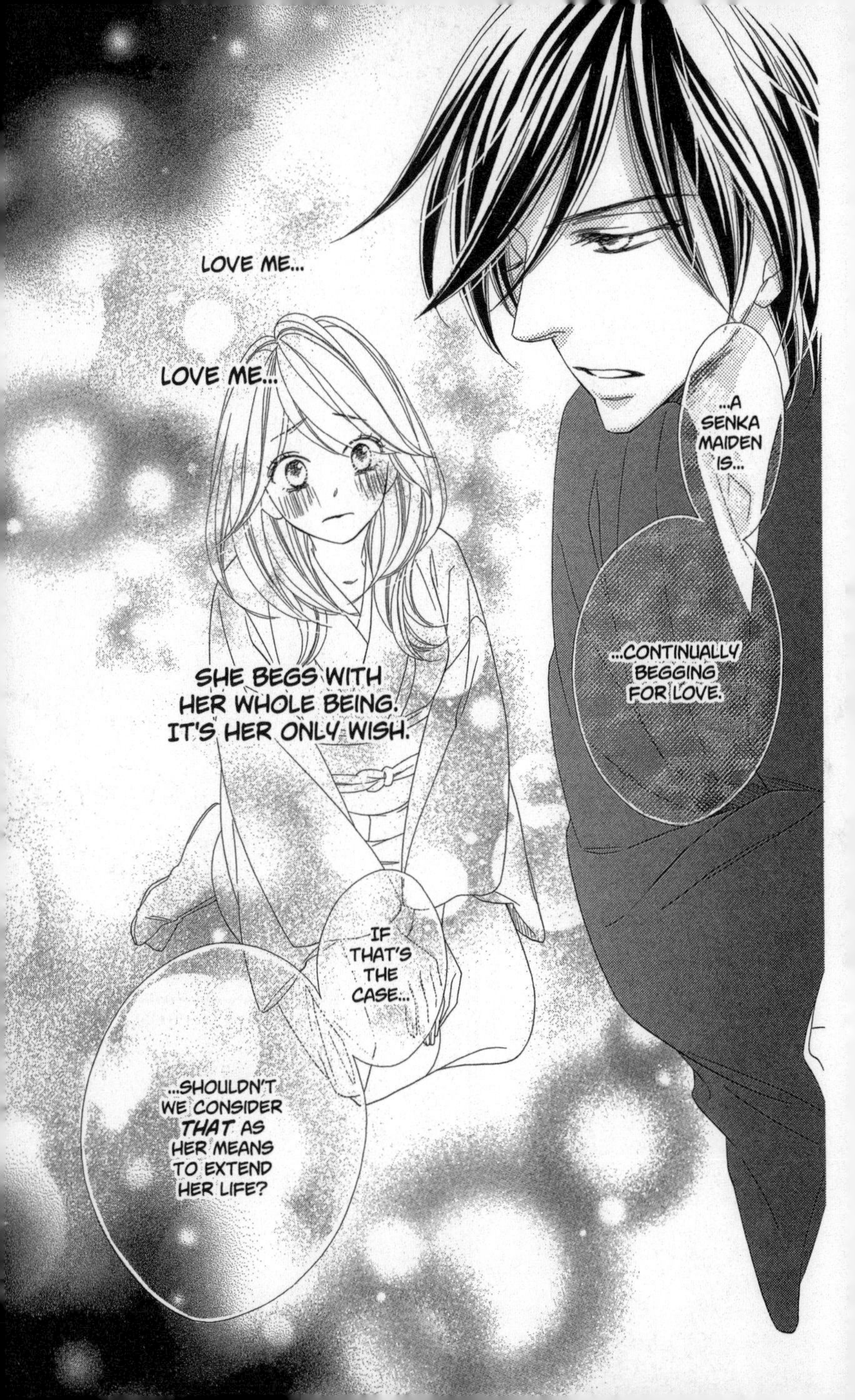
...A SENKA MAIDEN IS...
...CONTINUALLY BEGGING FOR LOVE.
LOVE ME...
LOVE ME...
SHE BEGS WITH HER WHOLE BEING. IT'S HER ONLY WISH.
IF THAT'S THE CASE...
...SHOULDN'T WE CONSIDER *THAT* AS HER MEANS TO EXTEND HER LIFE?

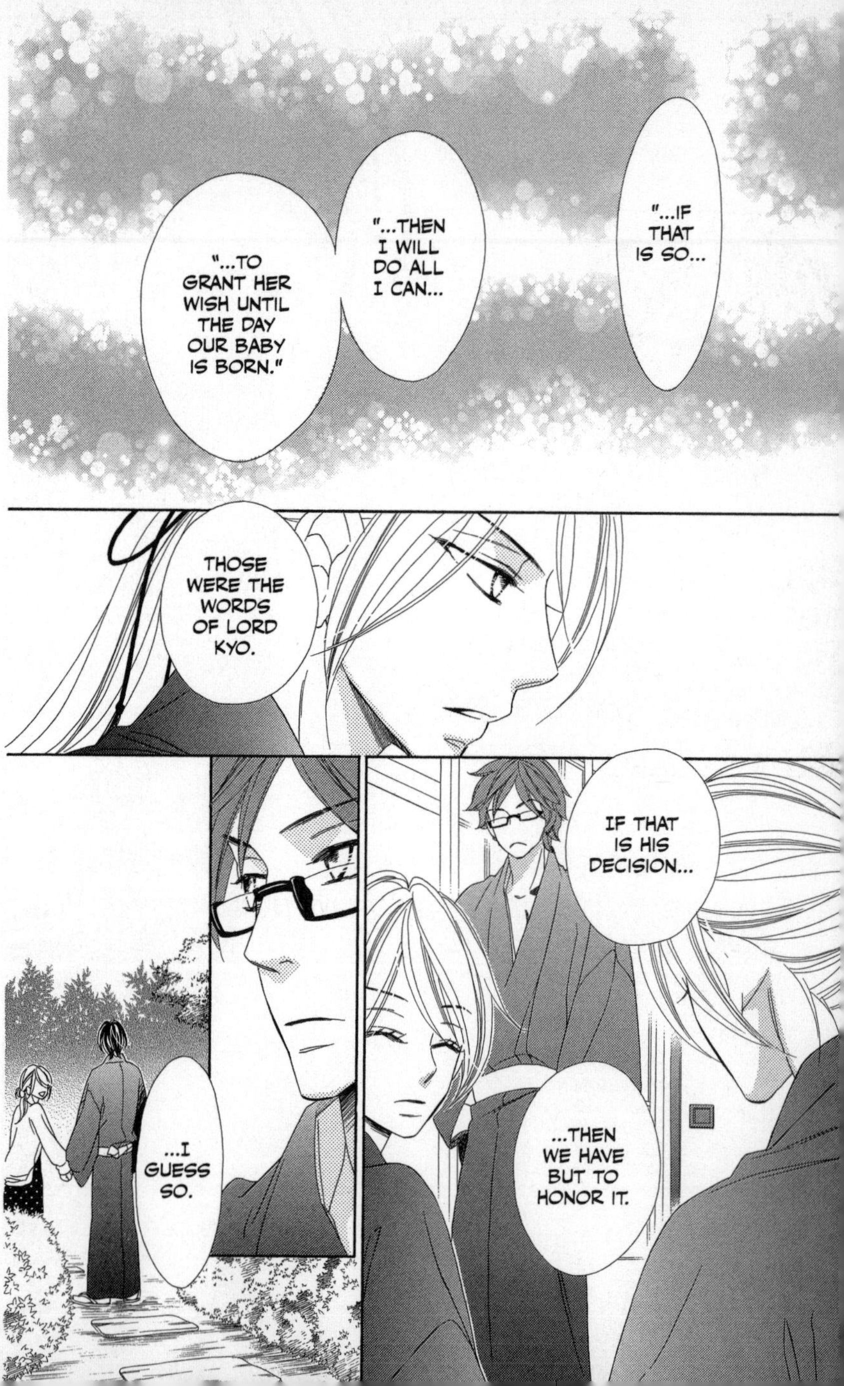
"...IF THAT IS SO...
"...THEN I WILL DO ALL I CAN...
"...TO GRANT HER WISH UNTIL THE DAY OUR BABY IS BORN."
THOSE WERE THE WORDS OF LORD KYO.
IF THAT IS HIS DECISION...
...THEN WE HAVE BUT TO HONOR IT.
...I GUESS SO.

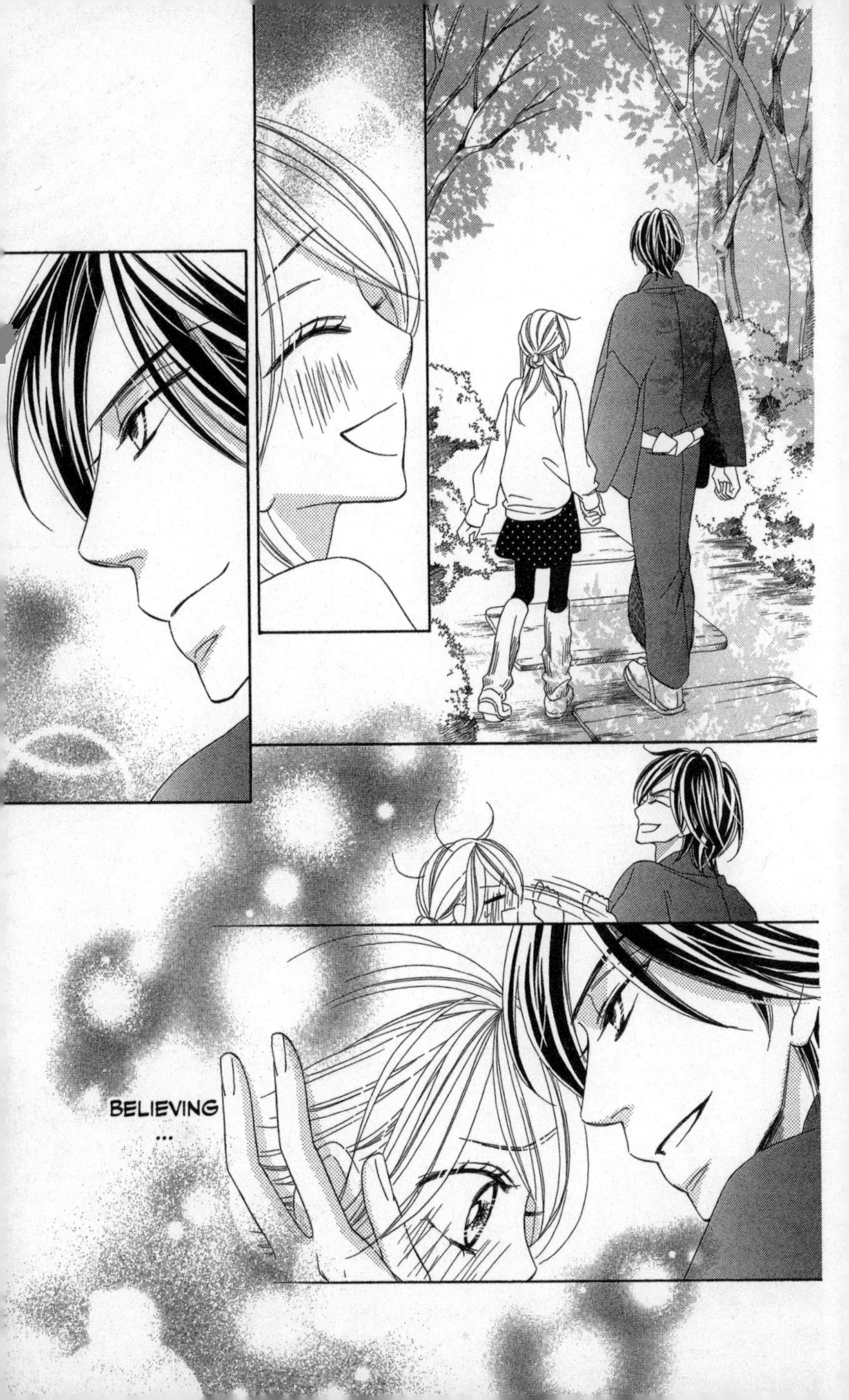
BELIEVING
...

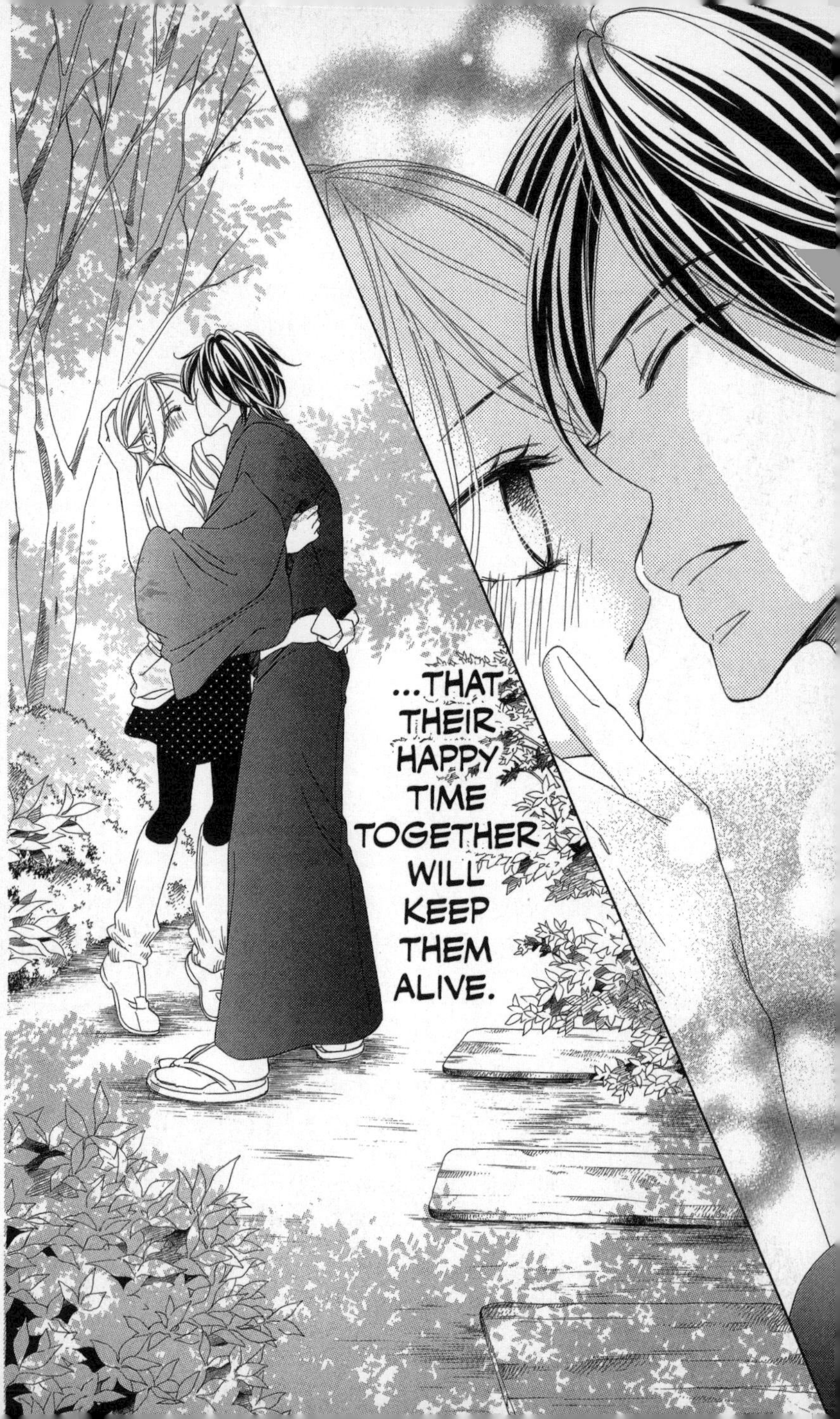
...THAT THEIR HAPPY TIME TOGETHER WILL KEEP THEM ALIVE.

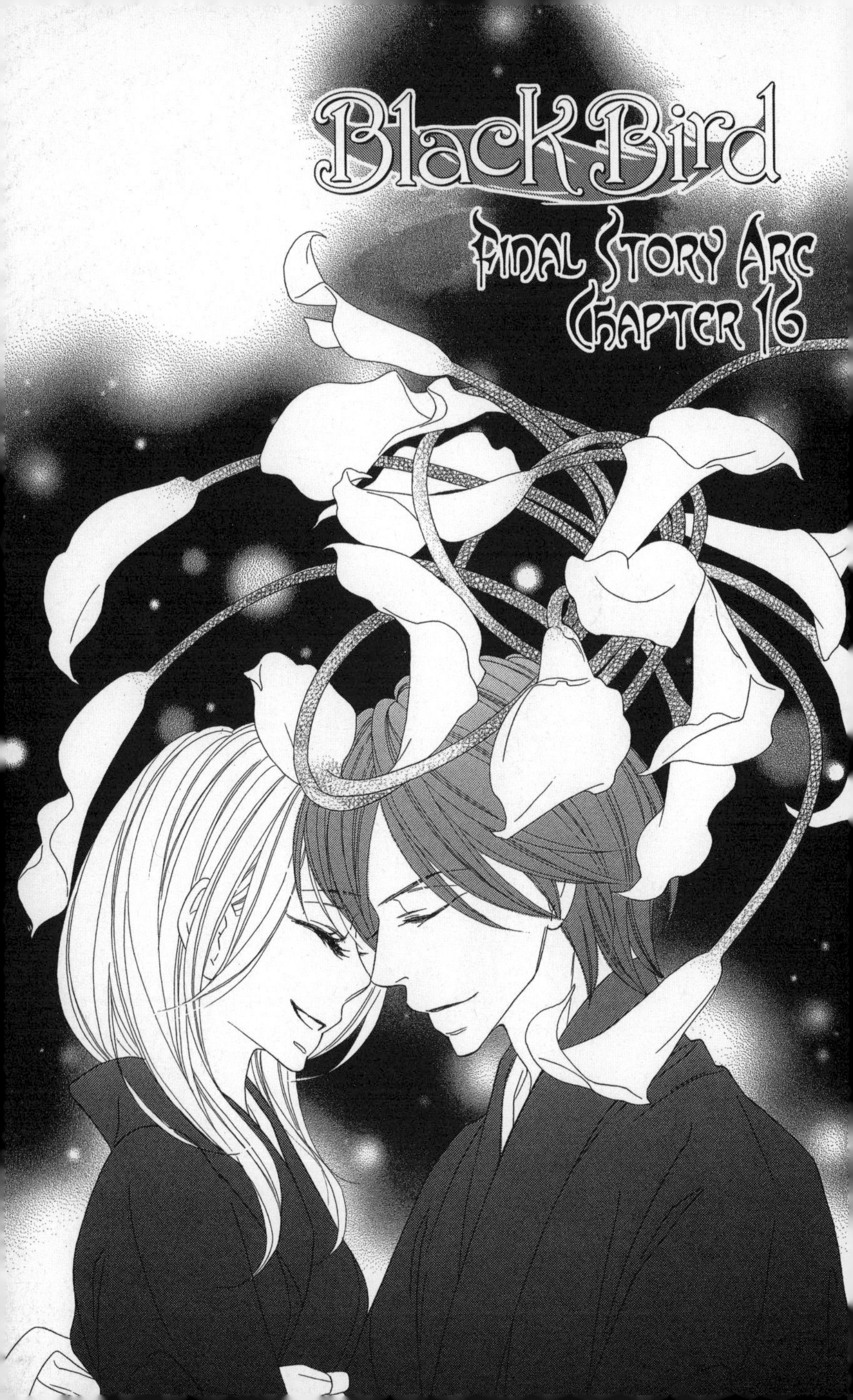
Black Bird
Final Story Arc
Chapter 16

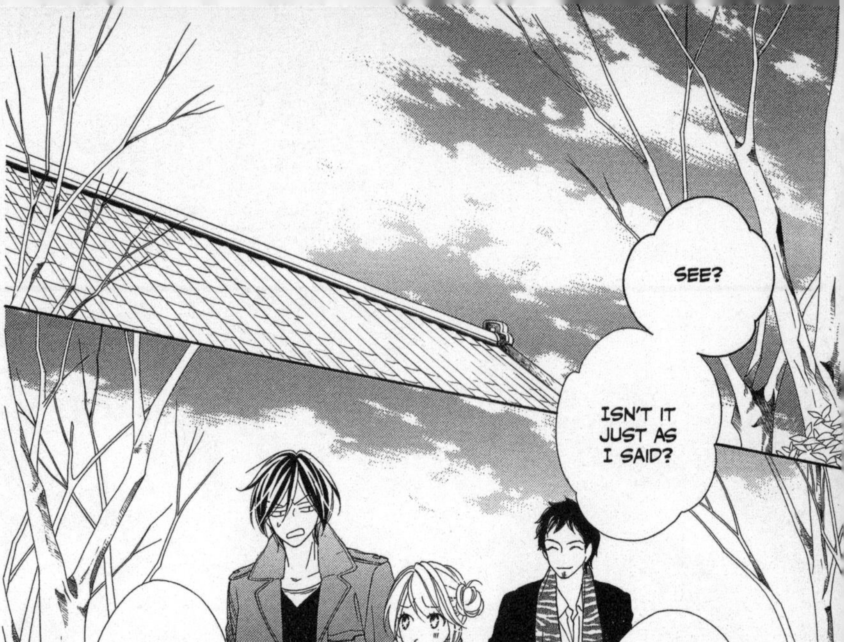
SEE?
ISN'T IT JUST AS I SAID?
I SWORE I MET HIM, BUT KYO...
WHO COULD BLAME ME FOR NOT BELIEVING...
...SOME-THING YOU SAW IN A DREAM...?

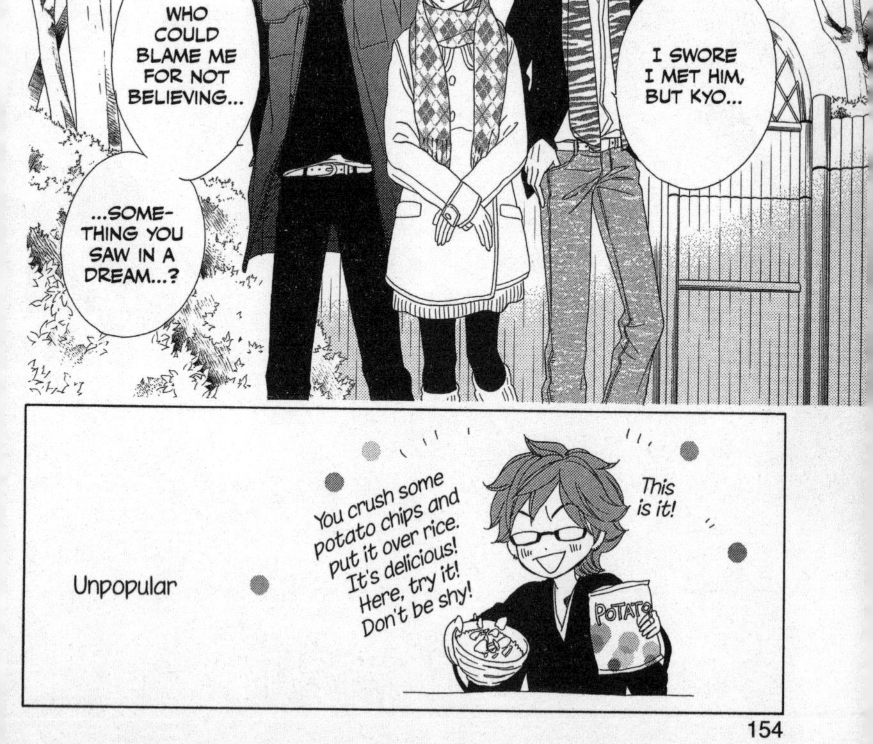
This is it!
You crush some potato chips and put it over rice. It's delicious! Here, try it! Don't be shy!
POTATO
Unpopular

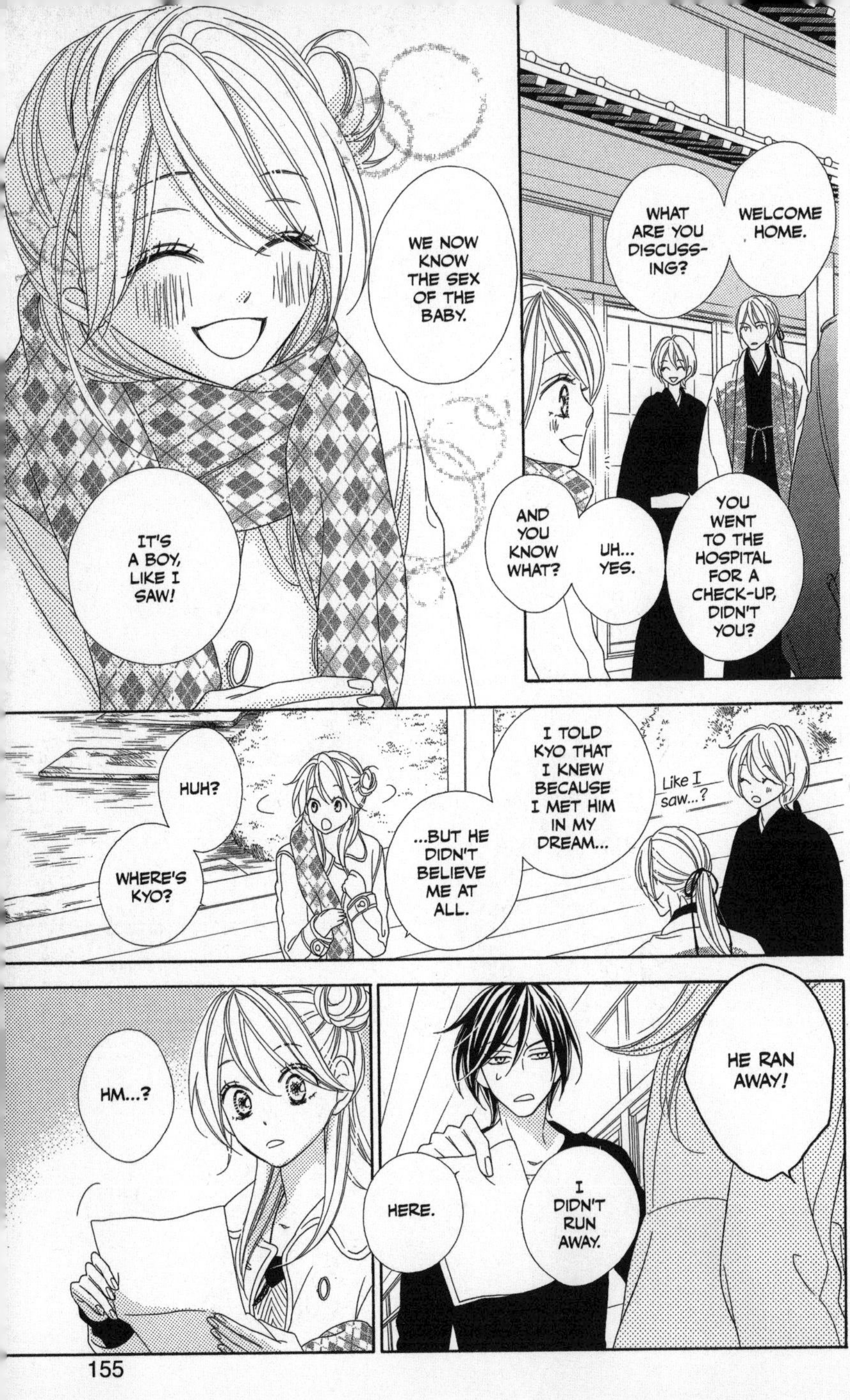

WELCOME HOME.
WHAT ARE YOU DISCUSS-ING?
YOU WENT TO THE HOSPITAL FOR A CHECK-UP, DIDN'T YOU?
UH... YES.
AND YOU KNOW WHAT?
WE NOW KNOW THE SEX OF THE BABY.
IT'S A BOY, LIKE I SAW!
Like I saw...?
I TOLD KYO THAT I KNEW BECAUSE I MET HIM IN MY DREAM...
...BUT HE DIDN'T BELIEVE ME AT ALL.
HUH?
WHERE'S KYO?
HE RAN AWAY!
I DIDN'T RUN AWAY.
HERE.
HM...?

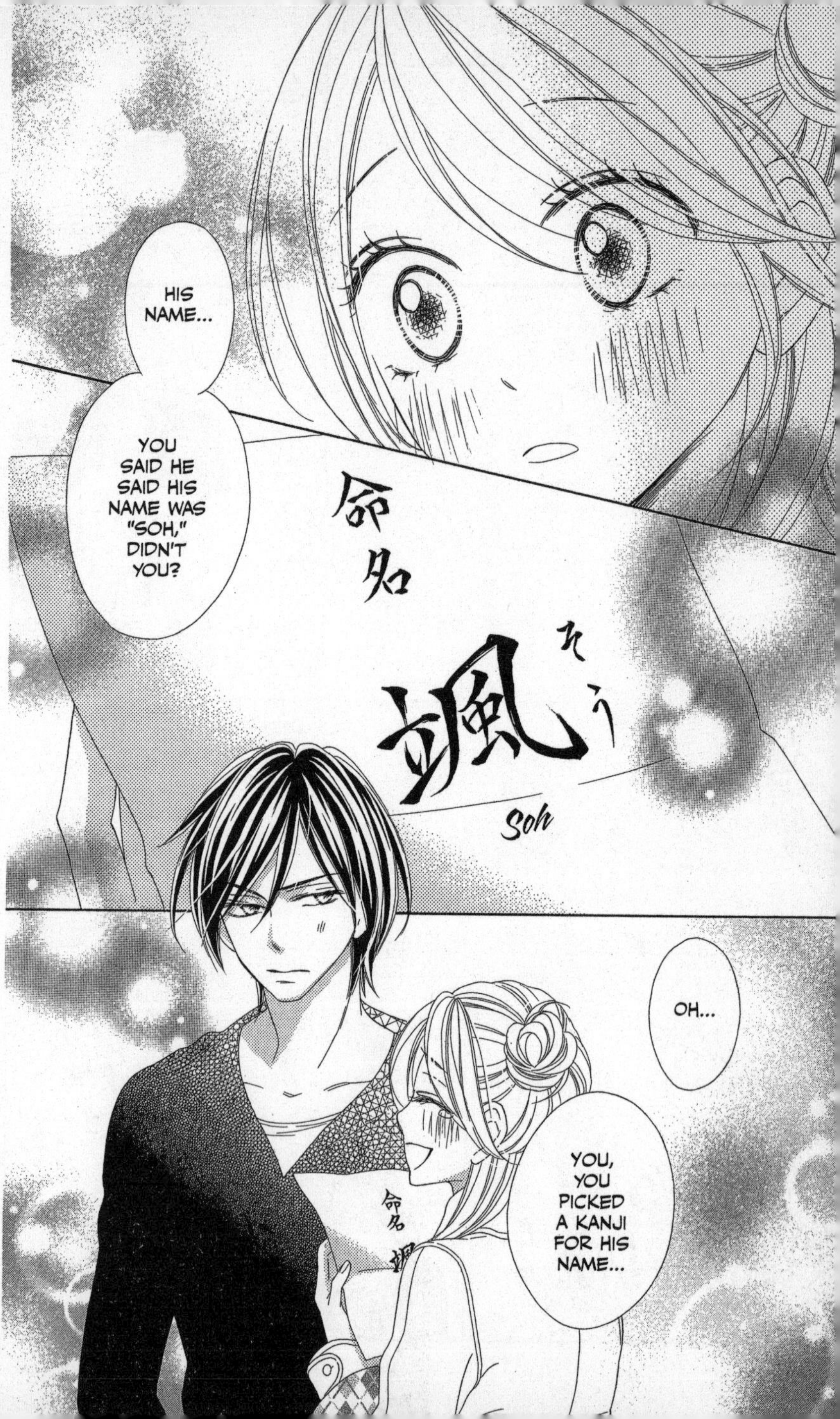
HIS NAME...
YOU SAID HE SAID HIS NAME WAS "SOH," DIDN'T YOU?
命名
颯
Soh
OH...
YOU, YOU PICKED A KANJI FOR HIS NAME...

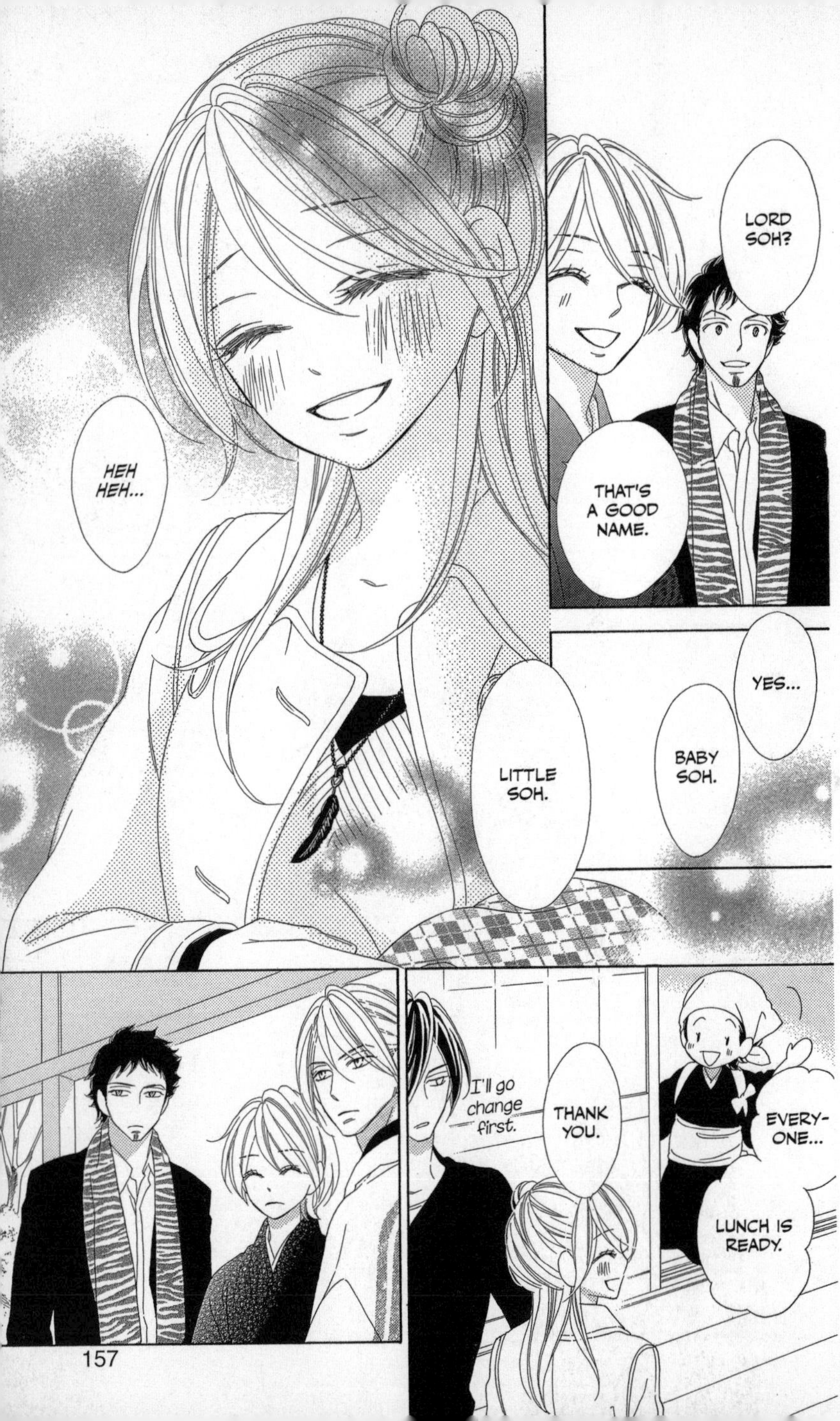
LORD SOH?
THAT'S A GOOD NAME.
YES...
BABY SOH.
LITTLE SOH.
HEH HEH...
EVERY-ONE...
LUNCH IS READY.
THANK YOU.
I'll go change first.

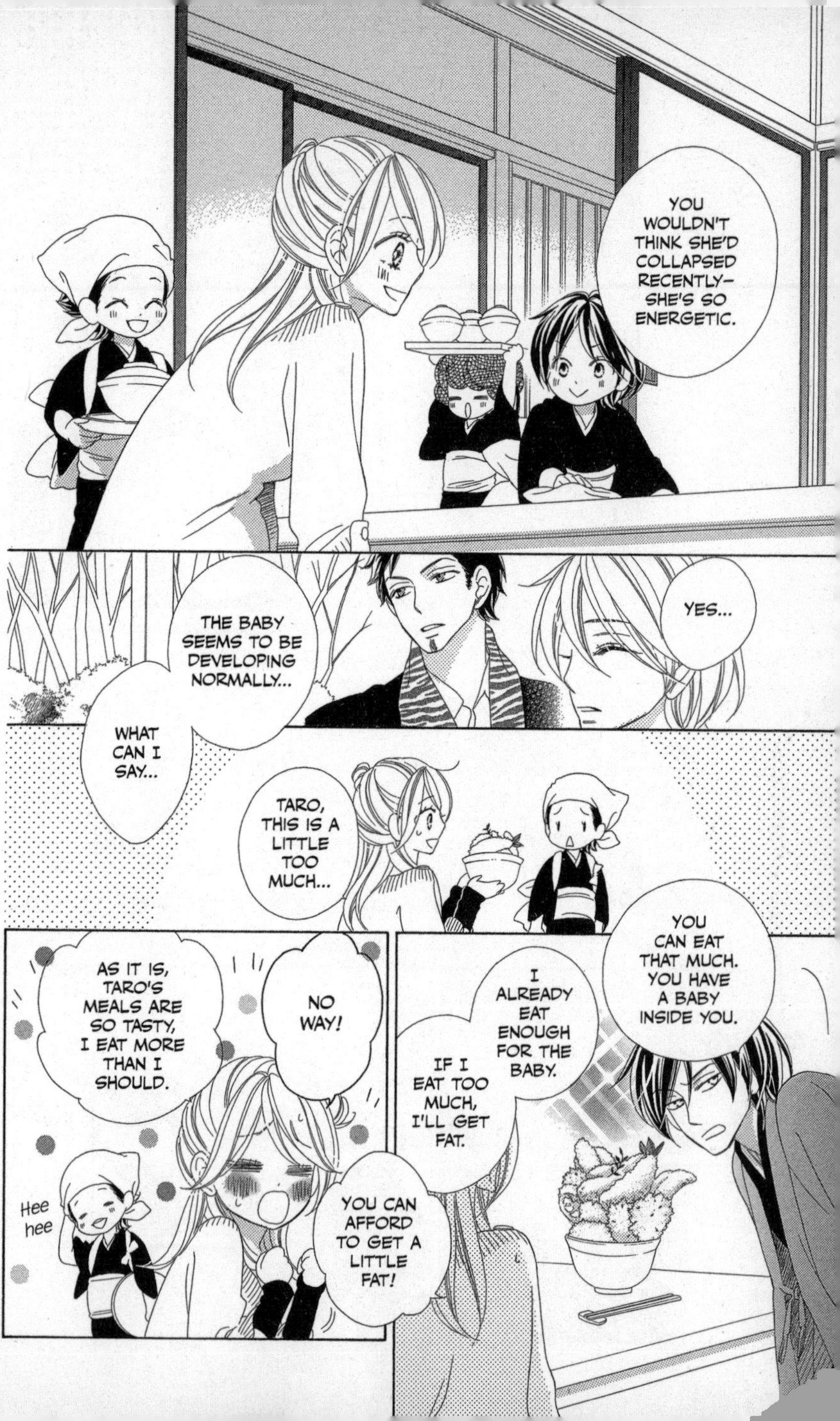
YOU WOULDN'T THINK SHE'D COLLAPSED RECENTLY— SHE'S SO ENERGETIC.
YES...
THE BABY SEEMS TO BE DEVELOPING NORMALLY...
WHAT CAN I SAY...
TARO, THIS IS A LITTLE TOO MUCH...
YOU CAN EAT THAT MUCH. YOU HAVE A BABY INSIDE YOU.
I ALREADY EAT ENOUGH FOR THE BABY.
IF I EAT TOO MUCH, I'LL GET FAT.
YOU CAN AFFORD TO GET A LITTLE FAT!
NO WAY!
AS IT IS, TARO'S MEALS ARE SO TASTY, I EAT MORE THAN I SHOULD.
Hee hee

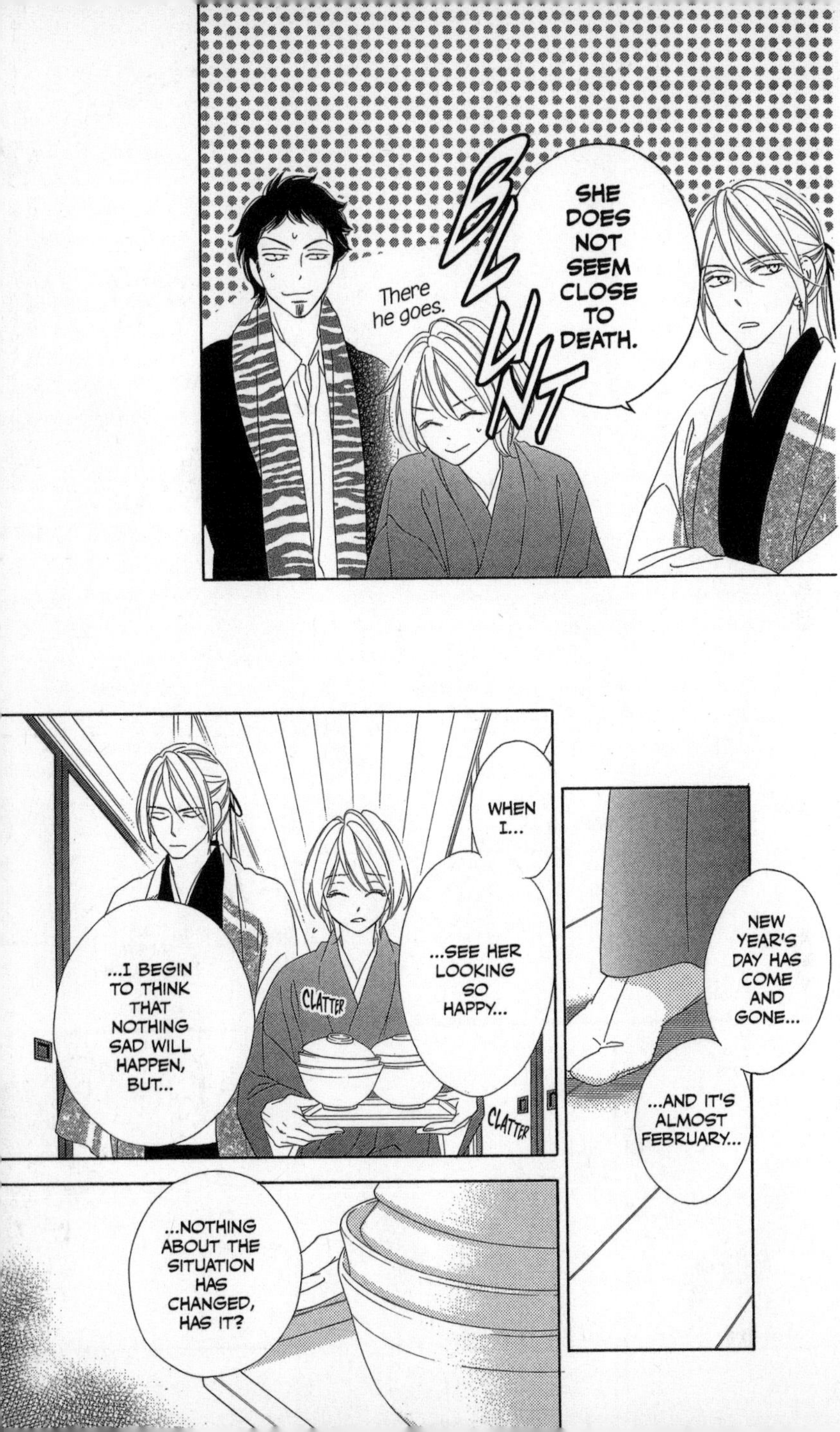
SHE DOES NOT SEEM CLOSE TO DEATH.
BLUNT
There he goes.
NEW YEAR'S DAY HAS COME AND GONE...
...AND IT'S ALMOST FEBRUARY...
WHEN I...
...SEE HER LOOKING SO HAPPY...
...I BEGIN TO THINK THAT NOTHING SAD WILL HAPPEN, BUT...
CLATTER
CLATTER
...NOTHING ABOUT THE SITUATION HAS CHANGED, HAS IT?

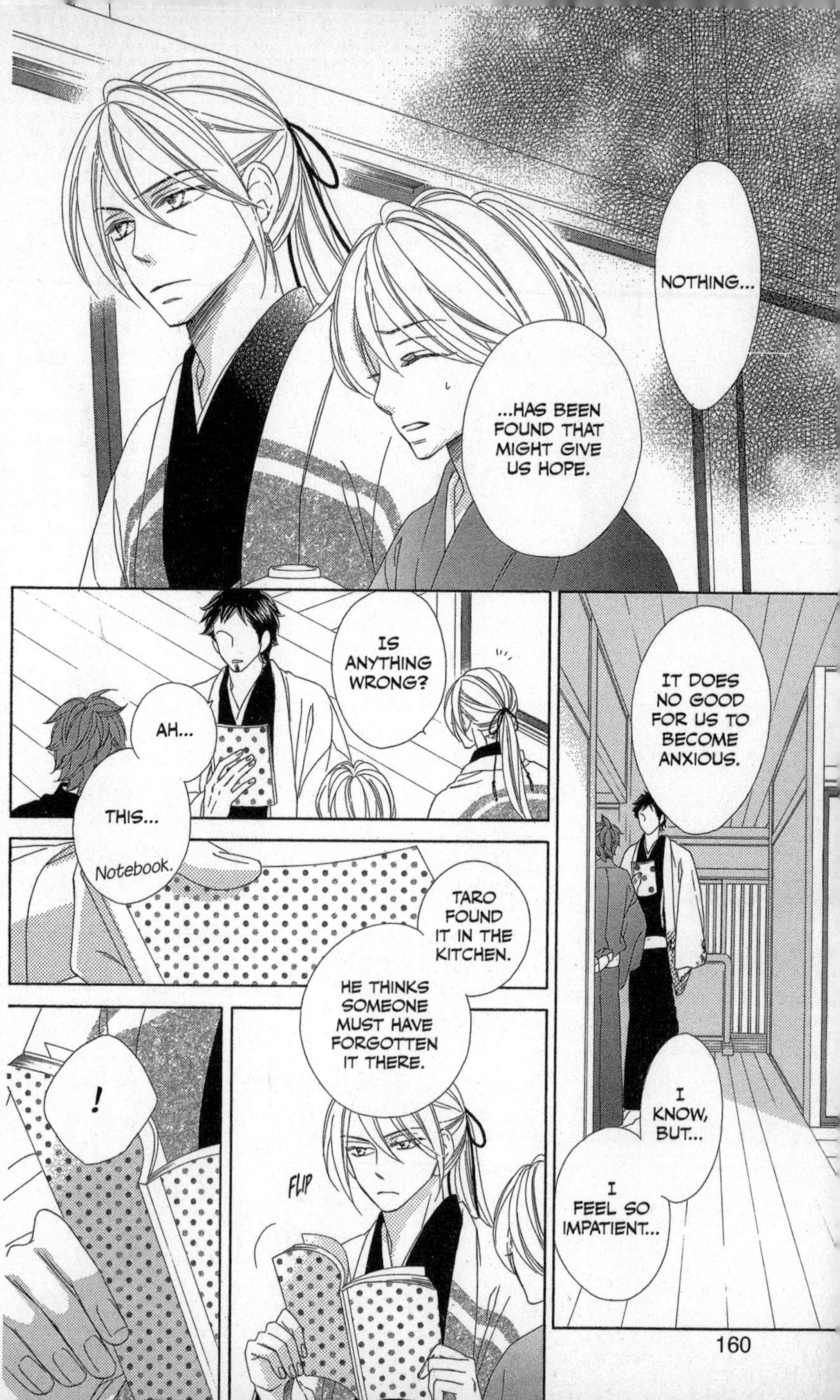

NOTHING...
...HAS BEEN FOUND THAT MIGHT GIVE US HOPE.
IT DOES NO GOOD FOR US TO BECOME ANXIOUS.
I KNOW, BUT...
I FEEL SO IMPATIENT...
IS ANYTHING WRONG?
AH...
THIS...
Notebook.
TARO FOUND IT IN THE KITCHEN.
HE THINKS SOMEONE MUST HAVE FORGOTTEN IT THERE.
FLIP
!

THE LADY MISAO...
YEAH...
A DIARY...
...NO...
December 6
Soh, you were very good today. Mommy had an easy time. I talk to you every day. Can you hea me? Today, I watched my favorite comedy DVD. I laughed out loud. Your dad said he couldn't understand. I hope I can watch it with you someday, Soh.
IT'S A LETTER...!
I talk to you every day.
IF SOMETHING HAPPENS TO HER...
...I GUESS SHE THINKS HE'LL UNDER-STAND HER FEELINGS FOR HIM, BUT...
ber 12
You've gotten quite big, Soh. Every day, you move a little. You'll probably grow into a very healthy boy. ...I look forward to it! strong and gentle like
I love you, my darling Soh.
I'll always be
Soh
THIS ISN'T GOOD.

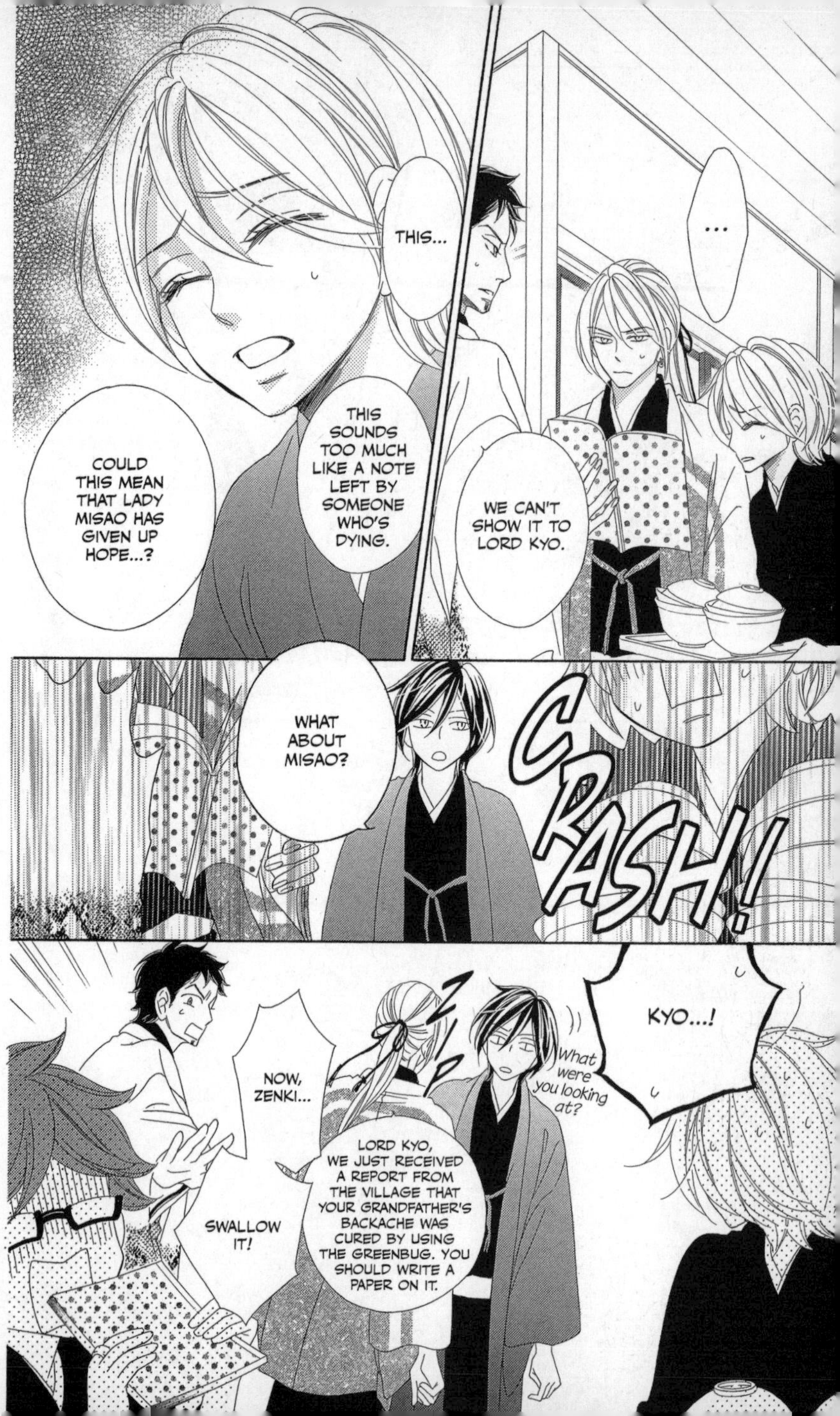
...
THIS...
WE CAN'T SHOW IT TO LORD KYO.
THIS SOUNDS TOO MUCH LIKE A NOTE LEFT BY SOMEONE WHO'S DYING.
COULD THIS MEAN THAT LADY MISAO HAS GIVEN UP HOPE...?
CRASH!
WHAT ABOUT MISAO?
KYO...!
What were you looking at?
ZIP
LORD KYO, WE JUST RECEIVED A REPORT FROM THE VILLAGE THAT YOUR GRANDFATHER'S BACKACHE WAS CURED BY USING THE GREENBUG. YOU SHOULD WRITE A PAPER ON IT.
NOW, ZENKI...
SWALLOW IT!

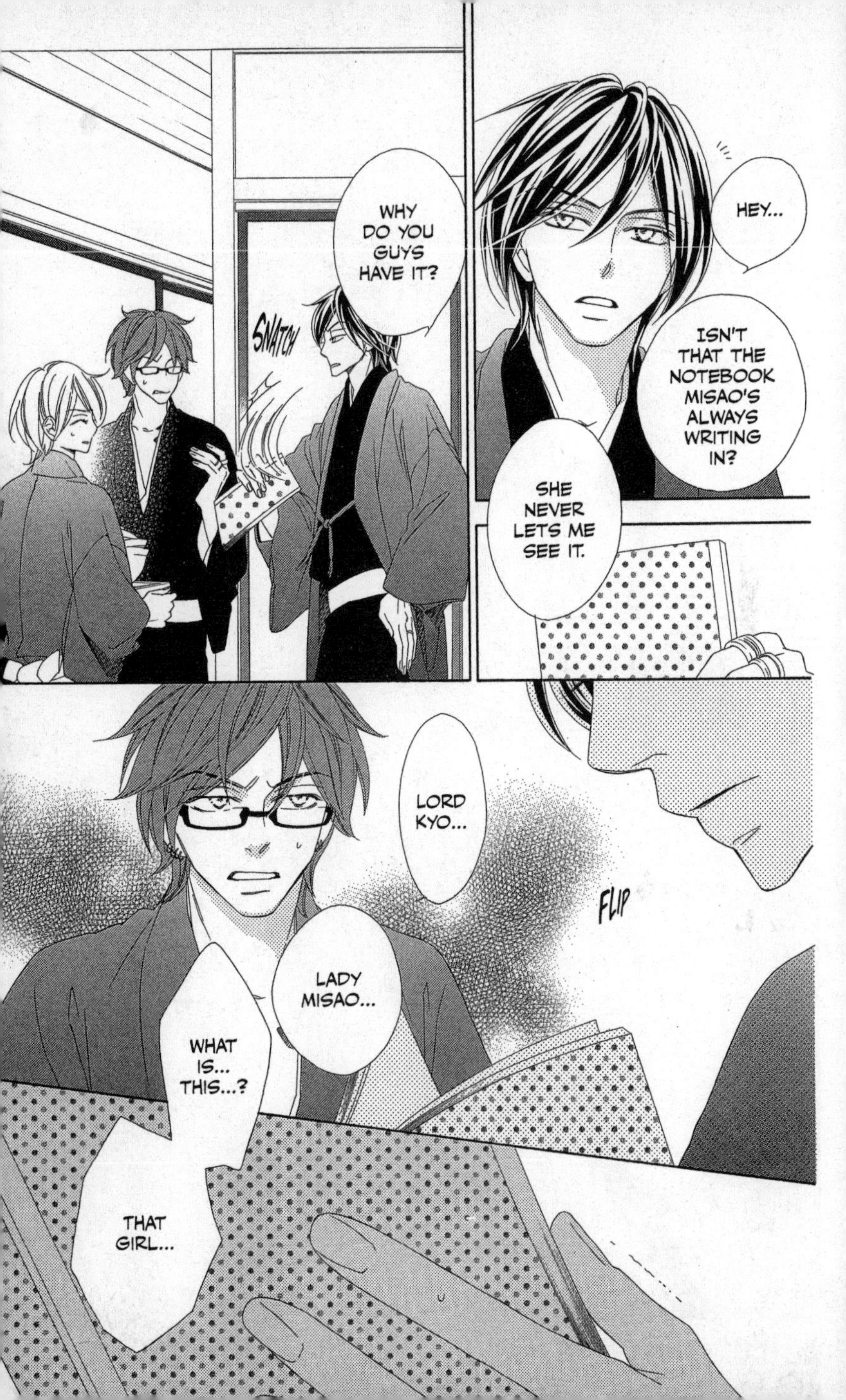
HEY...
ISN'T THAT THE NOTEBOOK MISAO'S ALWAYS WRITING IN?
SHE NEVER LETS ME SEE IT.
WHY DO YOU GUYS HAVE IT?
SNATCH
FLIP
LORD KYO...
LADY MISAO...
WHAT IS... THIS...?
THAT GIRL...

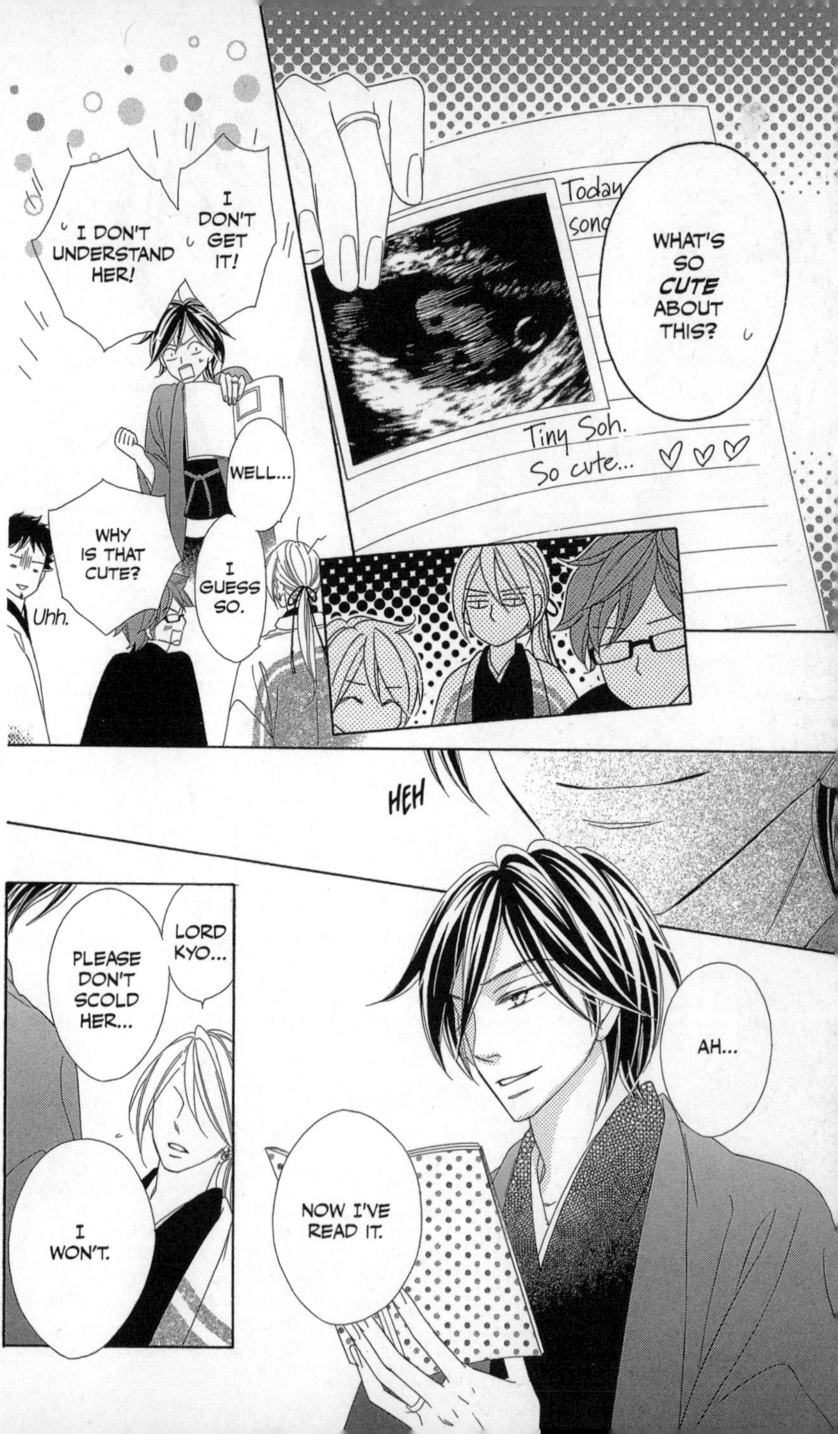
Today
song
Tiny Soh.
So cute...
WHAT'S SO CUTE ABOUT THIS?
I DON'T GET IT!
I DON'T UNDERSTAND HER!
WELL...
I GUESS SO.
WHY IS THAT CUTE?
Uhh.
HEH
AH...
NOW I'VE READ IT.
LORD KYO...
PLEASE DON'T SCOLD HER...
I WON'T.

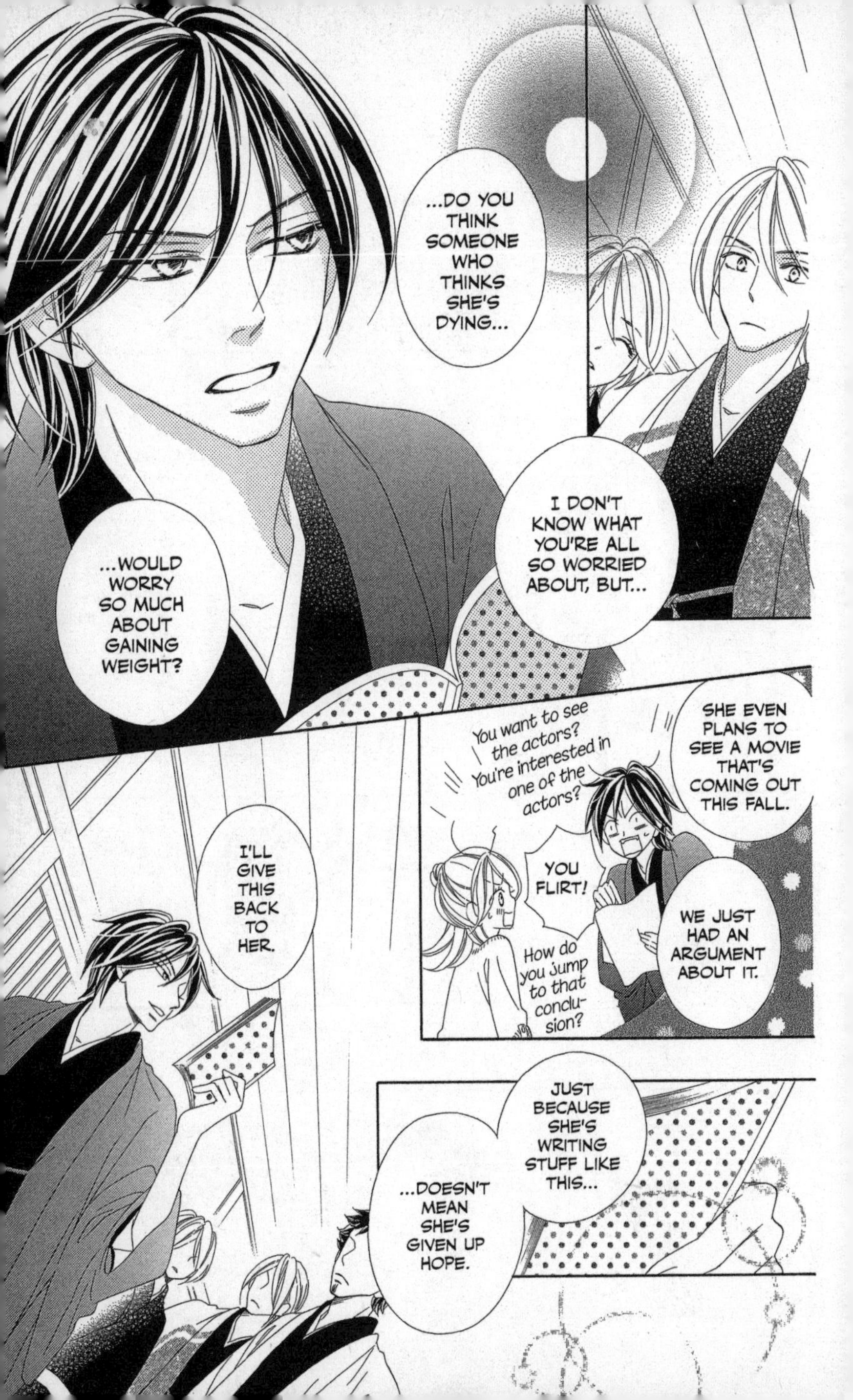
I DON'T KNOW WHAT YOU'RE ALL SO WORRIED ABOUT, BUT...
...DO YOU THINK SOMEONE WHO THINKS SHE'S DYING...
...WOULD WORRY SO MUCH ABOUT GAINING WEIGHT?
SHE EVEN PLANS TO SEE A MOVIE THAT'S COMING OUT THIS FALL.
You want to see the actors? You're interested in one of the actors?
YOU FLIRT!
How do you jump to that conclusion?
WE JUST HAD AN ARGUMENT ABOUT IT.
JUST BECAUSE SHE'S WRITING STUFF LIKE THIS...
...DOESN'T MEAN SHE'S GIVEN UP HOPE.
I'LL GIVE THIS BACK TO HER.

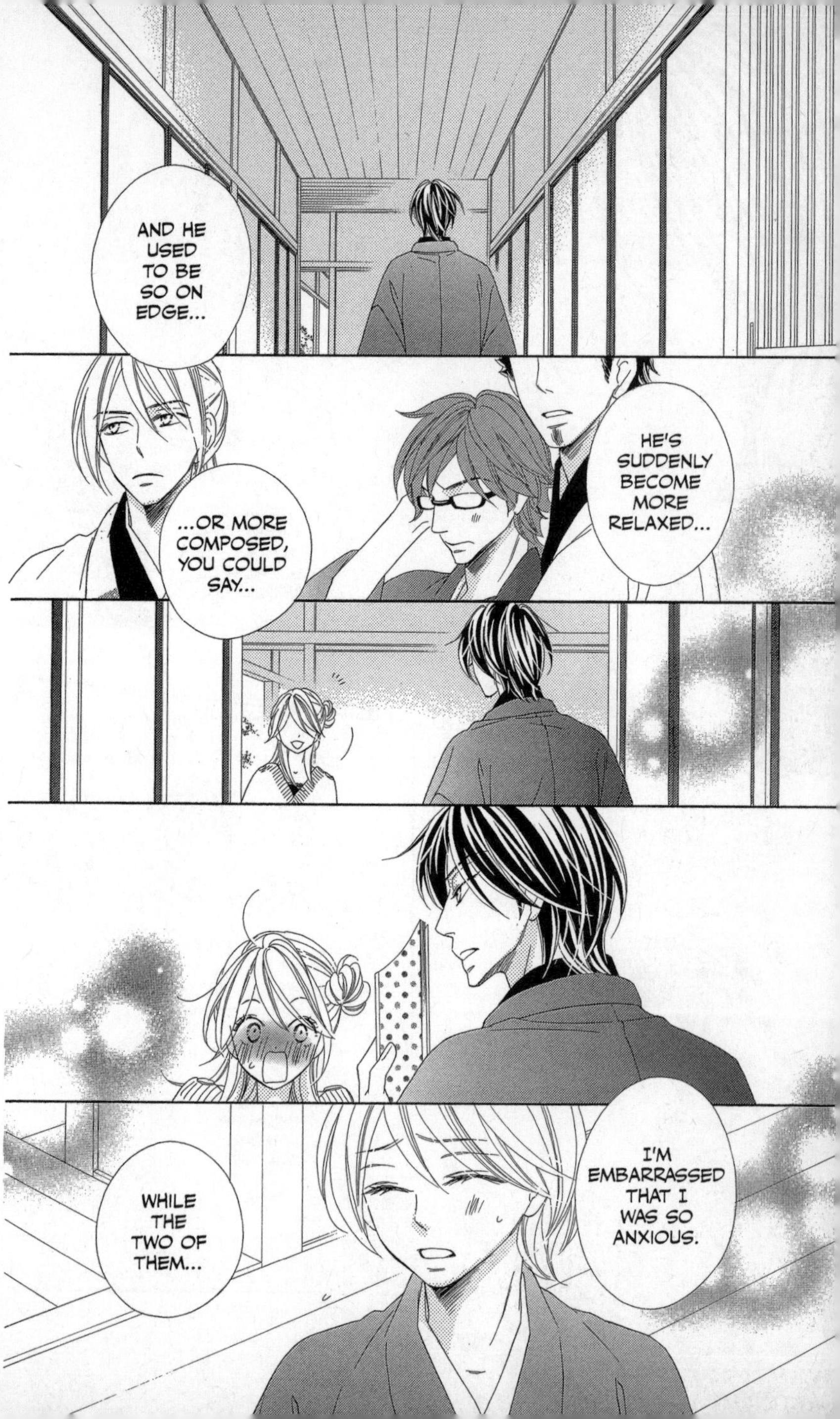
AND HE USED TO BE SO ON EDGE...
HE'S SUDDENLY BECOME MORE RELAXED...
...OR MORE COMPOSED, YOU COULD SAY...
I'M EMBARRASSED THAT I WAS SO ANXIOUS.
WHILE THE TWO OF THEM...

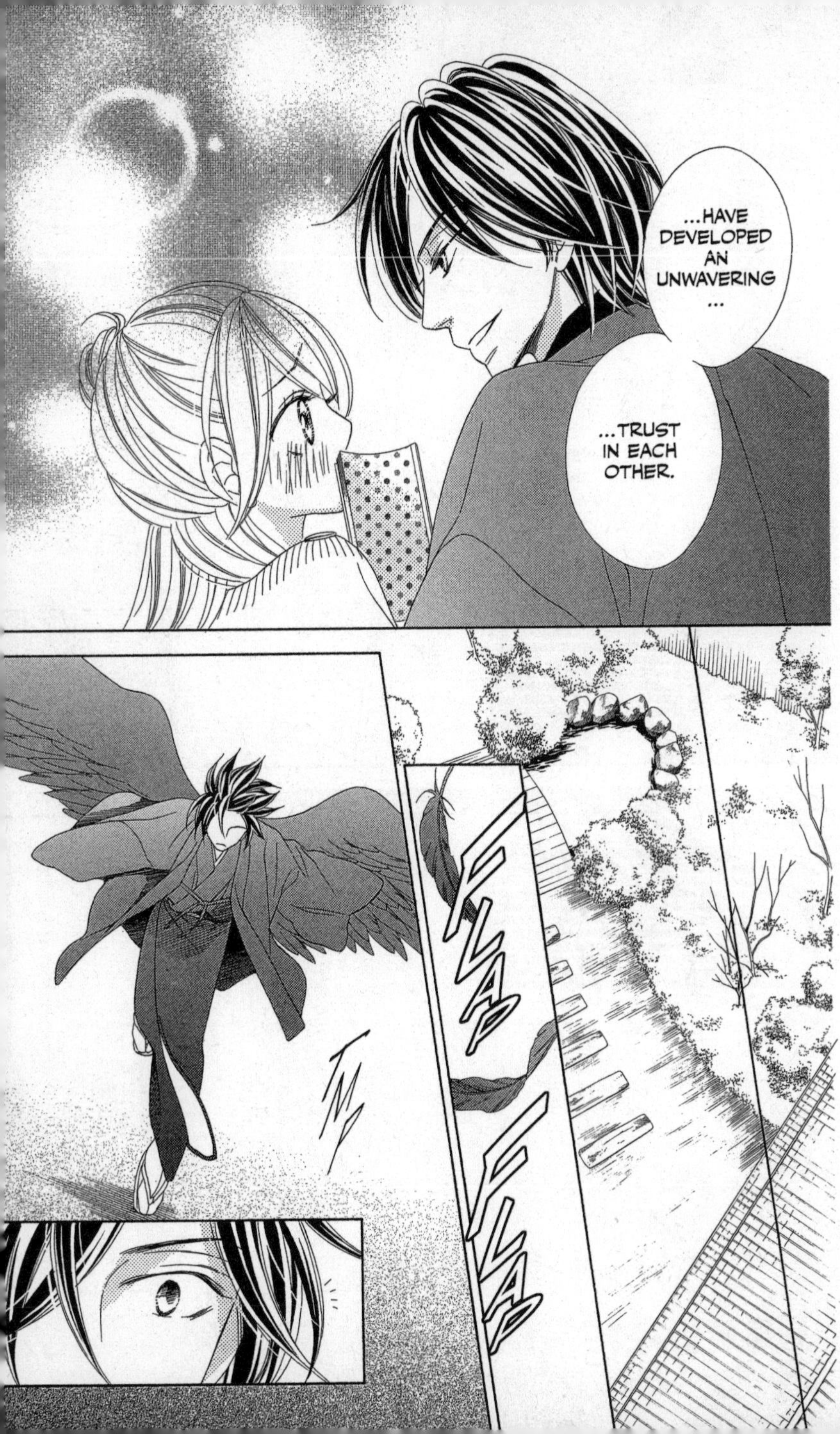
...HAVE DEVELOPED AN UNWAVERING ...
...TRUST IN EACH OTHER.

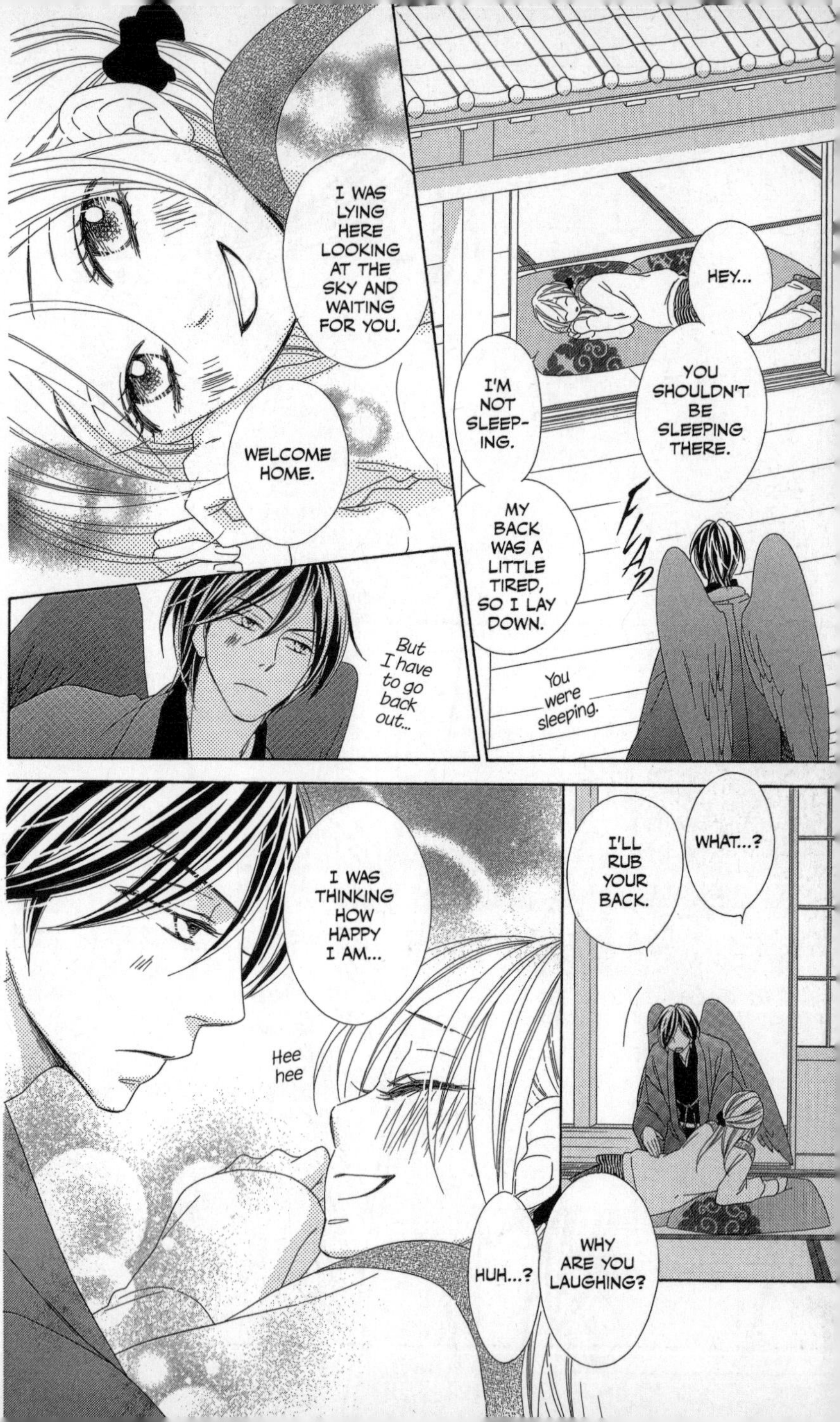
HEY...
YOU SHOULDN'T BE SLEEPING THERE.
I'M NOT SLEEPING.
FLAP
MY BACK WAS A LITTLE TIRED, SO I LAY DOWN.
You were sleeping.
I WAS LYING HERE LOOKING AT THE SKY AND WAITING FOR YOU.
WELCOME HOME.
But I have to go back out...
WHAT...?
I'LL RUB YOUR BACK.
WHY ARE YOU LAUGHING?
HUH...?
I WAS THINKING HOW HAPPY I AM...
Hee hee

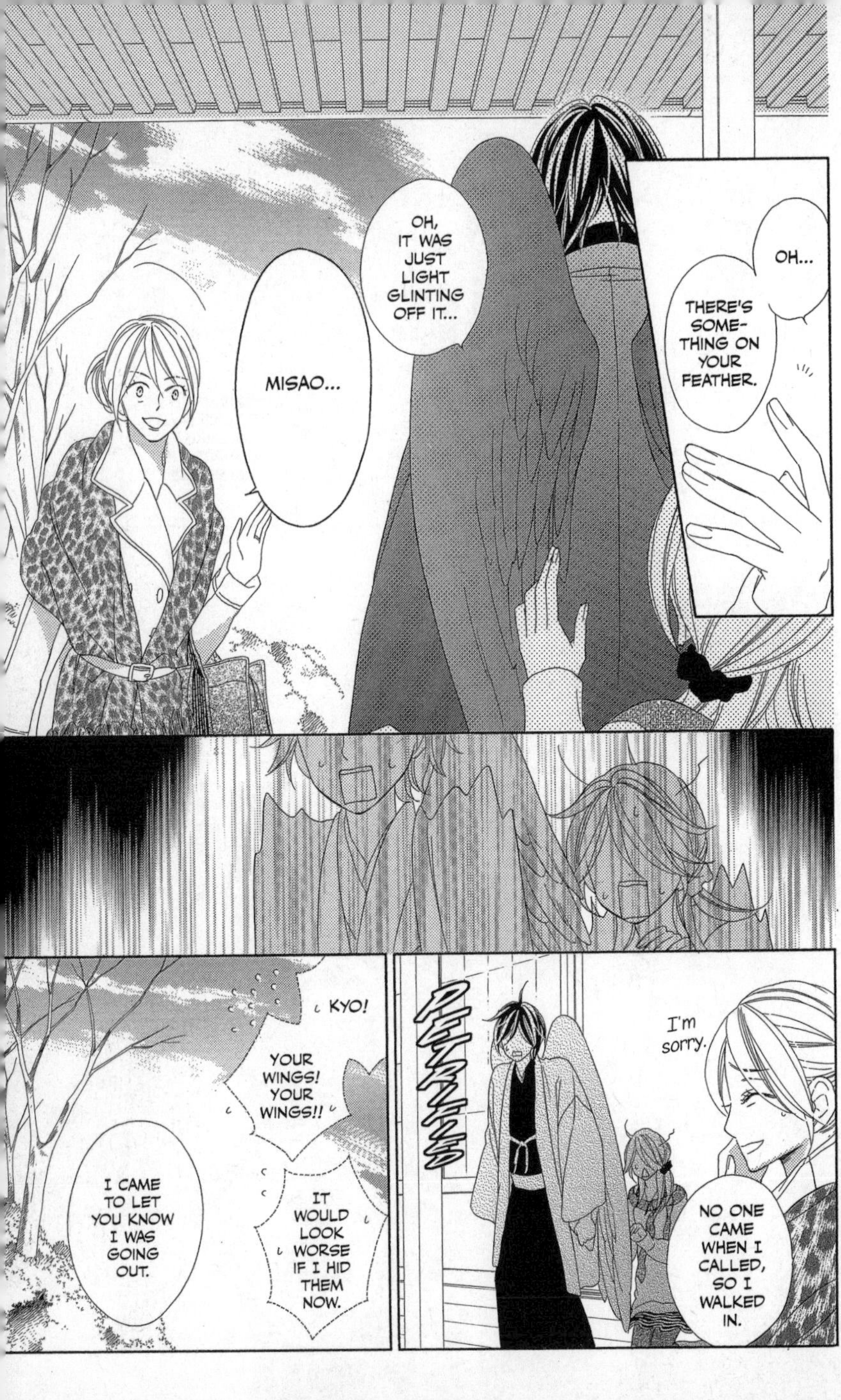
OH...
THERE'S SOME-THING ON YOUR FEATHER.
OH, IT WAS JUST LIGHT GLINTING OFF IT...
MISAO...
I'm sorry.
NO ONE CAME WHEN I CALLED, SO I WALKED IN.
KYO!
YOUR WINGS! YOUR WINGS!!
IT WOULD LOOK WORSE IF I HID THEM NOW.
I CAME TO LET YOU KNOW I WAS GOING OUT.

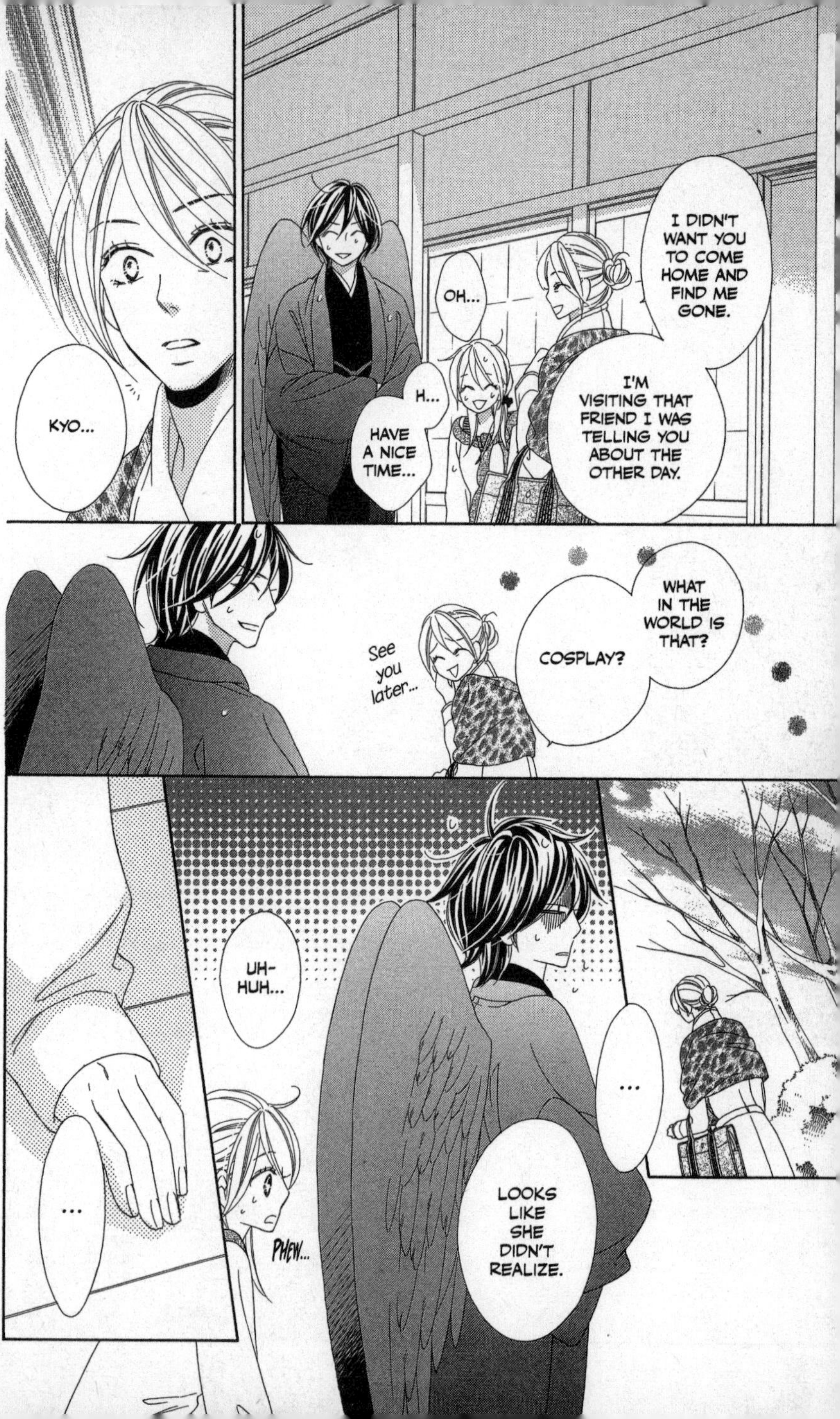
I DIDN'T WANT YOU TO COME HOME AND FIND ME GONE.
I'M VISITING THAT FRIEND I WAS TELLING YOU ABOUT THE OTHER DAY.
OH...
H... HAVE A NICE TIME...
KYO...
WHAT IN THE WORLD IS THAT?
COSPLAY?
See you later...
UH-HUH...
...
LOOKS LIKE SHE DIDN'T REALIZE.
PHEW...
...

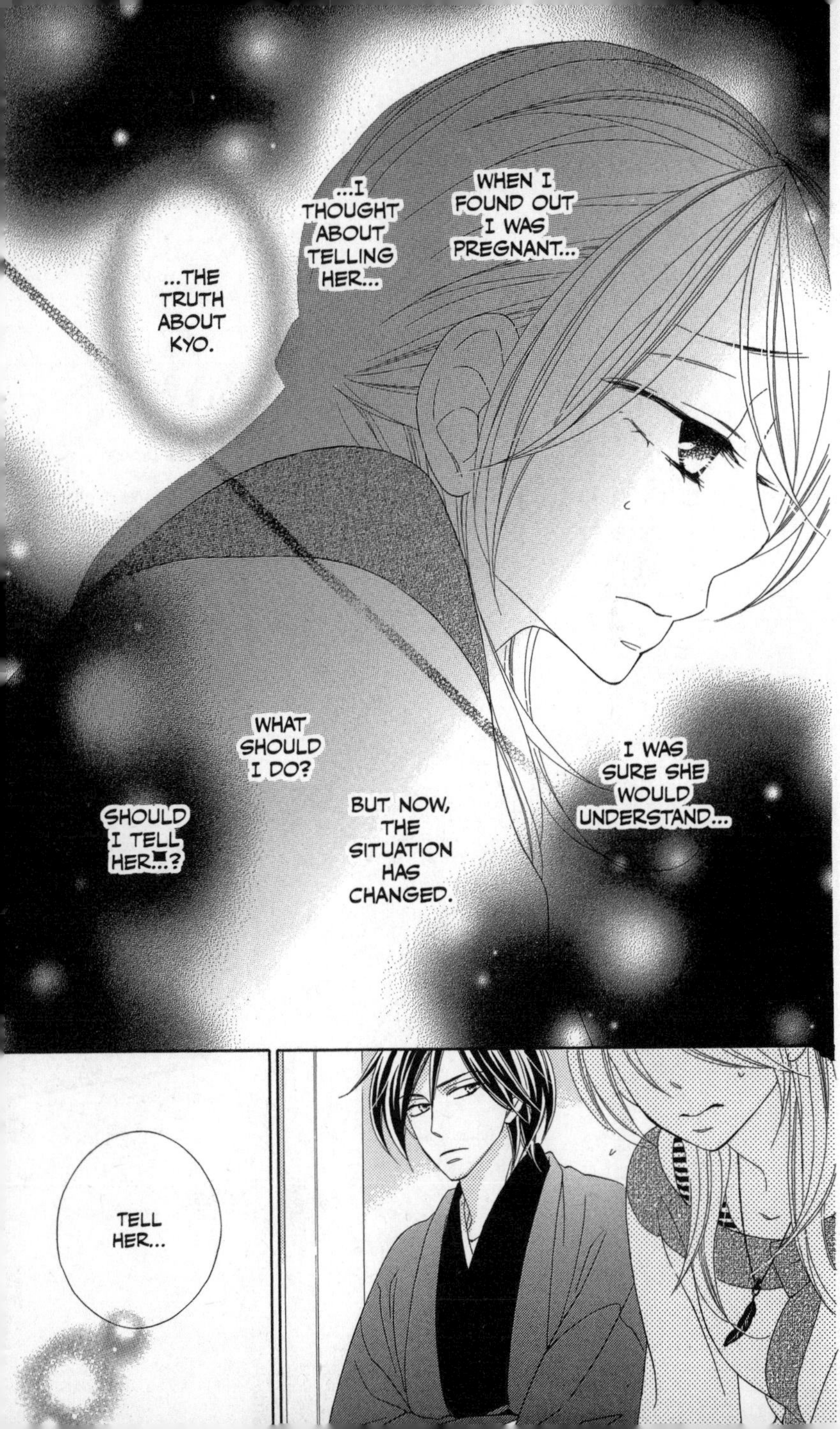
WHEN I FOUND OUT I WAS PREGNANT...
...I THOUGHT ABOUT TELLING HER...
...THE TRUTH ABOUT KYO.
I WAS SURE SHE WOULD UNDERSTAND...
BUT NOW, THE SITUATION HAS CHANGED.
WHAT SHOULD I DO?
SHOULD I TELL HER...?
TELL HER...

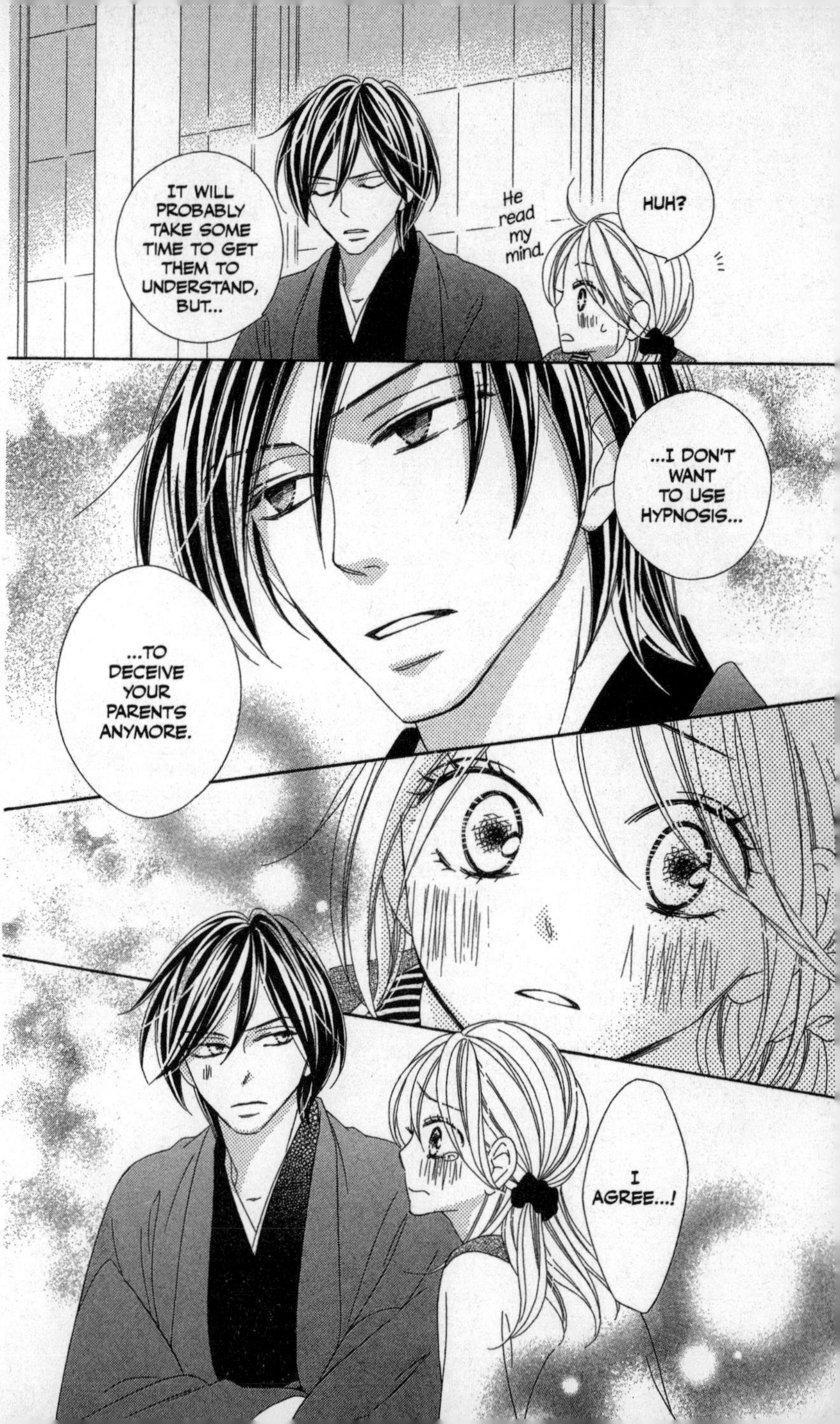
HUH?
He read my mind.
IT WILL PROBABLY TAKE SOME TIME TO GET THEM TO UNDERSTAND, BUT...
...I DON'T WANT TO USE HYPNOSIS...
...TO DECEIVE YOUR PARENTS ANYMORE.
I AGREE...!

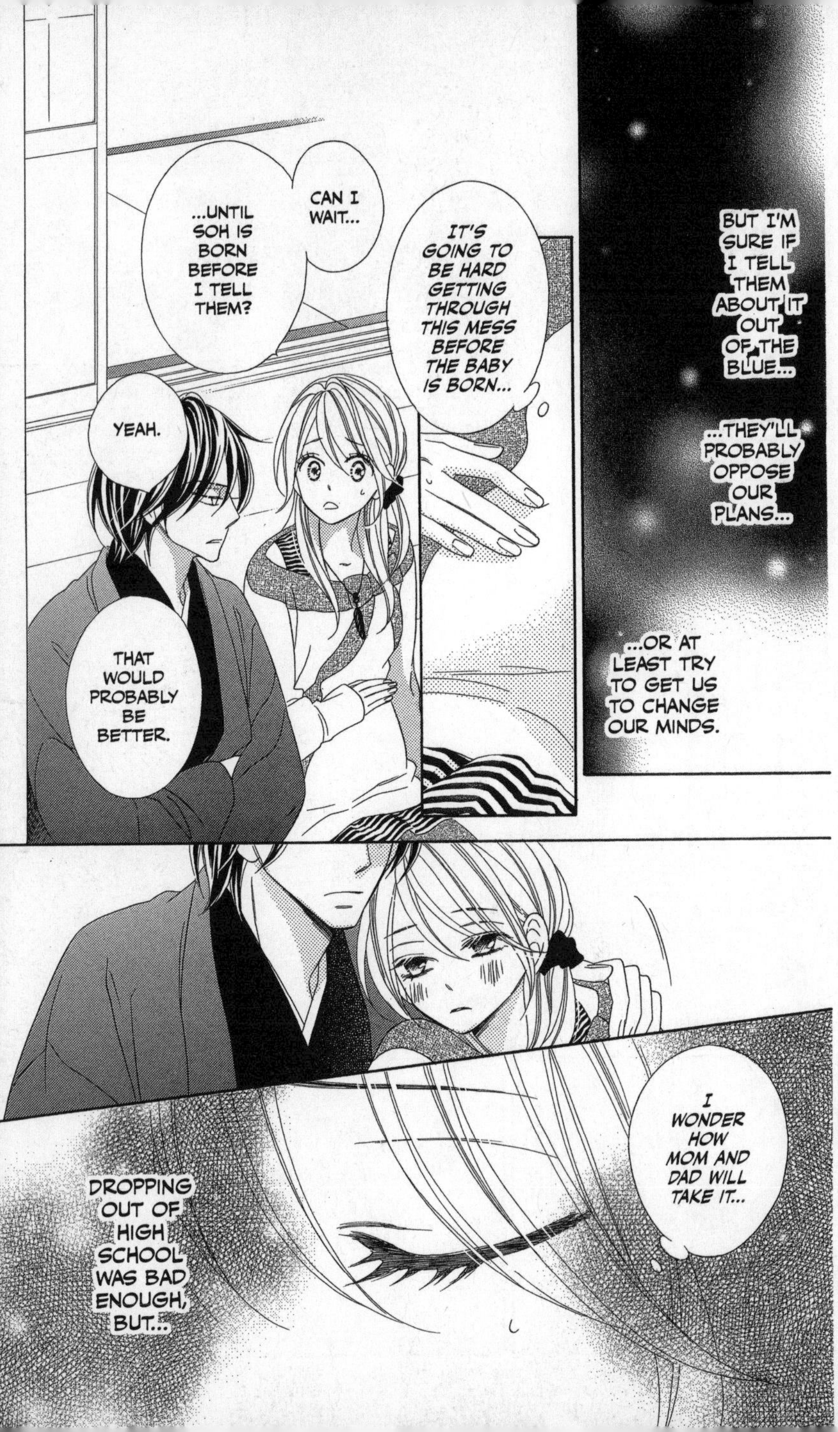
BUT I'M SURE IF I TELL THEM ABOUT IT OUT OF THE BLUE...
...THEY'LL PROBABLY OPPOSE OUR PLANS...
...OR AT LEAST TRY TO GET US TO CHANGE OUR MINDS.
IT'S GOING TO BE HARD GETTING THROUGH THIS MESS BEFORE THE BABY IS BORN...
CAN I WAIT...
...UNTIL SOH IS BORN BEFORE I TELL THEM?
YEAH.
THAT WOULD PROBABLY BE BETTER.
I WONDER HOW MOM AND DAD WILL TAKE IT...
DROPPING OUT OF HIGH SCHOOL WAS BAD ENOUGH, BUT...

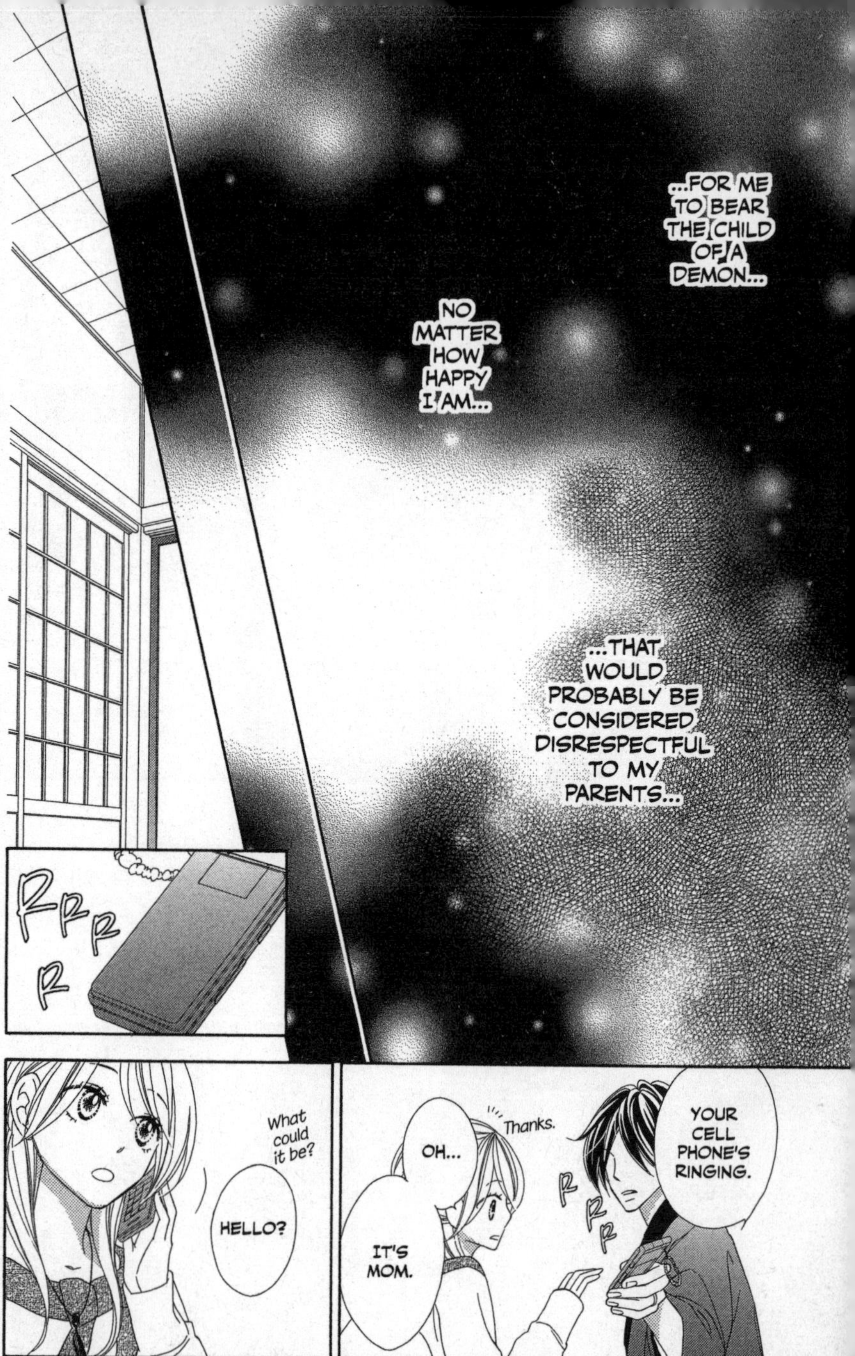
...FOR ME TO BEAR THE CHILD OF A DEMON...
NO MATTER HOW HAPPY I AM...
...THAT WOULD PROBABLY BE CONSIDERED DISRESPECTFUL TO MY PARENTS...
Rrrr
YOUR CELL PHONE'S RINGING.
Thanks.
OH...
IT'S MOM.
What could it be?
HELLO?

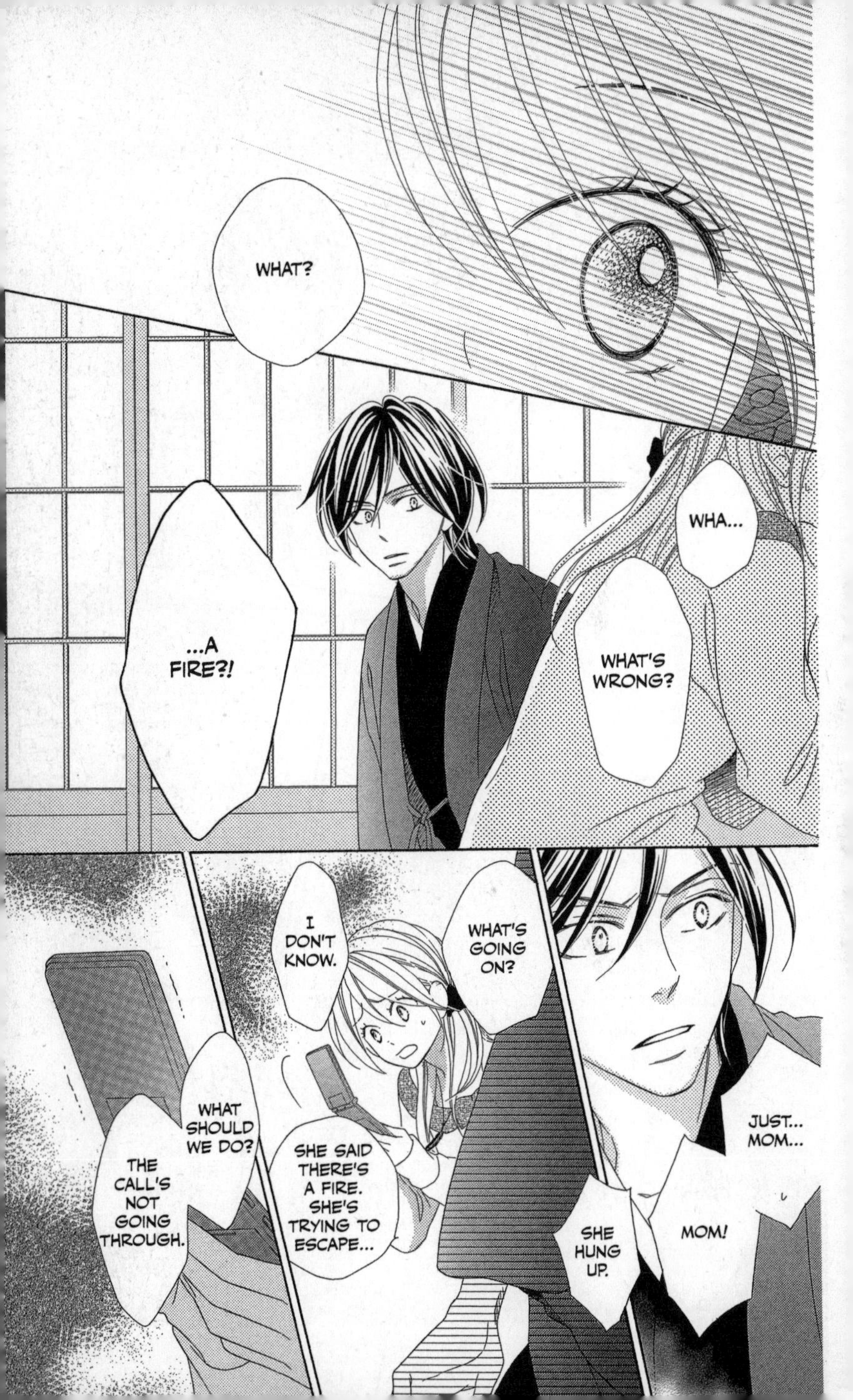
WHAT?
WHA...
WHAT'S WRONG?
...A FIRE?!
JUST... MOM...
MOM!
SHE HUNG UP.
WHAT'S GOING ON?
I DON'T KNOW.
SHE SAID THERE'S A FIRE. SHE'S TRYING TO ESCAPE...
WHAT SHOULD WE DO?
THE CALL'S NOT GOING THROUGH.

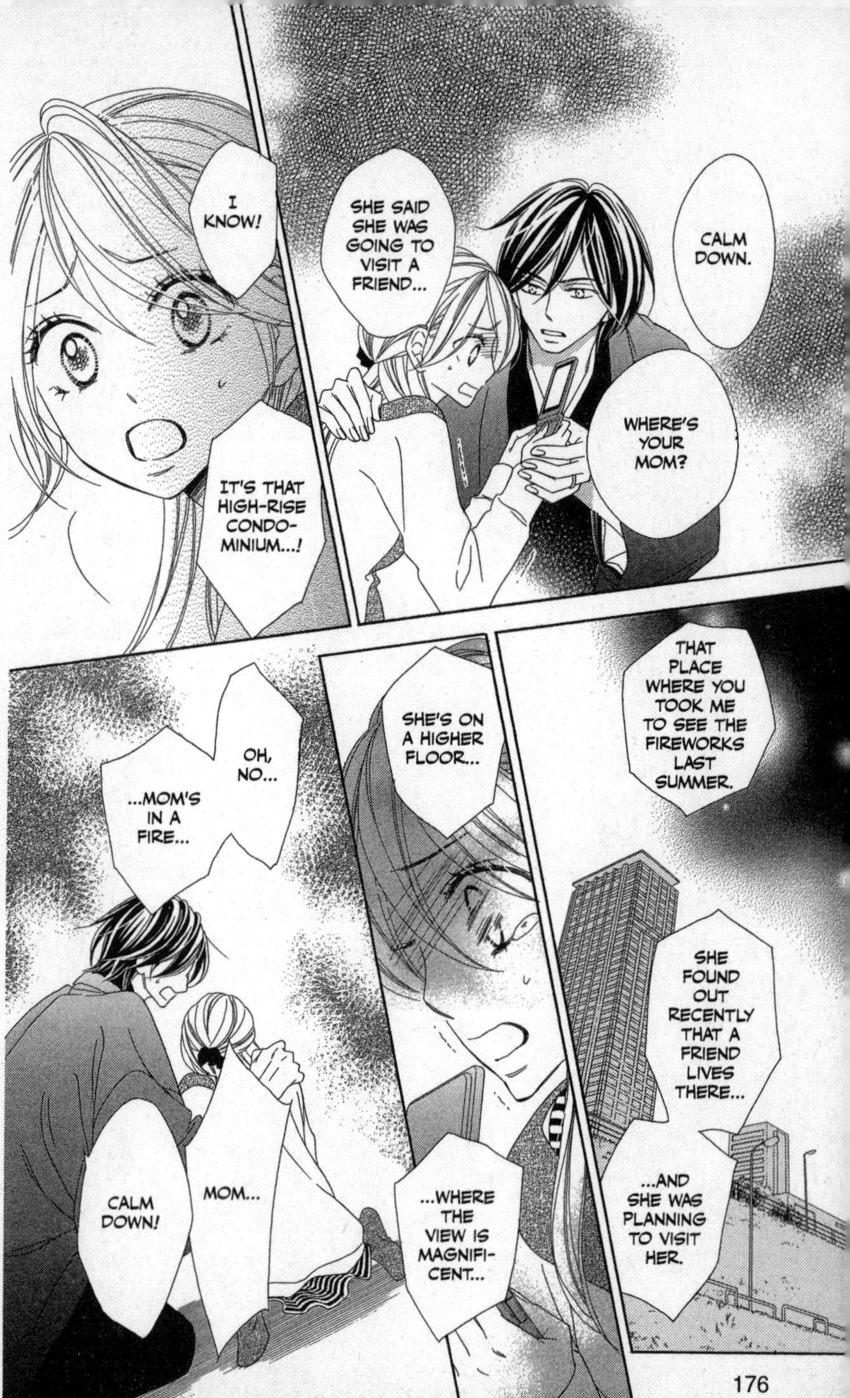

CALM DOWN.
WHERE'S YOUR MOM?
SHE SAID SHE WAS GOING TO VISIT A FRIEND...
I KNOW!
IT'S THAT HIGH-RISE CONDO-MINIUM...!
THAT PLACE WHERE YOU TOOK ME TO SEE THE FIREWORKS LAST SUMMER.
SHE FOUND OUT RECENTLY THAT A FRIEND LIVES THERE...
...AND SHE WAS PLANNING TO VISIT HER.
SHE'S ON A HIGHER FLOOR...
...WHERE THE VIEW IS MAGNIFI-CENT...
OH, NO...
...MOM'S IN A FIRE...
MOM...
CALM DOWN!

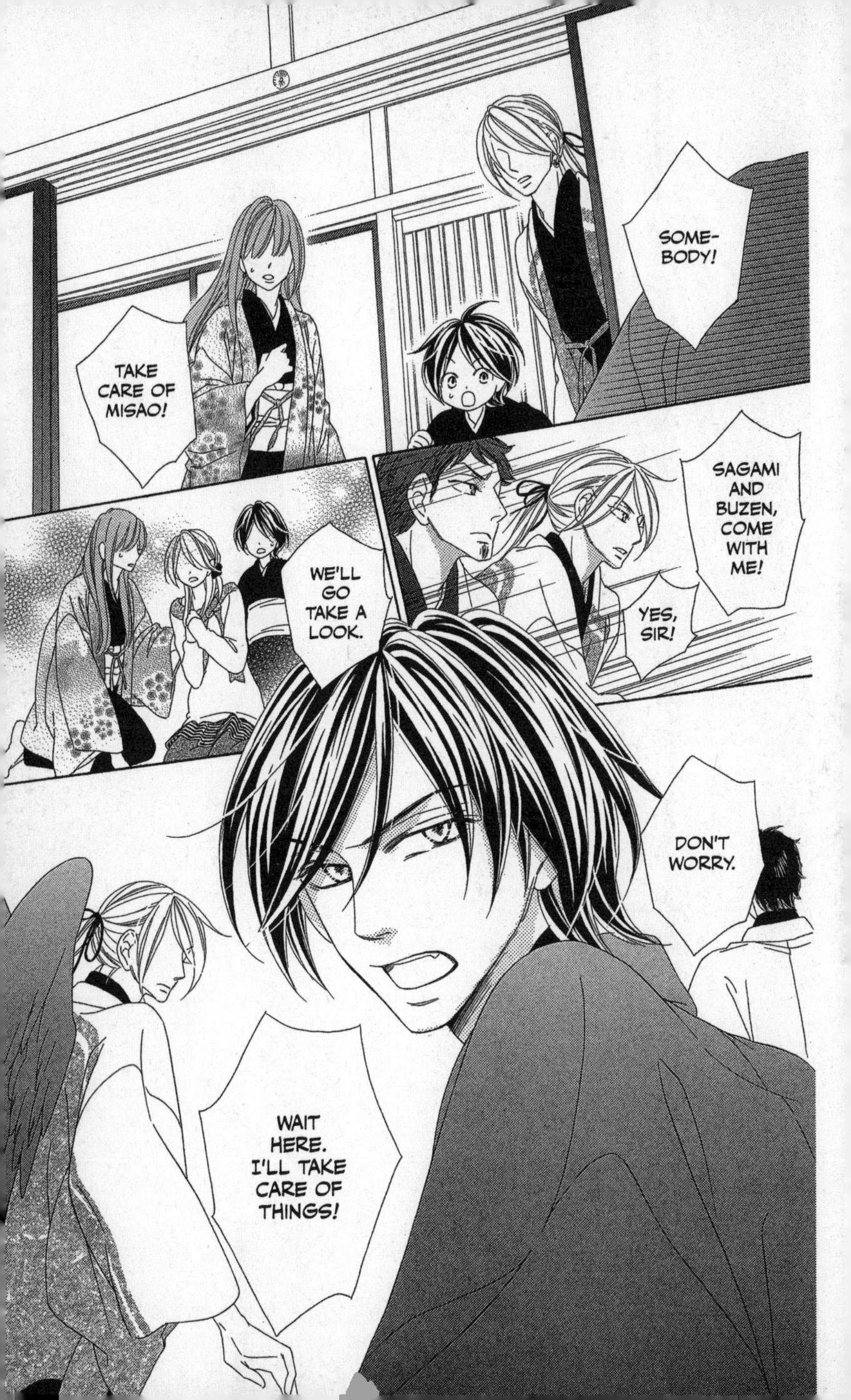
SOME-BODY!
TAKE CARE OF MISAO!
SAGAMI AND BUZEN, COME WITH ME!
YES, SIR!
WE'LL GO TAKE A LOOK.
DON'T WORRY.
WAIT HERE. I'LL TAKE CARE OF THINGS!

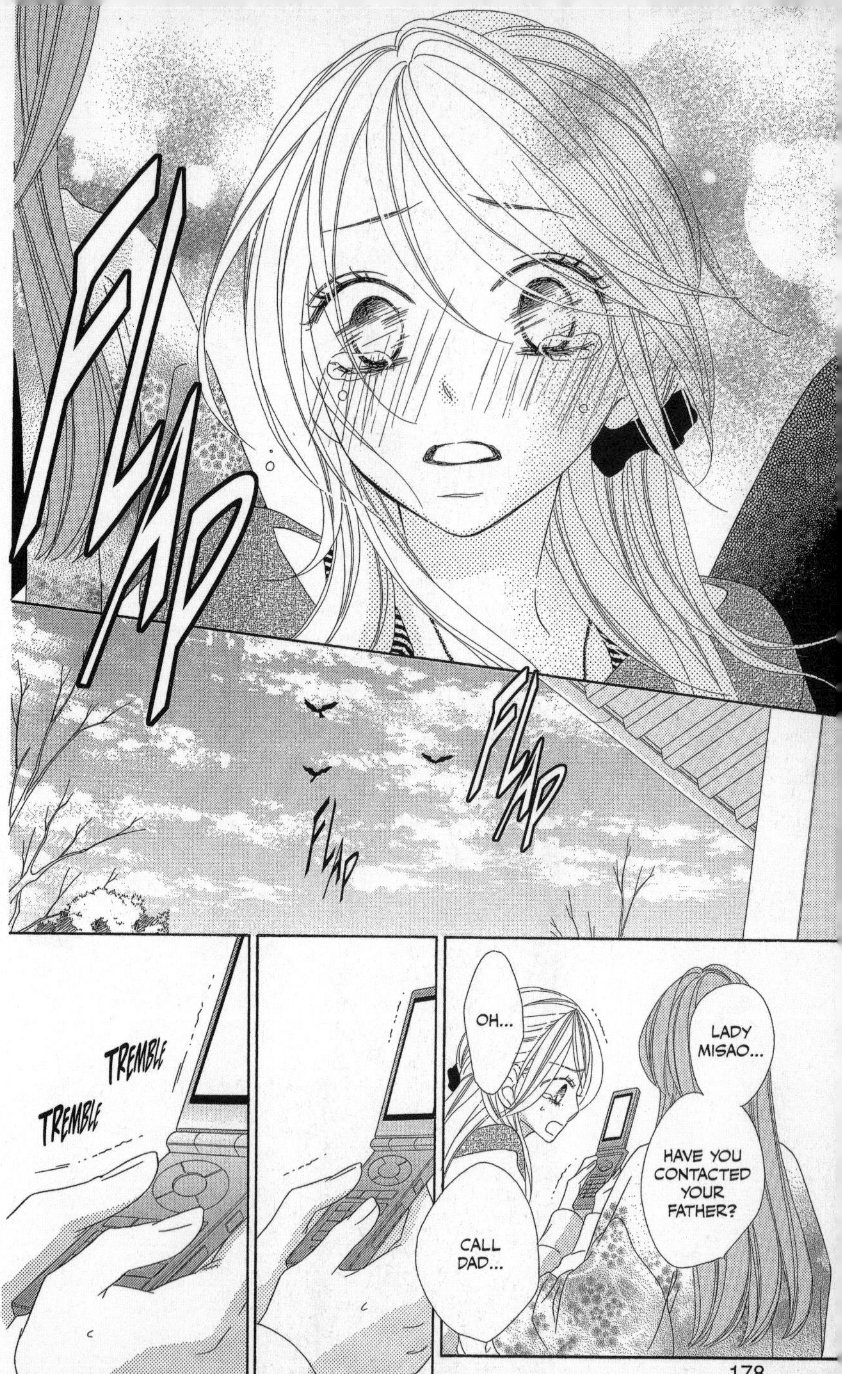
FLAP
FLAP
FLAP
FLAP
LADY MISAO...
OH...
HAVE YOU CONTACTED YOUR FATHER?
CALL DAD...
TREMBLE
TREMBLE

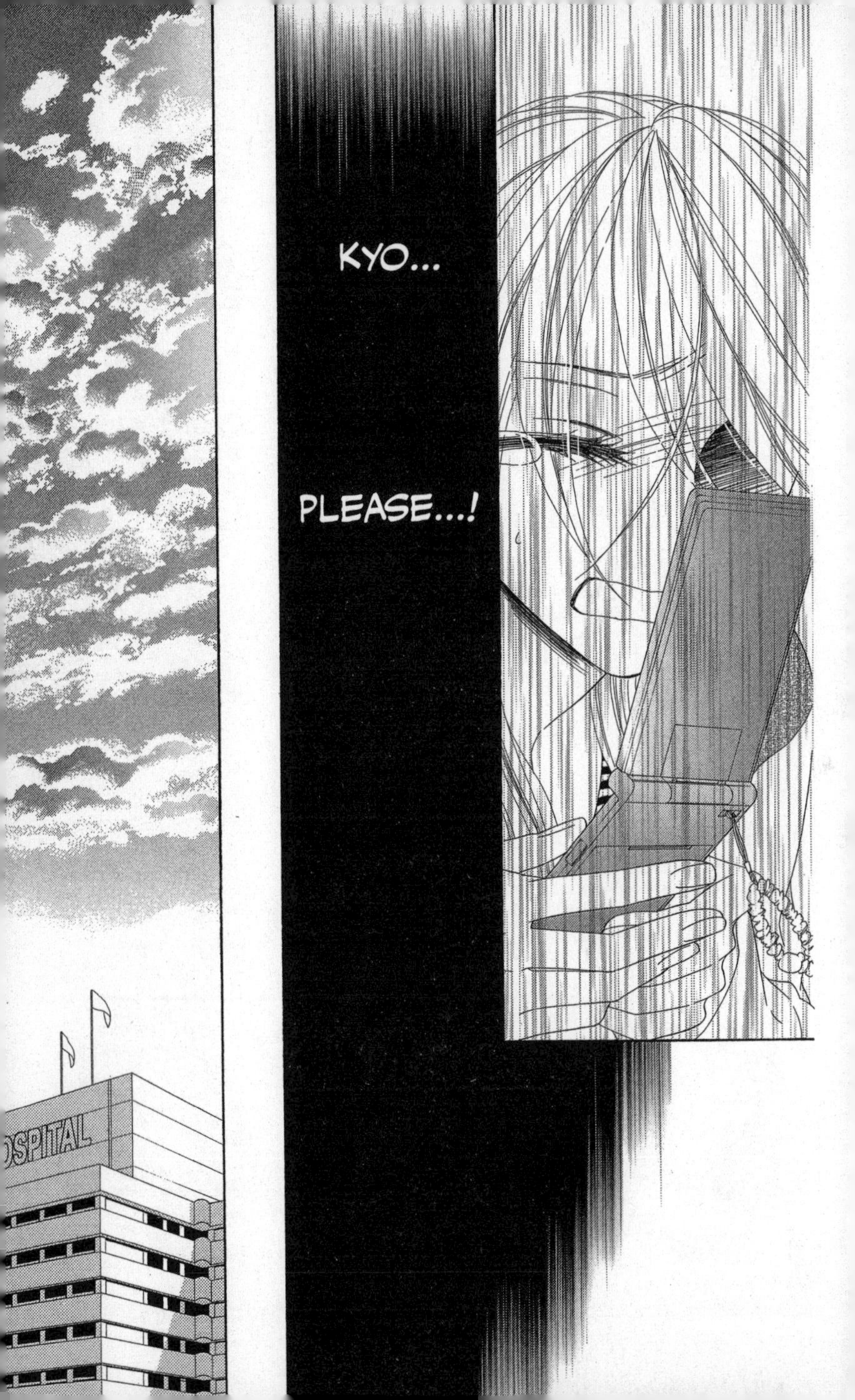
KYO...
PLEASE...!
OSPITAL

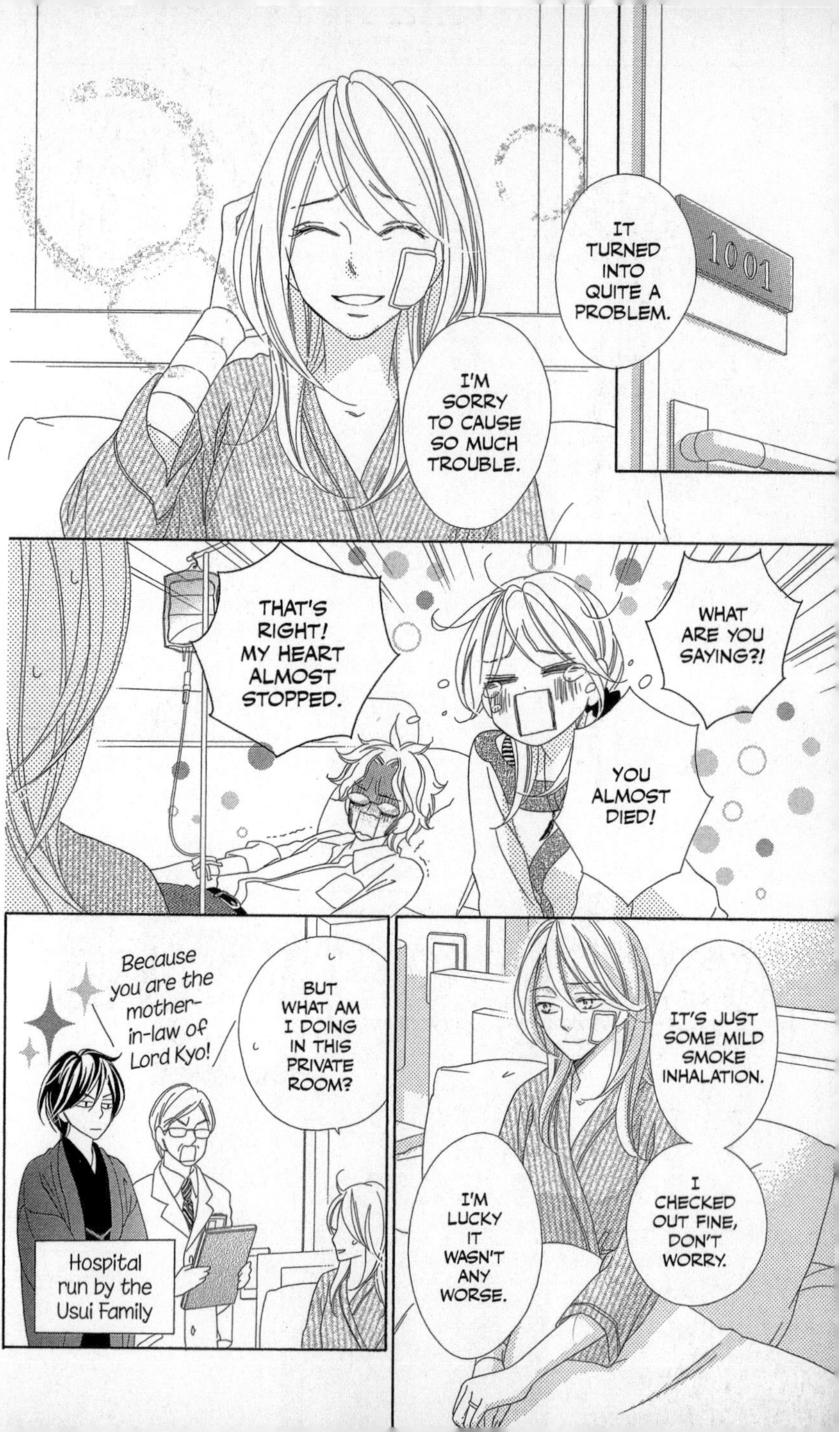
1001
IT TURNED INTO QUITE A PROBLEM.
I'M SORRY TO CAUSE SO MUCH TROUBLE.
WHAT ARE YOU SAYING?!
YOU ALMOST DIED!
THAT'S RIGHT! MY HEART ALMOST STOPPED.
IT'S JUST SOME MILD SMOKE INHALATION.
I CHECKED OUT FINE, DON'T WORRY.
I'M LUCKY IT WASN'T ANY WORSE.
BUT WHAT AM I DOING IN THIS PRIVATE ROOM?
Because you are the mother-in-law of Lord Kyo!
Hospital run by the Usui Family

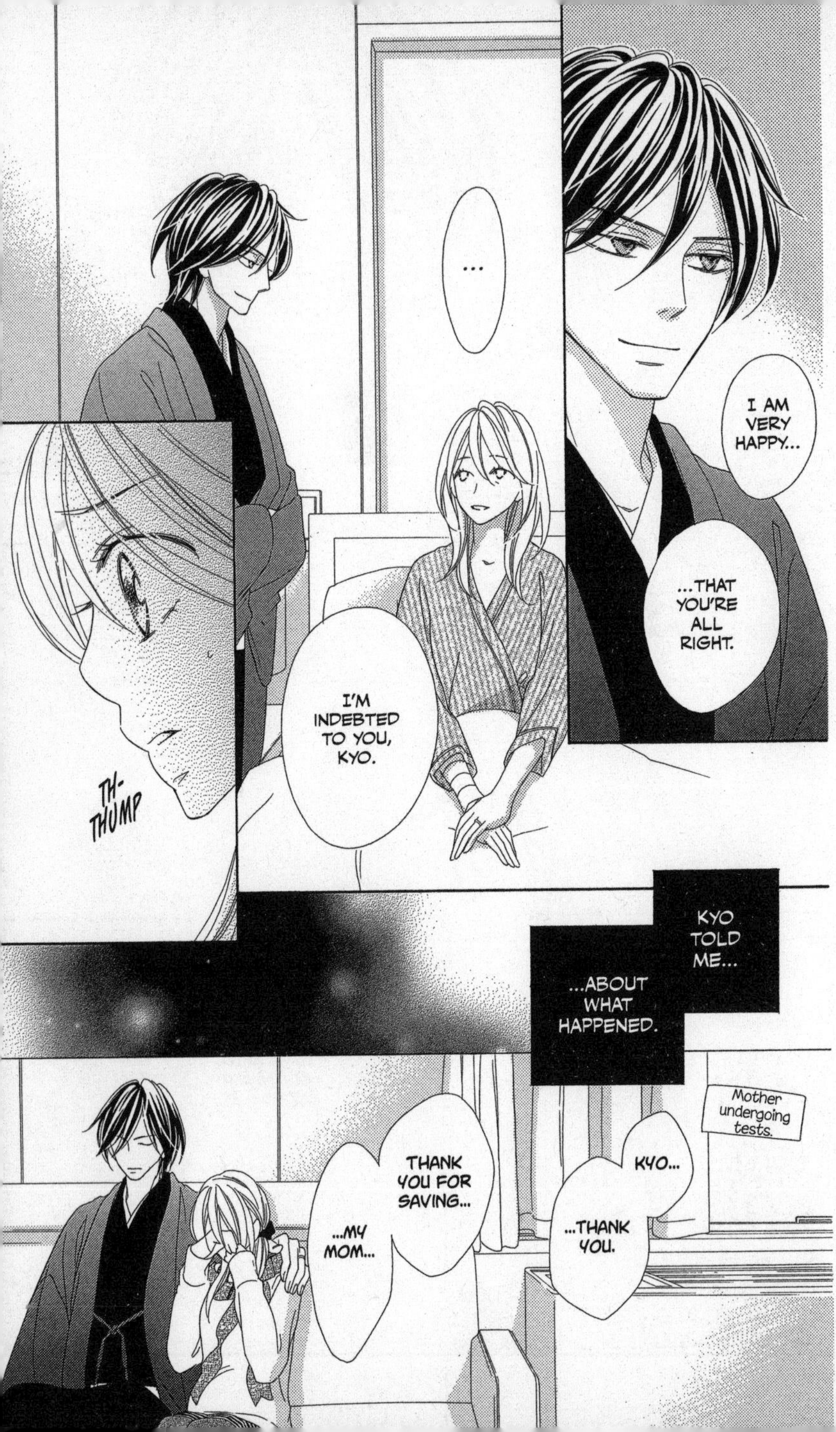
...
I'M INDEBTED TO YOU, KYO.
I AM VERY HAPPY...
...THAT YOU'RE ALL RIGHT.
TH-THUMP
KYO TOLD ME...
...ABOUT WHAT HAPPENED.
Mother undergoing tests.
KYO...
...THANK YOU.
THANK YOU FOR SAVING...
...MY MOM...

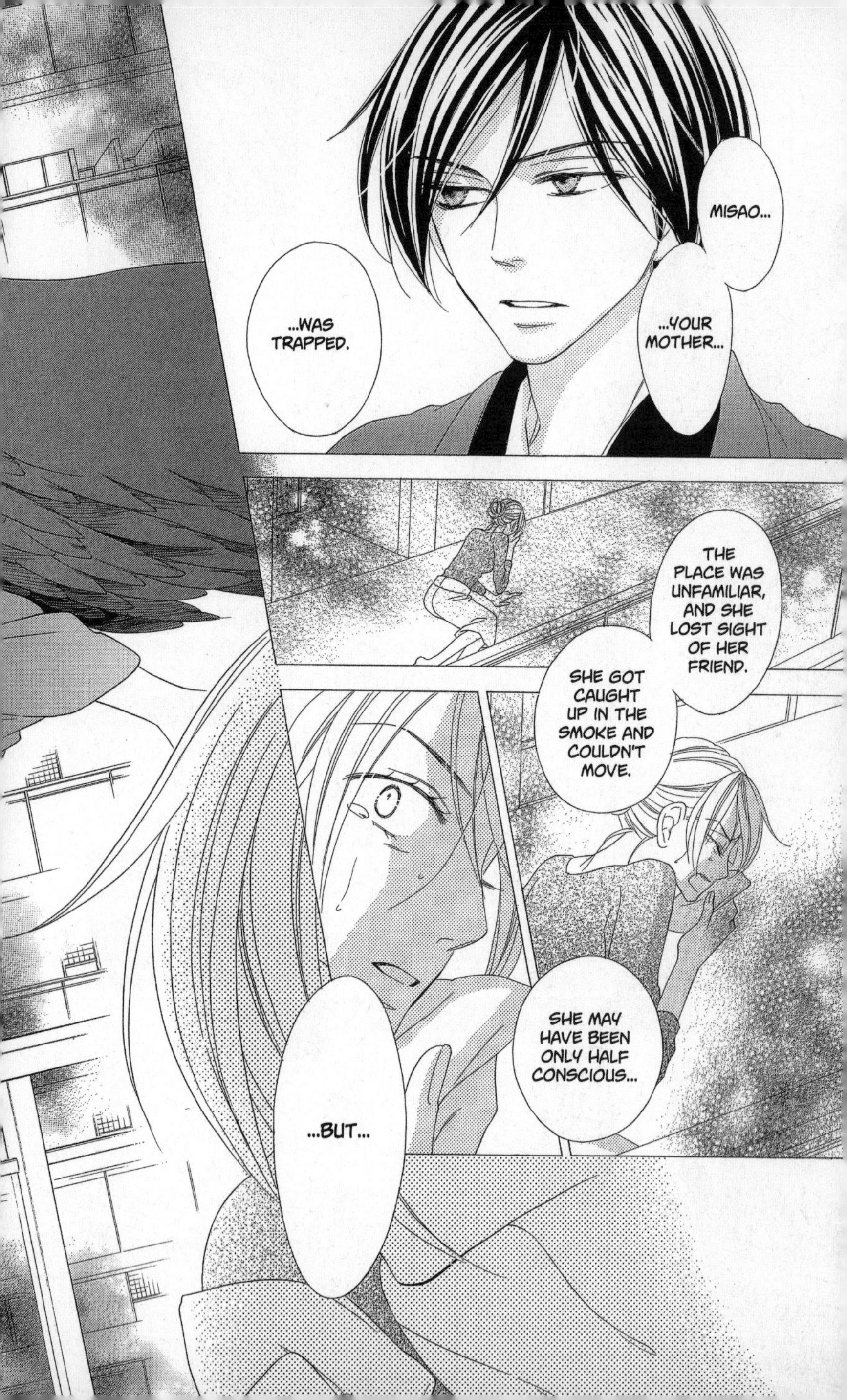
MISAO...
...YOUR MOTHER...
...WAS TRAPPED.
THE PLACE WAS UNFAMILIAR, AND SHE LOST SIGHT OF HER FRIEND.
SHE GOT CAUGHT UP IN THE SMOKE AND COULDN'T MOVE.
SHE MAY HAVE BEEN ONLY HALF CONSCIOUS...
...BUT...

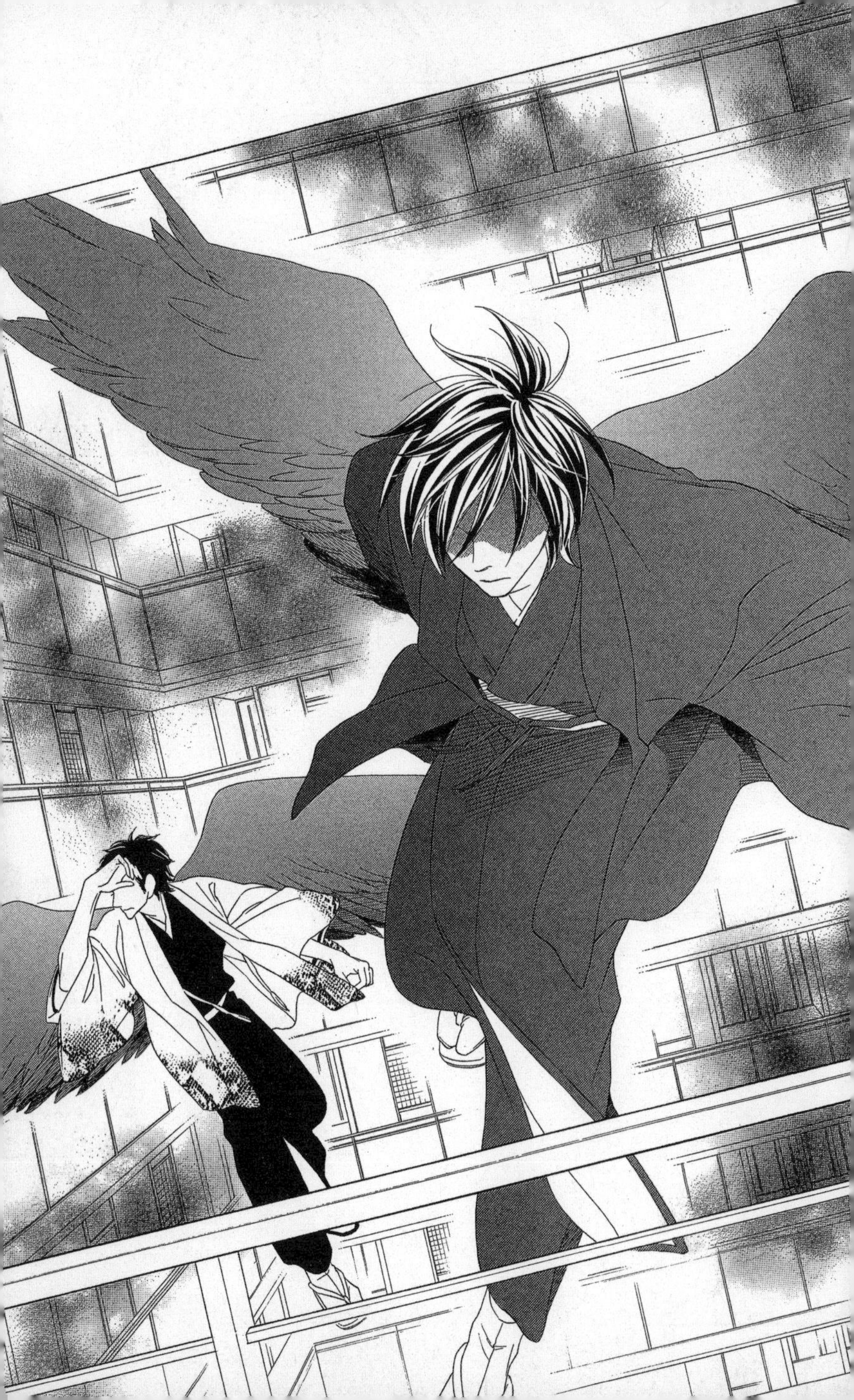

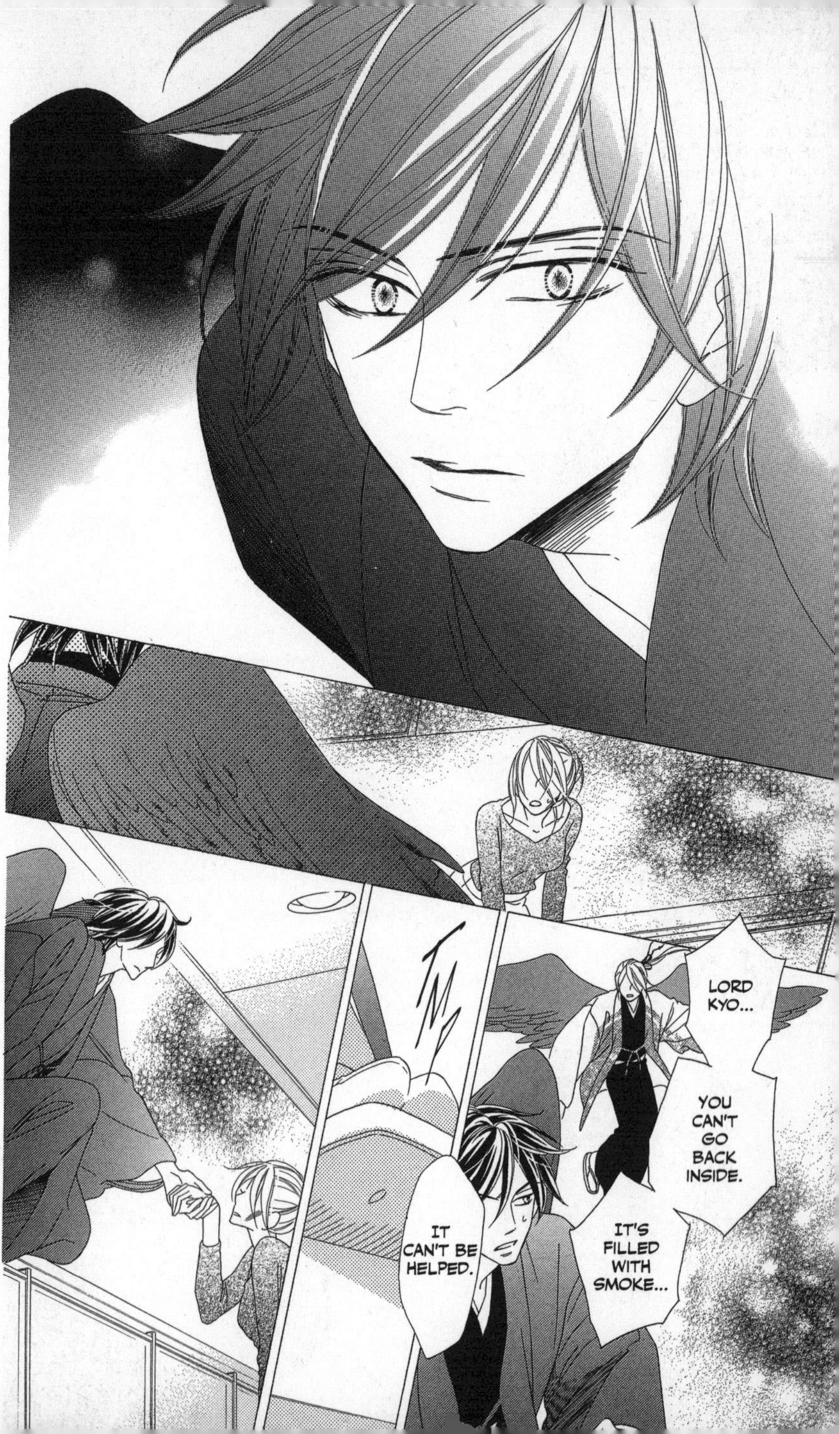
LORD KYO...
YOU CAN'T GO BACK INSIDE.
IT'S FILLED WITH SMOKE...
IT CAN'T BE HELPED.

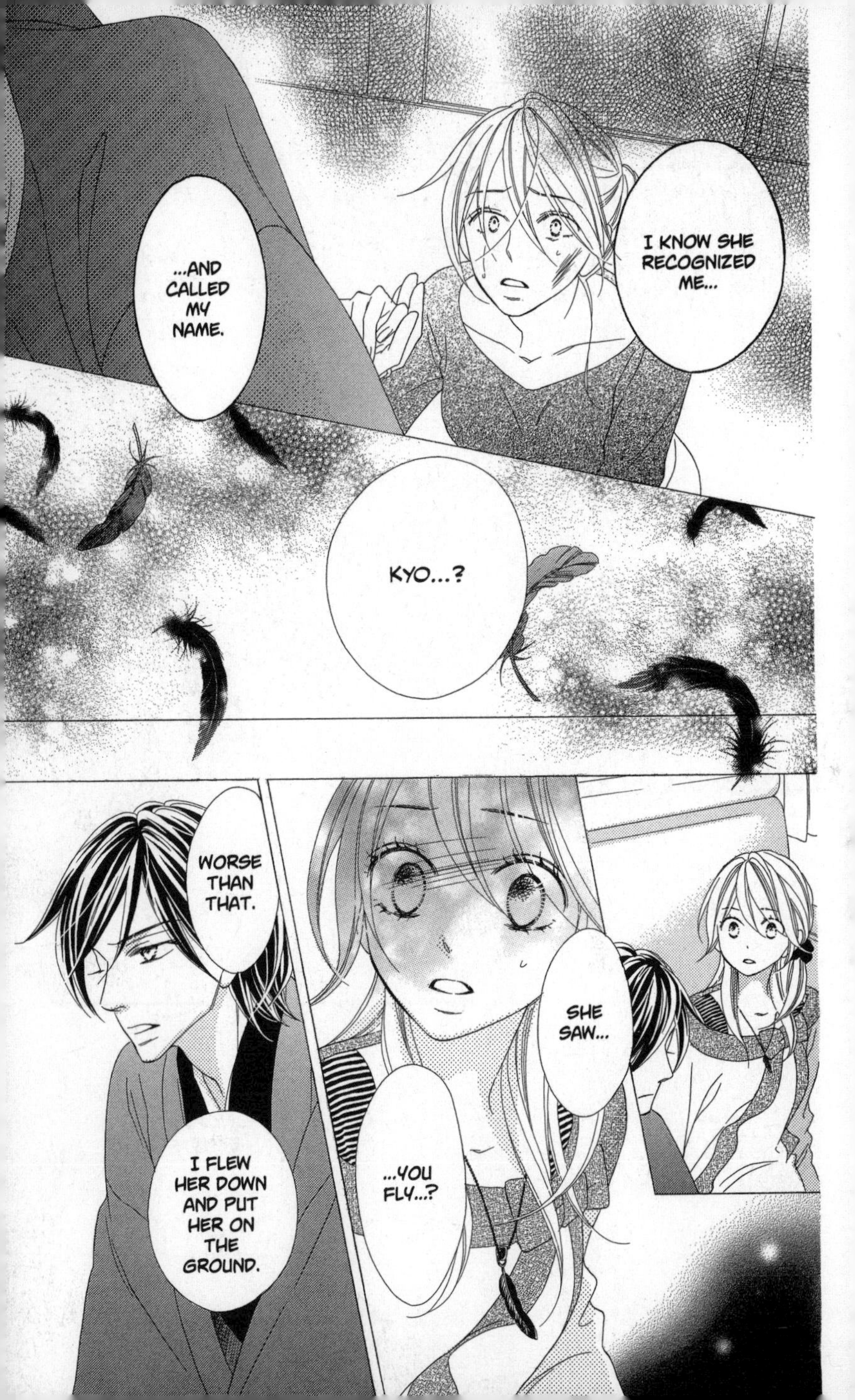
I KNOW SHE RECOGNIZED ME...
...AND CALLED MY NAME.
KYO...?
SHE SAW...
...YOU FLY...?
WORSE THAN THAT.
I FLEW HER DOWN AND PUT HER ON THE GROUND.

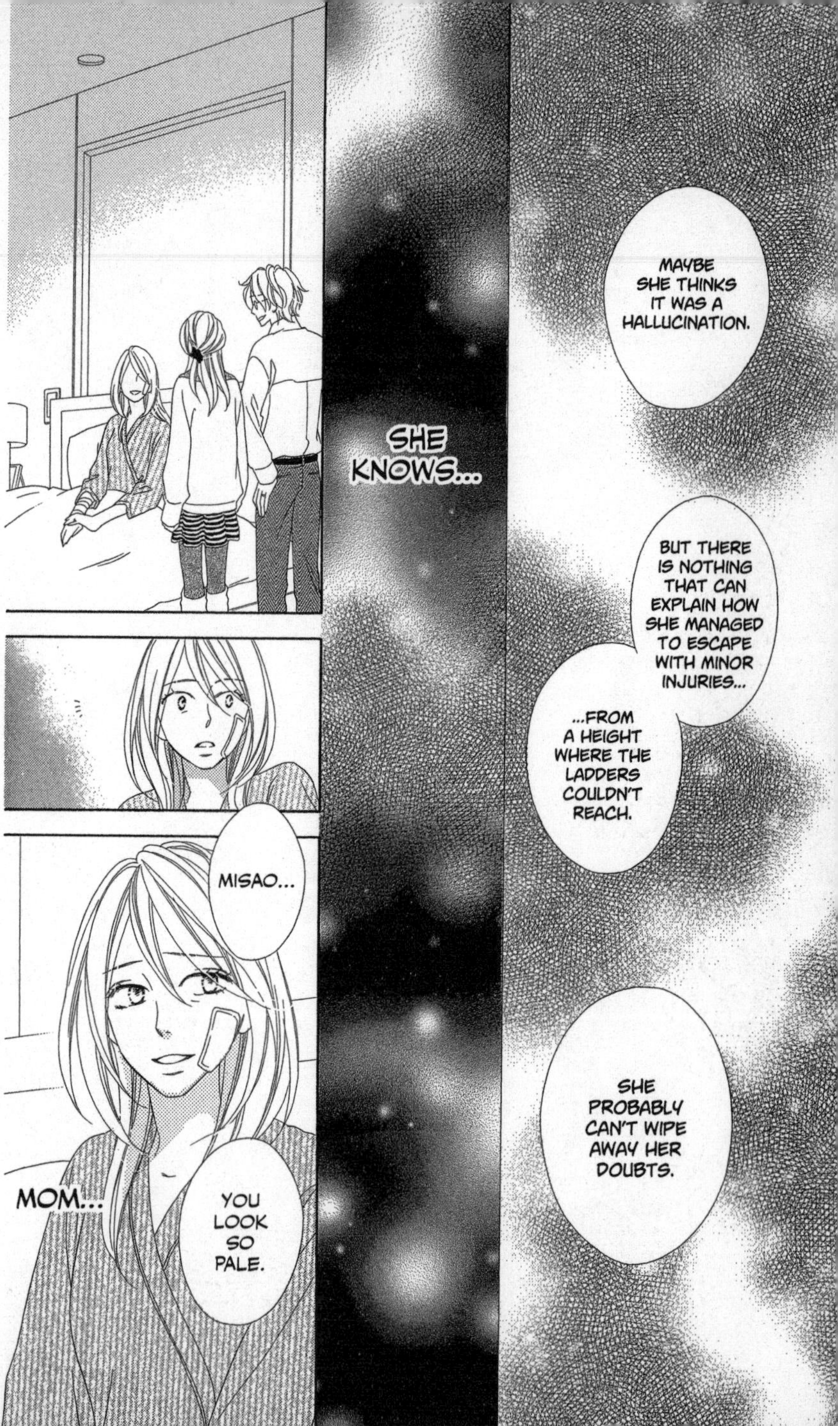
MAYBE SHE THINKS IT WAS A HALLUCINATION.
BUT THERE IS NOTHING THAT CAN EXPLAIN HOW SHE MANAGED TO ESCAPE WITH MINOR INJURIES...
...FROM A HEIGHT WHERE THE LADDERS COULDN'T REACH.
SHE PROBABLY CAN'T WIPE AWAY HER DOUBTS.
SHE KNOWS...
MISAO...
YOU LOOK SO PALE.
MOM...

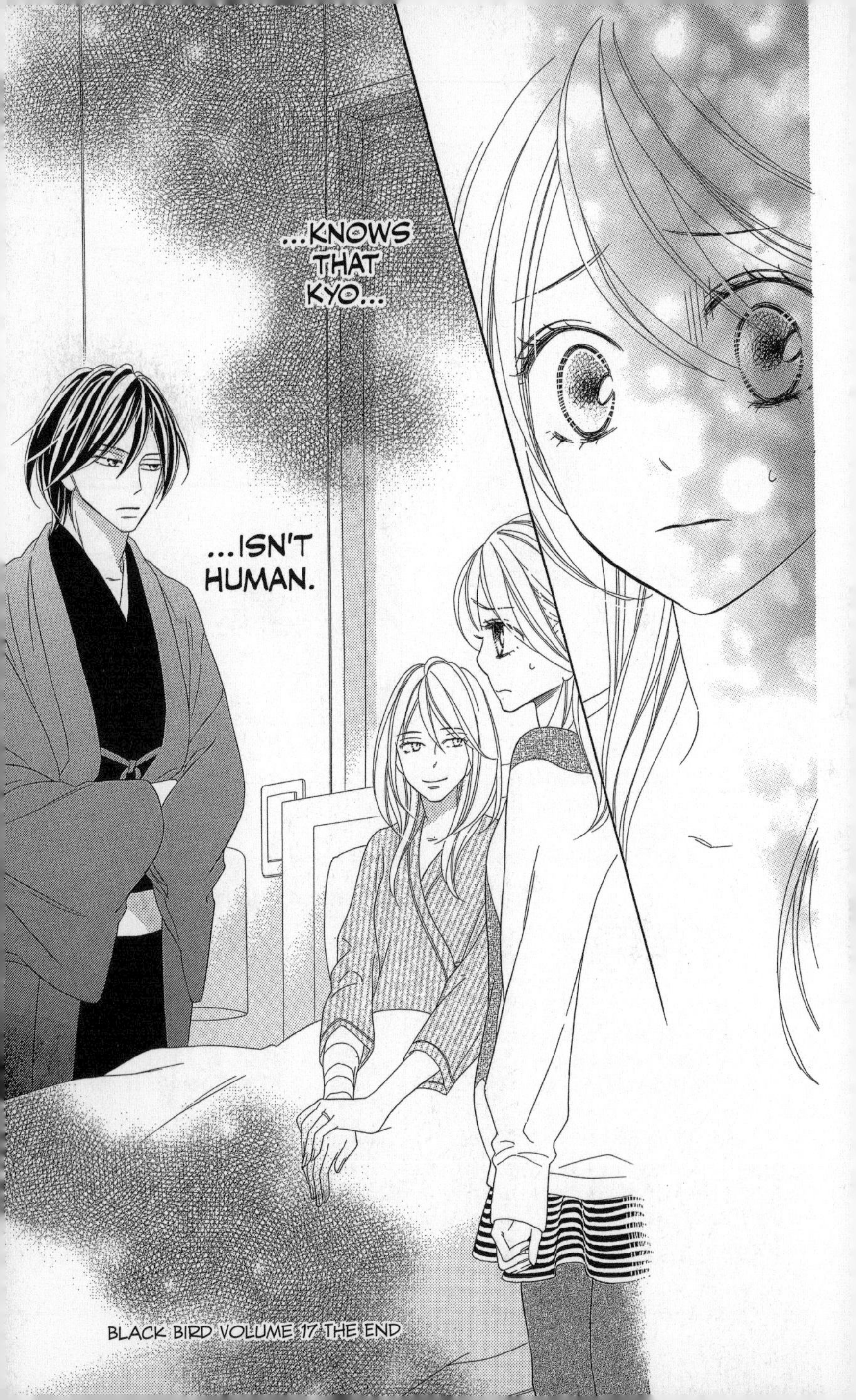
...KNOWS THAT KYO...
...ISN'T HUMAN.
BLACK BIRD VOLUME 17 THE END

YOU CAN COOK, MR. HARADA?
GIRLS LOVE IT. ☆
I'LL TEACH YOU THE RECIPE THAT MADE YOKO FALL FOR ME!
I LOST MY MOTHER WHEN I WAS YOUNG...
...SO I TOOK CARE OF THE COOKING. It was just my dad and me.
MY DAD DIED WHEN I WAS IN GRADUATE SCHOOL.
THIS IS THE LAST MEAL I PREPARED FOR HIM...
She raved about how good it was.
...
YOUR SAD STORY WAS PROBABLY AN EFFECTIVE SPICE.

This is the last dish I prepared for my mother...
You're lying... It's a good story, but... you're probably lying.

Natto on Rice

Thank you very much for reading this volume. The story is nearing its conclusion. I hope you will stay with me to the end.

The *Black Bird Fan Book* is out! It is full of fun reading! There are many never-before-published 4-panel comics, too! Please read it along with the rest of this series.♡

An auspicious day, Oct 2012

Kanako Sakurakouji

桜小路かのこ

Kanoko Sakurakouji was born in downtown Tokyo, and her hobbies include reading, watching plays, traveling and shopping. Her debut title, *Raibu ga Hanetara*, ran in *Bessatsu Shojo Comic* (currently called *Bestucomi)* in 2000, and her 2004 *Bestucomi* title *Backstage Prince* was serialized in VIZ Media's *Shojo Beat* magazine. She won the 54th Shogakukan Manga Award for *Black Bird*.

**BLACK BIRD**
VOL. 17
Shojo Beat Edition

## Story and Art by KANOKO SAKURAKOUJI

BLACK BIRD Vol. 17
by Kanoko SAKURAKOUJI
© 2007 Kanoko SAKURAKOUJI
All rights reserved.
Original Japanese edition published by SHOGAKUKAN.
English translation rights in the United States of America, Canada, the United
Kingdom and Ireland arranged with SHOGAKUKAN.

**TRANSLATION** JN Productions
**TOUCH-UP ART & LETTERING** Gia Cam Luc
**DESIGN** Amy Martin
**EDITOR** Pancha Diaz

Printed in the U.S.A.

Published by VIZ Media, LLC
P.O. Box 77010
San Francisco, CA 94107

10 9 8 7 6 5 4 3 2 1
First printing, October 2013

# SURPRISE

## You may be reading the wrong way!

It's true: In keeping with the original Japanese comic format, this book reads from right to left—so action, sound effects, and word balloons are completely reversed. This preserves the orientation of the original artwork—plus, it's fun! Check out the diagram shown here to get the hang of things, and then turn to the other side of the book to get started!

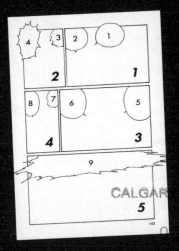